D0504187

Pieces of My Mind

FRANK KERMODE

Pieces of My Mind

WRITINGS 1958–2002

ALLEN LANE
an imprint of
PENGUIN BOOKS

ALLEN LANE
THE PENGUIN PRESS

Published by the Penguin Group
Penguin Books Ltd, 80 Strand, London WC2R 0RL, England
Penguin Putnam Inc., 375 Hudson Street, New York, New York 10014, USA
Penguin Books Australia Ltd, 250 Camberwell Road, Camberwell, Victoria 3124, Australia
Penguin Books Canada Ltd, 10 Alcorn Avenue, Toronto, Ontario, Canada M4V 3B2
Penguin Books India (P) Ltd, 11 Community Centre, Panchsheel Park, New Delhi – 110 017, India
Penguin Books (NZ) Ltd, Cnr Rosedale and Airborne Roads, Albany, Auckland, New Zealand
Penguin Books (South Africa) (Pty) Ltd, 24 Sturdee Avenue, Rosebank 2196, South Africa

Penguin Books Ltd, Registered Offices: 80 Strand, London WC2R 0RL, England

www.penguin.com

First published 2003
1

Set in 10.5/14 pt PostScript Linotype Sabon
Typeset by Rowland Phototypesetting Ltd, Bury St Edmunds, Suffolk
Printed and bound in Great Britain by Clays Ltd, St Ives plc
Cover repro and printing by Concise Cover Printers

ISBN 0–713–99673–0

To Anne and Al Alvarez

Contents

CONTENTS

SHORTER NOTICES

Acknowledgements

'Poet and Dancer Before Diaghilev' appeared first in *Partisan Review* and in *Puzzles and Epiphanies* (Routledge & Kegan Paul, 1962).

'Between Time and Eternity' (from the longer essay 'World Without End or Beginning') and 'Solitary Confinement' are parts of *The Sense of an Ending* (Oxford University Press, 1967, 2001).

'Hawthorne and the Types' and '*Wuthering Heights as a Classic*' are from *The Classic* (Faber, 1975).

'The Man in the Macintosh' is from *The Genesis of Secrecy* (Harvard University Press, 1979).

'Dwelling Poetically in Connecticut' is from *Wallace Stevens: A Celebration*, ed. Frank Doggett and Robert Buttell (Princeton University Press, 1980).

'Botticelli Recovered' and 'Cornelius and Voltemand' are from *Forms of Attention* (Chicago University Press, 1985).

'The Plain Sense of Things' is from *Midrash and Literature*, ed. Geoffrey H. Hartman and Stanford Budick (Yale University Press, 1986).

'Mixed Feelings' and 'Eros, Builder of Cities' are from *History and Value* (OUP, 1988).

'Literary Criticism, Old and New Styles' is from *Essays in Criticism*, Vol. LI, no. 2 (April 2001).

All the reviews are from the *London Review of Books* between 1994 and 2001.

Preface

All the essays in this book were written after 1958, and it is meant to give some idea of what a particular critic has been up to in those years. It cannot give a very full idea, since it does not include a large number of essays and reviews manifestly more ephemeral than these, though I should not claim that everything in this book can escape the imputation of ephemerality. Very little literary criticism achieves that. Fashions change, and they have of late changed more rapidly than usual. The number of persons now practising the craft, overwhelmingly less from desire than out of professional necessity, is large, and most of them seem understandably keen to clear a space for themselves. They will not be giving much time to subtle distinctions between what ought and what ought not to be let go. I believe such distinctions to exist. Indeed they seem fairly clear to me, and so I have tried to make them clear.

Io non sono che un critico, says Iago in Verdi's opera: 'I'm only a critic.' It is a mischievous translation of a remark of Shakespeare's Iago: 'I am nothing if not critical'; Boito and Verdi having good reason to dislike critics. In that respect they do not differ much from artists and writers generally. If we respond with the old claim that criticism is or may be an art, we shall do so in some embarrassment, for most criticism is now produced on academic assembly lines and is usually derivative, mechanical and very hard to read, which in any case you do only when you have to. So the claim needs to be toned down, though not to the extent of altogether conceding that critics are cuckoos in the nests of art. Indeed they are in certain ways indispensable; the business of explanation – of elucidation and comparison – has to go on as long as art goes on, for not being able to speak for itself it always needs someone to speak for it, about it. The clearer and more lucid the commentary the better for art. So criticism can be quite humbly and sometimes even quite magnificently useful. And in paying tribute, or even when cavilling, it can, it must, also give pleasure, like the other arts.

It may be agreed that the most immediately effective criticism occurs in reviews, which have a more worldly function – *Tageskritik* the Germans call it – than longer, more maturely considered studies, which are usually devoted to authors already established. First reviews are closer to news, as befits their place in newspapers and periodicals. They often deal with books which come to them trailing few clouds of glory beyond those provided by the publishers, and they must seek to entertain or amuse, as well as to inform, the cursory reader.

Reviewing is actually a rather unselfish occupation; the product is barely remembered a week after publication, after the Sunday papers are thrown out. Ideally it has already done its job of sorting, commending, reprehending, possibly even puffing and damning, and it accepts the fate of ephemerality as a condition of the employment. The bulk of this book consists of essays much longer than most editors could allow reviews to be; but of recent years there has been a change of influential editorial opinion on this point, and the editors of the *London Review of Books*, the journal for which much of my reviewing has been done in the past twenty-odd years, take an intelligently liberal view of length. It is a privilege to write for that journal pieces that fall comfortably between the newspaper notice and the seven-thousand-word lecture or essay. The genre has many virtues, and some writers, myself included, find it more congenial than any other. I admit this is in part because it offers such an agreeable contrast to what can seem the interminable labour of writing a book, but that is not the only reason.

Anyway, I have appended to the main body of the book seven reviews, all of which appeared in the *London Review*. To each of the longer pieces that precede these reviews I have added a few words by way of preface. I have preferred a chronological to a thematic arrangement, partly because of the unsystematic variety of the topics treated, partly because it may appeal to some readers as a glimpse of what it is like to spend forty years in the wilderness of criticism. I made one exception to this rule, putting together an essay on memory with one on forgetting. They were separated only because I had put aside the draft of 'Forgetting', forgotten it, and taken it up unfinished only when the act of writing about memory, six years later, jogged my memory. Otherwise the book is arranged chronologically as evidence, offered indifferently to defence and prosecution, of the way in which a now quite long professional life has been spent.

A few chapters, including those on memory and forgetting and the lecture on Shakespeare and Boito, have not been published before in any form. One or two of the others have appeared in the various collections I have made over the years, and some are rescued from books which were made up of lecture series. Their origins are disclosed in my headnotes.

ESSAYS

I

Poet and Dancer Before Diaghilev

In the summer of 1955 I wrote a short book called Romantic Image, *published in 1957, inspired largely by love of W. B. Yeats. Yeats was keen on dancers, and the book has a chapter called 'The Dancer', which is partly about the excited response of some* fin de siècle *poets – English and French, and notably, Mallarmé – to dancers, actual, historical and mythical. The object of their admiration might be Salome, the most fascinating of them all, but they could also worship the music-hall dancers of the moment, lavishly courted by poets and reviewers both as performers and as exotically strange women. Dowson and Symons, friends of Yeats, haunted the stage doors. The mysteriously neurotic Jane Avril, familiar from the posters of Toulouse-Lautrec, was one famous name, and there were a good many others, not least among them Loïe Fuller, in whom Yeats seems to have had a particular interest.*

The cult of the Diaghilev Ballets Russes, of Fokine and Nijinsky and the composers and painters who became famous in that context, is a familiar theme, but this somewhat earlier cult of the dance and dancers had been half forgotten by the time this essay was written. My book said something about Fuller, and was adorned by a striking image of her, the work of Thomas Theodor Heine. Then I resolved to find out more about her, making the leisurely library visits I mention below. In the end it was by pure accident I got most of the information I was looking for, and the essay eventually appeared in Partisan Review, *with some striking photographs in the American journal* Theatre Arts, *and later in a collection called* Puzzles and Epiphanies *(1962). When I returned the extremely useful material he had lent me I sent a copy of the article to Mr Nicol, who did not acknowledge it. I had used it, along with documents I found in the files of French periodicals and in the great collection at the Victoria and Albert Museum, to say something of the dancer's contemporary reputation, and of how she achieved her remarkable theatrical effects. But I'm afraid that Mr Nicol, who had himself, as a very young person, been a member of a Fuller troupe (she had given up solo dancing in favour of ensemble work) may have wanted a biography, which it had never been in my mind to produce.*

It is now much too late to apologize for this misunderstanding. Whether by my efforts or those of other fans, the celebrity of Fuller was in part restored for a time, though it never quite matched the fame of her rival Isadora Duncan, in most respects inferior as an artist but having a livelier biography. Duncan was celebrated in a successful movie, Fuller had to be content with the gorgeous tributes of Mallarmé. For a year or two Jonathan Miller and I gave some quite serious thought to the prospect of mounting an exhibition, but when there was one it was not of our making, and was shown in California and in Paris, but not in London. A pity, and the fame of Fuller is in consequence a little dimmer than it might have been. Anyway, I think of my essay not only as an appendix to Romantic Image *but as retaining some interest as a first attempt to revive interest in a remarkable dancer.*

Diaghilev figures in the title simply as a terminus; he arrived in Paris in 1909, and everybody knows what happened. '*Le rêve de Mallarmé se réalise*', said Ghéon. What dream of Mallarmé? That which found a true theatrical sonority, a stage liberated from cardboard falsities; which emerged from a confluence of the other arts and yet remained, as Wagner did not, theatre. The Ballets Russes demonstrated the correspondence of the arts so wonderfully that in comparison Wagner's effort was, said Camille Mauclair, '*une gaucherie barbare*'. Diaghilev arrived, not a moment too soon, in response to prayers from both sides of the Channel. One could trace the developments in taste which prepared his reception – not only in the limited sphere of the dance, but in writings on actors (the cult of Duse, for example), in the fashionable admiration for oriental art and theatre, in avant-garde agitation for theatrical reform. In March 1908, *The Mask*, a quarterly dedicated to this end and strongly under the influence of Gordon Craig, prayed in its opening editorial for a religion that did not 'rest upon knowledge nor rely upon the Word' but rather brought together 'Music, Architecture, and Movement' to heal 'the Evil . . . which has separated these three Arts and which leaves the world without a belief'. The editor can hardly have expected his prayers to be answered so soon – not precisely by the theatrical reforms he had in mind, but by the Russian dancers, prophets of that Concord and Renaissance he so earnestly requested. Havelock Ellis, with his usual wide view, put the situation thus in *The Dance of Life* (1923): 'If it is significant that Descartes appeared a few years after the death of Malherbe, it is equally significant that Einstein was immediately preceded by the Russian Ballet.'

Ellis makes Diaghilev a John the Baptist of a 'classico-mathematical Renaissance', and the notion that this was a renaissance of some kind or other was evidently in the air. However, such credit as is due to its heralds should not all be awarded to the Russian ballet. There was, obviously, Isadora Duncan; but Isadora doesn't take us to the root of the matter. Where, for my purposes, that lies, I can perhaps suggest in this way: what Camille Mauclair said of Diaghilev was somewhat disloyally said, for he had used almost the same words years before of the American dancer Loïe Fuller. Art, he declared, was one homogeneous essence lying at the root of the diversified arts, not a fusion of them; and Loïe Fuller was *it*, 'a spectacle . . . which defies all definition . . . Art, nameless, radiant . . . a homogeneous and complete place . . . indefinable, absolute . . . a fire above all dogmas'. The language is Mallarméan; as we shall see, it was all but impossible to write of Loïe Fuller otherwise unless you were very naïve. Still, not even Mallarmé could start a renaissance single-handed, and there has to be a word or two here about whatever it was that predisposed everybody to get excited in this particular way about dancers.

The peculiar prestige of dancing over the past seventy or eighty years has, I think, much to do with the notion that it somehow represents art in an undissociated and unspecialized form – a notion made explicit by Yeats and hinted at by Valéry. The notion is essentially primitivist; it depends upon the assumption that mind and body, form and matter, image and discourse have undergone a process of dissociation, which it is the business of art momentarily to mend. Consequently dancing is credited with a sacred priority over the other arts, as by Havelock Ellis (whose essay is valuable as a summary of the theoretical development I am now discussing) and, with less rhapsody and more philosophy, by Mrs Langer in the twelfth chapter of *Feeling and Form* and (more flatly) in the opening essay of *Problems of Art*. In view of this primitivizing, it is worth remembering that the increase of prestige was contemporaneous with a major effort by anthropologists, liturgiologists, and folklorists to discover the roots of the dance in ritual of all kinds, and also with the development of a certain medical interest in dancing. We are all familiar with the interest shown by the generation of Valéry and that of Eliot in these matters; and from Eliot, at the time when he was busy with Jane Harrison and Frazer, we can get some notion of how they struck the literary imagination. Here, for instance, is a passage from an uncollected *Criterion* review of two books on dancing:

Anyone who would contribute to our imagination of what the ballet may perform in future . . . should begin by a close study of dancing among primitive peoples . . . He should also have studied the evolution of Christian and other liturgy. For is not the High Mass—as performed, for instance, at the Madeleine in Paris—one of the highest developments of dancing? And finally, he should track down the secrets of rhythm in the still undeveloped science of neurology.

Mr Eliot found the Noh plays exciting and praised Massine for providing in the ignorant modern theatre that rhythm regarded as essential by Aristotle. But the peculiar modern view could hardly have been developed before dancing became an accredited fine art; and the date for this seems to be 1746, when Batteux included it among the five with music, poetry, painting and sculpture. The general and developing Romantic tendency was to give music pre-eminence as being non-discursive, 'autonomous' as the word now is, referring to nothing outside itself for meaning; poems would be like that if there were not a basic flaw in their medium, the habit that words have of meaning something in ordinary usage. But some of this prestige was undoubtedly captured by dancing; it is more 'natural' and more 'primitive' than music, more obviously expressive of what Mrs Langer calls 'patterns of sentience' and 'the mythic consciousness'. I use this late terminology because it is careful enough to avoid certain radical confusions. The dance, though expressive, is impersonal, like a Symbolist poem that comes off. Miss Deirdre Pridden[1] finds the proper word to be Ortega y Gasset's 'dehumanization'; the dancer *'vide la danse, autant que faire se peut, de son humaine matière'*. Something might here be said about organicist theories of expressiveness in Modern Dance, opposed not only to conventional ballet (as Fuller and Duncan and Yeats were) but sometimes even to the use of music, as irrelevant to the *Gestalt* of the dance; the source of these theories is Delsarte, but they have been much refined. However, there is no disagreement from the fundamental principle that dance is the most primitive, non-discursive art, offering a pre-scientific image of life, an intuitive truth. Thus it is the emblem of the Romantic image. Dance belongs to a period before the self and the world were divided, and so achieves naturally that 'original unity' which, according to Barfield for instance, modern poetry can produce only by a great and exhausting effort of fusion.

The Nineties poets wrote endlessly about dancers, welcomed foreign troupes and prepared the way for the serious impact of the Japanese Noh in the next decade.[2] But they also enjoyed the dancers themselves, and regularly fell in love with them. Symons and his friends would meet the Alhambra girls after the show and take them along to the Crown for drink and serious talk; serious not because of what Symons called the 'learned fury' of these 'mænads of the decadence', but in a humbler way. This was the epoch of the Church and Stage Guild, Stewart Headlam's club for clergy and actors. Headlam believed 'in the Mass, the Ballet, and the Single Tax' and such was his balletolatry that he wrote a book on ballet technique. But he also believed that the liturgy must not continue to be deprived of dancing, and so laboured to make the stage respectable, that the stigma on dancing might be removed. Among the membership girls from the Empire and the Alhambra preponderated. Headlam was not original in his liturgical views, which may have gained currency from Anglo-Catholic propaganda for ceremonies not explicitly forbidden;[3] however, he gives one a pretty good idea of what must have been a common enough belief in this passage from an article he contributed to his own *Church Reformer* (October, 1884) in a series on the Catechism:

... to take an illustration from the art of dancing, which perhaps more than all other arts is an outward and visible sign of an inward and spiritual grace, ordained by the Word of God Himself, as a means whereby we receive the same and a pledge to assure us thereof; and which has suffered even more than the other arts from the utter antisacramentalism of British philistia. Your Manichean Protestant, and your superfine rationalist, reject the Dance as worldly, frivolous, sensual, and so forth; and your dull, stupid Sensualist sees legs, and grunts with some satisfaction: but your Sacramentalist knows something worth more than both of these. He knows what perhaps the dancer herself may be partially unconscious of, that we live now by faith and not by sight, and that the poetry of dance is the expression of unseen spiritual grace. 'She all her being flings into the dance.' 'None dare interpret all her limbs express.' These are the words of a genuine Sacramentalist ...

The poet is T. Gordon Hake. Headlam knew Symons well, and also Yeats and many other Nineties poets and painters. He seems, in his Guild and in writing of this kind, to reflect rather accurately the liturgical, poetic, and music-hall aspects of this renaissance of dancing. The liturgical ingredient developed luxuriously in the border country of Anglo-Catholicism; witness R. H. Benson's essay 'On the Dance as a Religious Exercise', an account of the Mass as a dramatic dance:

The Catholic ... is not ashamed to take his place with the worshippers of Isis and Cybele, with King David, and with the naked Fijean, and to dance with all his might before the Lord.

The antiquarian interest culminated in G. R. S. Mead's *The Sacred Dance of Jesus* (published in *The Quest* in 1910, but long excogitated). This was Havelock Ellis's chief source, and it is a work of great and curious learning, written in a long tradition of attempts to explain Matthew 11:17, 'We have piped unto you and ye have not danced'. Mead was most interested in the second-century *Hymn of Jesus*, but he deals with the Fathers and with medieval church dancing, with the liturgies of the Greek Orthodox and Armenian churches, and so forth. I doubt if Mead is taken very seriously by modern historians – he isn't cited in the large bibliography of Backman's *Religious Dances* (1952) – but for a while he mattered a lot. Yeats, for example, went to his lectures. He was by no means the only zealous dance-historian of the time. Toulouse-Lautrec, who was not interested in these matters, had an English *savant* thrown out of a dance-hall for plaguing him about antiquity; this could have been Mead, but not necessarily. At a time when it was relatively easy for a dancer to acquire a reputation for learning, Loïe Fuller was said on high authority (Anatole France) to be wise in the history of dancing; she took as her prototype Miriam, who, according to Philo, as quoted by Mead, symbolizes perfect sense, as Moses symbolizes perfect mind.

The presence of the *savant* in the *bal* tells us something about the seriousness with which music-hall dancing was taken on both sides of the Channel. From Symons and Goncourt one knows that it was so; and of course this was a period of close relations between London and Paris. Yvette Guilbert often appeared in London, Marie Lloyd and others in Paris; it was fashionable to treat them as very great artists. This cult of the music-hall has been persistent; there is a classic state-ment of it in Mr Eliot's essay on Marie Lloyd (1932), and it still goes on in a London which has only one or two feebly surviving halls, constantly threatened with demolition. Nothing distresses some Eng-lish intellectuals more than the closing of a music-hall. This attitude is a weakly descendant of a positive avant-garde reaction against commercial theatre in the Nineties; failing dance-drama or über-marionettes, there were still Marie Lloyd and Little Tich, defying cultural and social division, freely satirical, speaking with the voice of the belly. You could talk of Yvette Guilbert, who, according to André Raffalovitch, sang 'the sufferings of those the world calls vile', in the same breath as the Duse.

The Parisian music-halls were certainly not short of a similar intellec-tual *réclame*, and had their place, as part of the metropolitan experi-ence, with all the other pleasures devised for an élite that took its pleasures seriously – fine clothes, Japanese prints, neurasthenia. They are as important in the early history of modern art as folk-music and primitive painting, with which indeed they are obviously associated. Our received idea of this world owes more to Toulouse-Lautrec than anybody else, and there is no reason to think it very inaccurate. The circus, the vaudeville, the *bal*, were serious pleasures; the primitive, the ugly, the exotic were in demand. The brutal patter of Aristide

Bruant, La Goulue coarsely cheeking the Prince of Wales, the emaciated and psychopathic May Belfort, the cherished ugliness of Mme Abdala; all are characteristic. The mood is that of the violent Lautrec drawings of Guilbert and Jane Avril, of dancers calling themselves Grille d'Egout or La Goulue, of café-concerts with such names as Le Divan Japonais and prostitutes with such *noms de guerre* as Outamoro. In this atmosphere all the dancers I am concerned with did their work, and were treated very seriously.

Of a good many of them it was enough to say, as Symons did in his excited lines on Nini Patte-en-l'air, that they possessed

> The art of knowing how to be
> Part lewd, aesthetical in part,
> And *fin-de-siècle* essentially.

Symons was one of those Englishmen whose solemn Parisian pleasures were the admiration of Lautrec – Conder, the strangest of them, he often drew, superbly drunk in his fine evening clothes. But Symons was building an aesthetic in which dancing was to have a central place – the climactic essay is called 'The World as Ballet' – and so his interest was slightly different from the painter's. Lautrec was equally absorbed by La Goulue and Jane Avril; but for Symons the former, a Messalina who wore her heart embroidered on the bottom of her knickers, was less important than the latter, who demonstrated that the female body was 'Earth's most eloquent Music, divinest human harmony'.

Some time in the Thirties a French exhibition, devoted to life under the Third Republic, showed Jane Avril and Loïe Fuller as representing the Dance, and most of what follows is concerned with these dancers. Like Fuller, Avril had the reputation of literacy, and enjoyed the friendship of Lautrec, Renoir, Theodor Wyczewa, Maurice Barrès. It is clear from Lautrec's posters that what interested him was the lack of conventionality, almost the *gaucherie*, in her attitudes, her being set apart from all the other girls. She danced a good deal alone, and not only in the solo variations of the quadrille; she designed her own dresses, and got some of her effects by whirling movements possibly learned from the English dancer Kate Vaughan, also perhaps a source of inspiration to Fuller – she was well thought of in the Eighties and later for bringing back long skirts for dancers. Avril, again like Fuller, lacked formal training and mechanical predictability; Pierre Charron said she was like

> une fleur balancée, troublante
> Au souffle du vent chaud qui l'endort doucement . . .

Avril had special privileges at the Moulin Rouge; she alone was not required to take part in the quadrille. In the poster Toulouse-Lautrec did for her London season you see her waving a thin leg at a different angle from the other three dancers'; in other drawings she is alone, one leg seemingly twisted, the other held clumsily up, or circulating skinny and solitary in the shadow of La Goulue. Symons saw her dancing before the mirrors in the Moulin Rouge and wrote of her 'morbid, vague, ambiguous grace' in a poem called 'La Mélinite: Moulin Rouge', which Yeats in 1897 called 'one of the most perfect lyrics of our time'. The only possible explanation of this enormous over-estimate is the irresistible appeal of a poem combining the Salome of the Romantic Agony with Pater's Monna Lisa:

> Alone, apart, one dancer watches
> Her mirrored, morbid grace;
> Before the mirror face to face,
> Alone she watches
> Her morbid, vague, ambiguous grace,
> And enigmatically smiling
> In the mysterious night,
> She dances for her own delight.

But she had talent. Whereas La Goulue and others gambolled, says Francis Jourdain, Avril danced. *'L'arabesque tracée dans l'espace par une jambe inspirée, n'est plus un signe vain c'est une écriture'*, he says, echoing, perhaps unconsciously, a phrase of Mallarmé.

There is small doubt – and here lies much of her interest – that this dancer owed most to the air of morbidity of which Symons speaks, and specifically to the long time she spent in her teens as a patient of

Charcot at the Salpétrière. This hospital, and particularly the ward of the *grandes hystériques*, in which Avril had been treated for her chorea, was used as a kind of alternative to music-halls; Charcot and his patients welcomed visitors, and the symptoms of hysteria[4] were well known to a large public. Charcot is celebrated for having turned Freud 'from a neurologist into a psychopathologist', but despite his discovery that he could induce hysterical symptoms by hypnotism, and his observation that certain nervous disorders were always a question of '*la chose génitale*', Charcot himself did not know as much as Freud was to learn from watching him.[5] He was greatly impressed by the resemblance between the symptoms of his patients and medieval descriptions and representations of demoniac possession and obsessive dancing. He seems not to have known the theory, now, I gather, beyond dispute, that the saltatory epidemics were caused by ergotism, a disease brought on by eating blighted rye. As early as 1877 he wrote of an hysteria patient who had hallucinations of serpents and exhibited 'in an embryonic state and sporadic form, a specimen' of medieval dancing mania, emphasizing that the symptoms appeared 'in a rudimentary state' and were arrested by compression of the left ovary. In 1887 he wrote, with Paul Richer, a book called *Les Démoniaques dans l'art*, in which he tries to show that the convulsions and dances of the possessed are characteristic of various stages in the hysterical seizures he had observed, and of which he shows sketches. Avril was never permanently cured of chorea, and had ample opportunity to observe her fellow-patients; whether by accident or design she seems to have reproduced some of the symptoms of hysterical dancing, doubtless in a rudimentary form, and I have no doubt that Charcot would have found Lautrec's famous poster 'Jane Avril aux serpents' characteristic of hysteria (compare, for example, the sketch from Mazza da Bologna on p. 72 of *Les Démoniaques*). 'Ambiguous grace', certainly; but the ambiguity was agreeable to a public much interested in 'neurasthenia' (an American discovery, but rapidly naturalized in Paris). Considered in this light, as combining certain powerful aesthetic and pathological interests of the period, it is easy to see how Avril produced a *frisson nouveau* and encouraged the literati to love the highest when they saw it in the Moulin Rouge.

Under these conditions it is not surprising that a good many dancers came to be associated with avant-garde movements in the other arts, and there was to be an *idéiste* dancer, Valentine de Saint-Point, who performed against a screen upon which 'geometric shadows' were cast,[6] and a Cubist and Dadaist dancer, Nina Payne, whose dancing to jazz music greatly pleased the fastidious Levinson. The Cubism, he said, must have something to do with a strange cylindrical *couvrechef* she wore. There were also vaguely Vorticist dancers in Mme Strindberg's Cave of the Golden Calf in London just before the first war; we know that cut-outs and shadows were used (see F. M. Ford's novel, *The Marsden Case*) but the memoirs of the period are hazy about what went on, and Miss Margaret Morris, who certainly knows, will not say. Isadora Duncan was a 'symbolist' dancer; but it is sometimes forgotten that she derived much that was admirable in her dancing from Loïe Fuller, and this brings me to the most important of all these names, to the woman who seemed to be doing almost single-handed what Diaghilev was later to achieve only with the help of great painters, musicians, and dancers.

Many living people must have seen Loïe Fuller, but there is no book about her, except her own autobiography, and no powerful tradition, as there is for Isadora Duncan. The standard reference books are scanty and inaccurate, and so should I have been, had I not had the good luck to encounter Mr E. J. Nicol, a nephew of the Miss Nolan who not only backed Fuller but carried out the famous experiments in textiles and dyes which were associated with the dancer's vogue. Mr Nicol also belonged to Fuller's company as a child, and knows all about a great many matters which were kept secret, mostly of a technical sort. For all correct comments on such techniques in what follows Mr Nicol is responsible, and for none that is incorrect. The rest of the material comes from diaries, newspapers, theatre programmes, publicity hand-outs, and the like; and, of course, the autobiography, *Fifteen Years of a Dancer's Life* (French edition, 1908; English, 1913).

Loïe Fuller was born in Illinois in 1862, under trying circumstances: she claimed to have caught a cold at birth which was never cured. She used this claim in much the same way as Isadora insisted that her character was predetermined from the womb ('Before I was born my mother was in great agony of spirit and in a tragic situation. She could take no food except iced oysters and iced champagne'). Throughout her life, Fuller made much of her congenital ill-health and demanded certain extraordinary attentions. Mr Nicol does not think she was particularly frail. A talented child, she captivated audiences with her songs at the age of five, and at the age of thirteen with her temperance lectures, during which she exhibited coloured illustrations of the liver. Later she went on the stage. Her early career was undistinguished, but she gave a hint of things to come by forming her own company and taking it on a long, but disastrous, tour of South America. In 1889 she made her first London appearance in *Caprice*, which opened on the 22 October at the Gaiety and closed almost at once. She went back to New York. At this time she had played everything from Shakespeare to burlesque but she had never danced.

In the early days of what is called Modern Dance it seems to have been a convention that all the best things happened by accident, like Ruth St Denis's getting the idea of her oriental dancing from a cigarette packet. Loïe Fuller encouraged the idea that she developed from one happy accident to the next. The first radical bit of luck came when she was acting, at a small New York theatre, a part in which she was hypnotized. To get the atmosphere right the management arranged for the stage to be illuminated entirely by green footlights, while the orchestra played sad music. During this hurriedly mounted piece, Fuller found herself on stage wearing a gauzy Indian skirt that was much too long for her. She says in her book that it was a present from an heroic admirer who later fell in the Khyber Pass; and she told a French historian that she got it from another girl. Anyway, she hit upon the idea of gliding hypnotically about the stage, holding the skirt up. To her surprise there were pleased exclamations from the house: 'It's a butterfly!', 'It's an orchid!' She danced around amid applause and then dropped ecstatically at the hypnotist's feet, 'completely enveloped in a cloud of the light material'. Next day she put the skirt on again and was studying it in a looking-glass when she noticed that sunlight made it translucent. 'Golden reflections played in the folds of the sparkling silk, and in this light my body was revealed in a shadowy contour.' Thereupon, 'gently, almost religiously', she waved the silk about, and saw that she had 'obtained modulations of a character before unknown . . . Finally I reached a point where each movement of the body was expressed in the folds of the silk, in a play of colours and draperies that could be mathematically and systematically calculated.'[7]

Such was the basis of her original act. She whirled about with her arms aloft – later she extended them with sticks concealed in the drapery – as shown in Toulouse-Lautrec's lithograph – and the result-ant spiral or serpentine effect she differentiated into twelve character-istic motions or dances, each carried out with different lighting. The lighting was provided by an electric lantern with coloured glasses, another device she was later to develop to an extraordinary degree. The final dance was performed in total darkness save for a single ray of yellow light crossing the stage. From the outset she invited attention to these optical effects; she was never beautiful, and even in these days too plump for her shadowy contour to be an important part of her appeal. This was new, though she admits modestly that at this stage she was 'far from imagining that I had hold of a principle capable of revolutionizing a branch of aesthetics'. Her very ignorance of classical technique was to contribute, with the hypnotic attitudes, the resemblances to natural objects, and the optical illusions, to her establishment as a living emblem of a new aesthetic.

The act was almost immediately successful. 'Three cheers for the orchid, the cloud and the butterfly!' cried the New York audience. But the New York managers were full of greed and duplicity; she was at once plagued by imitators, some even using her name (a trouble she was to have for many years) and after certain vicissitudes and wanderings she found her true home in Paris, where she arrived in October 1892. She was engaged to dance at the Folies-Bergère, and with a programme of five dances including the Serpentine she achieved a fantastic success, which was augmented later in the decade when she returned with new items. All over Europe and America she was imi-tated, but never successfully, largely because of the care she took to keep secret the technical apparatus upon which she depended. She was not overstating her triumph when she said that the usual audience at the Folies-Bergère was every evening 'lost amid a crowd composed of scholars, painters, sculptors, writers and ambassadors'. Outside the theatre, students pelted her with flowers and drew her carriage; the police, about to take brisk action against a procession obstructing circulation at the Madeleine, held their hands when they discovered that all was in honour of La Loïe Fuller.

At the time of her first success she was taken up by Rodin, who declared that she was 'a woman of genius, with all the resources of talent' and 'a Tanagra figurine in action'. She painted Nature, he said, in the colours of Turner; she was the woman on the famous Pompeian frieze. Anatole France, who wrote a preface for her autobiography in 1908, called her 'marvellously intelligent' but added that it was her unconscious that really counted. 'She is an artist . . . the chastest and most expressive of dancers, beautifully inspired, who reanimated within herself and restores to us the lost wonders of Greek mimicry, the art of those motions, at once voluptuous and mystical, which interpret the phenomena of nature and the life history of living things.' Other admirers were the Curies, to whom she later dedicated a remarkable dance. She knew anybody she cared to know. Pretty well all the theatrical artists of Paris represented her at this time, notably perhaps Steinlen and Toulouse-Lautrec, whose lithograph is probably the best of all; but she asked neither Lautrec nor Steinlen for posters, preferring their imitators. A pretty poster drawing by Chéret hung in her dressing-room. Perhaps she supposed herself too far from the real centre of Lautrec's interests; anyway, he soon moved on to more congenial subjects.

Loïe Fuller undoubtedly enjoyed all this. In a Paris that paid her 12,000 francs a month and was full of women wearing wide Loïe Fuller skirts, she expected a lot of attention. There is a note of rare disenchantment in an entry in Renard's diary (1901) which tells how he met Fuller in an omnibus, a shapeless figure too highly painted, sausage-fingered, with only the rings to make any divisions, an intermittent smile, as if everybody on the bus was the Public; vague myopic eyes. She was turned off the bus for not having her fare; Renard wanted to say, 'Mademoiselle, I know and admire you; *voilà dix sous!*' But he did not. It is surprising to hear of her using a bus; she lived extravagantly.

Her well-publicized hypochondria did not diminish. She took elaborate precautions against headache, and informed journalists that she was threatened with paralysis of the arms. Every performance ended in what looked like total collapse. Isadora Duncan, who never forgave Fuller for launching her, does nothing to spoil the picture of Fuller as agreeably mysterious, hypochondriacal and queer. She speaks of

16

visiting her in Berlin, where Fuller sat in a magnificent apartment at the Hotel Bristol, surrounded as usual by an entourage of beautiful girls who were 'alternately stroking her hands and kissing her'. 'Here,' says Isadora, 'was an atmosphere of such warmth as I had never met before.' Fuller complained of terrible pains in the spine, and the girls had to keep up a supply of icebags, which were placed between her back and the back of the chair. Judge Isadora's surprise when, after an expensive dinner, Fuller went off and danced. 'Had this luminous vision that we saw before us,' asks Isadora, 'any relation to the suffering patient of a few moments before?' Fuller was clearly one to keep separate suffering and creation. M. F. Jourdain also vouches for the icepack, but remembers it as wielded by the faithful Gaby, a Mlle Bloch who was for many years Fuller's companion-manager, and who kept the company going after Loïe's death in 1928. (It survived, though in decline, till 1940, when the Occupation put an end to it; but something called the Loïe Fuller ballet turned up in 1958 in a French film called *Femmes de Paris*.) M Jourdain testifies that every noise made Fuller suffer, even that of conversation; 'when the level of noise increased she would hastily apply the icepack to her neck, and, begging for silence with a gesture of supplication, she would stop her ears.' Once he saw her rehearse. She did not take off her coat, but sat on the stage, placed the icepack on her neck, stuck her fingers in her ears, and signalled the conductor to begin. She then followed his gestures with her eyes, taking care to hear as little as possible of the noise she had unleashed. Then she went back to her carriage. Naturally the performances were a little more tiring, and she was carried home to bed after every one of them. Mr Nicol says she had sinus trouble and loved overheated rooms; she was capable of arranging the kind of tableau Isadora came upon simply to impress visitors. As to rehearsal, she treated her company less tenderly than herself, wearing them out with all-night sessions. Mr Nicol was suspended from the company for inattention during a long rehearsal, at the age of five.

Fuller remained for a great many years enormously popular in the music-halls of Europe. She conquered London, as they say, in 1893, appearing during the interval of George Edwardes's *In Town*, a show distinguished by May Belfort's performance of 'Daddy wouldn't buy me a bow-wow'. But this did not prevent the English intelligentsia from taking her quite as seriously as the Parisian; for instance, there is an odd poem in French, in *The Cambridge ABC* of 11 June 1894 – it did not last long but had a cover by Beardsley – which refers to the '*Varicolore et multiforme*' Fuller, and uses such expressions as '*une volupté profonde . . . inquiétant mystère*', etc. The popular press found her both amazing and moral – her Mirror Dance showed *eight* Loïe Fullers 'dancing as if they were the fabled victims of the Tarantula, the whole forming an artistic spectacular effect that the world has never seen equalled'; yet she made no 'gesture or movement which would offend the susceptibilities of the most modest-minded of British matrons or maidens'. Her long skirts seemed to bring about a long-needed *rapprochement* of Art and Morality.

Quite early in her career she had built up a company, and her shows grew more elaborate. She had her own theatre at the Paris Exposition, and in it she introduced Sada Yacco to the European public. Yacco's success, unlike Fuller's, was not unmixed. Eventually Fuller built around Yacco her 'Japanese company' – I think Yeats had this company in mind when he spoke of her 'Chinese Dancers' in 'Nineteen Hundred and Nineteen', for she seems never to have had a Chinese troupe – and took them, with Isadora Duncan, on a tour of Germany. (Isadora left this 'troupe of beautiful but demented ladies' and struck out on her own, without ever rebutting the charges of immodesty, ingratitude, and treachery which Fuller laid against her.)

A French journal of the Exposition period describes her as '*parfaitement double . . . à la ville petite, à la scène grande . . .* a very pushing woman'. By this time Mr Tindall of *Pearson's Weekly* was willing to claim that 'she had given the world such ideas of colour as had never been conceived before; look at the pictures in the Paris salons if you would see some of the more striking effects of Loïe Fuller's dancing . . . she ranks with the great geniuses of the ages'. But she went on appearing at the Coliseum, in (for example) a variety bill called 'La Miraculeuse Loïe Fuller in the Grand Musical Mystical Dances', which was itemized as follows:

(1) The Flight of the Butterflies (Radium)
(2) The Dance of the 1,000 Veils,

this in five tableaux: 'Storm at Sea – Wrecked, Lost'; 'The River of Death'; 'The Fire of Life'; 'Ave Maria'; 'The Land of Visions'. How two famous dances, 'The Butterfly' (subject of many photographs) and 'Radium', a dance in honour of the Curies, came to be conflated, I do not know. 'The Land of Visions', Mr Nicol surmises, was a way of using up some photographs she had had taken of the surface of the moon.

As time went by, she depended more and more on her company, but also upon ingenious optical effects. Before 1909 she had founded her School, and by 1912 the best dancers were allowed to take over her Lily, Serpentine, and Fire Dances. But the new dances were more and more abstract. Her troupe had a great success in London in 1923 with a shadow ballet called *Ombres Gigantesques*. There are some splendid photographs in the *Sketch* for the 13 December of that year, the eve of a charity performance to be attended by the King and Queen. An enormous shadow hand plucks at the cowering dancers; a vast foot descends to crush them. In other performances, for example in a ballet using Debussy's *La Mer*, the dancers were not seen at all, but simply heaved under a huge sea of silk. One late dance 'consisted solely of silver-sequined tassels being "dabbled" in a narrow horizontal shaft of light – the background and the performers being veiled in black' (E. J. Nicol). Other performers – Maud Allen is a notable though forgotten Salome – came and went; but Fuller remained in the front line till her death in 1928.

The career of Fuller is unintelligible without some reference to her technical repertory. She had, of course, her own aesthetic notions, and claimed to have brought about a revolution in the arts. At first she saw the dance as arising naturally from music, but expressing human emotion best when unimpeded by training. 'The moment you attempt to give dancing a trained element, naturalness disappears; Nature is truth, and art is artificial. For example, a child will never dance of its own accord with the toes pointing out.' Rodin expressly agreed, and Massenet was so struck with the doctrine that he gave Fuller unrestricted performing rights in his music without royalty. Debussy was also interested, and Florent Schmitt wrote Fuller's Salome music (1893). But she very often used commonplace music, and it is hard to believe that her mature doctrine was either musical or expressive. The line of

the body, never, as we have seen, the principal exhibit in her performance, grew less and less important, and in the end hardly counted at
all – witness those dances in which no human figure was perceptible
to the audience. The story she tells of her stumbling upon a new art of
illuminated drapes in motion – and this at the outset of her career –
has the germ at any rate of the truth. In a theoretical chapter of her
autobiography she has some reflections on Light and the Dance; she
was greatly concerned with the affective qualities of colour and its
relation to sounds and moods (speculations much in vogue at the time)
and was once thrown out of Notre Dame for waving a handkerchief
in front of a sunlit window. She maintained the opinion that 'motion
and not language is truthful', a view not likely to meet much opposition
among the poets of the time, but she did not mean the simple dancer's
motions or even those involuntary gestures organized into art which
are the basis of Modern Dance; she meant the manipulation of silk
and light. With them she could penetrate the spectator's mind and
'awaken his imagination that it may be prepared to receive the image'.

Fuller used in her publicity a remark by Pierre Roche that she was
unequalled as an electrician and used her coloured lights on silk with
a painter's art. In fact in the earliest days of theatrical electricity she
seems to have gone a remarkably long way towards realizing that
dream of a *Farbenkunst* which had been epidemic since the eighteenth
century. She was given great credit for her skill at the time, not only
by aesthetes who thought of the whole thing as a transcendent success
for cosmetics, but by practical theatre people. Sarah Bernhardt consulted her. There was growing interest in the spectacular possibilities
of electric light on cheap materials, but nobody else brought off what
Mallarmé called the 'industrial achievement' of substituting coloured
light for all other properties, '*instituant un lieu*'.

The means by which she did this were closely kept secrets. She put
it about that one very striking effect was discovered by accident, when
an electrician 'the worse for strong drink, threw two lights of different
colours on the stage together' (*Pearson's Weekly*). In fact, of course,
she was intensely preoccupied, and most ingenious, with light. She
used the carbon arc-lights and coloured gelatines with which the
theatres of the period were equipped, but with colours of her own
specification. More important, she designed large magic-lantern pro-

jectors with slides of plain or frosted glass. The slides, which she painted with liquefied gelatine, were the fundamental secret, and only Fuller and Miss Nolan had access to them. Theatre men were not allowed to work the projectors, and the Company had its own trusted electricians. It was on such slides that she printed the photographs of the moon for the 'Nuages' ballet. The bewildering 'Radium' dance was done by projecting iridescent colour on to silks using first one multi-coloured slide, then superimposing another, and then withdrawing the first. When one thinks of her influence on future stage lighting, one should remember not only the Lyceum pantomimes in which she was regularly copied, but also that, as Mr Nicol says, 'our whole modern system of projected stage lighting owes its origin to her ingenious mind'. Experiments with coloured shadows on the cyclorama, and also with mirrors, were natural developments of such interests.

Her innovations were not confined to the lighting. She also did surprising things with silk. 'The idea of dyeing and painting silk in terms of abstract colour and not of pattern seems, undoubtedly, to have been Fuller's own', writes Mr Nicol. The work was carried out by Miss Nolan, and the dyed silks became a commercial success, still remembered as 'Liberty' silks. Mr Nicol would credit Fuller with an influence on Gordon Craig and others; certainly we have been underestimating her during all the years when her revolutionary innovations were forgotten. One has a clear picture of a performer who converted dancing into something quite other, whose scenes and machines were of a new theatrical epoch, and whose gifts lay primarily in such inventions. Writing of a performance at the Théâtre Champs-Elysées in June, 1922, Levinson said, 'Even though she has the insipid primary *plastique*, the scholarly *faux-héllenisme* of the Anglo-Saxon (which forms an apparent link between her school and Isadora's) her personality is none the less fascinating ... She is a great imaginative creator of forms. Her drapes animate and organize space, give her a dream-like *ambiance*, abolish geometrical space ... Whatever belongs to the dance is ordinary; but *tout ce qui tient de l'optique est plein d'intérêt.*' Levinson had no doubt that this was another matter entirely than '*les enfantillages caduces de Duncanisme et ces vaines danses d'expression*'.

It is a little surprising, therefore, that much of Fuller's fame derived from her ability to represent natural objects – moths, butterflies, lilies, etc. Dances of this kind were frequently photographed, and she kept them in her repertoire right into the Twenties. The Serpentine dance is part of the history of art nouveau; it would be tedious to make a list of the compliments paid her by distinguished men on her power to reveal fugitive aspects of nature. Certainly some of the photographs are impressively moth-like and lily-like. With this strain of compliment there was mingled a persistent note of praise for her Orientalism and her Hellenism too. Such contradictions, if they are so, may be reconciled in the aesthetic of a Mallarmé; he wrote that the dancer was not a woman dancing but a metaphor containing elemental aspects of our form, sword, cup, flower, etc. And Symons, in *The World as Ballet*, finds in the dance 'the evasive, winding turn of things . . . the intellectual as well as sensuous appeal of a living symbol'. She was a power like one of Nature's, and her creation had the same occult meanings.

The heart of this matter is, indeed, the chorus of poetic approval, and the terms in which it was couched. Consider, for example, the 'Fire Dance', a popular item from early days. She told the credulous Mr Tindall of *Pearson's Weekly* that this dance had its origin in an accident: when she was dancing her Salome at the Athénée (1893) she danced before Herod as 'the setting sun kissed the top of Solomon's temple'. But it also kissed her garments, and the public, always vocal, cried out and called it 'the fire-dance'. In fact this was merely another attempt to offset the cold electric calculations of Fuller. The *Danse du Feu* was lit from below stage, by a red lantern directed through a glassed-in trap. The effect was striking (*Pearson's Weekly* has some lurid coloured photographs). Fuller appeared to the music of the 'Ride of the Valkyries', shaking, we are told, and twisting in a torrent of incandescent lava, her long dress spouting flame and rolling around in burning spirals. She stood, says Jean Lorrain, in blazing embers, *and did not burn*; she exuded light, was herself a flame. Erect in her brazier she smiled, and her smile was the rictus of a mask under the red veil that enveloped her and which shook and waved like a flame along her lava-nakedness. Lorrain goes on to compare her with Herculaneum buried in cinders (it wasn't, of course), the Styx and its banks, Vesuvius with open throat spitting fire. Only thus, he argued, could one describe her motionless, smiling nakedness in the midst of a furnace, wearing the fires of heaven and hell as a veil. Gustave Fréville called her a nightmare sculpted in red clay. 'The fire caresses her dress, seizes her entirely, and, inexorable lover, is sated by nothing short of nothingness.' Years later Yeats was pretty certainly remembering this dance as well as Dante and a Noh play when he spoke in his 'Byzantium' of the dance as an emblem of art, caught up out of nature into the endless artifice of his Byzantium, the endless death-in-life of the mosaic:

> . . . blood-begotten spirits come
> And all complexities of fury leave;
> > Dying into a dance,
> > An agony of trance,
> An agony of flame that cannot singe a sleeve.

The 'Fire Dance' had all the qualities Yeats asked of the art, for not only was the dancer unconsumed, but she also wore the obligatory enigmatic smile. 'From this flame which does not burn', says Ménil in his *Histoire de la Danse* (1904), 'there leaps, between two volutes of light, the head of a woman wearing an enigmatic smile.' Ménil, as it happens, goes on – as Jourdain did – to question whether all this trickery of silk and electric light was really dancing at all, and he wonders how, from the vulgarity of the cheap glare and waving skirt, there could come this hashish-like experience. Goncourt's reaction was similar: 'What a great inventor of ideality man is!' he moralized, contemplating this 'vision of what is strange and supernatural' yet has its origin in common stuff and vulgar lights.

Other dances were greeted with equal rapture. Georges Rodenbach draws widely on Fuller's repertoire in his poem 'La Loïe Fuller', first published in *Figaro* in May 1896, and warmly praised by Mallarmé. It has fifty-eight lines, and is too long to quote in full, but here are some samples:

> Déchirant l'ombre, et brusque, elle est là: c'est l'aurore!
> D'un mauve de prélude enflé jusqu'au lilas,
> S'étant taillé des nuages en falbalas,
> Elle se décolore, elle se recolore.

Alors c'est le miracle opéré comme un jeu:
Sa robe tout à coup est un pays de brume;
C'est de l'alcool qui flambe et de l'encens qui fume;
Sa robe est un bûcher de lys qui sont en feu. . . .

Or, comme le volcan contient toutes ses laves,
Il semble que ce soit d'elle qu'elle ait déduit
Ces rivières de feu qui la suivent, esclaves,
Onduleuses, sur elle, en forme de serpents . . .
O tronc de la Tentation! O charmeresse!
Arbre du Paradis où nos désirs rampants
S'enlacent en serpents de couleurs qu'elle tresse! . . .

Un repos.
   Elle vient, les cheveux d'un vert roux
Influencés par ces nuances en démence;
On dirait que le vent du large recommence;
Car déjà, parmi les étoffes en remous,
Son corps perd son sillage; il fond en des volutes . . .
Propice obscurité, qu'est-ce donc que tu blutes
Pour faire de sa robe un océan de feu,
Toute phosphorescente avec des pierreries? . . .
Brunehilde, c'est toi, reine des Walkyries,
Dont pour être l'élu chacun se rêve un dieu. . . .

C'est fini.
   Brusquement l'air est cicatrisé
De cette plaie en fleur dont il saigna. L'étreinte
De l'Infini ne nous dure qu'un court moment;
Et l'ombre de la scène où la fresque fut peinte
Est noire comme notre âme, pensivement.

What Mallarmé liked about this was the recognition that Rodenbach restores to dancing its ancient character – it provides its own décor (*elle s'étoffe*). For Fuller's 'imaginative weavings are poured forth like an atmosphere' in contrast with the short-skirted coryphées of the ballet, who have no *ambiance* save what the orchestra provides.

   Everything conspires to bring Fuller's performance into the position of an emblem of the Image of art, 'self-begotten' in Yeats's favourite word; or like the body of a woman yet not in any natural sense alive (*prodige d'irréel*), enigmatic, having the power of election. The darkness of the stage at the end of the performance is the natural darkness of the modern soul which only the Image, hardly come by and evanescent, can illuminate: 'the embrace of eternity lasts us only a short moment'. This power of fusing body and soul, mending all our division, is celebrated even in *Pearson's Weekly*. More completely than any other dancer before her, Loïe Fuller seemed to represent in visible form the incomprehensible Image of art in the modern world,[8] as Mauclair said, 'The Symbol of Art itself, a fire above all dogmas'. And she remains the dancer of Symbolism, from Mallarmé to Yeats; a woman yet totally impersonal, 'dead, yet flesh and bone'; *poème dégagé de tout appareil du scribe*. 'Thanks to her,' said Roger Marx, 'the dance has once more become the "poem without words" of Simonides . . . above all one is grateful to her for giving substance to that ideal spectacle of which Mallarmé once dreamed – a mute spectacle, which escaped the limits of space and time alike, and of which the influence, powerful over all, ravishes in one common ecstasy the proud and the humble.'

In February 1893, Mallarmé went to the Folies-Bergère to see Loïe Fuller. It was an historic evening. André Levinson, complaining in the early Twenties of the exaggerated deference paid in literary circles to the music-hall, credits the Goncourts and Huysmans with beginning the vogue, but goes on: 'One day Stéphane Mallarmé, aesthetician of the absolute, was seen pencilling, in his seat at the Folies-Bergère, his luminous *aperçus* on the so-called serpentine dances of Loïe Fuller, *fontaine intarissable d'elle-même*. Since then the whole world has followed . . .' What Mallarmé was writing emerges as a passage of prose notably difficult even for him, but the centre, indeed the source in most cases, of contemporary poetic comment on Fuller. Concerning her, he says, and the way in which she uses the fabrics in which she is dressed, the articles of contemporary enthusiasts – which may sometimes be called poems – leave little to be said. 'Her performance, *sui generis*, is at once an artistic intoxication and an industrial achievement. In that terrible bath of materials swoons the radiant, cold dancer, illustrating countless themes of gyration. From her proceeds an expanding web – giant butterflies and petals, unfoldings – everything of a pure and elemental order. She blends with the rapidly changing colours which vary their limelit phantasmagoria of twilight and grotto, their rapid emotional changes – delight, mourning, anger; and to set these off, prismatic, either violent or dilute as they are, there must be the dizziness of soul made visible by an artifice.' He goes on to suggest that in this kind of dancing, in which the dancer seems to have the power infinitely to expand the dance through her dress, there is a lesson for the theatre, in which there is always a banality that rises up between dance and spectator. Loïe Fuller makes one see how the subtleties inherent in the dance have been neglected. 'Some restored aesthetic,' says Mallarmé, 'will one day go beyond these marginal notes'; but he can at least use this insight to denounce a common error concerning staging, 'helped as I unexpectedly am by the solution unfolded for me in the mere flutter of her gown by my unconscious and unwitting inspirer'. And he speaks of the dancer's power to create on the boards of the stage her own previously unthought-of milieu. The *décor* lies latent in the orchestra, to come forth like a lightning stroke at the sight of the dancer who represents the idea. And this 'transition from sonorities to materials . . . is the one and only skill of Loïe Fuller, who does it by instinct, exaggeratedly, the movements of skirt or wing instituting a place . . . The enchantress makes the ambience, produces it from herself and retracts it into a silence rustling with *crêpe de Chine*. Presently there will disappear, what is in these circumstances an inanity, that traditional plantation of permanent sets which conflict with choreographic mobility. Opaque frames, intrusive cardboard, to the scrap-heap! Here, if ever, is atmosphere, that is nothingness, given back to ballet, visions no sooner known than scattered, limpid evocation. The pure result will be a liberated stage, at the will of fictions, emanating from the play of a veil with attitude or gesture.' He sees the dance of Fuller as 'multiple emanations round a nakedness' which is central, 'summed up by an act of will ecstatically stretched to the extremity of each wing, her statuesque figure strict, upright; made dead by the effort of condensing out of this virtual self-liberation delayed decorative leaps of skies and seas, evenings, scent and foam'. And he concludes, 'I thought it necessary, whatever fashion may make of this miraculous contemporary development, to extract its summary sense and its significance for the art as a whole.'

There is dispute among students of Mallarmé as to the place of dancing in his unsystematic system, and less attention than might be expected is paid to this tribute to Loïe Fuller. But there seems to be no very good reason for discounting what it says: that she represented for him at least the spirit of an unborn aesthetic; that she offered a kind of spatial equivalent of music; that she stands for the victory of what he called the Constellation over what he called Chance, '*le couronnement du labeur humain*', as Bonniet describes it in his Preface to *Igitur*. Like the archetype of Art, the Book, Fuller eliminated *hasard*. Thibaudet, indeed, believed that the whole concept of the Book owed something to Mallarmé's meditations on the dance; so did Levinson, arguing that Mallarmé glimpsed in the ballet 'a revelation of the definitive Œuvre, which would sum up and transcend man'; so, more recently, does M Guy Delfel. The fitness of the dance as an emblem of true poetry is clear. Valéry was expanding the views of Mallarmé when he made his famous comparison between them (poetry is to prose as dancing is to walking). Mallarmé's growing concern for syntax, so irrefutably demonstrated by L. J. Austin, does not militate against this view that the dance took over in his mind some of the importance of music; for syntax is the purposeful movement of language and such movement has, in either art, to be assimilated to the necessarily autonomous condition of the Image. The dance is more perfectly devoid of ideas, less hampered by its means, than poetry, since it has not the strong antipathy of language towards illogic; yet it is not absolutely pure; the dancer is not inhuman. Mallarmé deals with precisely this point in the opening article of *Crayonné au Théâtre* (before 1887) when he discusses the ambiguous position of the dancer, half impersonal; very like the position of the poet ('The pure work requires that the poet vanish from the utterance' in so far as he can). But Fuller was more purely emptied of personality: an apparition, a vision of eternity for Rodenbach; for Mallarmé '*l'incorporation visuelle de l'idée*'.

If it seemed necessary, as it did, for poets to reclaim their heritage from music, the dance provided something more exactly fitting as an emblem of what was aspired to; and in a sense Fuller can stand for the liberation of Symbolism from Wagner. She is much more properly the

Symbolist dancer than any orthodox ballerina; and there is a clear discontinuity between the general admiration for dancers of French poets earlier than Mallarmé and his praise of Fuller. In Baudelaire the 'human and palpable element' counts for much; in Gautier also. But in the new age, the age of Mallarmé and Yeats, what matters is that the dancer 'is not a woman'; that she is 'dead, yet flesh and bone'. The difference constitutes a shift in the whole climate of poetry, represented by the shift in English poetic from Symons to Pound, from Symbolism as primarily an elaborate system of suggestion, of naming by not naming, to the dynamism of the Vortex and the Ideogram. For Fuller is a kind of Ideogram: *l'incorporation visuelle de l'idée*, a spectacle defying all definition, radiant, homogeneous.

Such, at any rate, was the way those people saw Fuller who saw her with eyes opened to dance as a *majestueuse ouverture* on a reality beyond flux. They saw in her *'la voyante de l'infini'*. When Diaghilev came, defying the *genres*, overwhelming the senses with music and colour and movement, one or two people perhaps remembered her as having been the first to do it. I am convinced that Valéry did. Again and again he returns to the dance as a satisfactory emblem of a desirable poetry. It best illustrates what he calls non-usage – 'the *not* saying "it is raining" – this is the language of poetry; and movement which is not instrumental, having no end outside itself, is the language of dancing. Poetry, like dancing, is action without an end.' As the dancer makes an image of art out of the quotidian motions of her body, so the poet must 'draw a pure, ideal Voice, capable of communicating without weakness, without apparent effort, without offence to the ear, and without breaking the ephemeral sphere of the poetic universe, an idea of some Self miraculously superior to Myself'. The Dance makes of an activity of the body – sweat, straining muscle, heaving chest – an idea, a diagram of a high reality. Valéry called his dialogue, *L'Ame et la Danse*, of 1921, 'a sort of ballet of which the Image and the Idea are Coryphaeus in turn'. The dialogue embodies in language of refined wit and gaudy elegance the essence of our post-Wagnerian aesthetic. Athiktè, the central figure, is usually thought of as a conventional ballet dancer; and she does dance on her points. But, as Levinson said in his pamphlet on the dialogue (*Paul Valéry, poète de la danse*, 1927) the *tourbillon*, her ecstatic finale, is not merely a ballet step, it is the whirling of a mystic's dance. Though Valéry collected ballet photo-graphs, they were of a special sort, *chronophotographies*; the plates were exposed in darkness, the dancers carrying lights; and the result was a whirl of white lines, a record of the pattern of aimless poetical acts. In any case, we need not suppose him so devoted to the ballet as to have forgotten Loïe Fuller. He was on the point of refusing the invitation to write the dance dialogue because he 'considered . . . that Mallarmé had exhausted the subject' and undertook it finally with the resolve that he would make Mallarmé's prodigious writings on the subject 'a peculiar condition of my work'. So I believe that when he came to write the passage comparing the dancer with a salamander – living 'completely at ease, in an element comparable to fire – he was remembering Fuller. The passage culminates in a long, rhapsodical speech from Socrates: 'what is a flame . . . if not *the moment itself*? . . . Flame is the act of that moment which is between earth and heaven . . . the flame sings wildly between matter and ether . . . we can no longer speak of movement . . . nor distinguish any longer its acts from its limbs'. Phaedrus replies that 'she flings her gestures like scintillations . . . she filches impossible attitudes, even under the very eye of Time!' Eryximachus sums it up: 'Instant engenders form, and form makes the instant visible.' And when the dancer speaks, she says she is neither dead nor alive, and ends: 'Refuge, refuge, O my refuge, O Whirlwind! I was in thee, O movement – outside all things . . .' A Bergsonian dancer almost, '*révélatrice du réel*' as Levinson says.

The propriety of yoking together Avril and Fuller as I have done here is now, perhaps, self-evident. Avril is a smaller figure altogether, but she demonstrates the strength of the link between dancing and poetry, as well as the important pathological element in the dancer's appeal. Fuller deserves, one would have thought, some of the attention that has gone to Isadora. Levinson, who repeatedly declares his faith in classical dancing as the one discipline '*féconde, complète, créatrice*', respected Fuller, but despised Duncan as having no technique, no beauty, no suppleness, her feet flattened and enlarged by years of barefoot prancing, her music primitive. The fact is that Duncan was much more the Tanagra figurine, the dancer from the Pompeian fresco, than Fuller, who earned these descriptions in her early days. And Duncan certainly did not submerge her personality in strange disguises and unnatural lights. The Modern Dance has developed theories sufficiently impersonal to make it intensely interesting to Mrs Langer, creating a symbolic reality independent of nature. But it depends always upon the body – upon the power of the body not to express emotion but to objectify a pattern of sentience. Fuller with her long sticks, her strange optical devices, her burying the human figure in masses of silk, achieved impersonality at a stroke. Her world was discontinuous from nature; and this discontinuity Valéry, speaking of his Symbolist ancestry, described as 'an almost inhuman state'. She withdrew from the work; if to do otherwise is human, said Valéry, 'I must declare myself essentially inhuman'.

This is the doctrine of impersonality in art with which T. E. Hulme and T. S. Eliot among many others have made everybody familiar. 'The progress of an artist is a continual self-sacrifice, a continual extinction of personality ... the more perfect the artist the more completely separate in him will be the man who suffers and the mind which creates.' Thomas Parkinson, commenting on Ortega y Gasset's 'dehumanization' – 'a point can be reached in which the human content has grown so thin that it is negligible' – remarks acutely that the confused reception accorded to Pound's *Pisan Cantos* was due to critical shock at their identification of the sufferer and the creator. Pound, in leaving off his 'ironic covering', simply broke with a rule of poetic that he himself had done much to enforce. Mr Parkinson is glad; he wants to let 'the Reek of Humanity' back into poetry, where he thinks it belongs, and he seems to regard the impersonality doctrine as a lengthy but temporary deviation from some true 'romantic aesthetic'. I am not sure that he is right, or how far he misunderstands the human relevance of what the impersonal artist attempts. Mrs Langer could answer him, and I am quite sure that there Pound does not show the way back to reeking humanity. In Mr Eliot, in Valéry, we surely are aware of what Stevens called 'the thing that is incessantly overlooked: the artist, the presence of the determining personality'.

However this may be, Fuller's progressive extinction of the dancing body was a necessary component of her success as an emblem of the Image, out of nature. The imagination of the spectator fed upon her, independently of what she intended (she once caught sight of herself in a glass when dancing, and was surprised that what she saw bore no relation to her intention). She is abstract, clear of the human mess, dead and yet perfect being, as on some Byzantine dancing floor; entirely independent of normal action, out of time. It is a highflown way of talking about an affected music-hall dancer with an interest in stage-lighting; and, but for the example of Mallarmé, we should hardly venture it. Yet she was not a mere freak; dancers are always striving to become, like poems, machines for producing poetic states; 'they labour daily', as Levinson says, 'to prevent a relapse into their pristine humanity'. Only when the body is objectified in this way does it function, in the words of Whitehead, as 'the great central ground underlying all symbolic reference'. Also, it dies; and in so far as it is permitted to appear like something that does, it cannot represent victory over *hasard*, perfect being, the truth behind the deceptive veil of intellect. How is this to be overcome? 'Slash it with sharp instruments, rub ashes into a wound to make a keloid, daub it with clay, paint it with berry juices. This thing that terrifies us, this face upon which we lay so much stress, is something they have always wanted to deform, by hair, shading, by every possible means. Why? To remove from it the terror of death, by making it a work of art.' So William Carlos Williams on primitive ways into the artifice of eternity. Fuller's dehumanization was another way; it is very closely related to a critical moment in the history of modern poetic, but it is also, and this is as we ought to expect, rooted in the terror and joy of the obscure primitive ground from which modern poets draw strength for their archaic art.

2

Between Time and Eternity

The Sense of an Ending, *in which this and the following essay first appeared, was published in 1967, having been given as the Mary Flexner lectures at Bryn Mawr College in 1965. The title of the book derives from an expression used in its course; and whatever may be said of the book as a whole, the title seems to have caught on.*

The first of these two essays is drawn from a longer one called 'World Without End or Beginning', which started with a discussion of the difficulties that existed, at a time when it was important to reconcile Christian doctrine (the world was made out of nothing) with the philosophy of Aristotle, between the biblical account of the Creation and the Aristotelian belief that nothing could come of nothing. The ensuing compromises did not solve the discrepancy between time and eternity, but St Thomas Aquinas argued for a third term of duration between these two, which he called aevum, *the time of the angels, who were not pure being yet not material; not 'simple' as God is, yet not material and subject to time. This third order of duration proved to have secular uses, for instance it could be thought of as the order in which corporations exist, which is not eternity yet not subject to the ordinary action of time (individuals, who are, expire, but the institution to which they belong continues).*

Unsure whether it would interest readers as much as it did me, I have here omitted this rather abstruse discussion, along with a passage about the poet Spenser's interest in the aevum *as exhibited in the generative cycle. The reference to tock looks back to an argument earlier in the lectures to the way in which, to satisfy an appetite for endings, we mark off the period between two ticks by calling – and even hearing – the second one as 'tock'.*

One of the differences between doing philosophy and writing poetry is that in the former activity you defeat your object if you imitate the confusion inherent in an unsystematic view of your subject, whereas in the second you must in some measure imitate what is extreme and scattering bright, or else lose touch with that feeling of bright confusion. Thus the schoolmen struggled, when they discussed God, for a pure idea of simplicity, which became for them a very complex but still rational issue: for example, an angel is less simple than God but simpler than man, because a species is less simple than pure being but simpler than an individual. But when a poet discusses such matters, as in say 'Air and Angels', he is making some human point, in fact he is making something which is, rather than discusses, an angel – something simple that grows subtle in the hands of commentators. This is why we cannot say the Garden of Adonis is wrong as the Faculty of Paris could say the Averroists were wrong. And Donne's conclusion is more a joke about women than a truth about angels. Spenser, though his understanding of the expression was doubtless inferior to that of St Thomas, made in the Garden stanzas something 'more simple' than any section of the *Summa*. It was also more sensuous and more passionate. Milton used the word in his formula as Aquinas used it of angels; poetry is more simple, and accordingly more difficult to talk about, even though there are in poetry ideas which may be labelled 'philosophical'.

All the same, poets think, and are of their time; so that poets of Spenser's time, though they might feel as Bacon did about the 'vermicular questions' of the schoolmen, owed much to their conquests. As De Wulf observed, the scholastic synthesis is too faithful a reflection of the Western mind for complete abandonment – it 'remained in all men a fixed point of reference for their sensibilities'. And the change they made in the human way of feeling time affected not only philosophical poetry like Spenser's. Stevens admired, and for good reason, a remark of Jean Paulhan's, that the poet 'creates confidence in the world' – '*la confiance que le poète fait naturellement – et nous invite à faire – au monde*'. But he added that this is not in itself one of the differentiae between poets and philosophers, because in a different way philosophers also are concerned in the creation of this confidence, in the humanizing of the world by such fictions as causality, or angels. And

33

if times changed as they did, we should expect to find this in the greatest creator of confidence, Shakespeare.

The subject being so enormous, I ask you to consider only one or two brief points. I have said that tragedy may be thought of as the successor of apocalypse, and this is evidently in accord with the notion of an endless world. In *King Lear* everything tends towards a conclusion that does not occur; even personal death, for Lear, is terribly delayed. Beyond the apparent worst there is a worse suffering, and when the end comes it is not only more appalling than anybody expected, but a mere image of that horror, not the thing itself. The end is now a matter of immanence; tragedy assumes the figurations of apocalypse, of death and judgement, heaven and hell; but the world goes forward in the hands of exhausted survivors. Edgar haplessly assumes the dignity; only the king's natural body is at rest. This is the tragedy of sempiternity; apocalypse is translated out of time into the *aevum*. The world may, as Gloucester supposes, exhibit all the symptoms of decay and change, all the terrors of an approaching end, but when the end comes it is not an end, and both suffering and the need for patience are perpetual. We discover a new aspect of our quasi-immortality; without the notion of *aevum*, and the doctrine of kingship as a duality, existing in it and in time, such tragedy would not be possible.

What temporal image of the world do we derive from *Macbeth*? It is, to use the word the play forces on us, equivocal. The play, uniquely concerned with prophecy, begins with a question about the future: 'When shall we three meet again?' The speaker adds, without much apparent sense: 'In thunder, lightning, or in rain?' But these are three conditions which flourish, so to say, in the same hedgerow; they do not differ so completely as to be presentable as mutually exclusive alternatives. For a demon who can see into the cause of things a forecast of bad weather in Scotland is no great enterprise, and the either-ors of the question merely include, in an ironical way, a pointless selection of some aspects of futurity at the expense of others. The answer to the question is:

> When the hurlyburly's done,
> When the battle's lost and won.

Hurlies are to burlies as thunder to lightning, and lost battles are normally also won. The future is split by man-made antitheses, absurdly doubled or trebled in a parody of the uncertainties of human prediction. 'Fair is foul and foul is fair'; it depends upon the nature of the observer's attention, or on the estimate he makes of his own interest.

This is what L. C. Knights called 'metaphysical pitch and toss', a good phrase, because pitch is to toss as hurly is to burly. It is also a parody of prophetic equivocation, a device as ancient as the Delphic oracle. All plots have something in common with prophecy, for they must appear to educe from the prime matter of the situation the forms of a future. The best of them, thought Aristotle, include a peripeteia no less dependent than the other parts upon 'our rule of probability or necessity' but arising from that in the original situation to which we have given less attention; peripeteia is equivocating plot, and it has been compared, with some justice, to irony.[1] Now *Macbeth* is above all others a play of prophecy; it not only enacts prophecies, it is obsessed by them. It is concerned with the desire to feel the future in the instant, to be transported beyond the ignorant present. It is about failures to attend to the part of equivoque which lacks immediate interest (as if one should attend to hurly and not to burly). It is concerned, too, with the equivocations inherent in language. Hebrew could manage with one word for 'I am' and 'I shall be'; Macbeth is a man of a different temporal order. The world feeds his fictions of the future. When he asks the sisters 'what are you?' their answer is to tell him what he *will* be.

Macbeth, more than any other of Shakespeare's plays, is a play of crisis, and its opening is a figure for the seemingly atemporal agony of a moment when times cross; when our usual apprehension of successive past and future is translated into another order of time. Perhaps one can convey this best by a glance at an earlier and prototypical chooser, St Augustine. He wrote about this moment, when one is confronted by the lost and won of the future; a moment when the gap between desire and act is wide. Though certain of the end desired, he was 'at strife' with himself; the choices to be made were 'all meeting together in the same juncture of time'. He said within himself, 'Be it done now, be it done now'; but he still hesitated between fair and foul, and cried,

'How long? How long? Tomorrow and tomorrow?' This is the time when the soul distends itself to include past and future; and the similarities of language and feeling remind us that Macbeth had also to examine the relation between what may be willed and what is predicted. Throughout the early scenes we are being prepared by triple questions and double answers for the soliloquy at the end of the first Act, which is the speech of a man at this same juncture of time. The equivocating witches conflate past, present, and future; Glamis, Cawdor, Scotland. They are themselves, like the future, fantasies capable of objective shape. Fair and foul, they say; lost and won; lesser and greater, less happy and much happier. They dress the present in the borrowed robes of the future, in the equivoques of prophecy. The prophecies, as Macbeth notes, are in themselves neither good nor ill; but they bring him images of horror that swamp the present, so that 'nothing is / But what is not.' They bring him to that juncture of time so sharply defined by Brutus – the time 'Between the acting of a dreadful thing / And the first motion' – as being like a hideous dream. It is an interim in which the patient is denied the relief of time's successiveness; it seems never to end. His life is balanced on the point of nightmare, and so is time. Hence the see-saw language: *highly–holily, fair–foul, good–ill.*

The great soliloquy begins by wishing away the perpetuity of this moment. It is curious that we should have made a proverb of the expression 'be-all and end-all'. It was not proverbial for Shakespeare – he invented it; it grows out of the theme and language of the play. To be and to end are, in time, antithetical; their identity belongs to eternity, the *nunc stans*. In another way, the phrase is a pregnant conflation of crisis and an end immanent in it. Macbeth would select one aspect of the equivocal future and make it a perpetual present, and Shakespeare gives him the right crisis-word, the see-saw of be-all and end-all. He did use a proverb in the speech, at its very outset; you will find the source of 'If it were done when 'tis done' in Tilley ('the thing that is done is not to do')[2] if you are sure that Shakespeare is not remembering Augustine (or Jesus: 'That thou doest do quickly' John 13:27).

Macbeth is saying that if an act could be without succession, without temporal consequence, one would welcome it out of a possible future into actuality; it would be like having *hurly* without *burly*. But acts without 'success' are a property of the *aevum*. Nothing in time can, in that sense be *done*, freed of consequence or equivocal aspects. Prophecy by its very forms admits this, and so do plots. It is a truism confirmed later by Lady Macbeth: 'What's done cannot be undone.' The act is not an end. Macbeth, in the rapt, triple manner of the play, three times wishes it were: if the doing were an end, he says; if surcease cancelled success, if 'be' were 'end'. But only the angels make their choices in non-successive time, and 'be' and 'end' are one only in God. Macbeth moves to abandon the project. He is dissuaded by his wife in a speech which brings past, present, and future tenses to bear at one juncture: '*Was* the hope drunk . . . ? . . . *Art* thou afeard / To be the same in . . . act . . . as . . . in desire? . . . *Will* you let "I dare not" wait upon "I would" . . . ?' She seeks the abolition of the interim between desire and act, the shrinking allowance of time in which men are permitted to consider their desires in terms of God's time as well as their own.

The distinction is ancient. Christ waited for his *kairos*, refusing to anticipate the will of his Father; that is what he meant when he said 'Tempt not the Lord thy God'. So Irenaeus explains; and when we sin we act against God's time and 'arrogate to ourselves a sort of eternity, to "take the long view" and "make sure of things"', as Clement observed. Hence, according to Hans Urs von Balthasar, 'the restoration of order by the Son of God had to be the annulment of that premature snatching at knowledge . . . the repentant return from a false, swift transfer into eternity to a true, slow confinement in time'. The choice is between time and eternity. There is, in life, no such third order as that Macbeth wishes for. In snatching at a future he has to take *hurly* with *burly*.

The whole of *Macbeth* is penetrated by the language of times, seasons, prophecies; after the interim, the acting of the dreadful thing brings Macbeth under the rule of time again, it anticipates his dread exploits, mangles him to the point where he can no longer even pretend to understand its movement. Of Time's revenges, of the great temporal equivocations in this play I cannot now speak. But it is true that the crisis of Macbeth's choice, as surely as the dead King, is 'the great Doom's image'; that the choice of angelic or divine time was his presumption, and that he accordingly suffers in time, having chosen

37

his end at the moment of crisis. To await the season, as Jesus did ('the time prefixed I waited',[3] as he says in Milton) or as Gloucester must learn to do in *Lear*, and as Hamlet also learns, is another solution than Macbeth's.

For *Hamlet* is another play of protracted crisis, and I think one could show there also the deliberate clash of *chronos* and *kairos*, the obsessive collocation of past, present, and future at a moment that seems to require action the outcome of which can only be ambiguously predicted. Finally it is known that the readiness is all; that our choices have their season, which is another time from that in which we feel we live, though, like the time of angels, it intersects our time. The *kairos* arrives, the moment when at last the time is free, by means of a divine peripeteia, by accidental judgements and purposes mistook; we cannot make ready for it simply by 'taking the long view'. And when it comes it is an end, in so far as human affairs have ends. It is not a universal end, merely an image of it. In the central tragedy, *Lear*, universality is explicitly disavowed; we have an image of an end, but the dignity survives into a kind of eternity, an *aevum*. This has no necessary implications of happiness; not only Malcolm but Edgar, as princes, and not only princes but the damned in hell, inhabit the *aevum*.

What, then, can Shakespearean tragedy, on this brief view, tell us about human time in an eternal world? It offers imagery of crisis, of futures equivocally offered, by prediction and by action, as actualities; as a confrontation of human time with other orders, and the disastrous attempt to impose limited designs upon the time of the world. What emerges from *Hamlet* is – after much futile, illusory action – the need of patience and readiness. The 'bloody period' of *Othello* is the end of a life ruined by unseasonable curiosity. The millennial ending of *Macbeth*, the broken apocalypse of *Lear*, are false endings, human periods in an eternal world. They are researches into death in an age too late for apocalypse, too critical for prophecy; an age more aware that its fictions are themselves models of the human design on the world. But it was still an age which felt the human need for ends consonant with the past, the kind of end Othello tries to achieve by his final speech; complete, concordant. As usual, Shakespeare allows him his *tock*; but he will not pretend that the clock does not go forward. The human perpetuity which Spenser set against our imagery of the end is represented here also by the kingly announcements of Malcolm, the election of Fortinbras, the bleak resolution of Edgar.

In apocalypse there are two orders of time, and the earthly runs to a stop; the cry of woe to the inhabitants of the earth means the end of their time; henceforth 'time shall be no more'. In tragedy the cry of woe does not end succession; the great crises and ends of human life do not stop time. And if we want them to serve our needs as we stand in the middest we must give them patterns, understood relations as Macbeth calls them, that defy time. The concords of past, present, and future towards which the soul extends itself are out of time, and belong to the duration which was invented for angels when it seemed difficult to deny that the world in which men suffer their ends is dissonant in being eternal. To close that great gap we use fictions of complementarity. They may now be novels or philosophical poems, as they once were tragedies, and before that, angels.

3

Solitary Confinement

This is the sixth and final lecture of the Bryn Mawr College series, and opens with an announcement to that effect, and a rather florid allusion to Wallace Stevens, a poet I was in love with at the time, as indeed I still am. 'Life / As it is, in the intricate evasions of as' is a thought that makes plausible the view that 'the theory of poetry is the theory of life'. Stevens is a presence in the lectures, and crops up again, as the poet of metaphysical poverty, in the next paragraph. He has often been criticized for having too little to say about actual poverty, but I think he included the idea of it in his musings, though of course without direct experience of it. The expression 'what will suffice' is also a quotation from Stevens, who calls the poem the act of the mind in finding what will suffice. Later I refer to his 'weather' – he used the word in a very individual way, meaning, among other things, external reality as it happened to be when one encountered it. 'Conversions of our Lumpenwelt' *is another, possibly less happy, invention of Stevens. Sartre's* La Nausée *had been examined in the previous lecture.*

Christopher Burney is not among the Burneys celebrated in the latest edition of The Oxford Companion to English Literature *(2000) so it appears that such fame as he had did not survive into the new millennium. And yet* Solitary Confinement *is a great book. The reference to George Herbert is to his remarkable sonnet 'Prayer', a list of metaphors for prayer that includes the two here mentioned.*

My treatment of Wordsworth's 'Resolution and Independence' has been criticized because of what it says about the relation between actual and metaphysical poverty, as if, like Stevens, I showed insufficient solicitude for the former. Over the years this wonderful poem has attracted a large number of interpretations which I am sure many readers, including the authors, prefer to my own. However, my version remains part of what Stevens calls the make of the mind, and to repeat it here is a simple act of self-loyalty.

The views of Ortega y Gasset, as expounded in his Meditations on Don Quixote, *were discussed earlier in the book. I cannot remember the source of William Phillips' observation on Kafka. The final lines are, as might be expected, by Wallace Stevens.*

In this lecture, which is my last, I shall try to touch upon most of the themes proposed in the earlier ones, though I do not hope to provide in it the marvellous clue that would make all the rest useful and systematic. I could only do that if I were the master described in the poem, that 'more severe, More harassing master' who

> would extemporize
> Subtler, more urgent proof that the theory
> Of poetry is the theory of life
>
> As it is, in the intricate evasions of as,
> In things seen and unseen, created from nothingness,
> The heavens, the hells, the worlds, the longed-for lands.

I have his programme but not his powers. 'Life / As it is, in the intricate evasions of as' is what I am talking about, as best I can; and I am glad that it was in my most recent talk that I discussed Sartre, who knew that fictions, though prone to absurdity, are necessary to life, and that they grow very intricate because we know so desolately that *as* and *is* are not really one. None of our fictions is a supreme fiction.

Our knowing this creates in us, to a most painful degree, the condition Sartre calls 'need' and Stevens 'poverty'. It may seem superfluous for me to admit that this poet, at this time, speaks more urgently and congenially to me than any other, especially when he speaks of the fictions which are the proper consolations of human loneliness:

> Natives of poverty, children of malheur,
> The gaiety of language is our seigneur.

This is a way of speaking about a newly realized imaginative poverty in terms of something much older, and which words will not mitigate; and yet the two situations sometimes run together and blur. To be alone and poor is, in a sense, everybody's fate; but some people have been alone and poor in a very literal sense, as most of us have not; and in solitary confinement some of them have tested the gaiety of language as a means of projecting their humanity on a hostile environment. And it is by speaking for a few moments about the book of one such man that I can best begin to say what I have to say in this final talk.

Christopher Burney, the author of *Solitary Confinement*,[1] was a British agent in occupied France, and the book begins after his capture, though at a time when he still found solitude and confinement mere notions with no real force. What follows is a study of those notions as they become real. I mustn't speak of Burney as if he were *Homo*, a man in every way able to represent Man. He is abnormally brave, abnormally intelligent, and, it is relevant to add, upper-class English. His 'project' is coloured by his education. A man educated on the French pattern, for example, could perhaps not have retained that metaphysical innocence in the air of which the philosophical fictions of his captivity attained their own unforeseen shapes. For this is a book about the world a man invents in real poverty and solitude, and with as little help as possible from prefabricated formulas. We may, by means of it, come to understand something of the way the world shapes itself in the mind of true poverty; certainly it will seem right to think of this author as one of those 'heroic children whom time breeds / Against the first idea'.

Burney in his cell has two main interests: his appetite and his thoughts. The first of these he controls in various ways, playing tricks on it, arranging its slow defeat through the hours of the day. But the second, his thinking, grows obsessive. When the man in the next cell tries to communicate by knocking on the wall he is rejected. The thinker wants no interference with his private figurations. Burney does not congratulate himself on this. He knew his own poverty, and might have found value in the knowledge of another's. 'To be able to combine solidarity of plight with diversity of state must be the highest achievement of the race', he says, and with much penetration; for such are the conditions of tragedy. What makes Burney's book as it were post-tragic is his need to understand his plight alone. In prison he found himself, paradoxically, free, within the limits set by hunger and 'the animal lust to roam'. In that freedom, which was the freedom of acceptance, of true poverty, his mind enabled him to impose his humanity on the world. Reality is transfigured by this act, as by an act of love. 'Down on the bedrock,' he writes, 'life becomes a love affair of the mind, and reality merely the eternally mysterious beloved.' The experience was terrible enough, but to be without the memory of it would be to forfeit also 'that strange and faithful fraternity of the windows and those moments when the mind's eye, like a restless prism, could see reality as no more than an outline against the faintly discerned light of truth'. Such are the consolations of poverty.

The courage and the intellectual integrity of this writer are far beyond what most of us would expect of ourselves, and yet we may legitimately look, in the motions of his mind, for certain characteristic fictions in a pure state. Let me mention some of these. He is aware that in his solitude and freedom he has made what he could not have made among the improvisations of normal life, an objective and ordered world; remembering *The Franklin's Tale*, he calls this structured world 'ful well corrected',

> As been his centris and his argumentz
> And his proportioneles convenientz
> For his equacions in every thyng.

Reflecting on the plenitude of this structure, the hero cannot avoid the problem of evil. He solves it by reinventing the theology of evil as privation. Pressing on with it, he rediscovers, in terms of the spectroscope, a Neo-Platonic philosophy of light. Another problem demands to be faced, the problem of determinism and free will. Mechanistic explanations are dismissed as fantastic, but as he considers free will in terms of his own practice (should I eat all my bread at once, or space it out?) he is forced to conclude that familiar explanations suffered from a fundamental misconception: 'it was held that the quality of an act was determined by an act of volition which supposedly preceded it, whereas I now believed that consciousness of the value of any action was essentially reflective, and could only be made crudely to precede the action by a process of forward imagination, in its turn an act of reflection . . . At this small discovery all the paradoxes of the freedom of human beings over against the omnipotence of God dissolved.' Thus, in poverty, on the bedrock, are the ancient problems restated, and the mind discovers 'what will suffice'.

Burney was required to produce two different varieties of fiction. As well as inventing his own 'equacions in every thyng', he had to make up stories for the Gestapo. These Gestapo stories had to fulfil certain conditions: without telling the truth, they were required to convince a sceptical audience. They were, in fact, experiments in novelistic *verismo*. They required absolutely plausible character, situation, and dialogue. If they failed, the novelist – we recall that he was literally poor as we are figuratively poor – would be bludgeoned by his critics. The requirement of verisimilitude presses like an evil on his narrative.

'When we arrived near Pau . . . an unhealed wound gave my companion so much trouble that we had to rest a while.' I nearly attributed the wound to myself, until I remembered that I had no suitable scar.

Under critical pressure he revises the story somewhat, until an acute but reasonably congenial interrogator can find no fault with it. In a sense, the moment of triumph in this exercise comes when the interrogator, shaking hands, says 'Goodbye, I don't believe a word you've told me'. It is what we might say to the Goncourts, if the street were time and they at the end of the street.

But in the cell again, fictional satisfactions are not to be had by compliance with the paradigms of *verismo*; it is harder to save one's humanity than to save one's life. It is a question, says Burney, of an abstract order obscured by the 'coarseness of actuality'. This obscuration is to be inferred not only of the physical world, but also of men, since every coarse and actual man is 'doubled by an abstract expression of himself'. Since ethics is the relation between this fictional giant and the human animal, ethical solutions are aesthetic; we are concerned with fictions of relation. Thus solitude is an 'exercise in liberty' and liberty is inventing, for all the casualty of life, fictions of relation.

Burney remarks that the movement of his mind often took him 'to Americas thickly populated by earlier Columbuses'. In this true poverty everything had to be reinvented – even the clock. He needed a clock not because the conventional divisions of time were of pressing importance, but for reasons closer to those of the monks who first made them. They needed clocks for the more devout observance of the offices, Burney because he needed to apprehend the increasing pressure of an approaching end. As long as his captivity was story-like in that its moments were to be given significance by an end, he needed to sense its imminence. 'One does not suffer the passing of empty time, but rather the slowness of the expected event which is to end it.' If time cannot be felt as successive, this end ceases to have effect; without the sense of passing time one is virtually ceasing to live, one loses 'contact with reality'. So the prisoner invents a clock, the shadow cast by a gable on a wall which he can see through the fretted glass of his high window. Time cannot be faced as coarse and actual, as a repository of the contingent; one humanizes it by fictions of orderly succession and end.

The final end, death, is something else that cannot be faced in its inhuman coarseness. Burney could have died any day, and thought daily of death. But 'Death is a word which presents no real target to the mind's eye', he notes. If you imagine yourself being shot, your body being rolled away in a barrow by soldiers, you are cheating yourself by substituting for your own body someone else's, or perhaps an impersonal dummy. Your own death lies hidden from you. This cheating, like the cheating I talked about in my last lecture, can be malignant or benign; in the malignant form it is exemplified by the doctor in *La Nausée*, but in its benign form it is tragedy, which at one time was our way of opening the subject of the hidden death to our reluctant imaginations. Burney goes back behind the tragedy, however, to a simpler eschatology. His fictions have to do with the 'hereafter'. To produce them, he remarks, is a process 'as natural as eating'. The reason for this is that 'we have a vacuum, a perfect secret, proposed to us as our end, and we immediately set about filling it up'.

Paradigmatic fictions, the heaven and hell of his childhood, press themselves upon his thought; but he rejects them. Why? For the reasons I have suggested elsewhere; our scepticism, our changed principles of reality, force us to discard the fictions that are too fully explanatory, too consoling. He develops a sense of the impotence of his fictions, but they continue with a rare truth to type. Lapsing into unclerical *naïveté*, like the apocalyptists of my first talk, he brusquely invents an end convenient to himself. 'One thing is out of the question. I cannot still be here at Christmas . . . This was an axiom.' When Christmas comes and he is still there, he notices the necessity of such disconfirmation – 'I had made it necessary for me to be wrong by setting the limit in the first place.' Yet he passes Christmas day in the manner of millennarian sects after disconfirmation – calculating this day afresh by estimating the time needed for the Allies to accumulate the required number of tanks and landing craft. 'The essential, though I did not know it at the time, was to have a boundary which would make time finite and comprehensible.' It seems to be an essential, whether one's poverty is real or figurative; tracts of time unpunctuated by meaning derived from the end are not to be borne.

All the types of fiction, inherited or invented, naïve or sophisticated, run together in the mind that seeks freedom in poverty. They are all part of the world of words, of the cheat which gives life to the world. Burney considered language and isolated an aspect of it which reminded him of a family joke or game, a way of short-circuiting the unintelligible complexities by letting a shared word work in the varying contexts: love, for example, which is moved up from the flesh to heaven and down again. He thought a good deal about the great family jokes which seem mutually contradictory and unstable in meaning, the parables of the New Testament, for example; they seem in their con-flicting senses to be divorced from the consolatory gospels in which they are found, calling upon us to make the effort of concordance; cold, hungry men sitting in a cell thinking about the prodigal son and the lilies of the field. Was he the prodigal son or the man who fell among thieves? One fed hope, the other not. 'The whole Gospel became more and more a structure of paradoxes, carefully balanced so that each statement could be invalidated by another, none having absolute precedence. The lost sheep, the foolish virgins; the prodigal son and the man with one talent; they made an impenetrable maze.' Another phrase in the same book spoke direct sense: 'For all our days are passed away in Thy wrath; we spend our years as a tale that is told.' That the concordant tale should include irony and paradox and peripeteia, that making sense of what goes to make sense should be an activity that includes the acceptance of inexplicable patterns, mazes of contradiction, is a condition of humanly satisfactory explanation.

The epigraph to *Solitary Confinement* is a passage from the last act of *Richard II*, and I will confess that it never made such exquisite sense to me before I read Burney's book.

> For no thought is contented. The better sort,
> As thoughts of things divine, are intermix'd
> With scruples, and do set the word itself
> Against the word:
> As thus—*Come, little ones*; and then again—
> *It is as hard to come, as for a camel*
> *To thread the postern of a small needle's eye.*
> Thoughts tending to ambition, they do plot
> Unlikely wonders: how these vain weak nails
> May tear a passage through the flinty ribs
> Of this hard world, my ragged prison walls;
> And for they cannot, die in their own pride.

These reflections arise out of Richard's 'study' to 'compare / This prison where I live unto the world'. Burney studies similarly, desiring to find the sense that, when ambitious thoughts fail, poverty can make of the world, and the sense of the fictions of poverty. The evidence is paradoxical, contradictory, the language unstable; the word is set against the word; above all the appetite for hope and consolation is invincible. And the question that must always be asked of whatever offers hope and consolation is equally human and imperious, and without it nothing will for long make sense: it is whether these explanations and consolations can be 'reconciled with that pan of putrid soup'.

I have been talking about Burney in this discursive way so that we can, if we like, think of his book as a model of a more general solitary confinement, of the fictions and interpretations of human beings 'doing time', imagining ends and concords. 'Men die because they cannot join the beginning to the end', but living is trying to do it. We give ourselves meaning by inventing critical time, like the shadow of the gable. Fictions in the end fail under the pressure of what James is said, in his

47

last words, to have called 'at last, the real distinguished thing'; but meanwhile we have our predictive games, our family jokes like *Lear*, our anthropomorphic paradigms of apocalypse; we have a common project, truth in poverty, and a common need, solidarity of plight in diversity of state. The free imagination makes endless plots on reality, attempts to make our proportionals convenient for our equations in everything; our common sense makes us see that without paradox and contradiction our parables will be too simple for a complex poverty, too consolatory to console. Our study, like Richard's, must have a certain complexity and a sense of failure. 'I cannot do it; yet I'll hammer it out', he says.

So here we are in the middest, and like Richard reinventing the world from inside a prison. Perhaps the autonomy of forms, of which we hear so much in Romantic, Symbolist, and Post-Symbolist criticism, is another reminder of incarceration; perhaps the autonomous forms which are called researches into the autonomy of forms – so much modern poetry, we complain, is about modern poetry, and the new novel is a research into novels – reflect our consciousness that deep in the cell we are using the shadows only, because we have lost the kind of confidence that enabled us to be interested in the apparent facts as well as in the human concords. George Herbert, making metaphors for prayer, called it that which in an hour transformed the six-days world, and he also called it 'a kind of tune'. It was a six-days world because God made it in six days. Music had six notes, one for each day of the creation, of which every tune reflected the harmony. All harmony has this hexameral structure. (Now it may have the structure of twelve tones in the arbitrary sequence invented in the cell.) In much the same way, encyclopaedists used to arrange the whole of human knowledge as a commentary on the six days of creation. To arrange it in terms of an alphabet is to make it conform to an arbitrary human formulation, and one that is obsolete in so far as what is sought in knowledge is concord, proportion, equation, seen from a cell set about by absurdity. The grand universal order of Genesis gave way to the spacious firmament of Newton, and this in turn yields to the subtle complementarities of modern physics; the Gospels submitted to the elaborate harmonies of patristic scholarship, and then to the refined synoptic concordance of the moderns; medieval randomness is transformed by the logic of Aristotelian plot, which is modified by the counter-logical devices of the modern novel, treating time and cause as it is treated by a totalitarian interrogator.

This, of course, is once again to overstate the case. Even if it were true that the forms which interest us were merely the architecture of our own cells (and it is never quite true) we should have to make allowances for the fact that they do, after all, please us, even perhaps bless us; and this does not emerge from the tone of what I have just been saying. Even if we prefer to find out about ourselves less by encountering what both Williams and Stevens call 'the weather' than by brooding over the darkening recesses of a Piranesi prison, we feel we have found our subject and for the moment ourselves; and that for us, as for everybody else, our world has point and structure. We are conscious of our cheating, and set the word against the word; but this only means that the concord we still desire is harder to achieve. When we achieve it, whatever the circumstances, we feel we have found a reality which is for the moment at any rate proof against sceptical research; even in an endless, shapeless world this reality has – to borrow a strange phrase from Josef Pieper – 'the character of being-directed-towards-the-End'. What makes the triumph difficult is that it has to take account of the world as we experience it; we have a loving–hating affair with reality, we 'keep coming back to the real'; and this continually impoverishes us because it is at odds with such concords as we have achieved. So it seems that we move always with less and less freedom, have less and less use for inherited wealth.

One reason for this impoverishment, for the growing difficulty of access to the paradigms, is simply that it is much harder now than it was even quite recently to imagine a relation between the time of a life and the time of a world. I talked in my third lecture about this problem in an earlier form. The modern version is probably much more upsetting. Fictional paradigms really belong to a world in which the relation of beginning and end is not too tenuous – a six-days world, the tight world-scheme of Augustine, the limited time-scale of Ussher. The quite sudden and enormous lengthening of the scale of history has been far more worrying than the Copernican revolution, of which one hears so much in literary discussion. The six-days world was still perfectly acceptable to intelligent contemporaries of Jane Austen.

When it collapsed, the sciences were liberated; what was for the arts a difficulty presented the sciences with a new dimension in which they could luxuriate.

For the sciences one after another turned to the temporal. Geology was first, and then in mid-century Darwin temporalized the spatial classifications of biology. The other sciences, including astronomy, followed. In every case, as Toulmin and Goodfield[2] show in their interesting book, the switch caused some shock; even in science there can be an emotional attachment to the paradigms. Meanwhile, for everybody, the origin and the end of the world receded. 'No Vestige of a Beginning – no Prospect of an End', said James Hutton, as early as 1790. For literature and its criticism this created problems we have not yet solved, though it is obviously relevant that the novel developed as the time of the world expanded, and that the facts are related.

We probably have to accept, though without making too much of it, an historical transition, related to this protraction of time, from a literature which assumed that it was imitating an order to a literature which assumes that it has to create an order, unique and self-dependent, and possibly attainable only after a critical process that might be called 'decreation'. (It is a further question whether we may not now have another attempt to shift to the position that no order need be created because the consumer will do this without help if he is given the right encouragement and set in the right situation. But that, I believe, is a mistake.) There are many ways of describing this shift, some of them much too simple and dramatic, full of lamentation and extravagant inference. For myself, I value some pages of Earl Wasserman's book *The Subtler Language*[3] as offering an acceptable way of talking about it. In his terms this transition is a transition from imitation to something more or less like mathematics – from mimesis to mathesis, or from proposition to surd. Thus the *concordia discors* of 'Cooper's Hill'[4] reflects the political philosophy of limited monarchy and implies a universe ordered by similar checks and balances. The 'subtler language' of 'The Sensitive Plant' is founded on a different assumption: that the reality of the senses and the reality of metaphor meet much more remotely, at some point unimaginable by the human mind. After such a change the experience of being isolated from reality, or of moving about in worlds not realized – or fallings from us, vanishings, of gates that one desperately clutches in order to disprove their insubstantiality – becomes much more commonplace, much more frequently a matter for enquiry. Indeed, it is the very matter-of-factness of Wordsworth that so effectively familiarizes us with a dimension-less, limitless world, resistant to paradigmatic mimesis, requiring the decreation of old forms and old ways of speaking, operating in a temporal mode. He sounds one of the characteristic notes of modern literature, and begins to make the quasi-spatial mode as inappropriate to literature as it was becoming to the sciences.

The discipline of fear is as much a matter of fact as the discipline of love: it is founded on a sense of remoteness and estrangement, as the other upon identity and comfort. One sees why Wordsworth dwelt so much upon those practically motionless old men, useless, utterly poor, but somehow identified with the earth they bowed towards, and so as mysterious as poems. Poems move, for him, out of fear into a moment of love; but they must acknowledge the pressure of fact, and so the best of Wordsworth's poems *contain* a vertiginous estrangement, a sense of what was later called the absurd, but transfigure it with joy. This is, I suppose, a way of stamping the 'characters of great apoca-lypse' on the terrifying limitlessness of time. The hiding places of power, for Wordsworth as for Proust, are the agents of time's defeat; discovered by involuntary memory, pure of discursive significance like the girl with the pitcher, they provide the structure and meaning and pleasure which constitute our deliverance from the long, meaningless attrition of time. The kinds of life here created Wordsworth curiously and beautifully speaks of as 'existences . . . like angels stopped upon the wing by sound'. They belong to the *aevum*, if you like, sempiternal moments that transcend the giddy successiveness of world-time. These necessary 'conversions of our *Lumpenwelt*', as Stevens calls them, are necessarily the work of necessary angels.

One such 'existence' is 'Resolution and Independence', to my mind both a very great and a very modern poem. The peculiar pains that attended the transfiguration of a commonplace but disquieting incident can be inferred from Wordsworth's letter of 14 June 1802 to Sara Hutchinson, and from Dorothy Wordsworth's Journal for the early part of May, and for 2 July of that year. The actual encounter with the leech-gatherer had occurred almost two years earlier, in October

1800. The man was bent double; he had suffered some accident in a cart, which had left him partly incapacitated. John Wordsworth wondered if he was a Jew. His occupation was technologically more primitive even than hill-farming; and nature, by growing parsimonious with leeches, has reduced him to utter poverty and at the same time made him a mysterious part of the landscape. They met the old man near Ambleside, 'late in the evening, when the light was just going away'.

The kind of interest this scarecrow figure aroused in Wordsworth was of the sort that only a poem could satisfy. He has great difficulty in talking about it, and great difficulty in writing the poem, largely because the old man talks, and what he says has something to do with the case, but only in the oblique way that matters of fact have to do with poems. He needs to put into the poem what the old man says; of course it is a bit tedious, but how can the poem work without it? Sara Hutchinson told him she did not like the end of the poem. He is forced to attempt an explanation of how she has gone wrong. 'It is in the character of the old man to tell his story in a manner which an *impatient* reader must necessarily feel as tedious. But Good God! Such a figure, in such a place . . .!' The old man must say something (say a lot) – it is the fact of the matter that he does so, irreducibly – and yet he must *be* something quite different, rather like a poem. For Wordsworth the task is to explain the power of this image, a man 'travelling alone among the mountains and all lonely places, carrying with him his own fortitude and the necessities which an unjust state of society has entailed upon him'.

But the poem says little about such matters, and is in fact not 'about' the leech gatherer at all. It is, as Wordsworth says to Sara Hutchinson, about 'a young Poet . . . overwhelmed by the thought of the miserable reverses that have befallen the happiest of men, viz. Poets'; and about 'an interposition of Providence' that gave this young man a degree of resolution and independence, the power to contemplate a certain poverty. In the poem the old man appears at a dreamlike moment when the poet's mind and the morning landscape suddenly darken. His tedious talk is not attended to, although it is reported in the poem, until a movement of the poet's mind convinces him that this may be a peculiar grace, a leading from above; the old man merges with the pool, and is metamorphosed into the great stone; the poem is never asking you to attend directly to the old man, but to its own transfiguration. It has an end which could pass as the end of a simpler, even of a bad poem; but here it is a fake, a cheat in the plotting. It says the poet will henceforth, when he is miserable, be able to think of this old man. There's always somebody worse off than yourself.

Yet even in the simpler *faux-naïf* of the *Lyrical Ballads* Wordsworth is asking the reader to sophisticate the narrative for him. Here he puts everything into the poem. In fact, its true end is the proof that from time to time, as now, we are by our own spirits deified; peculiar grace is the property not so much of grave livers, as of poems. Out of the intangible age and obscurity of the real world proceeds this extraordinary moment, with its complex perspectives of past and future. The poem begins with the loss of joy, and proceeds through a confrontation with the mystery of poverty and tedious age – a confrontation without communication, setting the word against the word.

The point is not even Wordsworth's continual anguish, that nature, which was once as plentiful a provider of poems as of leeches, will also be leaving it to the poet, as it has to the leech-gatherer, to 'persevere and find them where I may'. It is true that here is the first great confrontation of metaphorical with actual poverty, and that this is what produced the dream and the poem. Hence the extraordinary complexity of the end: the old man's poverty is unchanged, and he remains motionless on the moor; there is obviously nothing the poet can do with his except hope to endure it; and all this is said. But the poem ends in joy, the joy of its own success in giving a true and original human shape to poverty.

This poem mimes, as it were, that movement which Ortega sees in the novel also, out of an objective world of myth into the subjective consciousness working in time.[5] That the old world is still represented in it – that you can find a simple plot in the poem – is testimony to the strength, perhaps to the indispensability of the paradigms. But they are transfigured; and one of the forces that go to make this change is certainly Wordsworth's sense of the past, the need to find power in temporal 'hiding-places'. The growth of a poet's mind, for him the true subject of an epic, is no longer a process of grasping the spatial relations of a six-days world, turning oneself into a curious and universal scholar, but the process of finding oneself, by some peculiar grace, in lost time.

In this dark backward there are no limits for the form to imitate. It was a preoccupation of De Quincey's, this absence of a given design, this new power of fortuity. In this situation he called time a 'greater mystery' than space, and as J. Hillis Miller explains in his fine essay on this author,[6] the longing for an experience which would charge the present moment with the intangible powers of past and future, was a longing satisfied by what he called 'the apocalypse of the world within me' – a fake end, when time shall be no more, produced by opium. This is the triumph over time; in his attempts to reflect in syntax and argument this defeat of successiveness, De Quincey looks forward to many later artists, to the poetry of the apocalyptic image and the spatialized moment, even to that rescue from *chronos* of sempiternal events which we find in Proust. Here are anticipations of a literature of perpetual crisis, as in Kafka, who (in William Phillips's phrase) 'loads each particular experience with the sum of all experience'. But De Quincey, longing for external evidence of such sempiternity, admitted that one cannot write against the text of time a perpetually iterated *stet*; he sinks back 'into an impotent misery', says Mr Miller, 'a misery in which the self is once again a solitary point', and when the 'visionary morning life' consents to be summoned up, it is 'relived on a background of funereal darkness'. Certainly De Quincey saw the horror, where others see the depth, of the prison of modern form, the place where we accept the knowledge that our inherited ways of echoing the structure of the world have no concord with it, but only, and then under conditions of great difficulty, with the desires of our own minds.

Let me return a moment to Christopher Burney in his cell. He discovered this image of modern art: inconceivable diversity of state without solidarity of plight. What kind of fictions would you expect from this? Fictions as far as possible from ritual, certainly, or even from the forms that derive from ritual, such as tragedy. As for *verismo*, in these circumstances it is strictly for the police. Burney's fictions were of time, and of a world where the word is set against the next word. Such fictions will be complex, certainly, proof against discursive reduction; but they will live in time and change, because these are necessary to the sense of life, the more so when the spatial diagrams of the world have given way to temporal ones. Which brings me, finally, to the defence of time and change.

In so far as there is an art of the timeless prison, it is poetry; that so many critical techniques are also of the timeless prison may be historically accounted for by the fact that 'formal' criticism is much more closely associated with poems than novels. *The Waste Land* is intended to be outside time, though of course it has a temporal aspect; this is progressive form, as Kenneth Burke talks about it, a 'temporizing of essence'[7]. Novels, however, no matter how much they shift time, put slices of it layer on layer in search of intemporal concord, are always in some way bound to what Sartre calls its 'manifest irreversibility'. Their beginnings, middles, and ends, however refined, however distorted from the paradigm, will always join it somewhere.

It is a familiar problem. 'Beginnings are always troublesome', says George Eliot; and 'conclusions are the weak point of most authors', she adds, noting that 'some of the fault lies in the very nature of a conclusion, which is at best a negation'.[8] Fielding, who detested epistolary form, allowed it one advantage: it set the writer free 'from regular beginnings and conclusions'. History separates from chronicle, providing its own structures; the novel separates from the simple narrative. The problem of beginnings and ends in a form which, paradigmatically, imitates the form of the world, is created. So the best beginnings are the best faked, as in the perfect opening sentence of *A Passage to India*; in the irony of the opening of *Wuthering Heights* (the 'solitary neighbour I shall be troubled with'). Ends are ends only when they are not negative but frankly transfigure the events in which they were immanent.

The end of *Anna Karenina*, for instance: it recapitulates the domestic beginning. You remember the opening: 'All happy families are alike but an unhappy family is unhappy after its own fashion. Everything had gone wrong in the Oblonsky household . . .' A thousand pages later, in the Levin household, 'everyone is in the most amiable frame of mind'. Levin is listening to Koznyshev's theory about a new world epoch inaugurated by the Slavonic races when he is summoned to the nursery by his wife. On the way he thinks of other large arguments concerning God and providence, problems to which he has not formulated the answer. In the nursery his wife merely wants to tell him that the baby can now recognize them. A thing which had formerly seemed to Levin so pitiable that it merely added to the general stock of anxiety had become a loved person. On the way back to his guests in the drawing room Levin again worries about God, and the salvation of the heathen. But the kind of truth he has just seen in the nursery is the only kind in his grasp. Now Kitty interrupts him, sends him on an errand. He does not tell her he has made a discovery, of the solidarity of human plight; instead, happy as all families are happy, his will give him the same kind of life, full of contradictions, of words set against words, prayer and quarrelling; now he can say this: 'my whole life, independently of anything that can happen to me, every minute of it is no longer meaningless as it was before, but has a positive meaning of goodness with which I have the power to invest it'. In this conclusion, Levin speaks for the book; as much as he, it needs a happy family at its close; it needs characters who cease to be things and become persons; it needs to be invested by a power which will transfigure the verisimilar events of which its temporal course is made. And as for Levin, this power is a human power providing a human truth, as inaccurate maybe as our way of talking about the stars or as the prophecies of apocalyptic pan-Slavism. Perhaps, as Dostoevsky guessed, Levin will 'destroy his faith again . . . tear himself on some mental nail of his own making'. But we are concerned with the end, not of Levin, but of *Anna Karenina*, with the humanly necessary fake. 'Really, universally,' says James in the preface to *Roderick Hudson*, 'relations stop nowhere, and the exquisite problem of the artist is eternally to draw, by a geometry of his own, the circle in which they shall happily *appear* to do so.' And he goes on thus, very aptly to our purpose: 'He is in the perpetual predicament that the continuity of things is the whole matter for him, of comedy and tragedy; that this continuity is never broken, and that, to do anything at all, he has at once intensely to consult and intensely to ignore it.'

Here is the problem, the consulting and ignoring of continuity and especially the successiveness of time. Ignoring it, we fake to achieve the forms absent from the continuous world; we regress towards myth, out of this time into that time. Consulting it, we set the word against the word, and create the need for difficult concords in our fictions. But we ignore it at great peril; when, as Virginia Woolf puts it, 'the skin of the day has been cast into the hedge', the novel is dead, Joyce's day in *Ulysses* retains plenty of skin; it seems very doubtful that he 'proceeded on the assumption that a unified spatial apprehension of his work would ultimately be possible', as Joseph Frank claims,[9] for the book is full of coincidences that are non-significant, and there is a real indeterminacy in character which can only imply, as Arnold Goldman remarks, a 'thickening web of contingency' – we are 'forced to carry ultimate explanations to the novel's end'.[10] There is a polarity of static and dynamic; there is a mimesis of change, potential, as well as a structure of the kind we call spatial. As the book goes forward the Odyssean design is less and less dominant; the data which limit Stephen's freedom are diminished. Time and change, to the disgust of Wyndham Lewis, thrust back into the arts; the assault on temporality in fiction succeeded in the 'luminous statis' of the Vortex, but it does not succeed with fiction. 'Our Vortex does not suck up to life,' said *Blast*. But the novel has to, in however refined a way; it cannot banish time as Lewis banished it, even to the degree that poems and criticism can; of course it cannot banish the form we like to think of as spatial, either.

I believe that Burney in his cell, watching the shadow of the gable, and including it in his attempts to make sense, makes more sense than spatial form. This has grown very systematic and elaborate since Joseph Frank first named it and studied its history. His 'new Laocoon' implied that although books are inescapably of the element of time, their formal organization is to be apprehended as spatial; one would read them twice, as it were, once for time and once for space. And Frank says quite rightly that a good deal of modern literature is designed to be apprehended thus. He adds of Proust that he 'stamps his novel indelibly with the form of time', as he promised to do; but that by various means he also 'forces the reader to juxtapose disparate images spatially' so that we get what Ramon Fernandez called a 'spatialization of time and memory'.

Used in this way, 'spatialization' is one of those metaphors which we tend to forget are metaphorical, like the metaphor of organic form. Marcel, when he considers those happenings which gave him the clue to his experience, and restored, as he says, his faith in literature, is not talking about spatial form. The portents of his climactic day make sense for him by a benefaction of meaning; the end makes a concord with what had preceded it. But the experiences reserved for permanent meaning, carried out of the flux of time, surely do not make a pattern in space; they punctuate that order of time, free of contingency, in which only the ur-novel wholly exists, the *durée* if you like, or the *aevum*.

Forms in space, we should remember, have more temporality than Lessing supposed, since we have to read them in sequence before we know they are there, and the relations between them. Forms in time have an almost negligible spatial aspect (the size of the book). Their interrelations had much better be studied by reference to our usual ways of relating past, present and future – ways upon which I touched in my second talk – than by the substitution of a counterfeit spatial for the temporal mode. The equation 'between an exodus and return in time through reversible space and an exodus and return in space through reversible time' is, as we are told in the 'Ithaca' section of *Ulysses*, unsatisfactory.

We have our vital interest in the structure of time, in the concords books arrange between beginning, middle, and end; and as the Chicago critics, with a quite different emphasis, would agree, we lose something by pretending that we have not. Our geometries, in James's word, are required to measure change, since it is on change, between remote or imaginary origins and ends, that our interests are fixed. In our perpetual crisis we have, at the proper seasons, under the pressure perhaps of our own end, dizzying perspectives upon the past and the future, in a freedom which is the freedom of a discordant reality. Such a vision of chaos or absurdity may be more than we can easily bear. Philip Larkin, though he speaks quietly, speaks of something terrible.[11]

> Truly, though our element is time,
> We are not suited to the long perspectives
> Open at each instant of our lives.
>   They link us to our losses . . .

Merely to give order to these perspectives is to provide consolation, as De Quincey's opium did; and simple fictions are the opium of the people. But fictions too easy we call 'escapist'; we want them not only to console but to make discoveries of the hard truth here and now, in the middest. We do not feel they are doing this if we cannot see the shadow of the gable, or hear the discoveries of dissonance, the word set against the word. The books which seal off the long perspectives, which sever us from our losses, which represent the world of potency as a world of act, these are the books which, when the drug wears off, go on to the dump with the other empty bottles. Those that continue to interest us move through time to an end, an end we must sense even if we cannot know it; they live in change, until, which is never, *as* and *is* are one.

Naturally every such fiction will in some measure repeat others, but always with a difference, because of the changes in our reality. Stevens talks about the moment out of poverty as 'an *hour* / Filled with expressible bliss, in which I have / No need'. But the hour passes; the need, our interest in our loss, returns; and out of another experience of chaos grows another form – a form in time – that satisfies both by being a repetition and by being new. So two things seem to be true: first, that the poet is right to speak of his giant as 'ever changing, living in change'; and secondly, that he is right to say that 'the man-hero is not the exceptional monster, / But he that of repetition is most master'. Moreover, he is right about another thing, which for us who are medium men, living in a reality which is always February, is the most important of all. If he were wrong here we should have to close up our books of poetry and read somebody on Necessity:

> Medium man
> In February hears the imagination's hymns
> And sees its images, its motions
> And multitudes of motions
>
> And feels the imagination's mercies. . . .

4

The English Novel, *Circa* 1907

This essay was commissioned by Harvard College for a collection of studies on fiction. I was interested in the stirrings of modernity at a time when, as nearly always, the commercially successful novels had no concern with such questions. The year 1907 seemed a good choice, when in the course of a season Elinor Glyn published a silly best-seller and Conrad a masterpiece, variously but on the whole respectfully misunderstood by reviewers.

I took the opportunity to read William de Morgan, who belonged neither to the popular party nor to the modernists. At a time when there was much speculation about the Condition of England, the Prefaces of Henry James explored the condition of the novel. With Ford Madox Ford as an inspiration, novelists had become absorbed in questions of technique, but these were of no interest to Elinor Glyn or Florence Barclay.

Around 1907 great changes, we may confidently announce, were either occurring or pending, both in English society and in the English novel. Joyce and Lawrence were already at work; so was Gertrude Stein. James was publishing his Prefaces, and Ford, who had worked with Conrad, was excogitating a new theory of the novel. Arnold Bennett was writing *The Old Wives' Tale* on what seemed to him sound French principles. 1907 wasn't a bad year for novels, for it saw the publication of both *The Secret Agent* and *The Longest Journey*. Who would read them? Three years earlier a public had been found for both *Nostromo* and *The Golden Bowl*; the next year they would accept, though at first without enthusiasm, Bennett's novel, as well as *The Man Who Was Thursday*, *The War in the Air*, and *A Room with a View*. There were

Wagnerites and Ibsenites in the audience: William Archer's translations started to appear in 1907 and so, as I've suggested, did the New York edition of James. Many people had read some Flaubert and Tolstoy, Nietzsche and Whitman; a few had encountered *The Interpretation of Dreams*. Husserl was little known, but Russell was famous. The climate, at first glance, seems one in which there might have been an audience for fictions aspiring to art and seriousness.

Of the society more generally, it is necessary to say only that there were signs of a more critical attitude to the past, a developing habit of national self-examination. The fragility of the Empire had become more evident after the Boer War. The educated conscience had discovered the poor, whose plight, like that of women, troubled the liberal mind as much as the low standard of national health disturbed those whose property might, before long, be dependent on the country's ability to find fit men for the army. There was a powerful sense of transition, accompanied as always by mixed reactions to all the new evidence of decadence or of renovation, according to how one interpreted such signs of relaxation as the criticism of capitalism, the questioning of conventional sexual morality, and the treatment in literature of previously forbidden subjects. The early years of Edward's reign showed a real loss of nerve, which was in some measure recovered before its end. There was a feeling of crisis, that there was no telling how things might go; and this is caught in James's tragic retrospect at the outbreak of war in 1914: 'the plunge of civilisation into this abyss of blood and darkness ... is a thing that so gives away the whole long age in which we have supposed the world to be, with whatever abatement, gradually bettering, that to have to take it all now for what the treacherous years were all the while really making for and *meaning* is too tragic for any words.'[1]

How do such concerns affect the works of the time? There ought to be a relation between the Condition of England and the condition of the English novel. Such a relation would be not merely a matter of what novelists say about the state of the nation, and specific aspects of it – but how they go about doing so. Is there, so to say, a period lexicon? If so it should be easier to describe than a period syntax. Successful novels normally use language understood by many people. Let us glance first at a little group of novels that did well with the readers of 1907. In one way or another they might tell us something about the lexicon, and the grammar, of mid-Edwardian fiction. Of course we should remember that many of these readers were not fully extended by the works here discussed, since they could also read *The Secret Agent*, a work – to continue the figure – that made much severer linguistic demands.

Elinor Glyn's *Three Weeks* is, if not read, remembered still as a sexual fantasy, and in a way this is just; though the American preface defends the book against the charge that it is merely 'a sensual record of passion', and, in its fashion, it *is* more than that. The lovers are a young Englishman of great beauty and stupidity and the Imperatorskoye, a royal adventuress whose sensuality, at once mystical and practical, uplifts and exalts the young man, so that after the three weeks he spends with her – ending at the full of the moon – he finds himself transformed into a man of intellect and embarks on a career of distinguished public service. The Imperatorskoye separates love from all else, including domestic convenience and learning and art and 'feverish cravings for the impossible new', blaming such mixtures for the 'ceaseless unrest' now generally felt. ('"Yes," said Paul, and thought of his mother.') The consequence of all this is that the Empress bears Paul a son, but is murdered by her husband. He in turn falls to the hand of an avenging Kalmuck loyal to the Empress, and the child becomes, apparently, Czar or Czarevitch. Paul is able to attend his fifth birthday celebrations in the cathedral of the capital and sees his son, 'a fair, rosy-cheeked, golden-haired English child, future ruler by right'.

This curious and successful dream appealed to an increasingly felt need to abandon not only official morality but also cultural isolation. English virtue could reasonably be exchanged for alien virtuosity. The bedroom scenes, like the foreignness of the lady's manners, catch the exotic in an unserious way, or anyway in dreamlike fashion. The lady is 'beyond the ordinary laws of morality', and the novel offers the satisfaction of a solution in which this Nietzschean wickedness is paid for by death, yet contributes to the advancement of the real, that is the British, Empire. Paul is saved from his hearty English fiancée but nevertheless produces an heir, and a pure English heir for an empire previously the domain of foreigners; while he, purged by an admittedly unrepeatable sexual experience, returns to the true imperial centre, London. He is able to give it the benefit of all the knowledge and experience it had lost sight of during its protracted estrangement from Europe, for this is what he had acquired during his three weeks in an exotic but undeniably imperial bed.

Miss Glyn's rejection of middle-class English women may be seen as a measure of the desire of her female contemporaries to liberate themselves from the old roles, much as her rejection of the provincialism of the British Empire reflects a growing mood of the time. But she does not consider the possibility of asking the very considerable audience which was somehow ready for this kind of thing to abandon social and national assumptions inconsistent with the changes currently proposed. Her New Man is a boring Englishman transformed and liberated by coming into the knowledge, conveniently represented as sexual experience, which his own society denied him. He remains an upper-middle-class Englishman whose powers had been concealed, not destroyed, by the barrenness of his life, and he continues to behave in conformity with class conventions. The new Emperor is wholly English, apparently without genetic inheritance or early training from his foreign mother, who simply educated the husband, produced the son, and died. Thus the growing uneasiness lest imperialisms clash, a new awareness that British arrangements would have to be changed, defended, and perhaps even overthrown, that stupidities of education and rank urgently required correction, and that extreme sexual repression might be dangerous, are eased and calmed in a dream, in a best-seller. Taking it seriously is likely to seem odd or offensive because the text is not of a kind that advertises its connections with reality. They exist, perhaps inevitably; only sometimes the discrepancies are so huge as to conceal them.

The sense that one was entering a new age, in which some transformation of the British might be necessary if they were to maintain their hitherto effortless supremacy, inspired a whole range of invasion novels; and as the period wore on the outcome of these novels tended to change, first from easy victory to hard struggle, then to disaster. Erskine Childers, in the best of them, still showed some confidence in British racial superiority;[2] Wells, in a book serialized in 1907,[3] showed the coming world conflict through the eyes of an undereducated

English mechanic, but transferred the capital of the world to New York. But conscious enquiry into contemporary problems – as in Wells, or in *Major Barbara* (1905), or even in Galsworthy – isn't perhaps as good a guide to the capacities and needs of the audience as fiction which has no such explicit purpose. Florence Barclay's *The Rosary*, of 1908, will serve as an example of such fiction. This extraordinarily bad book was still being reprinted in my youth, and I read it somewhere around 1933 in a cheap edition; apparently it went on satisfying a public, albeit an unsophisticated one, for a quarter of a century.

The American publishers claimed that it was a modern book; ('modern' was already a hard-sell word); it is in fact a dream of the new woman, in this case represented as having been a nurse in the Boer War, a golfer, and very strong and healthy. She gives up an affair with an exquisite painter because she is too old and plain for him. The setting is a ducal home, and the upper-class dialogue works because the author has learned how to do it from, among others, Oscar Wilde. The poor are represented by a railway porter who when heavily tipped by the heroine imagines her an angel sent from heaven to provide delicacies for his sick wife. This fantasy about the poor is contemporary, it should be remembered, with the conscience-stricken sociological enquiries into their lot that were well under way with Fabianism and with the fear of rioting mentioned by Shaw in *Major Barbara*. Galsworthy surrounded his rich with a frieze of poor in attitudes of misery and sickness. Chesterton professed to regard them as the champions of a gay Christendom. Conrad knew they were exactly what the police existed to control. But Miss Barclay's new woman still treats them as beneficiaries of upper-class generosity, and this social imperceptiveness fairly represents the general level of her imagination.

Her artist goes blind and, incognito, she nurses him, pulls him through his worst time, and not only marries him but assists his completely effortless translation from painter into composer. Problems of art become, in this imaginative light, as simple as those of poverty. The impassioned dénouement, incidentally, is visible a mile off, and is an emblem of the easy gratifications expected of popular fiction.

Yet the success of the book transcended that of the ordinary cheap romance; it was taken more seriously. What is of some interest is the coexistence of decent, even accomplished, upper-class dialogue and an immense vulgarity of imagination and technique. It was possible to learn to do certain things, which probably sounded quite modern, without the slightest notion that there was a crisis in the relations between fiction and society which had already elicited much more radical modernization. And to have them taken seriously; one American reviewer, gratefully quoted by the publisher, called *The Rosary* a book that 'strengthens faith in the outcome of the great experiment of putting humanity on earth' and held that it was one of those unusual stories that appealed to 'all classes of readers of fiction'. This credits it with powers which were at the time much sought after, for example by Conrad. There existed a real desire to maintain the popularity of fiction while modernizing it.

But the urgency of technical innovation as a means to modern truth is felt by novelists rather than their readers. In general people probably wanted then, as in a measure they still do, old techniques applied to genial, or anyway familiar, materials. 1907 produced one novel worth examining in this light, William de Morgan's *Alice-for-Short*. De Morgan had been an associate of Morris in the pottery business and was himself a distinguished artist; only when at sixty-five he lost his studio did he turn to writing long novels, the first and most successful being *Joseph Vance* (1906).

De Morgan's manner was deliberately archaic. In a message to his readers at the end of *It Can Never Happen Again* (1909) he says, excusing himself for a particularly cosy, omniscient chat: 'I know that gossiping with one's readers is a disreputably Early Victorian practice, and far from Modern, which everything ought to be . . .' In *Alice-for-Short* he does much the same thing: 'We are dwelling (to your disgust, we doubt not) on these points because we really want to take you into our confidence about Charles and Alice, and what they thought and felt. Never you mind how we come to know these things! We answer for their accuracy. Be content with that!' (p. 464). The jocose unease of these interpolations suggests that the Modern was a trouble to de Morgan, and its presence in his thoughts produces some odd twists in his novels. *Alice* is about a waif brought up as an adopted daughter by a good family; eventually, despite their long adherence to the notion that their feelings are purely fraternal, she and the son of the house marry. The facetious chapter heads and the waggishly archaic tone don't quite gloss over the fact that much of the story is about death, broken marriage, drink, and slums, 'the great hells of civilisation', the stunted, abandoned children of the very poor. The time of the action is the early Victorian period, and there are obvious sources in Dickens; but to anybody interested, de Morgan is talking about Edwardian slums – his date and his tone exempt whoever does not want them from disagreeably topical reactions.

That he was conscious of doing more than producing a pastiche is indicated by the subtitle of his book, 'a dichronism'. Not content with a complicated Victorian plot, he makes unusual play with a character called Mrs Verrinder, whose basic narrative function is to bring the lovers together. But Mrs Verrinder is also the agent of further festoons of plotting. Having been knocked on the head at the age of twenty, sixty years before, she has only now come to; there is a good scene when she first sees herself in a looking glass, but the interest really lies in her being a sort of human time machine. Also we are told of her views on the art of fiction. She is surprised to learn that the poet Scott has turned to novel writing and, since the lovers cannot persuade her of the merits of Dickens and Thackeray, she reverts, in her search for entertainment, to *The Vicar of Wakefield*.

Since de Morgan was a man of intellect and imagination, this book poses some odd questions. Nowhere else, so far as I know, can one point to novels that please by a deliberate thematic and technical archaism, yet at the same time carry within them an awareness of technical change and the complex action of time on the authenticity of narrative.[4] De Morgan doesn't of course propose this as the main interest of his book; but his object is to give to readers who feel about the Victorian novel what Mrs Verrinder felt about *The Vicar of Wakefield* more of what they wanted, with as little change as time and conscience permitted. *Alice-for-Short* is therefore an example of a number of complex relationships – of changes in the life of forms in art, changes in the relations of writer to reader – all of which, given practised intelligence and practised conscience, continue to occur even in situations where they are for other reasons not wanted. A book caught like this, reluctantly but consciously, in an inevitable change of period, may well be something of a monster, and probably a short-lived one; but it has its interest.

The three books I've mentioned so far all illustrate, in different ways, the pressure of the times – of the Condition of England – on popular fiction. None of them was written on the assumption that serious changes in technique might be required to accommodate the dimly perceived new shape of the world; de Morgan's awareness that this might be so was deliberately dulled by his archaism. Yet this was also a time in which the technique of fiction was a matter of intense concern, not only because men wanted, as artists, to refine the instruments they had inherited, but because they felt with much urgency that the condition of the world required kinds of understanding which could not be provided otherwise than by technical innovation. There was even a characteristically patriotic motive, since it was not thought right to allow the English novel to remain technically inferior to the foreign. This was the age of the Dreadnought; one needed to overgo Flaubert and Maupassant as one needed to keep ahead of the German navy.

Much of the history of the novel in the twentieth century is dominated by the notion that technical changes of a radical kind are necessary to preserve a living relation between the book and the world. Here I am concerned only with the earlier stages of this technical research. Serious writers lived not only with the knowledge of the problems of naturalism but also with the example of James. The marvellous Prefaces were appearing. James had failed to interest a large popular audience, but had written, and commented upon, novels of great importance to technicians, who certainly did not believe that the interest of these works was limited to the area of professional know-how. *What Maisie Knew* was especially venerated and not only for its 'technique'. It was a model of how technique is necessary to imaginative apprehension of the times. And James's audience was not confined to practitioners; he could not, in the early years of the century, have repeated his complaint of 1884 that 'the "serious" idea of the novel appeals apparently to no one'. In 1897 the *Academy* reviewer greeted *Maisie* with 'amazement and delight'. In the opinion of the *Edinburgh Review*, James so far succeeded in his determination to achieve 'an immense correspondence with life' as to have 'added a new conception of reality to the art of fiction'. The *Saturday Review* said that this novel was 'very easily followed'; and many echoed the views of Oliver Elton in his fine essay of 1903 associating James with a specifically *modern* beauty and significance. Elton was a professor of English, and we would not ordinarily associate him with desperately adventurous opinions.[5]

These and similar observations imply a newly developed interest, confined no doubt to a smallish circle of readers, in the technical and theoretical aspects of fiction. Brownell, in a remarkable long essay published in the *Atlantic Monthly* in 1905, observed acutely that 'the present time may fairly be called the reign of theory in fiction ... and Mr James's art is in nothing more modern than in being theoretic'. Admittedly he goes on to complain that James is obsessed with theory to a damaging degree, 'palpably withholding from us the expected, the needful exposition and explanation'.[6] But this is the normal reaction against technical developments which proceed from an understanding that the routine product often has features which, on rigorous inspection, turn out to be archaic, redundant, and falsifying. Those features served no purpose relevant to the nature of the novel as it was coming to be understood, but they did give assurances to the normally inactive reader that whatever was going on matched his own comfortable and quite arbitrary expectations, so that he, unlike the new novelist, mistook them for the main business of the art. In short, the more reflexive, the more technique- and theory-obsessed the fiction, the more it asked its readers to give up and the more it asked them to supply;[7] so the 'new' novel demanded a large increase in that art of collaboration which was of course always needed but by convention mitigated and understated. Hence the assertion that the reader of *What Maisie Knew* or *The Golden Bowl* was called on to develop a sharper and more subtle feeling for *relevance*. This was identified as modern and attributed to a modern increase of 'general consciousness'. The point was taken, even by opponents of James – by Wells, for example. So the new techniques were firmly associated with the new changed times; both were abandoning some certainties, looking into attitudes and devices that had come to seem false, and facing a new situation in which more things had to be thought about and in different contexts of relevance.

And here we have to consider Conrad, who was responsible for much of this radical enquiry. By 1907 he had abandoned hope of

popular success, supposing that the public was incapable of the sacri-
fices he required, for example, in the matter of endings – a most
important matter, for the 'full close', the 'nail hit on the head', was
among the most falsifying of the time-honoured conventions, as well
as the one that seemed especially dear to ordinary readers 'in their
inconceivable stupidity'.[8] By a freak which astonished and possibly
annoyed Henry James, but which is of a kind we have later grown
more familiar with, Conrad did in 1913 slip into the best-seller list
with *Chance*, a book obsessed with method, theory, technique to
the point where even hardened Conradians begin to protest. This is
testimony either to a rather rapid evolution of public taste or to the
truth of Conrad's own view that the public will swallow anything,
even occasionally and fortuitously something that is properly 'done'.
Earlier, Conrad shared the view of his collaborator Ford that there
was a genuine though obscure relation between techniques and the
times, the condition of fiction and the Condition of England. Ford
regarded James not only as a great technician but also as a great
historian of the culture. He may already have been contemplating *The
Good Soldier*, which is not only a profoundly researched novel as
to its techniques but precisely intended as a history of the culture.
Ford's friend Masterman, as Wiley reminds us, had written in his
book *The Condition of England* of the need to diagnose 'the hidden
life of England' and suggested that fiction might be the instrument
employed.[9] The development of that instrument, Ford was sure, would
require study of alien examples rather than of the indigenous novel
– a cosmopolitanism acquired for reasons of national health and
security in a manner analogous, though remotely, to that dreamed of
by Elinor Glyn.

Techniques developed in order to study so great a subject without
looseness and bagginess are likely to be of the sort that can propose
without explicitness the symptomatic quality of a fictive event. The
circumscribed 'affair' used by Ford in *The Good Soldier*, and so much
admired by him in *What Maisie Knew*, should reverberate within the
chambers of the reader's attention in such a way as to induce him to
select, from an indeterminate range of possible inferences, those that
have significance. Their number is not to be limited by the conventional
coding of the old novel, by, for example, the formal close or by

steadiness of tone, or by what James called Bennett's 'hugging the shore of the real' or by the vouched-for authenticity of narrator, because these are no longer relevant except in so far as the disappointment of illegitimate expectations on the part of the reader may be a legitimately suggestive device.

It is easy enough to see why other writers who were capable of understanding the new thing – Bennett and Wells, for example – nevertheless rejected it. Finally the difference of opinion comes down to incompatible estimates of the rights and duties of the reading public, and to the question of whether the dismantling of all expectation-satisfying devices isn't in the last analysis the dismantling of the novel. The true heirs of Conrad are the modern French, with their demand for full collaboration from the reader in an act – all *lexis*, no *logos* – that can scarcely any longer be called fiction, so that the *roman* slips undifferentiated into *écriture*. But that was a long way off, and both Ford and Conrad cherished some hope of winning the attention of *la cour et la ville*, of a general reading public that might be induced to collaborate in the techniques required by the times. To some extent it was so induced. The outcry over the ending of *Jude* was evidence, as Alan Friedman says,[10] of the fact that tampering with the closed ending was tampering with public morality. But in the years that followed there was a change, and the famous hung ending of *Women in Love* seems not in itself to have upset people. There was a change, a recognition that totality, solidity, *rondure* may falsify the truth, especially when not achieved with the laborious sophistication displayed in *Nostromo* and *The Good Soldier*. Bennett, though perhaps he had more natural endowment than Ford or Conrad, was wrong about what was needed. Whether one thinks of such changes in terms of technology or in terms of grammar, they did make possible a modern and in some sense a more truthful fiction.

As an instance of how a writer, one who may be said to be of serious intent but of less natural ability than Bennett and less intelligence than Conrad or Ford, can fail significantly at such a moment, consider Galsworthy's novel *The Country House*. It appeared in 1907, a year after *The Man of Property*, which is rightly, for all its faults, the more celebrated. The easiest way to say what's wrong with *The Country House* is to declare, perhaps unreasonably, that it ought to be a Fordian novel. It is about a single 'affair' – the prevention of a divorce suit – but is much concerned with the Condition of England. Galsworthy is writing about an upper-class family and the troubles that come upon it when the son and heir gets involved with a New Woman whose husband threatens to cite him in divorce proceedings. The author knew the divorce law from personal experience and was writing at a moment when campaigns to change it had made it a prominent issue in the understanding of the new England.[11] But Galsworthy's hero escapes all the humiliation and obloquy, and does so by a quite deplorable bit of novelism.

His affair is conducted in a London which certainly contains poor people – they stand outside his club in Piccadilly; sick and weary, they wait on him in the discreet restaurant where he takes his wicked lady; at Newmarket they are jockeys in the pay of unscrupulous masters. But the affair of the book is essentially an affair of the rich, for since divorce was for the rich alone it could hurt only them. They are never focused in relation to the sufferers who crowd around; that there is no sorrow like that of the rich is written into the book's texture. This inability to focus may have disturbed the tender-hearted author – and it certainly makes a hash of his story, which, though rumpled and torn by ineffective ironies, arrives at a conclusion in which almost everything of interest in it is ignored or betrayed. What is certainly true is that there is a relation between this social falsity and failures of tone in the writing.

The boy's father, Mr Pendyce, is a collector:

His collection of rare, almost extinct birds' eggs was one of the finest in the 'three kingdoms'. One egg especially he would point to with pride as the last obtainable of that particular breed. 'This was procured,' he would say, 'by my dear old gillie Angus out of the bird's very nest. There was just the single egg. The species,' he added, tenderly handling the delicate porcelain-like oval in his brown hand covered with very fine blackish hairs, 'is now extinct.' He was, in fact, a true bird-lover, condemning cockneys, or rough, ignorant persons who, with no collections of their own, wantonly destroyed kingfishers or other scarce birds of any sort, out of pure stupidity. 'I would have them flogged,' he would say. . . . Whenever a rare, winged stranger appeared on his own estate, it was talked of as an event, and preserved alive with the very greatest care, in the hope that it might breed and be handed down with the property; but if it were personally known to belong to Mr Fuller or Lord Quarryman, whose estates abutted on Worsted Skeynes, and there was grave and imminent danger of its going back, it was promptly shot and stuffed, that it might not be lost to posterity.

(All quotations from *The Country House* are from the 1907 edition.)

This is firm enough, a little too sarcastic perhaps, but well made, down to the 'very fine blackish hairs'. There is no posterity save one's own; if Pendyce cannot possess the egg or the bird the species might as well die. The delicacy with which his animal hand touches the egg, his privileged knowledge of it, do not in the end distinguish his barbarity from that of the vandals. In itself it is not inconsistent with a desire to flog such people. This, though not subtle, is quite clear and sharp. Later we see him as a Justice of the Peace:

There were occasions . . . when they brought him tramps to deal with, to whom his one remark would be: 'Hold out your hands, my man,' which, being found unwarped by honest toil, were promptly sent to gaol. When found so warped, Mr Pendyce was at a loss, and would walk up and down, earnestly trying to discover what his duty was to them. There were days too . . . when many classes of offender came before him, to whom he meted justice according to the heinousness of the offence, from poaching at the top down to wife-beating at the bottom; for though a humane man, tradition did not suffer him to look on this form of sport as really criminal – at any rate not in the country.

It was true that all these matters could have been settled in a fraction of the time by a young and trained intelligence, but this would have wronged tradition, disturbed the Squire's settled conviction that he was doing his duty, and given cause for slanderous tongues to hint at idleness. And though, further, it was true that all this daily labour was devoted directly or indirectly to interests of his own, what was that but doing his duty to the country and asserting the prerogative of every Englishman at all costs to be provincial?

Here the sarcasm produces tired locutions, even very clumsy sentences; but the focus is again sharp enough, both as to the way the poor are judged and as to the assumption that the preservation of his own property is the sole important task the world sets a man. And the only reason for our hearing so much about the Squire is that his son's behaviour is a threat to his interests and pleasures, but also to the perpetuation of his property; so there is some expectation that this heavy 'placing' of him will tell when the plot begins to question him. There are matters within his upper-class competence, as when, with the Parson, he charges like an officer at the head of his troops to put out a fire in a tenant's barn. But the New Amoral Woman and Divorce should confront him with more difficult problems. Galsworthy, however, has a novelist's trick to play. Mrs Pendyce is a dull lady and no New Woman, but she is as highly bred as her husband; and by acting with ladylike decision she settles everything satisfactorily. She leaves her husband, thereby shaking momentarily his notions of property and propriety, goes to London, interviews her son and his mistress (who has by this time given the boy up), and then visits the lady's husband, who is still threatening proceedings. He is persuaded to drop them on the sole ground that Mrs Pendyce *is* a lady. So she sorts out the entire imbroglio at no cost save the speaking of a few sentences she would rather not have uttered.

When this has been done we hear no more of the poor or of bullied jockeys, for Mrs Pendyce returns home, where all is restored to its prelapsarian calm. The cloud has lifted (even the actual weather is fine) and in the garden are the Squire and the Parson looking at a tree; 'symbol of the subservient underworld – the spaniel John was seated on his tail, and he, too, was looking at the tree'. She notices weeds, but a word to the gardener will put that right. She picks one of her own white roses and kisses it. So the book ends. Later, no doubt, they will sit down to the modest seven-course dinner, served without champagne, which is all the family allows itself when alone.

This conclusion certainly proves that the rich can be lucky. Galsworthy wrote in a preface to *The Country House* that he had got the name of a revolutionary for speaking as he sometimes did about the upper classes, but argued that he was 'the least political of men. The constant endeavour of his pen has been to show Society that it has had luck; and if those who have had luck behaved as if they knew it, the chances of revolution would sink to zero.' Nothing else is done, and all the promises that something else will be done are frustrated, ignored. The ironies of the concluding tableau, in so far as they are effective at all, belong to a different book; it could have started from the same *données* and contained the passages on Mr Pendyce's collecting, but its middle would have been less lucky. It may be worth adding that Galsworthy himself owned a spaniel called John and treated him as the lucky should treat the poor; for when his conscience prevented him any longer taking part in blood sports, he sent John every summer to Scotland for the shooting, that his instincts should not go unsatisfied.[12]

It is curious that in the much more inclusive and more finely imagined *Man of Property* Galsworthy should have made Soames a 'great novel reader'; this prompted him to write a somewhat satirical passage on the ways in which novels 'coloured his [Soames's] view of life', giving him the false expectation that Irene would eventually come round to him again. Galsworthy, in *The Country House*, takes refuge in Soames's kind of expectation, having created expectations of another kind. His irony creates an amusing problem for interpreters, for its undoubted existence in some places creates a presumption that it may be found in others, whether he wanted it or not; as when Mrs Pendyce, seeking knowledge of her son, writes a solicitous letter ostensibly concerning the misfortunes of a poor girl in whom she is interested. We hear no more about the girl, whether she got into the home or not, any more than we hear of the worn-out waiters who so adored the adulterous rich young couple. She uses this pitiful case as a cover for the really serious business of her letter, and this is clear to her correspondent. Our hearing no more of the girl is part of the way things are, the way the lucky behave. What we hear about is how upper-class virtues saved the heir of a great estate from the consequences of his own conduct; and we hear it in no such way as to persuade us that the serving poor, the underworld, are still there in the text. The spaniel John does pastoral duty for them.

One sees in Galsworthy how it may be possible for a writer to command to admiration some traditional technical devices without knowing that the sort of honest dealing with the world he wanted to achieve might require him to control much more machinery, some of it very new. It was nine years later that Ford showed the way in another story of adultery; his narration hardly glances at the poor at all – only describing, as he says, the death of a mouse by cancer, but in such a way as to make it imply the sack of Rome.

Most would agree that the best novel of 1907 was *The Secret Agent*, a story with an enormous hole in the plot; so this particular kind of invitation to exceptionally strenuous hermeneutic activity on the part of the reader must be attributed to Conrad and not to Alain Robbe-Grillet, who has an admittedly more difficult hole in *Le Voyeur*. This is not the place to compare these holes, nor to expatiate on *The Secret Agent*. Conrad in his subtitle called it 'a simple tale', but its simplicity is precisely of the kind that makes for interpretative difficulty, like the notion of angels as simple in substance. I shall say something instead of a book published in the following year: Chesterton's *The Man Who Was Thursday*, which may have been a response to Conrad's novel and surely, it must be said, a weak one. It is another tale of 'those old fears', of anarchist plots and terrorism. In *The Napoleon of Notting Hill* Chesterton sets his action in a London of the future identical with that of the present, a protest against social change which would presumably extend to those technical changes advocated by writers of less conservative and optimistic outlook. Chesterton would dislike 'cold mechanic happenings' as much in fiction as in life. 'The old trade of story-telling is a much older thing than the modern art of fiction', he believed.[13] He did, however, call *Thursday* a 'nightmare' – that is his subtitle, and it may be a comment on Conrad's – and thought it worth reminding people of this fact many years later. He was trying, he said, 'to describe the world of wild doubt and despair which the pessimists were generally describing at that date'.[14] Most of their fears are dissolved in the dream. Saffron (Bedford) Park was the centre for aesthetes of the Godwin kind, but also housed the anarchist Stepniak, who was killed there on a railway line;[15] Chesterton makes it a sort of Cockaigne where the anarchist Gregory and the policeman Syme, disguised as a poet, can meet. A believer in order, poetry, and life, Syme ousts Gregory and gets himself elected to the Central Anarchist Council, having first explained – it is Conrad's point but differently put – the similarities between anarchists and policemen, which make the war between them a holy one. Chesterton gets some strikingly stagy effects: the seven top anarchists meet on the glassed-in balcony of a Leicester Square restaurant and observe on the street below them not only a policeman, 'pillar of common sense and order', but also the poor, entertained by a barrel organ and full of the vivacity, vulgarity, and irrational valour of those 'who in all those unclean streets were . . . clinging to the decencies and charities of Christendom'. The sight fills Syme himself with 'supernatural valour'. Compare the extraordinary moment in *The Secret Agent* when the agent provocateur Verloc calls the policeman in the park; it is like the difference between fancy and imagination; it expresses a contrast between the modes of paradox and poetry. And it helps to distinguish the kind of inventiveness proper to a new form of novel from the kind of fantasy permitted in the old.

Conrad's London is the raw, dark, dirty middle of the world, where there is no structure in space or in time that enables men to know one another, or even to familiarize themselves with inanimate objects. In a Soho café his policeman knows nobody and nothing; human contact is arbitrary and fugitive. But Chesterton finds order and charity in the dirty city and uses a Soho café to bless its alien inhabitants. Conrad's anarchistic aristocrats are sleazy politicians, Chesterton's are heroes. He is answering Conrad with counter-assertions that are belied even by his own text with its fake ending; and his truth is of nightmare, which the paradoxes whitewash. Thus in Chesterton it is a joke that anarchists and policemen turn out to be 'just the Syme'. And the primary process of his book *is* nightmare. We remember not what the comically educated policeman says on the Embankment, but the essentially horrible pursuit of Syme through London by an immobile but nightmarishly speedy ancient in a snowstorm, or the duel with the bloodless marquis.

The difference between *The Secret Agent* and *The Man Who Was Thursday* is instructive in the context of the present discussion. Chesterton was convinced of the existence of evil as a permanent feature of life; it was a sort of world-conspiracy represented by Jewish adventurers who, as he believed, began the Boer War 'and set two simpler and braver peoples to kill each other for their profit'. But the answers were old and paradoxical, unlike those of the 'pack of dirty modern thinkers' he declared incompatible with 'the mass of ordinary men'.[16] Conrad's novel contains specimens of the dirty modern thinker, but he handles them so originally, with such disregard for the mass of ordinary men, that he is in his way a dirty modern thinker himself. Chesterton takes Conrad's mixture of anarchist and policeman, rich and poor coexisting uneasily at the heart of the world; but Chesterton wants it to be ultimately a benign mixture and a good place, and in the pageant with which he ends, time itself takes on a ritual character as the seven policemen anarchists become days of the week and a mimesis of a good and ordered creation. For Conrad the attempt on the Observatory where time and space are zero and the imperial city is the devourer of the world's light is all the more nihilistic in that it is carried out by an idiot at the instigation of an informer whose master is a corrupt and foolish politician. The frescoes in the pub, the journey of the decrepit cab horse, are nightmares that no paradox will tame; the term 'mystery' in this novel belongs in the newspapers that further soil the filthy streets and corrupt the mind, not to a traditional theodicy. Empire, the English poor, the impact on Englishness of alien and often horrible thoughts are as much Conrad's concern as Chesterton's, but his way of seeing them belongs to another world.

Thus it was the alien who saw that the Condition of England was but a shadow of a deeper condition, which could only be diagnosed with transformed instruments. So radical is the change that in order to understand it we should have to look back at least to Nietzsche to discover how a text might have to stand in a new relation to reality to be truthful; and forward, half a century or more, to see more fully its technical implications for fiction. All we can say on this evidence is that it is one thing to know about or sense the issues – in a way, Elinor Glyn did that for those who shared her language and her expectations – and another to research the means by which a text might be caused to illuminate them. The need was felt by de Morgan, but the new novel was still a little too hard for Englishmen of 1907; it was for them too modern a way of rephrasing a proposition they might, at heart, accept: that the critical condition of England was the critical condition of life, if one had the means to know it.

5

Hawthorne and the Types

This essay originated as part of the second of four lectures given as the T. S. Eliot Memorial Lectures at the University of Kent at Canterbury in 1973. It begins with some pages on American classicism, and goes on to consider the interest of Americans in the idea of a providentially structured history and in types – historical events and persons identified as prophetic when complemented by later events or persons, their antitypes. Types were not always so strictly differentiated from allegory, and were not always strictly religious, as one sees from Hawthorne's remark about the steam engine.

Hawthorne was interested in types, and in the latest thing in types, the daguerreotype, which had its heyday in the 1840s. Since the principal figure in The House of the Seven Gables *is a daguerreotypist called Holgrave (he who engraves the whole), and the names of Maule and Pyncheon derive from the tools of an earlier kind of type, I began to see this odd book as full of reticent allegories or typologies, and went on to explore the controversy about types in evolutionary theory as a way of explaining, among other things, the shrunken Pyncheon hens.*

I greatly enjoyed this piece of research and continue to believe it is right, although I have to admit that so far as I know the Hawthorne experts have taken no notice of it. There is much pleasure to be had in simply finding things out, and I did something towards earning that pleasure in this and in the following chapter, on Emily Brontë.

Types are essentially what Auerbach has in mind when he speaks of *figurae*, events or persons that are themselves, but may presage others. Their purpose, to put it too simply, is to accommodate the events and persons of a superseded order of time to a new one. A writer conscious of standing on a watershed between past and present might well be interested in typology, though his use of the word 'type' might not have the exactness required by scholars, and he might let it be contaminated by other devices for accommodating an old veiled sense to a new order of time. Hawthorne, who *uses* the word frequently, certainly uses it loosely, and on occasion allows it to run into the senses of others, such as 'allegory' and 'emblem'.

In any case, Americans had already loosened up the concept – Jonathan Edwards, a student of Locke and Newton, extended it to natural phenomena, and influenced the Transcendentalism of Emerson, who influenced Hawthorne. For Emerson the agency by which the types were recognized was not theological; it was the imagination – 'a second sight', looking through facts, and using them as types or words for thoughts which they signify.[1] Thus types manifest themselves in nature no longer with the exact and clear fulfilment demanded by the ancestors but as the expression in natural form of something belonging to a higher realm. Another sentence of Emerson's is characteristic not only in the application of the word 'type', but also in that of the word 'influence': 'Throw a stone into the stream, and the circles that propagate themselves are the beautiful type of all influence.'[2]

Hawthorne, though he knew about Mather's stricter typology, was capable of calling the steam engine 'the type of all that go ahead', which has an Emersonian fluidity of designation. He was thus not alone in seeing the past in the light not of inherited certainties, but rather of cultivated uncertainties, the light of the imagination. Hawthorne was not concerned with the novelist's devices of verisimilar representation, which are an obeisance to a principle of reality incompatible with his purposes. As he says in the Preface to *The House of the Seven Gables*, he wrote Romances intended 'to connect a bygone age with the very present that is flitting away from us, with the legend that is 'prolonging itself . . . down into our own broad daylight', its significance rendered by that daylight dubious and obscure, suggestive and not positive.

In 'My Kinsman Major Molineux' he had spoken of 'the moon creating, like the imaginative power, a beautiful strangeness in familiar objects', a Coleridgean or Emersonian figure appropriate to the intellectual freedom he must exercise to see the shadow of the past – history, tradition and legend – as it lies on the critical present. It shares with, and imparts, a tremulous character to the passing moment, to the uncertainties of the present as it seeks the future in the past. Hawthorne has, in extraordinary degree, the 'modernist' sense of a future whose relation to the past is far more than ever before ambiguous; which makes his own moment typical of a transition from one structure of society, and one system of belief and knowledge, to another, in which the past and its types must be transformed.

For the word itself implies an event to be fulfilled in the future, and that future no one could now predict. Consequently its current senses imposed themselves in very curious ways on the old ones. Etymologically 'type' derives from the Greek *tuptein*, to incise or inscribe; for centuries it was believed that God had provided two books, the Bible and Nature, and that Nature too was inscribed with divine hints – the plants bore each a sign indicating its use, just as history revealed God's will to men. Before those times were effectively over the characters of printing had come to be called types; each was inscribed with the letter which was its function. And since the type is the fount of innumerable identical letters, the word has also the sense of the central or original member of its class.

Types were engraved with an instrument called a puncheon ('an instrument driven so as to make a hole or impression', says Johnson's *Dictionary*) and one tapped it with a mallet or maul. These tools provide the family names used by Hawthorne in *The House of the Seven Gables*, Pyncheon and Maule.[3] So Hawthorne was, for his purposes, punning discreetly on the printing sense of 'type'. But the word lent itself to all manner of uses beyond printing – in numismatics and botany, in philosophy, and more generally, says the *OED*, for the general form of a class of beings, such as a family: thus Motley can say, 'His face had lost all resemblance to the type of his heroic ancestors.' It was also used to mean 'armorial bearings'.

The earliest photographers called their plates 'types', partly no doubt because they were in a sense engraved by light, partly because they were the source of many identical examples. Daguerre's method, invented in 1839, does not allow of replication, but he called his device the daguerreotype; it was a silver plate sensitized by iodine, exposed to light, and developed by exposure to mercury. Daguerreotypes enjoyed a great vogue in the Forties; one made of Hawthorne in 1848 survives.[4]

They were valued for their delicacy, but also for their accuracy; they eliminated the style and flattery of the portrait painter, on the fallibility of whom Hawthorne commented, while sitting for his own portrait in May 1850: 'There is no such thing as a true portrait; they are all delusions and I never saw any two alike.'[5] This was written three months after he finished *The Scarlet Letter*, and shortly before he began *The House of the Seven Gables*. The daguerreotype also made unnecessary that sequence of operations by which a portrait is made reproducible in the form of an engraving, every workman in the chain adding his own distortions. Hawthorne was to complain, in *The Marble Faun*, of the loss entailed in the sculptor's use of assistants who worked on the marble, and to argue for the force and accuracy of the hasty sketch as against the finished work. The daguerreotype required no intervention whatsoever of human art; Hawthorne valued it for the same reasons as those later advanced in Ivins's remarkable book:[6] only in the photograph does one abolish the need *to accommodate the image to the syntax of the medium*. Without intervention by the human mind the truth is *wholly* inscribed; hence a daguerreotypist might well name himself Holgrave. This is the modern version of Maule (which was his original name); the maul made reliable types in an older fashion. Holgrave works with broad daylight, not with the wavering, hesitating, varying means used by artists in the past. The old picture of the Colonel changes, or rather 'tradition', that great agent of hesitation, of the tentative, in Hawthorne, alleges that it does, much as the types change and hesitate in the modern age to which they so doubtfully belong. But Holgrave, with his new techniques, seems to stand for a present and a future which will disown such mystery and uncertainty.

So the names of his principal characters assure us that, in *The House of the Seven Gables*, Hawthorne was brooding on past and present types. However, the time of that book was a time of other speculations on type, and these involved altogether new views both of the past and the future. Recall that the novel was published in the same year as *In Memoriam*, 1850, and you will at once remember Tennyson's types. First he laments the apparent cruelty of Nature:

> . . . so careful of the type she seems,
> So careless of the single life—

and then he retracts this, denying Nature even this degree of care:

> So careful of the type? But no.
> From scarped cliff and quarried stone
> She cries, A thousand types are gone,
> I care for nothing, all shall go.
>
> *(In Memoriam*, lv, lvi)

These lines were probably written in 1839, and the editors explain the importance of Lyell's *Geology*, first published in 1830. Later came Chambers's *Vestiges of the Creation* (1844); and the types, in Tennyson's sense, were henceforth of general concern. Fossil evidence of the extinction of types grew incontrovertible; the doctrine of special creation – each unchangeable type brought into existence simultaneously by a divine fiat about 6,000 years ago – grew much harder to defend. The past suddenly lengthened enormously. Yet there was room for optimism; there might in a future also inconceivably lengthened be better types. So Tennyson in his Epilogue to the poem reflects on Hallam as 'a nobler type, / Appearing ere the time was ripe', a piece of metabiological thinking that had both antecedents and successors.[7]

There was severe opposition to such speculations, not only from those who were committed to special creation for fundamentalist reasons, but also from scientists of great distinction. Cuvier died in 1832, but his doctrine of the immutability of species was strongly supported; this 'fixist' position required as a geological corollary the theory that fixed types were eliminated by catastrophes (of which he counted up to twenty) each followed by a new special creation, there being no continuity between these new types and the fossil remains of their predecessors. A pupil of Cuvier's, Louis Agassiz, having already made a reputation as a geologist and biologist, emigrated to the United States. He settled in Boston, and at once grew famous, giving, between 1846 and 1850, a series of immensely popular lectures on biology at the Lowell Institute.

Hawthorne, like everyone else of any note, knew Agassiz, who shortly became an important Harvard professor and the best known (if not the best) of American palaeontologists. He followed Cuvier in declaring that no evidence existed to indicate that one animal could develop from another, or to show that there was any genetic connection between the species of successive strata. 'Species,' he said, 'do not pass insensibly one into another, but . . . appear and disappear unexpectedly, without direct relation to their precursors.'[8] The form of each species he calls the *type*, explaining in the preface to his textbook that this was common parlance.[9] He reconciled his science with the Bible: 'The records of the Bible, together with human tradition, teach us that man and the animals associated with him were created by the word of God . . . and this truth is confirmed by the revelations of science, which unequivocally indicate the direct interventions of creative power.'[10] There is thus no parental line of descent between the faunas of different epochs, and none, of course, between animals and man.

Agassiz, though a valued correspondent of Darwin, not surprisingly rejected *The Origin of Species*; in a posthumously published paper he finally reasserted the truth of all species to their type, and denied analogies from embryology, arguing that the metamorphoses of the foetus 'have never been known to lead to any transition of one species into another'.[11] The metamorphoses of the embryo simply culminate in its compliance with its type. Striking at Darwin's weakest point, he affirmed that the mechanisms of heredity were badly understood, and that 'qualities both good and bad are dropped as well as acquired, and the process ends sometimes with the degradation of the type, and the survival of the unfit rather than the fittest'. Sexual selection may have had no regard for strength or beauty: 'fine progeny are not infrequently the offspring of weak parents, and vice versa'.

In allowing himself to speak of acquired characteristics Agassiz has in mind variations within the species, deviations from the type. He changed his views a little, but did not give them up; a great practical scientist, he stood uneasily at the end of one age and the beginning of another, as much in glaciology (he discovered the Ice Age but denied the inferences others made from his work) as in zoology. So great was his influence in America (especially in the South, where his characterization of Negroes as of a different type from Caucasians made him popular for essentially non-scientific reasons) that he delayed the American reception of Darwinism.[12] After his death in 1873, commerce, which had, as we have seen, already been chosen by evangelists as the agent of the millennium, exploited the Spencerian 'survival of the fittest' in its philosophy of Social Darwinism; though Richard Hofstadter, the historian of that movement, argues that it would have happened anyway, since Agassiz was losing his following, and his Harvard colleague Asa Gray, somewhat eclipsed by the glamour of the Swiss naturalist, was taking it over; he had attacked Agassiz openly in his review of *The Origin of Species*.[13]

With Agassiz departed the last hope of a science which could regard natural history as a phenomenal representation of the operations of divine providence; which thought of itself as 'interpreting a system that is his not ours', a system which is a record either of God's deeds or of his prophecies.[14] No longer could the types be regarded as divine inscriptions, as parts of a mystery both stable and divinely systematic. But for a few years in the late Forties, immediately before Hawthorne wrote *The Scarlet Letter* and *The House of the Seven Gables*, the acknowledged scientific leader of the New England community, though already under attack from more revolutionary biologists, argued with every appearance of modernity and authority that they could. And so the types of Agassiz might join, in a man's mind, with those of Emerson and those of Cotton Mather and those of Daguerre; a unique and critical moment in the history of the concept, on the threshold of a new age and a new order.

It is curious that the general opinion of Hawthorne scholars should be that expressed by E. Wagenknecht when he remarks that although Hawthorne knew Agassiz personally he had 'no more interest than Dickens' in 'the great scientific discoveries and speculations of the nineteenth century'.[15] One could begin the refutation of this view by mentioning Hawthorne's indisputable interest in mesmerism and phrenology; for these were both of great general interest at the time, and were regarded by many intelligent people as sciences. The fact that they have since been stripped of this distinction is not to the point. It is true that he was most concerned with the social and moral or imaginative aspects of these pseudo-sciences, but that is what one would expect. His fiancée, Sophia Peabody, was treated for her headaches by a mesmerist who, being also a dentist, is reflected in Holgrave. Hawthorne was troubled by the sexual suggestiveness of this therapeutic situation, wondering, in a letter to Sophia, whether it did not amount to 'an intrusion into thy holy of holies'[16] – an unpardonable sin, whatever the scientific status of the practice; and, says Taylor Stoehr in his important article, 'During the 1840's Hawthorne returned again and again, in his stories and his notebooks, to this idea of one soul immorally dominating another, by means of some mysterious exercise of the will.'[17] He did so again in all his major novels, from *The Scarlet Letter* to *The Marble Faun*.

However, the present point is not Hawthorne's interest in this moment of medical science, but the probability that he was far from indifferent to the new senses given to the concept of types by the authority of Agassiz, which had come to complicate the older typologics. The proof is to be found in *The House of the Seven Gables*. We have seen that the names of the characters – Pyncheon, Maule, Holgrave – all allude to aspects of that complicated word. A similarly oblique hint at another is provided by the Pyncheon hens.

These degenerate birds are ordinarily treated as a sort of arch decorative parallel to the Pyncheons, similarly declined; and indeed they are that; but there is so much about the hens in the novel that to limit their function thus is to call Hawthorne immoderate, tedious and obvious. What seems to have happened is this: when all Boston was discussing Agassiz and the fixity of types, Hawthorne remembered and returned to what had formerly been the *locus classicus* of such discussions among educated men, namely the *Natural History* of Buffon. Years before he had borrowed the fourth volume of the translation in the Salem Library[18] and so acquainted himself with views that were of special interest to Americans.

Buffon believed the types to be invariant – an elephant was always an elephant, and never turned into anything else – but allowed that within the type changes might be wrought by time. These changes were degenerative; thus an animal that was removed from its native habitat, or domesticated, would grow smaller. In particular he believed, and argued in his fourth volume, that this degeneration occurred in European species when they were transplanted to the New World.

Some of the celebrity, or notoriety, of these opinions was doubtless owing to Jefferson's careful refutation of them in his *Notes on Virginia*. Obviously Buffon's inversion of the familiar terms of the *translatio* was totally unacceptable to Jefferson, especially since man was included among the species that degenerated in the West. What about the mammoths? To forestall the damaging reply that there certainly *had* been mammoths, but that they existed no longer, Jefferson insists on the vastness of the continent, and the certainty that there are mammoths around somewhere, the species having been created invariant and inextinguishable;[19] and these alone refuted Buffon's contention that in America *'la nature vivante est beaucoup moins agissante, beaucoup moins forte'*.[20] And so Jefferson defended not only nature but America against 'this new theory of the tendency of nature to belittle her productions on this side the Atlantic'.[21] In doing so he produced a patriotic wartime version of the old *translatio* topic: England is in decline, 'The sun of her glory is fast descending to the horizon. Her philosophy has crossed the Channel, her freedom the Atlantic, and herself seems passing to that awful dissolution whose issue is not given human foresight to scan.'[22]

What has all this to do with the Pyncheon hens? Buffon, in his fourth volume, uses the domestic hen to illustrate his thesis. The hen, he explains, is not native to the New World, and this, in addition to decline by domestication, has caused it greatly to diminish in size. In the wild, he argues, the type is as large as a crow, but the American examples have shrunk to the size of a pigeon. The sexual force of the cocks is also much diminished by the Atlantic passage; ideally, each should have a seraglio of fifteen hens.[23] Buffon then passes to a consideration of the native turkey.

The House of the Seven Gables is undoubtedly a serious and topical book – which is what Melville meant when he spoke of its 'apprehension of the absolute condition of present things',[24] and Hawthorne was animated by a powerful sense of the historical crisis through which he was living, and to which he referred, with conscious geological extravagance, in *The Blithedale Romance*: 'It was impossible . . . not to imbibe the idea . . . that the crust of the earth in many places was broken, and its whole surface portentously heaving; that it was a day of crisis, and that we ourselves were in the critical vortex' (XVI). It is as if a Cuvierian catastrophe, an epochal alteration of types, was upon him.[25] Yet he also saw that there was an element of the ridiculous in what he was attempting in *The House of the Seven Gables*: 'Sometimes, when tired of it, it strikes me that the whole is an absurdity, from beginning to end; but the fact is, in writing a romance, a man is always, or always ought to be, careening on the utmost verge of a precipitous absurdity, and the skill lies in coming as close as possible, without actually tumbling over.'[26] The Pyncheon hens are an instance of such careening.

There had been no connection between the Pyncheons of the Old and the New Worlds for two centuries (IV), and the same is of course true of their hens. They were 'pure specimens of a breed which had been transmitted down as an heirloom in the Pyncheon family, and were said, while in their prime, to have attained almost the size of turkeys'. Hepzibah preserves an old eggshell almost as large as that of an ostrich. But now 'the hens were scarcely larger than pigeons', which made it 'evident that the race had degenerated, like many a noble race besides, in consequence of too strict a watchfulness to keep it pure'. Chanticleer has only two wives, and there is only one chicken. Thus the lapse of years, the lack of outbreeding, and 'a climate so unlike that which had fostered it', had 'wrought important changes in the physical system' of the hens as well as of Jaffrey, so much reduced in size from his ancestor or type, Judge Pyncheon (VIII).

The point is one that Hawthorne often makes in a more general way. The English breed has changed in New England, the people are more nervous, quicker. In *The Scarlet Letter* he contrasts the delicate modern Bostonian woman with her seventeenth-century ancestress; he has in mind a necessary degeneracy from all Old World types that Americans choose to preserve in the new habitat, whether they are noble families, their coats of arms, or their English gardens, across which might burst, as again in *The Scarlet Letter*, some enormous New World squash. But the hens make the point diagrammatic as well as comic. The cock is the size of a partridge, the hens the size of quails. The chicken looks small enough to be still in the egg, yet experienced enough to have been 'the founder of the antiquated race', a kind of walking embryo which has 'aggregated into itself the ages, not only of these living specimens of the breed, but of all its forefathers and foremothers'. It is, in short, the type, and it cannot but recall Agassiz's insistence on the typological importance of the embryo in the tenth chapter of his textbook, and his often repeated opinion that the embryo recapitulates the geological order of extinct types, at the same time being unambiguously what it now is.[27] Holgrave tells Phoebe that the chicken is 'a symbol of the life of the old house, embodying its interpretation likewise, although an unintelligible one, as such clews generally are. It was a feathered riddle, a mystery hatched out of an egg . . .' (X). The breed is saved by Phoebe; only what is *not* true to the Pyncheon type – as, we are told repeatedly, Phoebe and Clifford are not – can save the breed. Non-Pyncheon (i.e. American) women save the Old World stock of the Pyncheons from wickedness, degeneracy, and ultimately extinction.

For change is the law of the New World, and it is the failure to accept it, to avoid a habitual and too rigid reference back to the old, that hinders the fulfilment of a destiny appropriate, spiritually and materially only, to a new order. About these matters Hawthorne is complex and hesitant, as always; the shadows of that Old World are varyingly obtrusive, beyond elimination. Here his hesitancy is, in Henry James's sense, playful, but the play is on the old and new, on Buffonian degeneracy (which is an evolutionary instrument) and the acceptance of a world in which certain types ought not to survive – in which families decline from the patriciate to the proletariat, and it is reasonable to speak of the necessity to rebuild houses in every generation. Yet they do survive, in their riddling way, faded like the old carpets and the old claims to inheritance (the old map laying claim to the New World). Their degeneracy may be measured by the contrast between the feebleness of the bred-out Old World flowers ('the antique and hereditary flowers' (VI)) and the luxuriance of the ancient beans discovered by Holgrave, still true to the original type,[28] like the English cookbooks, and the ancient coffee-beans; or like Jaffrey, as base as, though less powerful than, his ancestor; or like the hereditary disease of the family, or their facial characteristics, transformed yet recognizable. These are the qualities that inhibit the future; which may mean that instead of offering a nomadic utopia of steam train and telegraph and loving spirituality, it may simply impose a journey back to a place very like the one where the journey began, as it is for Clifford and Hepzibah. Perhaps virtue grows under a republic; but change is more rapid and aimless, corruption easier.

There is another typological joke in *The House of the Seven Gables*; only as such can the repetitive theme of the urchin's visits to Hepzibah's shop be explained. He has designs on her whole stock of 'natural history', those gingerbread animals made in moulds, or types. All the Jim Crows come from one type (Hawthorne had some sympathy with Agassiz's view of the Negro question), though there may be an exemplar with a broken foot, or an elephant that collapses into untyped gingerbread. (Buffon, as I've said, held that an elephant was always only and completely an elephant, but that individual elephants, by time or accident, may diverge from the type.[29]) Hawthorne is playing a typological game with his gingerbreads, his lead soldiers, his sugar candies. With one of those tricks of explicitness that makes for reticence, by pretending to make a limited joke when he is making one of much broader implication, he says that 'this remarkable urchin, in truth, was the very emblem of old Father Time, in respect of his all-devouring appetite for men and things' (VIII). He 'ingulfs' creation. And finally, in the last chapter, Phoebe gives him the whole stock; no doubt the types, the moulds, remain, but as fossils of an older epoch; there are no more exemplars.

As an emblem of time the urchin is supported by Jaffrey's watch and by the sundial, whose 'shadow looks over the shoulder of the sunshine' (XIII).[30] Time destroys the exemplar; what resists it, though perhaps not without variation in the exemplar, is the type. This is, in a sense, Hawthorne's subject, the degree to which withered 'bygones' must be a part of the present and future. They are of the Old World, types of it, whether they are human, vegetable, social – for armorial bearings are types too, yet their owners preserve them, like genetic traits, into a plebeian future. One sees why Melville stressed the modernity of the book, and why Hawthorne used so many devices to foster its uncertainty, its ambiguity, its hesitancy, allowing the text to waver in authority, equivocating about tradition and history, falsely emphasizing some points and letting others slip by unstressed. So congenitally unassertive that one mistrusts all his assertions, he resigns the narrative to 'tradition' or to Holgrave, or, with quiet ostentation, withdraws all his authority, will not distinguish between tradition, history, truth. Certainly he inscribes the old types on his narrative, but it bears them not in the manner of a daguerreotype but as Clifford's soap-bubble bears the images of the world, which the reader must interpret as he can; in Hawthorne the reader's share is always a great one. These bubble inscriptions have none of the positiveness that characterizes a biblical type, or the old signature on a plant; they belong to modern books that are like bubbles, 'little impalpable worlds . . . with the big world depicted in hues bright as imagination, on the nothing of the surface'. The relation of these signifiers to what they signify is wholly problematic, and every man may look at them with pleasure or with anger, destroy them with the touch of a finger or a stick. To provide these fragile modern typologies is the work of the artist who inhabits a new world in flight from old certainties, an artist of the age of the steam engine, of mesmerism, of the new inconceivable past as well as the unknowable future.

Holgrave's arts – writing and daguerreotyping – don't occupy him entirely; he also does many jobs that are part of the materialism of the modern world. But though he is a modern worker, he has the inherited Maule powers, now redeemed from superstition and made scientific as mesmerism, yet still deriving 'from the type of his ancestors'. Hawthorne calls these powers 'sympathetic', and unlike his double in the inset tale, Holgrave will not use them to harm a Pyncheon woman. That he belongs to a new age, and enjoys its considerable discontinuity with the old, is frequently emphasized, at any rate until the book's strange conclusion. He is modern, rootless, so much so that the text takes on an unusual note of authority in condemning him for desiring too revolutionary a change, too violent an abandonment of the past, too ready a belief in the 'golden era' about to begin. 'Altogether in his culture, and want of culture – in his crude, wild and misty philosophy, and the practical experience that counteracted some of its tendencies; in his magnanimous zeal for man's welfare, and his recklessness of whatever the ages had established in man's behalf; in his faith and in his infidelity; in what he had, and in what he lacked – the artist might fitfully stand forth as the representative of many compeers in his native land' (XII). In Holgrave we see how millennial and translational myths survive the supersession of their Old World cultural and religious contexts. Henry James rightly found in him something of Hawthorne himself, 'American of the Americans', one whom 'the idea of long perpetuation and survival always appeared to have filled . . . with a kind of horror';[31] but he is also, like Hawthorne, shadowed by the perpetuities he has rejected.

Later Hawthorne was to meditate, in *The Marble Faun*, on Rome as an image of those perpetuities: timeless, the type of the City and of human civility, yet, in the aspect of time, a place of filth, corruption and superstition. In Holgrave's New England the perpetuities are less evident. The types survive in their shadowy way, culturally or genetically transmitted; but Holgrave is one who records the whole, on a modern photographic plate, with as little interference from past portraiture as may be. And yet his daguerreotypes of Jaffrey repeat the Gothic evil of the old portrait. And he himself, as I have said, inherits some of the dangerous powers of the old type of artist, now called 'magnetic' or 'sympathetic' or the like. It is by a story, a work of art, that he goes near to mesmerizing Phoebe; typically, it is a story *about* mesmerism. To be an artist at all is to involve oneself in making a new version of old types, to exercise the power that makes portraits, and some mirrors, so ominous. Holgrave's desire to destroy the past, dissolve the continuity between generations by destroying family houses, establish a democracy without a history, is frustrated in the end, though his present is to the past as daguerreotype is to portrait, the new house to the old, mesmerism, or 'magnetism', or 'influence', to witchcraft and Maule's curse.

The text of the novel imitates him in this; its Gothic materials – lost maps, inherited curses – its magic, its confusion of the 'traditionary' and the historical, its allegories cunningly too clear or too obscure – are all evasions of narrative authority, and imply that each man must make his own reading. The types inscribed on it are shifting, unstable, varying in force, to be fulfilled by the determinations of the reader; in strong contrast, then, to the old Puritan types. So the text belongs to its moment and implicitly declares that the modern classic is not, like the book of God or the old book of Nature, or the old accommodated classic, of which the senses, though perhaps hidden, are fully determined, there in full before the interpreter. In the making of it the reader must take his share. This is the sense in which *The House of the Seven Gables* justifies Henry James's remark that Hawthorne, though he inherited the Puritan conscience and some of its modes of operation, nevertheless altered it: in Hawthorne that conscience 'was only, as one may say, intellectual; it was not moral or theological. He played with it . . .'[32] Of course this is serious play, and the same qualification must be borne in mind when one endorses James's other observation, that Hawthorne's imagination is 'profane'.[33]

We are told twice that Holgrave lives by a new law; it is a profane law, typically related to the Covenant of Grace only as that was to the Covenant of Works; indeed less so, since the catastrophe of the times, represented by palpable changes in society, in history, in art, has made all typologies problematical. This is the topic with which Hawthorne plays in *The House of the Seven Gables*. He had done so with much more direct allusion to older typology in its greater predecessor, *The Scarlet Letter*. But that too is a bubble of fugitive typologies, consciously modern, carefully unauthoritative, open to multiple interpretation because the modern world is so.

The Letter itself is, of course, a type, variously engraved and susceptible to multiple interpretation. God may, as the characters of the novel believe, have inscribed the world with types; inscribing this world, the novel, with types is a much less certain proceeding. It is for the reader to make sense of the inscriptions, by his own imaginative collaboration. Once again, tradition is part of the chorus of voices that confuse all relations between the words of the text and what they refer to, much as the mirror distorts, and the armour, and the forest pool. In such a book text and reality stand in no enantiomorphic relation; the text continually questions its own references; the types with which it is inscribed are of very uncertain provenance and meaning, for the simple senses of the old typology and the old pneumatology are suspended. 'Indistinctness and duplicity of impression' are words applicable not only to Dimmesdale but to the text itself, and Hawthorne uses many means to enforce them. Here, then, is another work that contemplates the ancient assumptions from over the threshold of the modern; the old contracts between signifier and signified, between the authoritative maker and the reader certain that there is a right interpretation, are boldly broken. Such a text must continually draw attention to itself as something written, as open and plural, itself a type of things to come, in a time when all books must be read with a difference.

Chillingworth is a herbalist, expert therefore in the doctrine of signatures, belonging to a time in which nature proclaimed, to the scholar, its divinely instituted structures and senses – a world, then, very unlike what the intrusive voice in the text calls 'the opaque substance of today'. The types of the book of God have grown ambiguous. 'Awful hieroglyphics' are written on the cope of heaven – as our forefathers believed and tradition reports, but Dimmesdale interprets them in a sense peculiar to himself. He alone, says the text, was responsible for the reading. So with the text itself; the truths written on its firmament are the responsibility of each reader. We proceed, as it were, from truth to shadowy types. The letter itself varies in meaning; the text undercuts traditional interpretations in the light of what it calls 'modern incredulity', in the light of the 'refined present' and its lost certainties. The past grows obscure, like those 'half-obliterated coats of arms' brought over from the Old World, like the Governor's garden, dominated by the new, extra-systematic pumpkin. Whether it is a rosebush or the wilderness, the symbol hesitates, grows occult to the modern eye. The interpretative light falls differently, from the imagination and not from heaven.

Is the forest what the text will allow us to believe, an emblem or type of the 'moral wilderness', or of pastoral sympathy, which it also proposes? What are we encouraged to make of the brook, the old tree? Of the Black Man, through whom nature is associated with the demonic? Is Chillingworth diabolical, or is that a naïve opinion and what he himself, in a remarkable expression which, more than any other, tells us how Hawthorne must be read, calls a 'typical illusion'? 'The reader', says the text as it draws to its end, 'may choose among these theories.' May we choose to say that in associating nature and sex with evil, with the breaking of a law and a necessary punishment, the Old World erred? That its strict antithesis between nature and grace made no allowance for the extraordinary overdetermination of nature? All that is, at least, licit. Dimmesdale, returning from his moment with Hester in the mock-paradise of the forest, becomes almost comically an enemy of grace; and yet in his experience sin seems to produce a certain abundance of grace, and we can say (though we can also deny) that had he not sinned he could not have preached as he did.

Pearl is the crucial instance, embodying the oxymoron 'native grace', and variously proposed as elf, child of sin, witch-child, child of Misrule; a visitor, nevertheless, from the 'spiritual world' (XIII), and the agency by which her mother is prevented from founding a new Antinomian, and so in a measure naturalist, religion. The child is repeatedly associated with mirrors and reflections; the mirror is the type of the type, but in Hawthorne, it is usually mysterious or distorting, denying the possibility of a simple relation between image and reality, sign and referent. So we cannot know where we have her. Is she an allomorph of the ambiguous letter itself? A natural child excluded, for most of the book, from the human family that is held together by grace? A Florimell both true and false? Anyway, Pearl plays her part in enforcing the submission of Dimmesdale, and not only enters the restricted family of grace but disappears to the Old World, with its types of nobility, its dark armorial bearings; while Hester, still wearing her own type, rejoins the community on new terms. Pearl drifts back to the world of types; Hester is a prophetic type of the New World. The fulfilment of this type must be obscure, and between the theories that she is a type of natural disorder, or, like Holgrave, of 'a new order peculiar to herself', the text can only say 'the reader may choose'.

Out of these problematically inscribed types, and within certain limits, we make the book according to the order or disorder of our own imagination. Dimmesdale's sermon can be thought of as the true type of the text itself. Men may have a truth, we are told, but be unable to communicate it for lack of the Pentecostal gift, symbolizing, it would seem, not the power of speech in foreign and unknown languages, but that of addressing the whole human brotherhood in the heart's native language (XI). Dimmesdale, for all his black heart, admits to having this power (XVII). And when he preaches his sermon the text gives us not one word of it, in any language (XXII), though it speaks to each man in his own way, prophesying the high destiny of the New World. This Pentecostal sermon is the text's comment on itself; guilty, inspired, all things to all men, obscurely prophesying a future empire under a new law.

So the book speaks of itself, and, over and over again, of types (e.g. X, XIV, XXIII, XXIV) and typical illusions. Hester is 'a type of something to be sorrowed over, and looked upon with awe'; yet she is also, like Hallam, and in the spirit of a very modern typology, a prophetic type, shadowing a future woman free of the old law in a time when 'a new truth would be revealed, in order to establish the whole relation between man and woman on a surer ground of mutual happiness'; this Antinomian prophecy we are invited to associate with Anne Hutchinson. Prevented by her sin from establishing such a religion in her own time, Hester may be prophetess of another time, her type may find its antitype in a new world liberated from the past.[34] The text does not assert these prophecies and types; it is too deliberately unauthoritative to say anything so positive. Yet in the end Hester's A takes the place of the old armorial bearings on the tomb; a new type, a New World type, to be interpreted by the imagination, by the choosing reader, in place of the fixed senses of the old, though the inscription, ironically, uses the old precise heraldic language: 'On a field, sable, the letter A, gules.'[35]

Much more might be said of the deliberate hesitations of Hawthorne, the acuity of his sense of the transitional moment, and the manner in which he sought to invent a modern book, mimetic only in the most unstable way, aware of itself, pondering its relation to the past and also the future. In his last completed novel he undertook a more explicit encounter with the past at its imperial centre, the Rome of *The Marble Faun*, far from what he calls the 'broad and simple daylight' of modern New England. Since Hawthorne cannot have his Holgravian way, and every half-century destroy by fire a town's accumulation of guilt and filth, he sees the Eternal City as the Sibylline recipient of a 'grievous boon of immortality'. Coexistent with this immemorial and perpetually present past is the present of Kenyon's own new world: 'In that fortunate land, each generation has only its own sins and sorrows to bear. Here, it seems as if all the weary and dreary Past were piled upon the back of the Present' (XXXIII). Yet Rome is also the centre of 'that central clime, whither the eyes and the heart of every artist turn' (VI). Perhaps they ought not to; Hilda, by growing so perfect a copyist of the Old, abandons the gift with which she might have enriched her own New World.

What is remarkable is Hawthorne's double vision of Rome. It is the *urbs aeterna*, centre of perpetual Empire, beside which all other places are provincial (XXIV). It is the monument of a past when Italy was 'yet guiltless of Rome' (XXVI), stretching back to the date of the faun and dryad, and, in art, to the obelisk in the Piazza del Popolo, oldest of things, even in Rome (XII). It is the classic Rome, closer to us than those Gothic centuries between, which 'look further off than the

Augustan age' (XVIII). It is the Rome of St Peter's seen in its entirety, 'the world's cathedral' (XII). But it is also the Rome that 'lies, a long-decaying corpse' (XXXVI), among centuries of filth and squalor, amid 'the grime and corruption which paganism had left there, and a perverted Christianity had made more noisome' (XLV); the Rome of malaria, foul air; the Rome in which even the Carnival, though partaking of the city's perpetuity, is mean and degenerate. At the end of his career Hawthorne rediscovers the Rome that is timeless yet exists in the aspect of time.

Hilda's ambiguous relation with the art, and with the religion, of Rome, is that of the new to the old Empire, the one more spiritual but also, even in being less evil, less connected to humanity and to art. On the one hand there is the corruption of Donatello's nature, which is also the birth of his soul, and the creative decadence of Miriam;[36] on the other the priggishness of Kenyon, the New World chastity of Hilda. There is the provinciality of America, its obvious past never more than a generation or two back, with no use for marble, and a taste for vulgar and rootless iconographies, satirized by Kenyon when he jokes about a possible American equivalent for the fountain of Trevi – the ancient deities pulled down, and thirty-one spouts, one for each state, pouring into one vast basin, symbolizing 'the grand reservoir of national prosperity' (XVI). Yet Rome represents that heritage of sin, the loss of natural joy, which, it is suggested, though as usual the suggestion is contested, may make of history a fortunate fall, from which 'we might rise to a far loftier paradise' (L).

The law of the *imperium* was like that of the Puritans, powerful, persistent, yet requiring to be broken in the New World. As the great type of Empire, Rome is both beautiful and sinister, unforgettable and yet to be expelled from the memory. It is perpetual, only its dispositions changing; yet there is a modern empire, founded in the West by that 'handful of half-starved fanatics', which will reject this classic perpetuity and, changing essentially, make an art which is itself an art of change.

For the classic of the modern *imperium* cannot be, as the Bible had been, and Virgil too, a repository of certain, unchanging truths. Truth in art – itself a dangerous and perhaps ambiguously evil activity – will have the hesitancy, the instability, of the attitude struck by the New

World, provincial and unstable itself, towards the corrupt maturity of the metropolis. This is why one cannot even try to read Hawthorne, that great inventor of American attitudes to the metropolitan past, as one is still urged to read Virgil. To say that the meaning of *The Scarlet Letter*, or of *The House of the Seven Gables*, is the meaning Hawthorne meant, is pointless; his texts, with all their varying, fading voices, their controlled lapses into possible inauthenticity, are meant as invitations to co-production on the part of the reader.

In this sense it may be said that the texts of the once innocent new empire in the West of necessity lose their innocence; the accommodations needed by the old classics after a lapse of years are required by these modern classics from every reader, from the very beginning of their existence. This had to be so, if there were to be a New World art, which, itself reticent and opaque, could hint at the true relation between the old *imperium* and the new.

Here, then, is the classic of that *renovatio* that accompanied the westward translation of empire and learning; over it, in some always incalculable degree, lies the shadow of the past, as it lay over all former renovations; though here the forces of discontinuity are so much greater. This new classic is not an *Aeneid* that suffers, without openly inviting, accommodation, as times change and empires move; for without the co-operation of the reader's imagination it can hardly exist at all, except for readers so naïve as to be contented with what, as a simple tale, must seem ill-told.

By this route, we reach the modern classic, which offers itself only to readings which are encouraged by its failure to give a definitive account of itself. Unlike the old classic, which was expected to provide answers, this one poses a virtually infinite set of questions. And when we have learnt how to ask some of the questions we may discover that the same kinds of question can also be put to the old classic. The modern classic, and the modern way of reading the classic, are not to be separated. Some of the consequences of this change I shall discuss in the next chapter.

6

Wuthering Heights as a Classic

This essay also comes from the Eliot lecture series given at the University of Kent at Canterbury in 1973, published in 1975. I see on returning to this discourse that it will not be easy to read for anybody who hasn't read Wuthering Heights *pretty recently. I wrote it at a time when I was interested in ways of talking about narrative that were newly imported from Paris and, in the case of Wolfgang Iser, from Germany. If I were writing now I should not be tackling the issues in quite this way, but I think I was on the right lines and wonder still whether there was any other way to take on the job; which means, I suppose, that I couldn't, now, even pretend to do so.*

I have chosen *Wuthering Heights* for what I take to be good reasons. It meets the requirement that it is read in a generation far separated from the one it was presented to; and it has other less obvious advantages. It happens that I had not read the novel for many years; furthermore, although I could not be unaware that it had suffered a good deal of interpretation, and had been the centre of quarrels, I had also omitted to read any of this secondary material. These chances put me in a position unfamiliar to the teacher of literature; I could consider my own response to a classic more or less untrammelled by too frequent reading, and by knowledge of what it had proved possible, or become customary, to say about it. This strikes me as a happy situation, though some may call it shameful. Anyway, it is the best way I can think of to arrive at some general conclusions about the classic, though I daresay those conclusions will sound more like a programme for research than a true ending to this briefer exercise.

I begin, then, with a partial reading of *Wuthering Heights* which represents a straightforward encounter between a competent modern reader (the notion of competence is, I think, essential, however much you may think this demonstration falls short of it) and a classic text. However, in assuming this role, I could not avoid noticing some remarks that are not in the novel at all, but in Charlotte Brontë's Biographical Notice of her sisters, in which she singles out a contemporary critic as the only one who got her sister's book right. 'Too often,' she says, 'do reviewers remind us of the mob of Astrologers, Chaldeans and Soothsayers gathered before the "writing on the wall", and unable to read the characters or make known the interpretation.' One, however, has accurately read 'the Mene, Mene, Tekel, Upharsin of an original mind' and 'can say with confidence, "This is the interpretation thereof"'. This latterday Daniel was Sidney Dobell, but a modern reader who looks him up in the hope of coming upon what would after all be a very valuable piece of information is likely to be disappointed. Very few would dream of doing so; most would mistrust the critic for whom such claims were made, or the book which lent itself to them. Few would believe that such an interpretation exists, however frequently the critics produce new 'keys'. For we don't think of the novel as a code, or a nut, that can be broken; which contains or refers to a meaning all will agree upon if it can once be presented *en clair*. We need little persuasion to believe that a good novel is not a message at all. We assume in principle the rightness of the plurality of interpretations to which I now, in ignorance of all the others, but reasonably confident that I won't repeat them, now contribute.

When Lockwood first visits Wuthering Heights he notices, among otherwise irrelevant decorations carved above the door, the date *1500* and the name *Hareton Earnshaw*. It is quite clear that everybody read and reads this (on p. 2) as a sort of promise of something else to come. It is part of what is nowadays called a 'hermeneutic code'; something that promises, and perhaps after some delay provides, explanation. There is, of course, likely to be some measure of peripeteia or trick; you would be surprised if the explanation were not, in some way, surprising, or at any rate, at this stage unpredictable. And so it proves. The expectations aroused by these inscriptions are strictly *generic*; you must know things of this kind before you can entertain expectations of the sort I mention. Genre in this sense is what Leonard Meyer (writing of music) calls 'an internalized probability system'.[1] Such a system could, but perhaps shouldn't, be thought of as constituting some sort of contract between reader and writer. Either way, the inscriptions can be seen as something other than simple elements in a series of one damned thing after another, or even of events relative to a story as such. They reduce the range of probabilities, reduce randomness, and are expected to recur. There will be 'feedback'. This may not extinguish all the informational possibilities in the original stimulus, which may be, and in this case is, obscurer than we thought, 'higher', as the information theorists say, 'in entropy'. The narrative is more than merely a lengthy delay, after which a true descendant of Hareton Earnshaw reoccupies the ancestral house; though there is little delay before we hear about him, and can make a guess if we want.

When Hareton is first discussed, Nelly Dean rather oddly describes him as 'the late Mrs Linton's nephew'. Why not 'the late Mr Earnshaw's son'? It is only in the previous sentence that we have first heard the name Linton, when the family of that name is mentioned as having previously occupied Thrushcross Grange. Perhaps we are to wonder how Mrs Linton came to have a nephew named Earnshaw. At any rate, Nelly's obliquity thus serves to associate Hareton, in a hazy way, with the house on which his name is *not* carved, and with a family no longer in evidence. Only later do we discover that he is in the direct Earnshaw line, in fact, as Nelly says, 'the last of them'. So begins the provision of information which both fulfils and qualifies the early 'hermeneutic' promise; because, of course, Hareton, his inheritance restored, goes to live at the Grange. The two principal characters remaining at the end are Mr and Mrs Hareton Earnshaw. The other names, which have intruded on Earnshaw – Linton and Heathcliff – are extinct. In between there have been significant recursions to the original inscription – in Chapter XX Hareton cannot read it; in XXIV he can read the name but not the date.

We could say, I suppose, that this so far tells us nothing about *Wuthering Heights* that couldn't, with appropriate changes, be said of most novels. All of them contain the equivalent of such inscriptions; indeed all writing is a sort of inscription, cut memorably into the uncaused flux of event; and inscriptions of the kind I am talking about are interesting secondary clues about the nature of the writing in which they occur. They draw attention to the literariness of what we are reading, indicate that the story is a story, perhaps with beneficial effects on our normal powers of perception; above all they distinguish a *literary* system which has no constant relation to readers with interests and expectations altered by long passages of time. Or, to put it another way, Emily Brontë's contemporaries operated different probability systems from ours, and might well ignore whatever in a text did not comply with their generic expectations, dismissing the rest somehow – by skipping, by accusations of bad craftsmanship, inexperience, or the like. In short, their internalized probability systems survive them in altered and less stringent forms; we can read more of the text than they could, and of course read it differently. In fact, the only works we value enough to call classic are those which, as they demonstrate by surviving, are complex and indeterminate enough to allow us our necessary pluralities. That 'Mene, Mene, Tekel, Upharsin' has now many interpretations. It is in the nature of works of art to be open, in so far as they are 'good'; though it is in the nature of authors, and of readers, to close them.

The openness of *Wuthering Heights* might be somewhat more extensively illustrated by an inquiry into the passage describing Lockwood's bad night at the house, when, on his second visit, he was cut off from Thrushcross Grange by a storm. He is given an odd sort of bed in a bedroom-within-a-bedroom; Catherine Earnshaw slept in it and later Heathcliff would die in it. Both the bed and the lattice are subjects of very elaborate 'play'; but I want rather to consider the inscriptions Lockwood examines before retiring. There is writing on the wall, or on the ledge by his bed: it 'was nothing but a name repeated in all kinds of characters, large and small – *Catherine Earnshaw*, here and there varied to *Catherine Heathcliff*, and then again to *Catherine Linton*'. When he closes his eyes Lockwood is assailed by white letters 'which started from the dark, as vivid as spectres – the air swarmed with Catherines'. He has no idea whatever to whom these names belong, yet the expression 'nothing but a name' seems to suggest that they all belong to one person. Waking from a doze he finds the name *Catherine Earnshaw* inscribed in a book his candle has scorched.

It is true that Lockwood has earlier met a Mrs Heathcliff, and got into a tangle about who she was, taking first Heathcliff and then

Hareton Earnshaw for her husband, as indeed, we discover she, in a different sense, had also done or was to do. For she had a merely apparent kinship relation with Heathcliff – bearing his name as the wife of his impotent son and having to tolerate his ironic claim to fatherhood – as a prelude to the restoration of her true name, Earnshaw; it is her mother's story reversed. But Lockwood was not told her first name. Soon he is to encounter a ghost called Catherine Linton; but if the scribbled names signify one person he and we are obviously going to have to wait to find out who it is. Soon we learn that Mrs Heathcliff is Heathcliff's daughter-in-law, *née* Catherine Linton, and obviously not the ghost. Later it becomes evident that the scratcher must have been Catherine Earnshaw, later Linton, a girl long dead who might well have been Catherine Heathcliff, but wasn't.

When you have processed all the information you have been waiting for you see the point of the order of the scribbled names, as Lockwood gives them: *Catherine Earnshaw, Catherine Heathcliff, Catherine Linton*. Read from left to right they recapitulate Catherine Earnshaw's story; read from right to left, the story of her daughter, Catherine Linton. The names Catherine and Earnshaw begin and end the narrative. Of course some of the events needed to complete this pattern had not occurred when Lockwood slept in the little bedroom; indeed the marriage of Hareton and Catherine is still in the future when the novel ends. Still, this is an account of the movement of the book: away from Earnshaw and back, like the movement of the house itself. And all the movement must be *through* Heathcliff.

Charlotte Brontë remarks, from her own experience, that the writer says more than he knows, and was emphatic that this was so with Emily. 'Having formed these beings, she did not know what she had done.' Of course this strikes us as no more than common sense; though Charlotte chooses to attribute it to Emily's ignorance of the world. A narrative is not a transcription of something pre-existent. And this is precisely the situation represented by Lockwood's play with the names he does not understand, his constituting, out of many scribbles, a rebus for the plot of the novel he's in. The situation indicates the kind of work we must do when a narrative opens itself to us, and contains information in excess of what generic probability requires.

Consider the names again; of course they reflect the isolation of the society under consideration, but still it is remarkable that in a story whose principal characters all marry there are effectively only three surnames, all of which each Catherine assumes. Furthermore, the Earnshaw family makes do with only three Christian names, Catherine, Hindley, Hareton. Heathcliff is a family name also, but parsimoniously, serving as both Christian name and surname; always lacking one or the other, he wears his name as an indication of his difference, and this persists after death since his tombstone is inscribed with the one word *Heathcliff*. Like Frances, briefly the wife of Hindley, he is simply a sort of interruption in the Earnshaw system.

Heathcliff is then as it were between names, as between families (he is the door through which Earnshaw passes into Linton, and out again to Earnshaw). He is often introduced, as if characteristically, standing outside, or entering, or leaving, a door. He is in and out of the Earnshaw family simultaneously; servant and child of the family (like Hareton, whom he puts in the same position, he helps to indicate the archaic nature of the house's society, the lack of sharp social division, which is not characteristic of the Grange). His origins are equally betwixt and between: the gutter or the royal origin imagined for him by Nelly; prince or pauper, American or Lascar, child of God or devil. This betweenness persists, I think: Heathcliff, for instance, fluctuates between poverty and riches; also between virility and impotence. To Catherine he is between brother and lover; he slept with her as a child, and again in death, but not between latency and extinction. He has much force, yet fathers an exceptionally puny child. Domestic yet savage like the dogs, bleak yet full of fire like the house, he bestrides the great opposites: love and death (the necrophiliac confession), culture and nature ('half-civilized ferocity') in a posture that certainly cannot be explained by any generic formula ('Byronic' or 'Gothic').

He stands also between a past and a future; when his force expires the old Earnshaw family moves into the future associated with the civilized Grange, where the insane authoritarianism of the Heights is a thing of the past, where there are cultivated distinctions between gentle and simple – a new world in the more civil south. It was the Grange that first separated Heathcliff from Catherine, so that Earnshaws might eventually live there. Of the children – Hareton, Cathy, and Linton – none physically resembles Heathcliff; the first two have Catherine's eyes (XXXIII) and the other is, as his first name implies, a Linton. Cathy's two cousin-marriages – constituting an endogamous route to the civilized exogamy of the south – are the consequence of Heathcliff's standing between Earnshaw and Linton, north and south; earlier he had involuntarily saved the life of the baby Hareton. His ghost and Catherine's, at the end, are of interest only to the superstitious, the indigenous now to be dispossessed by a more rational culture.

If we look, once more, at Lockwood's inscriptions, we may read them thus (see facing page).

Earnshaws persist, but they must eventually do so within the Linton culture. Catherine burns up in her transit from left to right. The quasi-Earnshaw union of Heathcliff and Isabella leaves the younger Cathy an easier passage; she has only to get through Linton Heathcliff, who is replaced by Hareton Earnshaw; Hareton has suffered part of Heathcliff's fate, moved, as it were, from Earnshaw to Heathcliff, and replaced him as son-servant, as gratuitously cruel; but he is the last of the Earnshaws, and Cathy can both restore to him the house on which his name is carved, and take him on the now smooth path to Thrushcross Grange.

Novels, even this one, were read in houses more like the Grange than the Heights, as the emphasis on the ferocious piety of the Earnshaw library suggests. The order of the novel is a civilized order; it presupposes a reader in the midst of an educated family and habituated to novel reading; a reader, moreover, who believes in the possibility of effective ethical choices. And because this is the case, the author can allow herself to meet his proper expectations without imposing on the text or on him absolute generic control. She need not, that is, know all that she is saying. She can, in all manner of ways, invite the reader to collaborate, leave to him the supply of meaning where the text is indeterminate or discontinuous, where explanations are required to fill narrative lacunae.

Instances of this are provided by some of the dreams in the book.[2] Lockwood's brief dream of the spectral letters is followed by another about an interminable sermon, which develops from hints about Joseph in Catherine's Bible. The purport of this dream is obscure. The preacher Jabes Branderham takes a hint from his text and expands the

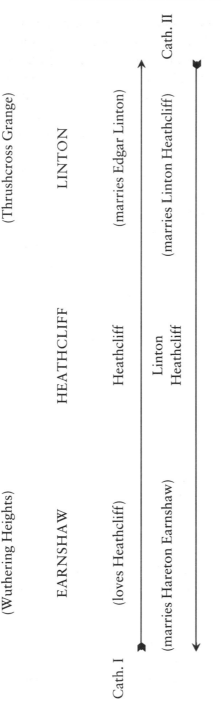

	EARNSHAW	HEATHCLIFF	LINTON	
(Wuthering Heights)				(Thrushcross Grange)
Cath. I	(loves Heathcliff)	Heathcliff		
		Linton Heathcliff		Cath. II
	(marries Hareton Earnshaw)		(marries Edgar Linton) (marries Linton Heathcliff)	

N.B. Heathcliff stands between Earnshaw and Linton as having Earnshaw origins but marrying Isabella Linton. He could also be represented as moving from left to right and right to left – into the Linton column, and then back to the Earnshaw when he usurps the hereditary position of Hareton. Hareton himself might be represented as having first been forced out of the Earnshaw column into the intermediate position when Heathcliff reduces him to a position resembling the one he himself started from, a savage and inferior member of the family. But he returns to the Earnshaw column with Cath. II. Finally they move together (without passing through the intermediate position, which has been abolished) from left to right, from Wuthering Heights to Thrushcross Grange.

seven deadly sins into seventy times seven plus one. It is when he reaches the last section that Lockwood's patience runs out, and he protests, with his own allusion to the Bible: 'He shall return no more to his house, neither shall his place know him any more.' Dreams in stories are usually given a measure of oneiric ambiguity, but stay fairly close to the narrative line, or if not, convey information otherwise useful; but this one does not appear to do so, except in so far as that text may bear obscurely and incorrectly on the question of where Hareton will end up. It is, however, given a naturalistic explanation: the rapping of the preacher on the pulpit is a dream version of the rapping of the fir tree on the window.

Lockwood once more falls asleep, but dreams again, and 'if possible, still more disagreeably than before'. Once more he hears the fir-bough, and rises to silence it; he breaks the window and finds himself clutching the cold hand of a child who calls herself Catherine Linton.

He speaks of this as a dream, indeed he ascribes to it 'the intense horror of nightmare', and the blood that runs down into the bedclothes may be explained by his having cut his hand as he broke the glass; but he does not say so, attributing it to his own cruelty in rubbing the child's wrist on the pane; and Heathcliff immediately makes it obvious that of the two choices the text has so far allowed us the more acceptable is that Lockwood was not dreaming at all.

So we cannot dismiss this dream as 'Gothic' ornament or commentary, or even as the kind of dream Lockwood has just had, in which the same fir-bough produced a comically extended dream-explanation of its presence. There remain all manner of puzzles: why is the visitant a child and, if a child, why Catherine *Linton*? The explanation, that this name got into Lockwood's dream from a scribble in the Bible, is one even he finds hard to accept. He hovers between an explanation involving 'ghosts and goblins', and the simpler one of nightmare; though he has no more doubt than Heathcliff that 'it' – the child – was trying to enter. For good measure he is greeted, on going downstairs, by a cat, a brindled cat, with its echo of Shakespearian witchcraft.

It seems plain, then, that the dream is not simply a transformation of the narrative, a commentary on another level, but an integral part of it. The Branderham dream is, in a sense, a trick, suggesting a measure of rationality in the earlier dream which we might want to transfer to the later experience, as Lockwood partly does. When we see that there is a considerable conflict in the clues as to how we should read the second tapping and relate it to the first we grow aware of further contrasts between the two, for the first is a comic treatment of 491 specific and resistible sins for which Lockwood is about to be punished by exile from his home, and the second is a more horrible spectral invasion of the womb-like or tomb-like room in which he is housed. There are doubtless many other observations to be made; it is not a question of deciding which is the single right reading, but of dealing, as reader, with a series of indeterminacies which the text will not resolve.

Nelly Dean refuses to listen to Catherine's dream, one of those which went through and through her 'like wine through water'; and of those dreams we hear nothing save this account of their power. 'We're dismal enough without conjuring up ghosts and visions to perplex us,' says Nelly – another speaking silence in the text, for it is implied that we are here denied relevant information. But she herself suffers a dream or vision. After Heathcliff's return she finds herself at the signpost: engraved in its sandstone – with all the permanence that Hareton's name has on the house – are 'Wuthering Heights' to the north, 'Gimmerton' to the east, and 'Thrushcross Grange' to the south. Soft south, harsh north, and the rough civility of the market town (something like that of Nelly herself) in between. As before, these inscriptions provoke a dream apparition, a vision of Hindley as a child. Fearing that he has come to harm, she rushes to the Heights and again sees the spectral child, but it turns out to be Hareton, Hindley's son. His appearance betwixt and between the Heights and the Grange was proleptic; now he is back at the Heights, a stone in his hand, threatening his old nurse, rejecting the Grange. And as Hindley turned into Hareton, so Hareton turns into Heathcliff, for the figure that appears in the doorway is Heathcliff.

This is very like a real dream in its transformations and displacements. It has no simple narrative function whatever, and an abridgement might leave it out. But the confusion of generations, and the double usurpation of Hindley by his son and Heathcliff, all three of them variants of the incivility of the Heights, gives a new relation to the agents, and qualifies our sense of all narrative explanations offered in the text. For it is worth remarking that no naturalistic explanation of Nelly's experience is offered; in this it is unlike the treatment of the later vision, when the little boy sees the ghost of Heathcliff and 'a woman', a passage which is a preparation for further ambiguities in the ending. Dreams, visions, ghosts – the whole pneumatology of the book is only indeterminately related to the 'natural' narrative. And this serves to muddle routine 'single' readings, to confound explanation and expectation, and to make necessary a full recognition of the intrinsic plurality of the text.

Would it be reasonable to say this: that the mingling of generic opposites – daylight and dream narratives – creates a need, which we must supply, for something that will mediate between them? If so, we can go on to argue that the text in our response to it is a provision of such mediators, between life and death, the barbaric and the civilized, family and sexual relations. The principal instrument of mediation may well be Heathcliff: neither inside nor out, neither wholly master nor wholly servant, the husband who is no husband, the brother who is no brother, the father who abuses his changeling child, the cousin without kin. And that the chain of narrators serves to mediate between the barbarism of the story and the civility of the reader – making the text itself an intermediate term between archaic and modern – must surely have been pointed out.

What we must not forget, however, is that it is in the completion of the text by the reader that these adjustments are made; and each reader will make them differently. Plurality is here not a prescription but a fact. There is so much that is blurred and tentative, incapable of decisive explanation; however we set about our reading, with a socio-logical or a pneumatological, a cultural or a narrative code uppermost in our minds, we must fall into division and discrepancy; the doors of communication are sometimes locked, sometimes open, and Heathcliff may be astride the threshold, opening, closing, breaking. And it is surely evident that the possibilities of interpretation increase as time goes on. The constraints of a period culture dissolve, generic presump-tions which concealed gaps disappear, and we now see that the book, as James thought novels should, truly 'glories in a gap', a hermeneutic gap in which the reader's imagination must operate, so that he speaks continuously in the text. For these reasons the rebus – *Catherine*

Earnshaw, Catherine Heathcliff, Catherine Linton – has exemplary significance. It is a riddle that the text answers only silently; for example it will neither urge nor forbid you to remember that it resembles the riddle of the Sphinx – what manner of person exists in these three forms? – to which the single acceptable and probable answer involves incest and ruin.

I have not found it possible to speak of *Wuthering Heights* in this light without, from time to time, hinting – in a word here, or a trick of procedure there – at the new French criticism. I am glad to acknowledge this affinity, but it also seems important to dissent from the opinion that such 'classic' texts as this – and the French will call them so, but with pejorative intent – are essentially naïve, and become in a measure plural only by accident. The number of choices is simply too large; it is impossible that even two competent readers should agree on an authorized naïve version. It is because texts are so naïve that they can become classics. It is true, as I have said, that time opens them up; if readers were immortal the classic would be much closer to change-lessness; their deaths do, in an important sense, liberate the texts. But to attribute the entire *potential* of plurality to that cause (or to the wisdom and cunning of later readers) is to fall into a mistake. The 'Catherines' of Lockwood's inscriptions may not have been attended to, but there they were in the text, just as ambiguous and plural as they are now. What happens is that methods of repairing such indeterminacy change; and, as Wolfgang Iser's neat formula has it, 'the repair of indeterminacy' is what gives rise 'to the generation of meaning'.[3]

Having meditated thus on *Wuthering Heights* I passed to the second part of my enterprise and began to read what people have been saying about the book. I discovered without surprise that no two readers saw it exactly alike; some seemed foolish and some clever, but whether they were of the party that claims to elucidate Emily Brontë's intention, or libertarians whose purpose is to astonish us, all were different. This secondary material is voluminous, but any hesitation I might have had about selecting from it was ended when I came upon an essay which in its mature authority dwarfs all the others: Q. D. Leavis's 'A Fresh Approach to *Wuthering Heights*'.[4]

Long-meditated, rich in insights, this work has a sober force that nothing I say could, or is intended to, diminish. Mrs Leavis remarks at the outset that merely to *assert* the classic status of such a book as *Wuthering Heights* is useless; that the task is not to be accomplished by ignoring 'recalcitrant elements' or providing sophistical explanations of them. One has to show 'the nature of its success'; and this, she at once proposes, means giving up some parts of the text. 'Of course, in general one attempts to achieve a reading of a text which includes all its elements, but here I believe we must be satisfied with being able to account for some of them and concentrate on what remains.' And she decides that Emily Brontë through inexperience, and trying to do too much, leaves in the final version vestiges of earlier creations, 'unregenerate writing', which is discordant with the true 'realistic novel' we should attend to.

She speaks of an earlier version deriving from *King Lear*, with Heathcliff as an Edmund figure, and attributes to this layer some contrived and unconvincing scenes of cruelty. Another layer is the fairy story, Heathcliff as the prince transformed into a beast; another is the Romantic incest-story: Heathcliff as brother-lover; and nearer the surface, a sociological novel, of which she has no difficulty in providing, with material from the text, a skilful account. These vestiges explain some of the incongruities and inconsistencies of the novel – for example, the ambiguity of the Catherine–Heathcliff relationship – and have the effect of obscuring its 'human centrality'. To summarize a long and substantial argument, this real novel, which we come upon clearly when the rest is cut away, is founded on the contrast between the two Catherines, the one willing her own destruction, the other educated by experience and avoiding the same fate. Not only does this cast a new light on such characters as Joseph and Nelly Dean as representatives of a culture that, as well as severity, inculcates a kind of natural piety, but enables us to see Emily Brontë as 'a true novelist . . . whose material was real life and whose concern was to promote a fine awareness of human relations and the problem of maturity'. And we can't see this unless we reject a good deal of the text as belonging more to 'self-indulgent story' than to the 'responsible piece of work' Emily was eventually able to perform. Heathcliff we are to regard as 'merely a convenience'; in a striking comparison with Dostoevsky's

Stavrogin, Mrs Leavis argues that he is 'enigmatic . . . only by reason of his creator's indecision', and that to find reasons for thinking otherwise is 'misguided critical industry'. By the same token the famous passages about Catherine's love for Heathcliff are dismissed as rhetorical excesses, obstacles to the 'real novel enacted so richly for us to grasp in all its complexity'.[5]

Now it seems very clear to me that the 'real novel' Mrs Leavis describes *is* there, in the text. It is also clear that she is aware of the danger in her own procedures, for she explains how easy it would be to account for *Wuthering Heights* as a sociological novel by discarding certain elements and concentrating on others, which, she says, would be 'misconceiving the novel and slighting it'. What she will not admit is that there is a sense in which all these versions are not only present but have a claim on our attention. She creates a hierarchy of elements, and does so by a peculiar archaeology of her own, for there is no *evidence* that the novel existed in the earlier forms which are supposed to have left vestiges in the only text we have, and there is no reason why the kind of speculation and conjecture on which her historical argument depends could not be practised with equal right by proponents of quite other theories. Nor can I explain why it seemed to her that the only way to establish hers as the central reading of the book was to explain the rest away; for there, after all, the others *are*. Digging and carbon-dating simply have no equivalents here; there is no way of distinguishing old signs from new; among readings which attend to the text it cannot be argued that one attends to a truer text than all the others.

It is true that 'a fine awareness of human relations', and a certain maturity, may be postulated as classic characteristics; Eliot found them in Virgil. But it is also true that the coexistence in a single text of a plurality of significances from which, in the nature of human attentiveness, every reader misses some – and, in the nature of human individuality, prefers one – is, empirically, a requirement and a distinguishing feature of the survivor, *centum qui perfecit annos*. All those little critics, each with his piece to say about *King Lear* or *Wuthering Heights*, may be touched by a venal professional despair, but at least their numbers and their variety serve to testify to the plurality of the documents on which they swarm; and though they may lack authority, sometimes perhaps even sense, many of them do point to what is *there* and ought not to be wished away.

A recognition of this plurality relieves us of the necessity of a *Wuthering Heights* without a Heathcliff, just as it does of a *Wuthering Heights* that 'really' ends with the death of Catherine, or for that matter an *Aeneid* which breaks off, as some of the moral allegorists would perhaps have liked it to, at the end of Book VI. A reading such as mine is of course extremely selective, but it has the negative virtue that it does not excommunicate from the text the material it does not employ; indeed, it assumes that it is one of the very large number of readings that may be generated from the text of the novel. They will of course overlap, as mine in some small measure does with that of Mrs Leavis.

And this brings me to the point: Mrs Leavis's reading is privileged; what conforms with it is complex, what does not is confused; and presumably all others would be more or less wrong, in so far as they treated the rejected portions as proper objects of attention. On the other hand, the view I propose does not in any way require me to reject Mrs Leavis's insights. It supposes that the reader's share in the novel is not so much a matter of knowing, by heroic efforts of intelligence and divination, what Emily Brontë really meant – knowing it, quite in the manner of Schleiermacher, better than she did – as of responding creatively to indeterminacies of meaning inherent in the text and possibly enlarged by the action of time.

We are entering, as you see, a familiar zone of dispute. Mrs Leavis is rightly concerned with what is 'timeless' in the classic, but for her this involves the detection and rejection of what exists, it seems to her irrelevantly or even damagingly, in the aspect of time. She is left, in the end, with something that, in her view, has not changed between the first writing and her reading. I, on the other hand, claimed to be reading a text that might well signify differently to different generations, and different persons within those generations. It is a less attractive view, I see; an encouragement to foolishness, a stick that might be used, quite illicitly as it happens, to beat history, and sever our communications with the dead. But it happens that I set a high value on these, and wish to preserve them. I think there is a substance that prevails, however powerful the agents of change; that *King Lear*, underlying a thousand dispositions, subsists in change, prevails, by being patient of interpretation; that my *Wuthering Heights*, sketchy and provocative as it is, relates as disposition to essence quite as surely as if I had tried to argue that it was Emily Brontë's authorized version, or rather what she intended and could not perfectly execute.

This 'tolerance to a wide variety of readings' is attacked, with considerable determination, by E. D. Hirsch, committed as he is to the doctrine that the object of interpretation is the verbal meaning of the author; I think he would be against me in all details of the present argument. For example, he says quite firmly that interpretations must be judged entire, that they stand or fall as wholes; so that he could not choose, as I do, both to accept Mrs Leavis's 'realist' reading and to reject her treatment of Heathcliff.[6] But Hirsch makes a mistake when he allows that the 'determinations' (*bestimmungen*) of literary texts are more constrained than those of legal texts; and a further difficulty arises over his too sharp distinction between criticism and interpretation. In any case he does not convince me that tolerance in these matters represents 'abject intellectual surrender'; and I was cheered to find him in a more eirenic mood in his later paper. He is surely right to allow, in the matter of meaning, some element of personal preference; the 'best meaning' is not uniform for all.

This being so one sees why it is thought possible, in theory at any rate, to practise what is called 'literary science' as distinct from criticism or interpretation: to consider the structure of a text as a system of signifiers, as in some sense 'empty', as what, by the intervention of the reader, takes on many possible significances.[7] To put this in a different way, one may speak of the text as a system of signifiers which always shows a surplus after meeting any particular restricted reading. It was Lévi-Strauss who first spoke of a 'surplus of signifier' in relation to shamanism, meaning that the patient is cured because the symbols and rituals of the doctor offer him not a specific cure but rather a language 'by means of which unexpressed, and otherwise inexpressible, psychic states can be immediately expressed'.[8] Lévi-Strauss goes on to make an elaborate comparison with modern psychoanalysis. But as Fredric Jameson remarks, the importance of the concept lies rather in its claim for the priority of the signifier over the signified: a change which itself seems to have offered a shamanistic opportunity for the expression of thoughts formerly repressed.[9]

The consequences for literary texts are much too large for me to enter on here; among them, of course, is the bypassing of all the old arguments about 'intention'. And even if we may hesitate to accept the semiological method in its entirety we can allow, I think, for the intuitive rightness of its rules about plurality. The gap between text and meaning, in which the reader operates, is always present and always different in extent.[10] It is true that authors try, or used to try, to close it; curiously enough, Barthes reserves the term 'classic' for texts in which they more or less succeed, thus limiting plurality and offering the reader, save as accident prevents him, merely a product, a consumable. In fact what Barthes calls 'modern' is very close to what I am calling 'classic', and what he calls 'classic' is very close to what I call 'dead'.

There is, in much of the debate on these matters, a quality of outrageousness, of the *outré*, and there is no reason why this should not be taken into account. We should, however, recall that in any *querelle* it is the modern that is going to display it most palpably. The prime modern instance is the row between Raymond Picard and Roland Barthes, which followed the publication of Barthes's *Racine* in 1963. The title of Picard's brisk pamphlet puts the point of the quarrel with a familiar emphasis: *Nouvelle Critique ou nouvelle imposture* (1965), and it contrives to make Barthes sound like the critic, deplored by all though read by few, who said that Nelly Dean stood for Evil. Barthes makes of the violent but modest drama of Racine something unrestrainedly sexual; if the text doesn't fit his theory he effects a 'transformation'; he uses neologisms to give scientific dignity to absurdities, and makes of the work under consideration 'an involuntary rebus, interesting only for what it doesn't say'.[11]

Barthes's reply is splendidly polemic; the old criticism takes for granted its ideology to the degree that it is unconscious of it; its vocabulary is that of a schoolgirl (specifically, Proust's Gisèle, Albertine's friend) seventy-five years ago. But the world has changed; if the history of philosophy and the history of history have been transformed, how can that of literature remain constant? Specifically the old criticism is the victim of a disease he calls *asymbolie*; any use of language that exceeds a narrow rationalism is beyond its understanding. But the moment one begins to consider a work as it is in itself, symbolic reading becomes unavoidable. You may be able to show that the reader has made his rules wrong or applied them wrongly, but errors of this kind do not invalidate the principle. And in the second more theoretical part of this very notable document Barthes explains that in his usage a symbol is not an image but a plurality of senses; the text will have many, not through the infirmity of readers who know less history than Professor Picard, but in its very nature as a structure of signifiers. 'L'œuvre propose; l'homme dispose.' Multiplicity of readings must result from the work's 'constitutive ambiguity', an expression Barthes borrows from Jakobson. And if that ambiguity itself does not exclude from the work the authority of its writer, then death will do so: 'By erasing the author's signature, death establishes the truth of the work, which is an enigma.'[12]

I have suggested that the death of readers is equally important, as a solvent of generic constraints. However much we know about history we cannot restore a situation in which a particular set of arbitrary rules of a probability system is taken for granted, internalized. To this extent I am firmly on Barthes's side in the dispute; and I have found much interest in his later attempts – which don't, however, command anything like total agreement – to describe the transcoding operations by which, in contemplating the classic, we filter out what can now be perceived as mere ideological deposits and contemplate the limited plurality that remains.[13]

Barthes denies the charge that on his view of the reading process one can say absolutely anything one likes about the work in question; but he is actually much less interested in defining constraints than in asserting liberties. There are some suggestive figures in his recent book *Le Plaisir du texte* (1973), from which we gather that authorial presence is somehow a ghostly necessity, like a dummy at bridge, or the shadow without which Die Frau ohne Schatten must remain sterile; and these are hints that diachrony, a knowledge of transient dispositions, may be necessary even to the *nouvelle critique* competently practised. Such restrictions on criticism *à outrance* can perhaps only be formulated in terms of a theory of competence and performance analogous to that of linguistics.

Though I am more than half-persuaded (largely by Dr Jonathan Culler) that such a theory could be constructed, I am certainly not to speak of it now. It will suffice to say that in so far as it is thought possible to teach people to read the classics it is assumed that knowledge of them is progressive. The nature of that knowledge is, however, as Barthes suggests, subject to change. Secularization multiplies the world's structures of probability, as the sociologists of religion tell us, and 'this plurality of religious legitimations is internalized in consciousness as a plurality of possibilities between which one may choose'.[14] It is this pluralism that, on the long view, denies the authoritative or authoritarian reading that insists on its identity with the intention of the author, or on its agreement with the readings of his contemporaries; or rather, it has opened up the possibilities, exploited most aggressively by the structuralists and semiologists, of regarding the text as the permanent locus of change; as something of which the permanence no longer legitimately suggests the presence and permanence of what it appears to designate.

I notice in a very recent book on *The Early Virgil* – though it is by no means a Formalist or Structuralist study – what seems a characteristic modern swerve in the interpretation of the Fourth Eclogue; the author believes that the *puer* is the poem itself, that the prophecy relates to a new golden age of poetry, an age which the Eclogue itself inaugurates; and this, like the author's remarks on the self-reflexiveness of the whole series of eclogues, seems modern, for it insists in some measure on the literarity of the work, its declared independence of the support of external reference. Even the arithmological elements in its construction serve to confirm it in this peculiar status.[15] And we see how sharply this form of poetic isolation differs from the privileged status accorded the Eclogue by the 'imperialist' critics: there would be, for Mr Berg, no question of Christian prophecy in the Eclogue – there is not even any question of a reference to some recent or impending political event involving Antony or Octavius or Pollio himself. By the same token no interpretation of Virgil which depends on the assumption, in however sophisticated a form it may be presented, that his *imperium* was to be transformed into the Christian Empire, his key words – *amor, fatum, pietas, labor* – given their full significance in an eternal pattern of which he could speak without actual knowledge, would be acceptable to this kind of criticism. When we say now that the writer speaks more than he knows we are merely using an archaism; what we mean is that the text is under the absolute control of no thinking subject, or that it is not a message from one mind to another.

The classic, we may say, has been secularized by a process which recognizes its status as a literary text; and that process inevitably pluralized it, or rather forced us to recognize its inherent plurality. We have changed our views on change. We may accept, in some form, the view proposed by Michel Foucault, that our period-discourse is controlled by certain unconscious constraints, which make it possible for us to think in some ways to the exclusion of others. However subtle we may be at reconstructing the constraints of past *epistèmes*, we cannot ordinarily move outside the tacit system of our own; it follows that except by extraordinary acts of divination we must remain out of close touch with the probability systems that operated for the first readers of the *Aeneid* or of *Wuthering Heights*. And even if one argues, as I do, that there is clearly less epistemic discontinuity than Foucault's crisis-philosophy proposes, it seems plausible enough that earlier assumptions about continuity were too naïve. The survival of the classic must therefore depend upon its possession of a surplus of signifiers; as in *King Lear* or *Wuthering Heights* this may expose them to the charge of confusion, for they must always signify more than is needed by any one interpreter or any one generation of interpreters. We may recall that, rather in the manner of Mrs Leavis discarding Heathcliff, George Orwell would have liked *King Lear* better without the Gloucester plot, and with Lear having only one wicked daughter – 'quite enough', he said.

If, finally, we compare this sketch of a modern version of the classic with the imperial classic that occupied me earlier, we see on the one hand that the modern view is necessarily tolerant of change and plurality whereas the older, regarding most forms of pluralism as heretical, holds fast to the time-transcending idea of Empire. Yet the new approach, though it could be said to secularize the old in an almost Feuerbachian way, may do so in a sense which preserves it in a form acceptable to changed probability systems. For what was thought of as beyond time, as the angels, or the *majestas populi Romani*, or the *imperium* were beyond time, inhabiting a fictive perpetuity, is now beyond time in a more human sense; it is here, frankly vernacular, and inhabiting the world where alone, we might say with Wordsworth, we find our happiness – our felicitous readings – or not at all. The language of the new Mercury may strike us as harsh after the songs of Apollo; but the work he contemplates stands there, in all its native plurality, liberated not extinguished by death, the death of writer and reader, unaffected by time yet offering itself to be read under our particular temporal disposition. 'The work proposes; man disposes.' Barthes's point depends upon our recalling that the proverb originally made God the disposer. The implication remains that the classic is an essence available to us under our dispositions, in the aspect of time. So the image of the imperial classic, beyond time, beyond vernacular corruption and change, had perhaps, after all, a measure of authenticity; all we need do is bring it down to earth.

7

The Man in the Macintosh

This was the third of the six Charles Eliot Norton lectures that I gave at Harvard in the academic year 1978–9. When invited, a year or so earlier, to give these lectures I was in the midst of a period in which, for obscure reasons, I was devoting much attention to New Testament scholarship. I read a good deal, consulted learned men, attended a fine lecture course by Dr John O'Neill in the Cambridge Divinity School, and worked at New Testament Greek. I found myself excited and impressed by the skill and also by the imaginative boldness of some of the biblical criticism produced in the centuries since its foundations were laid at the time of the German Enlightenment. I could think of no other subject for my Harvard lectures, most of which were written at Harvard, where I had further expert advice on such subjects as midrash, which is a Hebrew interpretative technique of great historical importance. It concerns the narrative interpretation of a narrative, and was used, in what is more correctly thought of as a proto-midrashic form, by the authors of the Gospels.

Since it was the nature of the gospel narrative that interested me my principal focus narrowed somewhat to Mark, as the first Gospel and the chief source of Matthew and Luke. When the lectures emerged as a book they attracted much more comment (and more approval) from biblical than from secular scholars, but of course my trade is literary criticism, and this chapter is an example of it. It brings together with a famous puzzle in Mark another famous puzzle in Joyce's Ulysses. Having used the enigmas of Mark and Joyce to make some points about interpretation generally, I turn to a yet bigger puzzle, the ending of Mark's Gospel.

My interest in biblical criticism continued – surprising even to me,

*since religion has no part in it – and I wrote several other studies of
the kind, and collaborated with the distinguished Hebraist Robert
Alter on a literary introduction to the whole Bible (Collins and Harvard
University Press: 1987). But then my interest faded, giving way to
other preoccupations.*

> *Where the deuce did he pop out of?*
> Ulysses

So far I have been unable to represent the lot of the interpreter as an
altogether happy one. Yet the world is full of interpreters; it is impossible to live in it without repeated, if minimal, acts of interpretation;
and a great many people obviously do much more than the minimum.
Interpretation is the principal concern of their waking lives. So the
question arises, why would we rather interpret than not? Or, why do
we prefer enigmas to muddles?

We may begin to consider the problem by thinking about James
Joyce's *Ulysses*. The institution controlling literary interpretation
thinks well of the book; and I, as a reasonably docile member of it,
endorse its valuation. I have taken no part in the exegetical labours
that are the inescapable consequence; but one doesn't need to have
done that to be aware that the work offers certain opportunities
to interpreters – opportunities which, fortunately for one's younger
colleagues, have every appearance of being inexhaustible. One such is
the riddle of the Man in the Macintosh. It is, if you like, an aporia of
the kind that declares itself when a text is scrutinized with an intensity
normally thought appropriate only after institutional endorsement.
Such scrutiny may originate in an enthusiastic cult, as it did in the
present instance; and in the early stages the establishment may be
hostile to the cult. But if it decides to take over the enterprise – as it
took over Joyce studies – it absorbs and routinizes that primitive
enthusiasm. There occurs a familiar transition from the charismatic to
the institutional.

Let me remind you about the Man in the Macintosh. He first turns
up at Paddy Dignam's funeral, in the Hades chapter. Bloom wonders
who he is. 'Now who is that lanky looking galoot over there in the
macintosh? Now who is he I'd like to know?' And Bloom reflects that

the presence of this stranger increases the number of mourners to thirteen, 'Death's number.' 'Where the deuce did he pop out of? He wasn't in the chapel, that I'll swear.' The newspaper reporter Hynes doesn't know the man either, and following a conversational mix-up records his name as M'Intosh. The stranger is thus given a spurious identity, a factitious proper name, by the same hand that distorts Bloom's by calling him Mr Boom – a diminution of identity.

Later, in 'The Wandering Rocks', a number of people are recorded as having taken note of or ignored the procession of the Lord Lieutenant. For example, Mr Simon Dedalus removed his hat; Blazes Boylan offered no salute, but eyed the ladies in the coach; and a pedestrian in a brown macintosh, eating dry bread, passed 'swiftly and unscathed across the viceroy's path'. Why 'unscathed'? Did he pass very close to the wheels? Is the Lord Lieutenant peculiarly dangerous to such persons? In 'Nausicaa' Bloom, wondering who the 'nobleman' may be who passes him on an evening stroll, again remembers the man, and now seems to know more about him, for he obscurely reminds himself that the man has 'corns on his kismet', which may mean 'is famous for being unlucky'. Appearing yet again at the end of 'The Oxen of the Sun', MacIntosh is described – though once more the sense is dubious – as poor and hungry. He is drinking Bovril, a viscous meat extract from which one makes a hot bouillon that is held to be fortifying, though preferred, in the ordinary way, by people of low income, and perhaps a plausible supplement to dry bread. Perhaps the stranger's eating habits are telling us something about him; perhaps we are to read them as indices of social standing and character. Yet it appears that MacIntosh has a grander cause for sorrow than simple poverty and habitual bad luck; for we are told that he 'loves a lady who is dead'. This might explain his presence at the funeral as well as his dietary carelessness and his reckless transit across the path of the viceroy.

He next turns up in a more positive, though phantasmagoric role: at the foundation of Bloomusalem in 'Circe' he springs up through a trapdoor and accuses Bloom of being in truth Leopold M'Intosh, or Higgins, a notorious fire-raiser. Bloom counters this further threat to his already shrunken and distorted identity by shooting M'Intosh; but later the man is observed going downstairs and taking his macintosh and hat from the rack, which understandably makes Bloom nervous.

And sure enough he returns; but only at the end of the novel, in the 'Ithaca' section, when Bloom, meditating the pattern of the day's events, or their lack of it, hears the timber of the table emit a loud, lone crack, and returns in his musings to the enigma of M'Intosh. Not for long, however; as he puts out his candle he is reminded of another and far more ancient enigma: 'Where was Moses when the candle went out?'

It can be argued[1] that MacIntosh is susceptible of explanation in terms of the known relations between Joyce's book and the *Odyssey* of Homer. He represents Homer's Theoclymenos, a character who turns up in the fifteenth book as an outlaw getting free passage with Telemachus, and then again, rather mysteriously, in the twentieth book, when the suitors, having mocked Telemachus for saying he won't coerce his mother into marrying one of them, suddenly grow sad. At this point 'the godlike Theoclymenos' offers a comment on their behaviour, and a dire prophecy. He tells the suitors that their faces and knees are veiled in night, that there is a sound of mourning in the air, that the walls are splashed with blood and the porch filled with ghosts on their way to Hades. The effect of these observations is to restore the good humour of the suitors, and no more is heard of the godlike outlaw.

One possible, though severe, opinion of the Homeric Theoclymenos is that his prophecy is banal and his presence in the story quite without point – in fact, that he is simply an intrusion, and does not belong to the poem at all. Can this be said to justify the presence of MacIntosh in *Ulysses*? One would then have to explain how the relevance of MacIntosh is established by the irrelevance of Theoclymenos. Certainly, however, they have something in common. MacIntosh's making the extra man and bringing the total of mourners to thirteen, and the occurrence of the funeral in the Hades chapter, chime with the funereal tone of the prophecy in Homer.

But there is still a lot left to explain. Perhaps Joyce, now imitating another famous precursor, was at his exercise of putting particular persons into his book, as Dante put certain people, in his case people of importance, into hell. So it has been proposed that MacIntosh is really a man called Wetherup, who is actually mentioned twice in *Ulysses* (with his name misspelled) and represented as given to the utterance of platitudes, though not as wearing a macintosh. Note also that MacIntosh is identified, by some scholars, with Mr James Duffy, a character in Joyce's story 'A Painful Case', which is to be found in *Dubliners*. Mr Duffy is a shadowy wanderer and the lover of a dead woman. He illustrates what Joyce called 'the hated brown Irish paralysis', if he really is the man in the macintosh it is appropriate that Bloom should forget all about him as soon as he climbs into Molly's bed. What is more, Duffy is partly based on Joyce's brother Stanislaus, who was puritanical about sex, and argued that its absence made friendship between man and man, and its presence friendship between man and woman, equally impossible. Stanislaus was aware that James had him in mind when he invented Mr Duffy, for he declared that Duffy was 'a portrait of what my brother imagined I should become in middle age'.[2]

Joyce vouched for none of this, but we know he liked jokes and riddles, and that he sometimes teased his admirers by asking them 'Who was the man in the macintosh?' Another view of the whole matter is that MacIntosh is absolutely gratuitous and fortuitous, a mere disturbance of the surface of the narrative. So Robert M. Adams, who says that Joyce is just playing with our 'unfulfilled curiosity', and that if the identification of MacIntosh with Wetherup, or presumably one of the other tedious possibilities I have outlined and some that I have not (for instance, that MacIntosh is Joyce himself), is correct, then 'we may be excused for feeling that the fewer answers we have for the novel's riddles, the better off we are'. Adams is persuaded that in the texture of this novel 'the meaningless is deeply interwoven with the meaningful' so that 'the book loses as much as it gains by being read closely'.[3]

I daresay there is a larger literature on this drab enigma than I have suggested – certainly there could be: why, for instance, the epidemic of misspelled names?[4] – but this is enough to be going on with. The real question is, why do we want to solve it anyway? Why does the view of Adams commend itself to us not at once, not as intuitively right, but as somehow more surprising and recondite than the attempts to make sense of MacIntosh? Why, in fact, does it require a more strenuous effort to believe that a narrative lacks coherence than to believe that somehow, if we could only find out, it doesn't?

Here is a cryptic and far from wholly satisfactory answer: within a text no part is less privileged than the other parts. All may receive the same quality and manner of attention; to prevent this one would need to use metatextual indicators (typographical variation, for instance) and there are no such indicators in the present instance. Why is this so? There must be supra-literary forces, cultural pressures, which tend to make us seek narrative coherence, just as we expect a conundrum to have an answer, and a joke a point. Our whole practice of reading is founded on such expectations, and of course the existence of genres such as the pointless joke and the deviant conundrum depends upon the prior existence of the normal sort. Just so do detective stories depend upon the coherence of elements in an occult plot that declares itself only as the book ends. There are detective novels, of which Robbe-Grillet's *Les Gommes* is the supreme example, which disobey this convention; but far from disregarding it, they depend upon it for their effect. In short: just as language games are determined by historical community use, so are plot games; and the subversion of the values of either depends on the prior existence of rules.

It is a prior expectation of consonance, the assumption that as readers we have to complete something capable of completion, that causes us to deal as we do with the man in the macintosh. We look for an occult relation (since there is no manifest relation) between all the references to him. It may be hidden in Homer, or in the larger body of Joyce's writing, or in his life, or in some myth; for we may well decide that MacIntosh is Death, or even that he is Hermes. Only when we are exhausted by our unprofitable struggle with the dry bread, the Bovril, the corns, the charge that Bloom himself is M'Intosh, do we relapse into a scepticism which is willing to entertain the notion of Robert Adams' nude emperor. We come to rest somewhere in the end, for the incoherence of the evidence can induce real anxiety. Perhaps, then, the appearances of MacIntosh lack coherence because they mime the fortuities of real life; a coherence related to another of our conventional expectations of narrative. Perhaps its satisfaction may sometimes entail the use of incoherences, devices by means of which, as Adams expresses it, the work of art may 'fracture its own surface'.[5]

There are current at present much bolder opinions than this one, which presupposes, rather conventionally, that some or much of a text can and should be processed into coherence, though some, if after careful interpretative effort it resists this treatment, may be left alone, or dealt with in a different way. One bolder view would be that an ideal text would be perfectly fortuitous, that only the fractures are of interest; that in establishing coherence we reduce the text to codes implanted in our minds by the arbitrary fiat of a culture or an institution, and are therefore the unconscious victims of ideological oppression. Freedom, the freedom to produce meaning, rests in fortuity, in the removal of constraints on sense. In so far as *Ulysses* is not a congeries of MacIntoshes it falls short of the ideal, though a determined reader may do much to correct it by resisting the codes. Newly liberated from conventional expectations first formulated by Plato, solidified by Aristotle, and powerfully reinforced over the past two centuries, we are no longer to seek unity or coherence, but by using the text wantonly, by inattention, by skipping even (every time you read *A la Recherche du temps perdu* it can be a new novel, says Roland Barthes, because you skip different parts each time[6]), by encouraging in ourselves perversities of every sort, we produce our own senses. The reason why Adams could give the establishment a bit of a shock without going anywhere near these Utopian extremes is simply that Joyce studies, and kindred literary researches, were already institutionalized – a paradigm was established, 'normal' research was in progress, to adapt Thomas Kuhn's terms[7] – so that even to propose that normal exegesis should be withheld from certain passages in *Ulysses* was unorthodox enough, close enough to the revolutionary, to cause a stir.

Let us now turn to the Boy in the Shirt (*sindōn*, a garment made of fine linen; not precisely a shirt, rather something you might put on for a summer evening, or wrap a dead body in, if you were rich enough). The Boy (actually a young man, *neaniskos*) is found only in Mark (14:51–2). At the moment of Jesus' arrest, says Mark – and Matthew agrees – all the disciples forsook him and fled. And both agree further that his captors then led him to the high priest. But between these two events Mark alone inserts another: 'And a young man followed him, with nothing but a linen cloth about his body; and they seized him, but he left the linen cloth and ran away naked.' And that is all Mark has to say about this young man.

The difficulty is to explain where the deuce he popped up from. One way of solving it is to eliminate him, to argue that he has no business in the text at all. Perhaps Mark was blindly following some source that gave an inconsistent account of these events, simply copying it without thought. Perhaps somebody, for reasons irrecoverably lost, and quite extraneous to the original account, inserted the young man later. Perhaps Matthew and Luke omitted him (if they had him in their copies of Mark) because the incident followed so awkwardly upon the statement that *all* had fled. (It is also conjectured that the Greek verb translated as 'followed', *sunēkolouthei*, might have the force of 'continued to follow', though all the rest had fled.[8] Anyway, why is the youth naked? Some ancient texts omit the phrase *epi gumnou*, which is not the usual way of saying 'about his body' and is sometimes called a scribal corruption; but that he ran away naked (*gumnos*) when his cloak was removed is not in doubt. So we have to deal with a young man who was out on a chilly spring night (fires were lit in the high priest's courtyard) wearing nothing but an expensive, though not a warm, shirt. 'Why', asks one commentator, 'should Mark insert such a trivial detail in so solemn a narrative?'[9] And, if the episode of the youth had some significance, why did Matthew and Luke omit it? We can without difficulty find meanings for other episodes in the tale (for instance, the kiss of Judas, or the forbidding of violent resistance, which makes the point that Jesus was not a militant revolutionist) but there is nothing clearly indicated by this one.

If the episode is not rejected altogether, it is usually explained in one of three ways. First, it refers to Mark's own presence at the arrest he is describing. Thus it is a sort of reticent signature, like Alfred Hitchcock's appearances in his own films, or Joyce's as MacIntosh. This is not widely believed, nor is it really credible. Secondly, it is meant to lend the whole story verisimilitude, an odd incident that looks as if it belongs to history-like fortuity rather than to a story coherently invented – the sort of confirmatory detail that only an eyewitness could have provided – a contribution to what is now sometimes called *l'effet du réel*. We may note in passing that such registrations of reality are a commonplace of *fiction*; in their most highly developed forms we call them realism. Thirdly, it is a piece of narrative developed (in a manner not unusual, of which I shall have something to say later) from Old Testament texts, notably Genesis 39:12 and Amos 2:16. Taylor, with

Cranfield concurring, calls this proposition 'desperate in the ex-treme'.[10] I suppose one should add a fourth option, which is, as with MacIntosh, to give up the whole thing as a pseudo-problem, or anyway insoluble; but although commentators sometimes mention this as a way out they are usually prevented by self-respect and professional commitment from taking it.

Now we have already noticed that Mark, for all the boldness of its opening proclamation ('The beginning of the good news of Jesus Christ') is, to say the least, a reticent text, whether its reserve is genuinely enigmatic or merely the consequence of muddle. Moreover, as I have suggested, where enigmas are credibly thought to exist in a text, it is virtually impossible to maintain that some parts of it are certainly not enigmatic. This is a principle important to the history of interpretation, and it was by carefully violating it with his fractured-surface theory that Robert Adams upset people. Let us then look at two attempts that have been made to treat the boy in the shirt as enigmatic and functional.

The first of these very well illustrates one alarming aspect of the business of interpretation, which is that by introducing new senses into a part of the text you affect the interpretation of the whole. And this 'whole' may be not simply Mark, but the history of early Christianity. It has lately been shown that there was more than one version of Mark. Morton Smith found, in a Judean monastery, an eighteenth-century Greek manuscript in which was copied a letter written by Clement of Alexandria at the end of the second century. After demonstrating that this letter was indeed written by Clement, Smith studies a passage in it that purports to be a quotation from Mark, though it is nowhere to be found in the gospel as we have it. The context is as follows: Clement is commending his correspondent Theodore for taking a firm line with the Carpocratian Gnostics, a contemporary libertine sect which believed it right to sin that grace might abound, indeed they were 'unafraid to stray into ... actions whose very names are unmentionable', as Irenaeus, speaking of Carpocratians and Cainites alike, reports.[11] Now Clement wishes to distinguish his authentic secret Mark from the inauthentic and conceivably licentious secret Mark of the Carpocratians. He explains that Mark first wrote his gospel in Rome, drawing on the reminiscences of Peter (we know from other evidence that Clement, like most other people, accepted this account of the origin of the gospel). But on that occasion Mark left out certain secrets. After Peter's martyrdom, says Clement, Mark went to Alexandria, where he 'composed a more spiritual gospel' for the exclusive use of those who were 'being initiated into the great mysteries'. Carpocrates had presumably taken over this secret gospel and adulterated it with his own interpretations. In the circumstances, says Clement, it will be best for the faithful to deny the very existence of a secret version.

He then quotes a passage from the authentic Alexandrian version. It must have come somewhere in the present tenth chapter of the gospel, and it tells of a visit to Bethany. In response to the plea of a woman, Jesus rolled back the door of a tomb and raised a rich young man from the dead. The young man, looking upon him, loved him, and begged to be with him. After six days he was commanded to go to Jesus at night. This he did, wearing a linen garment (*sindōn*) over his naked body (*epi gumnou*). During the night Jesus instructed the young man in 'the mystery of the kingdom of God'. Then the text continues at 10:35 as we now have it.

Clement goes out of his way to deny that the true, as distinct from the spurious, secret text contains the words *gumnos gumnou*, which might suggest that the master as well as the catechumen was naked. Whether this suggestion bore on baptismal practice, or had other magical and sexual import, is a matter for conjecture in the light of what is known of Carpocratian habits; for of course if Clement is telling the truth the words have no place in his genuine text, only in the spurious version of Carpocrates.

In Morton Smith's opinion the initiation in question was baptism. The story of the young man raised from the dead is obviously related to that of Lazarus, which occurs only in John, and Smith believes they have a common original older than the Mark we now have. He also thinks that our young man in the linen shirt is this same young man in Clement's gospel who had looked and loved and worn a *sindōn* over his naked body. In the extant gospels Jesus never baptizes, but in Clement's version of Mark baptism must have been a central rite; and Clement would want to preserve this initiation ceremony from contamination by the libertine Gnostics. Anyway, the young man in Mark's account of the arrest is on his way to be baptized; that is why he is naked under his *sindōn*, a garment appropriate to symbolic as well as to real burial, and appropriate also to symbolic resurrection, both to be enacted in the ceremony. His baptism would take place in a lonely garden, under cover of night. We know that Jesus set guards (on this theory, to prevent interruption) and we know that the guards fell asleep. He was then surprised with the naked youth.

Thus the entire narrative is altered to make sense of a part of it. But the account I have so far given is a very inadequate account of Smith's hypothesis. He also proposes the view that the secretiveness of Mark's Jesus almost throughout the gospel is related to this use of baptism as initiation into the mysteries of the kingdom. Jesus is here regarded as a magician or shaman, the Transfiguration is explained as a shamanistic ascent. Now the Gnostic libertine interpretation of the secret gospel can be seen as an attempt to preserve or recover an original mystery concealed by the expurgated 'Roman' version of Mark in general circulation. Like Clement, only more so, the Gnostics could think of the popular text as corrupt and imperfect in consequence of its attempt to keep the secrets. And whatever may be said about the provenance of these Alexandrian secret texts, they do provide a reason why the text as we have it appears both to reveal and proclaim, and at the same time to obscure and conceal.[12]

We see, then, that an interpretation of our two Marcan verses along the lines proposed by Morton Smith entails a drastic revision of the received idea of a much larger text. We might want to ask some low-level questions about plausibility: for example, why did the hand that so expertly curtailed the tenth chapter fail to deal with the anomalous verses about the young man in the shirt? And perhaps there could be other explanations for the repetition of *epi gumnou*. This, as I said, has been thought unacceptable; it is absent from some good manuscripts at 14:51, and Taylor drops it from his text; but its recurrence in Clement's letter must mean either that it was right, and that Mark used it twice, or that whoever wrote the secret version of Chapter 10 did so with the story of the young man in mind. At any rate it seems not unlikely that in the two verses we have been considering the secret gospel is showing through, a radiance of some kind, merely glimpsed by the outsider. And we should not be unduly surprised that the gospel, like its own parables, both reveals and conceals.

It is obvious by now that the story of the young man in the shirt cannot be *simply* interpreted; and complex interpretations, whether or not they have the seismic historical effects of Morton Smith's, will always have consequences that go far beyond the local problem. The most elegant interpretation known to me is that of Austin Farrer.[13] It uses as evidence Mark's linguistic habits, but it also finds in the gospel an occult plot, this time typological in style. Farrer was writing before the discovery of Clement's letter. It would probably have changed his argument in some ways, though he would doubtless have found useful to his purposes the occurrence, in the secret Mark, of the words *neaniskos* (not the most usual word for a young man) and *sindōn*. Mark uses *neaniskos*, in the public gospel, only for the young man who fled, and for the one who, at the end of the gospel, greets the women at Jesus' empty tomb.

Behind Farrer's interpretation is the knowledge that many of the crucial events in the gospel, especially in the Passion narrative, are closely related to Old Testament texts. They fulfill these texts, and the narrative as we have it records, and is in a considerable measure founded upon, such fulfilments. More of this later; for the moment it is sufficient that an event in the gospel stories may originate, and derive some of its value from, a relationship with an event in an earlier narrative. The force of the connection may be evident only if we are aware of the conditions governing such relationships, for example that the relation of Jesus to the Law, and of Christian to Jewish history, is always controlled by the myth of fulfilment in the time of the end, which is the time of the gospel narratives. If this is granted, there is always a possibility that the sort of relationship Taylor called 'desperate in the extreme' – between the story of the young man and the texts in Genesis and Amos – exists. Moreover, if the gospel contains allusions so delicate and recondite to earlier and uncited texts, why should there not be internal allusions and dependencies of equal subtlety? By seeking out such occult structural organizations one might confer upon Mark, after centuries of complaint at his disorderly construction, the kind of depth and closure one would hope to find in what has come to be accepted as the earliest and, in many ways, the most authoritative of the gospels.

Farrer's theories about Mark – numerological, typological, theological – are far too complicated to describe here, though to a secular critic they are exceptionally interesting. He himself altered them and then more or less gave them up, partly persuaded, no doubt, by criticisms of them as far-fetched, partly disturbed by the imputation that a narrative of the kind he professed to be discussing would be more a work of fiction than an account of a crucial historical event. Neither of these judgements seems to me well founded. But let me say briefly what he made of the young man in the cloak. He sets him in a literary pattern of events preceding and following the Passion: for example, the unknown woman anoints Jesus at Bethany, and he says this anointing is an early anointing for burial; afterwards the women make a futile attempt to anoint his corpse. The youth who flees in his *sindōn* forms a parallel with the youth (also *neaniskos*) the women find in the tomb. The first youth deserted Jesus; the second has evidently been with him since he rose. Furthermore, the linen in which Joseph of Arimathea wraps the body is called a *sindōn*, so there seems to be an intricate relationship between the *neaniskos* in his *sindōn* and the body in the tomb, now risen. As I say, the relation might have been made still more elaborate had Farrer known of the passage in Clement, which also involves a *neaniskos* in a tomb. He tells us that the punishment of a temple watcher who fell asleep on duty was to be beaten and stripped of his linen garment; which may have a bearing on the boy's losing his. He also accepts the affiliation which Taylor rejected, believing that the young man is related to (he does not say 'invented to accord with') two Old Testament types, one in Amos (2:16) – 'on that day the bravest of warriors shall be stripped of his arms and run away' – and the other in Genesis (39:12), where Joseph escapes from the seduction attempt of Potiphar's wife by running away and leaving his cloak in her hands.

In such patterns as these, Farrer detected delicate senses, many of them ironical. And since he was not an adherent of the latest school of hermeneutics, he believed that Mark must have intended these senses, and that he must have had an audience capable of perceiving them. So far from being a bungler, awkwardly cobbling together the material of the tradition, Mark developed these occult schemes 'to supplement logical connection', by which I take it Farrer meant something like 'narrative coherence'. He let his imagination play over the apparently flawed surface of Mark's narrative until what Adams calls fractures of the surface became parts of an elaborate design.

I do not doubt that Farrer's juggling with numbers gets out of hand. But even that has a basis in fact. He was confronting a problem that earlier exegetes had experienced. Since there is certainly a measure of arithmological and typological writing in the New Testament (twelve apostles and twelve tribes, Old Testament types sometimes openly cited, sometimes not) is there not reason to think that intensive application may disclose more of it than immediately meets the eye? Yet the more complex the purely literary structure is shown to be, the harder it is for most people to accept the narratives as naïvely transparent upon historical reality.

At one point Farrer even suggests that the young man deserting is a figure representing the falling off of all the others. This seems to me a fine interpretation. We have, at this moment in the narrative, three principal themes: Betrayal, Flight, and Denial. Judas is the agent of the first and Peter of the third. Peter, halfway through the gospel, was the first to acknowledge the Messiah, though the acknowledgement was at once followed by a gesture of dismissal by Jesus: 'Get behind me, Satan – you care not for the things of God but the things of man.' Now he apostasizes and perhaps even curses Jesus,[14] exactly at the moment when his master is for the first time asserting his true identity and purpose before the Sanhedrin. The implication, first made at the moment of recognition, and followed by the first prophecy of the Passion, is that the chief apostle will, when the Passion begins, deny the master. On both occasions he stands for the wholesale denial of Jesus, almost for Denial in the abstract. So too this young man, who is Desertion. The secret passage enhances this reading; the typical deserter is one who by baptism or some other rite of initiation has been reborn and received into the Kingdom. Nevertheless he flees. Thus we may find in this sequence of betrayal, desertion, and denial, a literary construction of considerable sophistication, one that has benefited from the grace that often attends the work of narration – a grace not always taken into account by scholars who seek to dissolve the text into its elements rather than to observe the fertility of their interrelations. It must, however, be said again that these narrative graces entail some disadvantages if one is looking more for an historical record than for a narrative of such elaborateness that it is hard not to think of it as fiction.

How do the interpretations of Smith and Farrer differ? The first assumes that Mark built up an esoteric plot, using material that was somehow also available to John, who developed it differently in the story of Lazarus and his sisters. The second argues that Mark worked an existing Passion narrative, presumably quite simple, into a complex narrative structure so recherché that between the first privileged audience and the modern interpreter himself no one ever understood it in its fullness. The frame of reference of the first is provided by the techniques of historiography, that of the second by literary criticism. Each is in its own way imaginative, though the quality of imagination differs greatly from one to the other. A Schweitzer might place Smith's work in the tradition of lives of Jesus, beginning two centuries ago with Bahrdt and Venturini,[15] which assumed that what made sense of the gospel narratives was something none of them ever mentioned: for example, that Jesus was the instrument of some secret society. As to Farrer, his work was rejected by the establishment, and eventually by himself, largely because it was so literary. The institution knew intuitively that such literary elaboration, such emphasis on elements that must be called fictive, was unacceptable because damaging to what remained of the idea that the gospel narratives were still, in some measure, transparent upon history.[16]

The constructions of Smith are historical; those of Farrer are literary. But they both assume that there is an enigmatic narrative concealed in the manifest one. Each suggests that an apparent lack of connection, the existence of narrative elements that cannot readily be seen to form part of a larger organization, must be explained in terms of that hidden plot, and not regarded as evidence of a fractured surface, or mere fortuities indicating that reality may be fortuitous. Joyce once said of *Ulysses*: 'I've put in so many enigmas and puzzles that it will keep the professors busy for centuries over what I meant, and that's the only way of ensuring one's immortality.'[17] This is a shrewd joke, but the suggestion that enigmas and puzzles have necessarily to be 'put in' is false. Joyce was only imitating the action of time. It would be more accurate to say that whatever remains within the purview of interpretation – whether by the fiat of the professors or of some other institutional force – will have its share of enigmas and puzzles. Whatever is preserved grows enigmatic; time, and the pressures of interpretation, which are the agents of preservation, will see to that. Who was the man in the macintosh? Mr Duffy, Stanislaus Joyce, Mr Wetherup, Bloom's doppelganger, Theoclymenos, Hermes, Death, a mere series of surface fractures? Each guess requires the construction of an enigmatic plot, or, failing that, a declaration that the text is enigmatically fortuitous. Who was the boy in the linen shirt, and where did he pop out of? The answers are very similar: a candidate for baptism, an image of desertion, a fortuity that makes the surface of narrative more like the surface of life.

So I return to the question I have already put: why do we labour to reduce fortuity first, before we decide that there is a way of looking which provides a place for it? I still have no satisfying answer; but it does appear that we are programmed to prefer fulfilment to disappointment, the closed to the open. It may be that this preference arises from our experience of language-learning; a language that lacked syntax and lacked redundancy would be practically unlearnable. We depend upon well-formedness – less so, it must be confessed, in oral than in written language: in the written story there is no visible gesture or immediate social context to help out the unarticulated sentence, the aposiopesis. There are modern critics who think our desire for the well-formed – or our wish to induce well-formedness where it is not apparent – is in bad faith. They hold that it is more honest to experience deception, disappointment, in our encounters with narrative. They have not yet prevailed; we are in love with the idea of fulfilment, and our interpretations show it. In this we resemble the writers of the New Testament and their immediate successors, who were, though much more strenuously, more exaltedly, in love with fulfilment; the verb meaning to fulfil, and the noun *pleroma*, full measure, plenitude, fulfilment, are endlessly repeated, and their senses extend from the fulfilment of prophecy and type to the complete attainment of faith.

Such expectations of fullness survive, though in attenuated form, in our habitual attitudes to endings. That we should have certain expectations of endings, just as we have certain expectations of the remainder of a sentence we have begun to read, has seemed so natural, so much a part of things as they are in language and literature, that (to the best of my knowledge) the modern study of them begins only fifty years ago, with the Russian Formalist Viktor Shklovsky. It was he who showed that we can derive the sense of fulfilled expectation, of satisfactory closure, from texts that actually do not provide what we ask, but give us instead something that, out of pure desire for completion, we are prepared to regard as a metaphor or a synecdoche for the ending that is not there: a description of the weather or the scenery, he says, will do,[18] say the rain at the end of Hemingway's *Farewell to Arms*, or the river at the end of Matthew Arnold's *Sohrab and Rustum*. These are matters that still require investigation; the fact that they do so testifies to the truth of the statement that we find it hardest to think about what we have most completely taken for granted.

Now it happens that Mark is never more enigmatic, or never more clumsy, than at the end of his gospel; and I can best bring together the arguments of this chapter by briefly considering that ending. Too briefly, no doubt; for whole books have been written about it, and it has been called 'the greatest of all literary mysteries'.[19] It is worth saying, to begin with, that nobody thought to call it that until after Mark had come to be accepted as the earliest gospel and Matthew's primary source; we do not recognize even the greatest literary mysteries until the text has gained full institutional approval. When Mark was thought to derive from Matthew it was easy to call his gospel a rather inept digest, as Augustine did; and then the abruptness of the ending was merely an effect of insensitive abridgement, and not a problem at all, much less a great mystery. Even now there are many who are impatient of mystery, and wish to dispose of it by asserting that the text did not originally end, or was not originally intended to end, at 16:8. But very few scholars dare to claim that the last twelve verses, 9–20, as we still have them in our Bibles, are authentic, for there is powerful and ancient testimony that they are not.

The gospel we are talking about ends at 16:8. In the previous verse the young man in the tomb gives the women a message for Peter and the disciples concerning their meeting with the risen Jesus. But they flee the tomb in terror and say nothing to anybody. This ending must soon have come to seem strange, which is why somebody added the extra twelve verses. We are not entitled to do anything of that kind; we can argue that the gospel was, for some reason, left unfinished; or we can interpret the ending as it stands.

The last words of the gospel are: 'for they were afraid', *ephobounto gar*. It used to be believed that you could not end even a sentence with such a construction; and to this day, when it is accepted that you could do so in popular Greek, nobody has been able to find an instance, apart from Mark, of its occurrence at the end of a whole book. It is an abnormality more striking even than ending an English book with the word 'Yes', as Joyce did. Joyce's explanations of why he did so are interestingly contradictory. *Ulysses*, he told his French translator, 'must end with the most positive word in the human language'.[20] Years later he told Louis Gillet something different: 'In *Ulysses*,' he said, 'to represent the babbling of a woman as she falls asleep, I tried to end with the least forceful word I could possibly find. I found the word *yes*, which is barely pronounced, which signifies acquiescence, self-abandonment, total relaxation, the end of all resistance.'[21] Here again Joyce gives the professors a licence to interpret which they would have had to take anyway. The only positive inference to be made from these two remarks is that Joyce knew, as Shklovsky did, that we all want to make a large interpretative investment in the end, and are inclined to think the last word may have a quite disproportionate influence over the entire text. Later he ended *Finnegans Wake* with the word *the*; in one sense it is as weak as Mark's enclitic *gar*, though in another it is definite though barely pronounced, and deriving strength from the great *ricorso*, which makes it the first word in the book as well as the last. These ambiguities are not unlike those of Mark's problematical ending.

Let us pass by the theories which say the book was never finished, that Mark died suddenly after writing 16:8, or that the last page of his manuscript fell off, or that there is only one missing verse which ties everything up (such a verse in fact survives, but it is not authentic and will probably not be in your Bible), or that Mark had intended to write a sequel, as Luke did, but was prevented. Let us also skirt round the more congenial theory of Jeremias, that Mark went no further because he thought that what happened next should be kept from pagan readers.[22] We can't deny that this fits in with a pattern of revelation and deception observable elsewhere in Mark; nor that there is evidence of secrets reserved to the initiate, or expressed very cryptically, as in Revelation. Still, it's hard to see why the gospel, which is a proclamation of the good news, should stop before it had fairly reached the part that seemed most important to Paul; by Mark's time it had been preached for an entire generation.

So let us assume that the text really does end, 'they were scared, you see', and with *gar* as the last word, 'the least forceful word' Mark 'could possibly find'. The scandal is, of course, much more than merely philological. Omitting any post-Easter appearance of Jesus, Mark has only this empty tomb and the terrified women. The final mention of Peter (omitted by Matthew) can only remind us that our last view of him was not as a champion of the faith but as the image of denial. Mark's book began with a trumpet call: 'This is the beginning of the gospel of Jesus Christ, the son of God'. It ends with this faint whisper of timid women. There are, as I say, ways of ending narratives that are not manifest and simple devices of closure, not the distribution of rewards, punishments, hands-in-marriage, or whatever satisfies our simpler intuitions of completeness. But this one seems at first sight wholly counter-intuitive, as it must have done to the man who added the twelve verses we now have at the end.

A main obstacle to our accepting 'for they were scared' as the true ending, and going about our business of finding internal validation for it, is simply that Mark is, or was, not supposed to be capable of the kinds of refinement we should have to postulate. The conclusion is either intolerably clumsy; or it is incredibly subtle. One distinguished scholar, dismissing this latter option, says it presupposes 'a degree of originality which would invalidate the whole method of form-criticism'.[23] This is an interesting objection. Form-criticism takes as little stock as possible in the notion of the evangelists as authors; they are held to be compiling, according to their lights, a compact written version of what has come to them in oral units. The idea that they shaped the material with some freedom and exercised on the tradition strong individual talents was therefore foreign to the mode of criticism which dominated the institution throughout the first half of the twentieth century. And that alone is sufficent to dispose of the idea as false. Now all interpretation proceeds from prejudice, and without prejudice there can be no interpretation; but this is to use an institutional prejudice in order to disarm exegesis founded on more interesting personal prejudices. If it comes to a choice between saying Mark is original and upholding 'the whole method of form-criticism' the judgement is unhesitating: Mark is not original. To be original at all he would have had to be original to a wholly incredible extent, doing things we know he had not the means to do, organizing, alluding, suggesting like a sort of ancient Henry James, rather than making a rather clumsy compilation in very undistinguished Greek.

Yet if we look back once more to the beginning of Mark, we might well have the impression that this brief text, so much shorter than any of the other gospels, at once gave promise of both economy and power. First, an exultant announcement of the subject, then the splendidly wrought narrative of John the Baptist, which, though heavy with typology, has memorable brevity and force. It is a world away from the overtures of the other gospels. Matthew and Luke were not content with it, perhaps it did not seem a true beginning, this irruption of a hero full grown and ready for action; so they prefixed their birth stories and genealogies. We are so used to mixing the gospels up in our memory into a smooth narrative paste that laymen rarely consider the differences between them, or reflect that if we had only Mark's account there would be no Christmas, no loving virgin mother, no preaching in the temple – nothing but a clamorous prologue, the Baptist crying in the wilderness, with his camel-skin coat and his wild honey. Matthew and Luke started earlier, with Jesus' ancestry, conception, and birth; John exceeded them both, and went back to the ultimate possible beginning, when, in the pre-existence of Jesus, only the Word was.

Mark, it appears, could not maintain this decisiveness, this directness. He grows awkward and reticent. There are some matters, it seems, that are not to be so unambiguously proclaimed. The story moves erratically, and not always forward; one thing follows another for no very evident reason. And a good deal of the story seems concerned with failure to understand the story. Then, after the relative sharpness and lucidity of the Passion narrative, the whole thing ends with what might be thought the greatest awkwardness of all, or the greatest instance of reticence: the empty tomb and the terrified women going away. The climactic miracle is greeted not with rejoicing, but with a silence unlike the silence enjoined, for the most part vainly, on the beneficiaries of earlier miracles – a stupid silence. The women have come to anoint a body already anointed and two days dead. Why are they so astonished? Jesus has three times predicted his resurrection. Perhaps they have not been told? Perhaps their being dismayed and silent is no stranger than that Peter should have been so disconcerted by the arrest and trial? He knew about *that* in advance. And we might go on in this way, without really touching the question.

Farrer, extending the argument I've already mentioned, finds the answer in the double pattern of events before and after the Crucifixion. Before it, Jesus said he would go to Galilee; spoke of the anointing; gave to the disciples at the Last Supper a sacramental body which should have made it clear to them that the walling up of a physical body was unimportant. The disciples fled before the Crucifixion, the women after it. And all in all, says Farrer, the last six verses of the gospel (3–8) form 'a strong complex refrain, answering to all the ends of previous sections in the Gospel to which we might expect it to answer'.[24] So for him the ending, like everything else in this strange tacit text, is part of an articulate and suggestive system of senses which lies latent under the seemingly disjointed chronicle, the brusquely described sequence of journeyings and miracles. Farrer may persuade us that even if he is wrong in detail there is an ending here at the empty tomb, and it is for us to make sense of it.

Earlier, in my first chapter, I used the term 'fore-understanding'. It is a translation of the German word *Vorverständnis*, and its value in hermeneutics is obvious. Even at the level of the sentence we have some ability to understand a statement before we have heard it all, or at any rate to follow it with a decent provisional sense of its outcome; and we can do this only because we bring to our interpretation of the sentence a pre-understanding of its totality. We may be wrong on detail, but not, as a rule, wholly wrong; there may be some unforeseen peripeteia or irony, but the effect even of that would depend upon our having had this prior provisional understanding. We must sense the genre of the utterance.

Fore-understanding is made possible by a measure of redundancy in the message which restricts, in whatever degree, the possible range of its sense. Some theorists, mostly French, hold that a fictive mark or reference inevitably pre-exists the determination of a structure; this idea is not so remote from *Vorverständnis* as it may sound, but it is so stated as to entitle the theorist to complain that such a centre must inevitably have an ideological bearing. 'Closure ... testifies to the presence of an ideology.'[25] To restrict or halt the free movement of senses within a text is therefore thought to be a kind of wickedness. It may be so; but it is our only means of reading until revolutionary new concepts of writing prevail; and meanwhile, remaining as aware as we can be of ideological and institutional constraints, we go about our business of freezing those senses into different patterns. Of course the inevitability of such constraints, which increase with every increase of ideological or institutional security, is a reason why outsiders may produce the most radiant interpretations.

The conviction that Mark *cannot* have meant this or that is a conviction of a kind likely to have been formed by an institution, and useful in normal research; the judgements of institutional competence remove the necessity of considering everything with the same degree of minute attention, though at some risk that a potential revolution may be mistaken for a mere freak of scholarly behaviour. But there are occasions when rigour turns to violence. The French scholar Etienne Trocmé, steeped in Marcan scholarship and the methods of modern biblical criticism, can argue that an understanding of the structure of Mark depends upon our seeing that in its original form it ended, not at 16:20, and not at 16:8 either, but at the end of the thirteenth chapter, which forms the so-called Marcan apocalypse, and immediately precedes the Passion narrative. Given the religious and political situation at the moment of writing, this is where the gospel ought to end, with an allusion to the genre of apocalypse current at that time, and a solemn injunction to watch, which refers to a particular first-century community of Christians and not to the historical narrative as such. If one accepts this position it becomes possible to show that the preceding part of the text is consonant with this ending; and what is not consonant can be explained as the work of the editor who later revised the gospel and added the Passion narrative for a 'second edition, revised and supplemented by a long appendix'.[26] By such means one may, without violating the institutional consensus, prepare a text that conforms with one's own rigid fore-understanding of its sense. On the other hand, Farrer's reading is condemned as it were by institutional intuition; we may therefore call it an outsider's interpretation. I find it preferable to interpretations that arise from the borrowed authority of the institutionalized corrector, and presuppose that the prime source of our knowledge of the founder of Christianity will necessarily be compliant with whatever, for the moment, are the institution's ideas of order.

Farrer's notions of order were literary, and although his tone is always reverent, and occasionally even pious, he makes bold to write about Mark as another man might write about Spenser, except that he has some difficulty with the problem of historicity, for he could certainly not accept Kant's word for it that the historical veracity of these accounts was a matter of complete indifference. Of course his motive for desiring fulfilment was related to his faith and his vocation. But his satisfaction of that desire was to be achieved by means familiar to all interpreters, and like the rest he sensed that despite, or even because of, the puzzles, the discontinuities, the amaze-ments of Mark (and the gospel is full of verbs meaning 'astonish', 'terrify', 'amaze', and the like), his text can be read as somehow hanging together.

If there is one belief (however the facts resist it) that unites us all, from the evangelists to those who argue away inconvenient portions of their texts, and those who spin large plots to accommodate the discrepancies and dissonances into some larger scheme, it is this convic-tion that somehow, in some occult fashion, if we could only detect it, everything will be found to hang together. When Robert Adams challenged this conviction he was thought bold. The French utopians challenge it in a different way, condemning the desire for order, for closure, a relic of bourgeois bad faith. But this is an announcement of revolutionary aims: they intend to change what is the case. Perhaps the case needs changing; but it is the case. We are all fulfilment men, *pleromatists*; we all seek the centre that will allow the senses to rest, at any rate for one interpreter, at any rate for one moment. If the text has a great many details that puzzle us, we ask where they popped up from. Our answers will be very diverse: Theoclymenos or Stanislaus, Mr Duffy or Death, a hooded phallus haunting tombs, a mimesis of fortuity and therefore not in itself fortuitous. Or perhaps: a candidate for baptism; a lover; a mimesis of actuality; a signature. We halt the movement of the senses, or try to. Sometimes the effort is great. Bloom failed with the man in the macintosh; the hour was late, too late for him to sort out carnal and spiritual, manifest and latent, revealed and concealed. He had had a long hard day and went, quite carnally, to bed. Perhaps he returned to the question later, as we must.

8

Dwelling Poetically in Connecticut

I wrote a little book on Stevens in 1960 (a new edition appeared in 1989) and was co-editor with Joan Richardson of the Library of America edition (1997). I also prepared an edition of Harmonium *but it was lost to the world when the United States changed its copyright rules; consequently copyright, thought to have expired, would not do so till 2018 or thereabouts, and the publisher withdrew the book. I think of this essay as my best tribute to the poet.*

The last poetry of Wallace Stevens, which may be his greatest, seems not to have found the critic who can speak for it. The present essay will not do so, for my purpose is the marginal one of reflecting on various interests that we know Stevens to have had in his last years, in the hope that they may have some relevance to those venerable poems. They are mostly poems of death, or of the achievement of a posture in which to meet it correctly. Stevens was a correct man. There was also a proper *mise en scène* for poetry; he cared for the physical presentation of his and other people's poems, as if their disclosures, even the most exalted, the closest to a final truth, required the art of the typographer and the gold, leather, and linen of the binder as accompaniments to revelation. Propriety is not always satisfied by greys and blacks; ideas, poems, and persons may need or deserve some decorous slash of vivid colour from the remoter parts of the lexicon, some gaiety. Or, if they do not deserve it, they should get it: 'Merit in poets is as boring as merit in people' (*Adagia, Opus Posthumous*, p. 157).[1]

In these years Stevens was also interested in Friedrich Hölderlin, who also knew that merit was not enough: 'Full of merit, yet poetically / Man dwells on the earth'. And because of Hölderlin he looked toward the poet's great explainer, the philosopher Martin Heidegger. Whether he ever found Heidegger is an interesting question. Between them, Hölderlin and Heidegger form a kind of model of that composite poet, virile youth and old tramp, who seized on Stevens' imagination. But Stevens himself was not very like them. For him the poetical, the supererogatory grace might be a gaiety, 'light or color, images', or a gilt-top edge. Like Hölderlin, he thought of the poet as 'the priest of the invisible'; but unlike him, he would choose a wild word with sane care and give his poems wry titles to make them self-ironical. Like Heidegger, he thought of poetry as a renovation of experience; unlike him, he thought that the truth in the end did not matter. And even as he grew old, Stevens was never the tramp, as he had never been the virile youth. The encounter of being with death was not far off, but there was time for these interests, the well-made typeface or rich binding, the Germans, mad and obscure.

As for the fine bindings and limited editions, Stevens came to like them more and more, and not only for his own poems. He wrote letters to printers and binders about the way books should be produced. He told his editor, Katharine Frazier, that he would rather rewrite lines in *Notes toward a Supreme Fiction* than have ugly turnovers in the printed copy (*Letters*, p. 407).[2] Later he had a bibliopegic correspondence with Victor Hammer a Viennese who operated first the Anvil Press in Lexington, Kentucky, and then the Aurora Press at Wells College. In 1946 he bought Janet Lewis' *The Earth-Bound*, beautifully published by Mr Hammer, and negotiated for a bookplate. On 22 January 1948, he wrote to Hammer ordering a copy of his limited edition (fifty-one copies only) of Hölderlin's *Poems 1796–1804* – 'I read German well enough,' he remarked – and he later thanked Hammer for the book in terms that bore entirely upon the beauty of the printing (*L*, pp. 576, 681). He spoke not of Hölderlin's art but of Mr Hammer's.

It was not unimportant to Stevens that Hammer was living in Kentucky. Reality changes, he observed, and 'in every place and at every time the imagination makes its way by reason of it'. He thought of this Viennese printer in Kentucky and reflected that 'a man is not bothered by the reality to which he is accustomed, that is to say, in the midst of which he has been born. He may be very much disturbed by reality elsewhere, but even as to that it would be only a question of time' (*L*, p. 577). He wondered whether Hammer could procure him a drawing of a necessary angel by Fritz Kredel. Mr Kredel was 'to state in the form of a drawing his idea of the surroundings in which poor people would be at rest and happy'. A few weeks later he explained why this was desirable, referring to his 'Angel Surrounded by Paysans': 'There must be in the world about us things that solace us quite as fully as any heavenly visitation could.' The plan was given up; perhaps Kredel could not see that particular angel (*L*, pp. 656, 661, 662–3).

Although he said nothing about the contents of Hammer's *Hölderlin*, Stevens was presumably interested in them. He had recently acquired a German edition of the *Gedichte*, published in 1949. This book is described in the catalogue of the Parke-Bernet sale of Stevens' books (March 1959) as a small folio, full niger morocco, gilt fillets on sides, gilt edges. 'In a morocco-edged linen slipcase . . . A SUMPTUOUS BOOK PRINTED WITH A SPECIALLY CUT TYPE-FACE AND PRINTED ON HAND-MADE PAPER.' Angels visiting the poor were, for Stevens, none the worse for top-edge gilt, even though they might themselves claim to have no 'wear of ore' and to 'live without a tepid aureole'. Still, he must have looked inside this splendid package. He was certainly reading *about* Hölderlin, for example, an essay by Bernard Groethuysen, which he read in May 1948. Four years later he discovered that 'Heidegger, the Swiss philosopher', had written a little work on Hölderlin, and he asked his Paris bookseller, Paule Vidal, to find him a copy. He would prefer, he said, a French translation, 'But I should rather have it even in German than not have it at all' (*L*, p. 758).

As it happens, his local bookseller could have provided him with the essay in English, for a translation of the *Erläuterung zu Hölderlins Dichtung* was included in a collection of essays by Heidegger, *Existence and Being*, in 1949. Perhaps its workaday appearance would not have suited Stevens in any case. He asked Mme Vidal for a copy from 'some bookseller at Fribourg'. Probably she did not find one, for when Stevens' Korean friend Peter H. Lee was in Freiburg in June 1954, Stevens wrote asking him about Heidegger in terms that do not suggest close acquaintance with his work: 'If you attend any of his lectures, or even see him, tell me about him because it will help to make him real. At the moment he is a myth, like so many things in philosophy.' At the end of September, still unsatisfied and still apparently under the impression that Heidegger was Swiss, he asked Lee whether the philosopher lectured in French or German (*L*, pp. 839, 846). That letter was written two days before the publication of *Collected Poems*, three before Stevens' seventy-fifth birthday, and less than a year before his death. At that late date his knowledge of Heidegger seems scanty enough, more myth than reality. The only certain fact is that Stevens was mixing up the Swiss and German Freiburgs, which is why he used the French form of the name of the city and referred to Heidegger as Swiss. He can therefore have known nothing of the philosopher's brief tenure as the Nazi-appointed rector of Freiburg University. It is an odd mistake, if one reflects that Heidegger spent about as much time outside of Germany as Stevens did out of the United States.

Still, he must have heard talk of Heidegger and the Hölderlin essays (though he mentions only one). His belated career as a lecturer and reader at colleges and universities had made him acquainted with philosophers – people who did their probing deliberately, he said, and not fortuitously, like poets. But we can be sure that he did not know Heidegger, even in French, as he knew, for example, Emerson, Santayana, and William James. Heidegger's was a book he did not, as a reader, 'become'. Years before, a philosophy professor had asked him why he did not take on a 'full-sized' philosopher, and, when asked by Stevens to name some, included C. S. Peirce on the list. In his relation of this episode to Theodore Weiss, Stevens added, 'I have always been curious about Pierce [*sic*], but have been obliged to save my eyesight for THE QUARTERLY REVIEW, etc' (*L*, p. 476). Since his correspondent was the editor of *The Quarterly Review*, we must take this as banter, but all the same, he probably meant that he preferred being curious about Peirce to reading him.

Perhaps for his purposes a smattering of knowledge was more useful than an understanding. Some image of Heidegger in his peasant clothes, darkly speculating upon his hero and supreme poet, precursor of the angel most necessary when, after the failure of the gods, our poverty is most complete, suited Stevens better than a whole philosophy, however vatic in expression. Perhaps the notion of this venerable man as having thought exhaustively about death and poetry and about the moment of their final encounter was enough. Stevens would try by his accustomed channels to acquire the sage's book, but if it did not come, it would still be interesting to know how he looked and what language he spoke in his Freiburg lecture room, in the midst of his accustomed reality.

It is sometimes argued that Stevens' poems are suffused with the philosophy of others, indeed, that they are sometimes virtually paraphrases of such philosophies, so that the sense of, say, 'The Bird with the Coppery, Keen Claws' must be sought in William James's *The Pluralistic Universe*.[3] However that may be, the focus here is on something else. Heidegger thinking about Hölderlin – his great poet of the Time Between the failure of God and the birth of a new age, and of the sense in which man dwells poetically on earth – was meditating on the essence of poetry, its disclosures of being and its relation with death, which completes and annihilates being. He was probing these matters as deliberately as his extraordinary pre-Socratic manner allowed, and the text he meditated was the text of a schizophrenic seer who also loved those philosophic origins and sought to subvert the civil languages that had supervened upon them. Perhaps, borrowing Housman's joke, one could say that Stevens was a better poet than Heidegger and a better philosopher than Hölderlin, and so found himself, in a manner, betwixt and between. But there he was in the accustomed reality of Connecticut, meditating these very problems, probing fortuitously, and commenting on his own text. The projects were related. It was a leaden time; when reality is death, the imagination can no longer press back against it. When you live in '*a world that does not move for the weight of its own heaviness*' (*The Necessary Angel*, p. 63),[4] you may imagine how differently it might appear to a young virile poet, but in the end you must find out for your ageing self how that weight is to be lifted, what fiction will transform death.

In 'The Poet's Vocation', Hölderlin calls upon the angel of the day (*des Tages Engel*) to awaken the people, stupefied by their world, and enable them to help the poet by interpreting him. But even if he is denied that help, he goes on all the same

> And needs no weapon and no wile till
> God's being missed in the end will help him.[5]

Stevens was capable of a fair degree of rapture at the poetic possibilities opened up by the death of God; indeed, on this point he is less gnomic than his precursor. But like Hölderlin, he also felt the cold: 'wozu Dichter in dürftiger Zeit?'[6] 'What are poets for in the time of poverty?' is a question he often asked in his own way. In his own way he also maintained, though his obscurities are not Hölderlin's, that 'Voll Verdienst, doch dichterisch, wohnet der Mensch auf dieser Erde' [full of merit (what would be a better translation?), yet poetically, man dwells on this earth].[7] Does the approach of death make this a little difficult to see?

In his essay 'Effects of Analogy' (1948), Stevens proposes: 'Take the case of a man for whom reality is enough, as, at the end of his life, he returns to it like a man returning from Nowhere to his village and to everything there that is tangible and visible, which he has come to cherish and wants to be near. He sees without images. But is he not seeing a clarified reality of his own? Does he not dwell in an analogy?' (NA, p. 129). He thinks that the being-toward-death, as Heidegger would call it, finds its form in the roofs, woods, and fields of a particular accustomed reality. It is a theme not altogether remote from that of Hölderlin's 'Homecoming' ('*Heimkunft*'). And it is central to Stevens. The place where the poet dwells, especially if it is his place of origin, will be his *mundo*, a clarified analogy of the earth he has lived in, the more so as death approaches. In the same essay he explains that a poet's sense of the world, his sense of place, will colour his dealings with death. James Thomson has a melancholy sense of the world; his place was a city of dreadful night, and he writes 'We yearn for speedy death in full fruition, / Dateless oblivion and divine repose'. Whitman, on the other hand, speaks of a 'free flight into the worldless, / Away from books, away from art, the day erased, the lesson done . . .'[8] Stevens does not enlarge upon these disclosures. They are effects of analogy; death is understood analogously, the last reality has the colour and the shapes of a clarified reality of one's own. In 'Imagination as Value', delivered as he approached his seventieth birthday, Stevens spoke of Pascal as one who, for all his hatred of the imagination ('this superb power, the enemy of reason'), clung 'in the very act of dying' to the faculty that, however 'delusive', might still create 'beauty, justice and happiness' (NA, pp. 135–6). As Pascal needed it to comprehend his death, so the poet needs it, especially in a time when 'the great poems of heaven and hell have been written and the great poem of the earth remains to be written' (*NA*, p. 142).

The point is Heideggerian; Stevens does not quote Heidegger here, one feels, only because he had not read him. Instead, he thinks of Santayana, whom he had known well at Harvard fifty years before. He thinks of him as one who gave the imagination a part in life similar to that which it plays in art. For the art of dying depends on our having dwelt poetically on earth. And so Santayana in old age 'dwells in the head of the world, in the company of devoted women, in their convent, and in the company of familiar saints, whose presence does so much to make any convent an appropriate refuge for a generous and human philosopher . . . there can be lives in which the value of the imagination is the same as its value in arts and letters and I exclude from consideration as part of that statement any thought of poverty or wealth, being a *bauer* or being a king, and so on, as irrelevant' (*NA*, p. 148). Reflecting on Santayana's death in a letter to Barbara Church (29 September 1952), he thinks again of one who abandoned poetry for thought but made this imaginative gesture, the choice, for a long old age, of a Roman convent, of a kind of poverty (he 'probably gave them all he had and asked them to keep him, body and soul' [*L*, p. 762]), of an image of oncoming death founded in the accustomed reality of prayer, liturgy, and the earthly city, which, being the heart of one world, may be the figure of another, the more so if, in dwelling poetically, we dwell in analogy. So the poem he might have written for Heidegger became a poem for Santayana.

'To an Old Philosopher in Rome' is about such dwelling, and about the moment when accustomed reality provides a language for death, invents it, as it invents its own angels, by analogy. The poem straddles the threshold, 'the figures in the street / Become the figures of heaven. . . . The threshold, Rome, and that more merciful Rome / Beyond, the two alike in the make of the mind' (*Collected Poems*, p. 508).[9] It is, one may say, a great poem, though perhaps not wholly characteristic of Stevens in the persistence with which it fills out its scenario of antitheses: 'The extreme of the known in the presence of the extreme / Of the unknown'; the candle and the celestial possible of which it is the symbol, life as a flame tearing at a wick; grandeur found in 'the afflatus of ruin', in the 'Profound poetry of the poor and of the dead'; splendour in poverty, death in life. It is language accommodating itself to that which ends and fulfils being, an image of that 'total grandeur'. This is a grandeur made of nothing but the bed, the chair, the moving nuns, the bells, and newsboys of the *civitas terrena*; but it is total, and the only image of a grandeur still unknown.

Note also that it is *easy*: 'How easily the blown banners change to wings'. Somehow it has become easy to find heaven in poverty's speech. The ease is the 'ease of mind' mentioned at the beginning of 'Prologues to What is Possible', where the rowers are sure of their way, and 'The boat was built of stones that had lost their weight and being no longer heavy / Had left in them only a brilliance, of unaccustomed origin' (*CP*, p. 515). The voyager easily passes into the unfamiliar – into death – as if it were the known. I do not mean that for Stevens this step is always easy, only that there is a kind of comfortable grace in some of his accounts of the threshold, an absence of what might be called, after Heidegger, *care* (to say nothing of dread), a grace that arises from acquiescence in the casual boons of the world of poverty, even at the moment when suffering caused by the absence of the gods might be most acute.

Heidegger called Hölderlin the poet of the Time Between – between the departure and the return of the gods – the midnight of the world's night. Stevens is consciously a poet of the same time. His answer to Hölderlin's question, *'wozu Dichter?'* (which Heidegger took as the title of his astonishing lecture on the twentieth anniversary of the death of Rainer Maria Rilke), would not be, in essence, different from either the poet's or the philosopher's. He had long been trying to make poetry out of commonplaces, for instance, in *Owl's Clover* in the Thirties, and in 1949 he said that in 'An Ordinary Evening in New Haven' his interest was 'to try to get as close to the ordinary, the commonplace and the ugly as it is possible for a poet to get. It is not a question of grim reality but of plain reality. The object is of course to purge oneself of anything false' (*L*, p. 636). At the end of that poem reality, plain reality, is given some of the imagery of death: 'It may be a shade that traverses / A dust, a force that traverses a shade' (*CP*, p. 489). Those 'edgings and inchings of final form', those statements tentatively closing in on the real, are in their way a figure for the imagination's edging and inching toward the comprehension of death. Hence, too, the idea of self-purgation; the moral and the poetic functions of imagination grow toward identity and in virtually the same way labour to include death in being. Death is a threshold, the common-place on one side of it, its transcendent analogue on the other, as the Santayana poem at once asserts. And that notion is much prefigured, for Stevens is a poet of thresholds: even summer is a threshold and, in 'Credences of Summer', an image of death. At the end of 'The Auroras of Autumn' the 'scholar of one candle' opens his door and sees across the threshold 'An Arctic effulgence flaring on the frame / Of everything he is. And he feels afraid' (CP, p. 417). Finally, the supreme poet understands, out of the partial fact that we are 'An unhappy people in a happy world':

> In these unhappy he meditates a whole,
> The full of fortune and the full of fate,
> As if he lived all lives, that he might know,
>
> In hall harridan, not hushful paradise,
> To a haggling of wind and weather, by these lights
> Like a blaze of summer straw, in winter's nick.   (CP, pp. 420–21)

Here all the accustomed realities are known and accommodated to a summerlike brilliance in an icy world. Hölderlin would have called this poet a servant of the wine god, bearing all such care, seeing that blaze on behalf of all, imagining everything for them, including death. Knowing poverty ('His poverty becomes his heart's strong core' [CP, p. 427]) is the means to find a way through the world, which 'Is more difficult to find than the way beyond it' (CP, p. 446). This is what Stevens calls the will to holiness. It is a favorite word of Hölderlin's. Wozu Dichter? They must dwell in their huts, their accustomed reality, framed by their commonplace thresholds, and do all that angels can – intimate, by use of a perhaps delusive faculty, what lies beyond, the fullness of the encounter when Being has inched and edged its way to death. Santayana's choice of Rome as a place to die is a poet's choice; he seeks out this central city as affording the structures, the rituals, even the ritual compassions, that, out of accustomedness, the imagination confers on death. 'These are poems', wrote Randall Jarrell of *The Rock*, 'from the other side of existence, the poems of someone who sees things in steady accustomedness, as we do not, and who sees their accustomedness, and them, as about to perish.'[10] Or, as Stevens himself puts it, 'The thing seen becomes the thing unseen' (*Adagia, OP*, p. 167). Nevertheless, as he states elsewhere in the *Adagia*, 'The poet is the intermediary between people and the world in which they live . . . but not between people and some other world' (*OP*, p. 162). Thus, in concerning himself with death, the poet must concern himself with the poverty of the accustomed, with the mystery of dwelling poetically in its midst. And perhaps, as Hölderlin remarked, 'God's being missed in the end will help him'. Perhaps it will also help him to see the poet's words comfortingly coated in the adventitious splendours of decorative bindings, rendered easy by sharp, clear type, the blessings of richness in poverty, of ease in the world of care.

Stevens was quite right to be curious about Heidegger and to want to know what the philosopher said about Hölderlin. The intense meditation on poetry that Heidegger produced in the series of works inaugurated by the 1936 essay on Hölderlin represents, in a way, the fulfilment of an ambition evident in Stevens' prose. Stevens could not achieve it fully for various reasons. The desire for ease could have been one. Then again, his philosophy, as he himself admitted, was a philosophy of collects, an amateur's philosophy. Heidegger was professional as well as incantatory; he thought as the pre-Socratics (or some of them) thought, poetically. But he thought accurately. Albert Hofstadter says that as a thinker Heidegger did what a poet does: *dichtet*.[11] Like the poet, he was concerned with 'the saying of world and earth', with their conflict – not unlike the conflict of world and *mundo* in Stevens – and so with the place of all nearness and remoteness of the gods. 'Poetry is the saying of the unconcealedness of what is. Actual language at any given moment is the happening of this saying.' This is the *truth*, for Heidegger looked to the etymological meaning of *alētheia*, which is 'unconcealedness'. Thus, although it sets up a world, the work of art also *lets the earth be an earth*. 'As a world opens itself the earth comes to rise up.' And so it happens that 'art is the becoming and happening of truth'. All art is in essence poetry, a disclosure of the earth, a 'setting-into-work of truth'. The appearance of this truth is beauty.[12]

There are times when Stevens would have recognized this voice as that of a remote kinsman in poetry, for example, in the 'thinking poem', 'Aus der Erfahrung des Denkens' ('The Thinker as Poet'):

> When the early morning light quietly
> grows above the mountains. . . .

> The world's darkening never reaches
> to the light of Being.

> We are too late for the gods and too
> early for Being. Being's poem,
> just begun, is man . . .[13]

Or, one can just imagine these aphorisms occurring in the *Adagia*:

> Poetry looks like a game and yet it is not.

> Poetry rouses the appearance of the unreal and of dream in the face of the palpable and clamorous reality, in which we believe ourselves at home. And yet . . . what the poet says and undertakes to be, is the real.[14]

Yet the affinity, I think, goes beyond these resemblances. It is of course mitigated by differences of a kind at which I have already hinted; Stevens was less bold, less willing to be oracular than Heidegger. And then there is the matter of those new typefaces and fine bindings: wear of ore for the angel of accustomedness, precursors of a transfigured commonplace, patches of Florida in the world of books. Likewise, there are the *trouvailles* and the collects and the fortuities of dizzle-dazzle that interrupt disclosures of pure poverty. But for all that, there is an affinity.[15]

If we think of the idea of dwelling and death we may come to understand this affinity. 'Poetically man dwells on this earth', said Hölderlin. In the poverty of the Time Between, one establishes this dwelling by finding the poetry of the commonplace, in the joy of Danes in Denmark, in the cackle of toucans in the place of toucans, in

Elizabeth Park and Ryan's Lunch. Stevens did it over and over again, observing the greater brilliancies of earth from his own doorstep. He dwelt in Connecticut as Santayana dwelt in the head of the world, as if it were origin as well as threshold. He wanted to establish Hölderlin's proposition, and every reader of Stevens will think of many more instances of his desire to do so. Freiburg, Fribourg, were elsewhere. The foyer, the dwelling place, might be Hartford or New Haven, Farmington or Haddam. The Captain and Bawda 'married well because the marriage-place / Was what they loved. It was neither heaven nor hell' (CP, p. 401). It was earth, and the poetry of the earth was what Hölderlin sought and Heidegger demanded. Stevens was always writing it and naming the spot to which it adhered. This is what poets are for in a time of need. They provide a cure of that ground; they give it health by disclosing it, in its true poverty, in the nothing that is. The hero of this world, redeemer of being, namer of the holy, is the poet. Stevens has many modest images of him, yet he is the centre. In that same central place Heidegger sets Hölderlin and adorns him with words that have special senses: *truth, angel, care, dwell.*

Heidegger gave the word *dwell* a special charge of meaning. Drawing on an old sense of the German word, he can say that 'Mortals dwell in that they can save the earth', that is, 'set it free in its own presencing', free, as Stevens would say, of its man-locked set. There is much more to dwelling,[16] but I will mention only that to dwell is to initiate one's own nature, one's being capable of death as death, 'into the use and practice of this capacity, so that there may be a good death'. Furthermore, 'as soon as man *gives thought* to his dwelling it is a misery no longer'; so out of its insecurity and poverty ('man dwells in huts and wraps himself in the bashful garment,' says Hölderlin;[17] 'a single shawl / Wrapped tightly round us, since we are poor . . .', says Stevens [CP, p. 524]) he can build, can make poetry.[18] For Heidegger is here meditating on Hölderlin's enigma, that we dwell poetically on this earth, even in a time of destitution, and that our doing so is somehow gratuitous, independent of our merits, a kind of grace.

Where one dwells is one's homeland, and to return to it is to see it in its candid kind. Heidegger's first essay on Hölderlin is about the elegy 'Homecoming', a poem of serenity and angels but also of the poet who names the town and makes it 'shine forth'. The angels are best summoned in one's homeland because the 'original essence of joy is the process of becoming at home in proximity to the source'.[19] The gods have failed; the poet 'without fear of the appearance of godlessness . . . must remain near the failure of the god until out of that proximity the word is granted which names the High One'. For he is the giant of the time that follows the default of the god. He is the first among men; others must help him by interpreting his word (which is the life of the world) so that each man may have his own homecoming.

In a second essay on Hölderlin, Heidegger deepens these apprehensions and speaks of the godlike power of his poet. Man has been given arbitrariness, and he has been given language, with which he creates and destroys and affirms what he is. What he affirms is that he 'belongs to the earth and gives it being: Only where there is language is there world'. (The 'words of the world,' says Stevens, 'are the life of the world' [*CP*, p. 474].) The naming of the gods ('This happy creature – It is he that invented the Gods' [*OP*, p. 167]) was only the first act by which language – poetry – established Being. To dwell poetically is to stand in the proximity of being; when the essence of things receives a name, as the gods once received a name in the first poetic act, things shine out.[20] These things are commonplace and accustomed till thus named: only then is it the case that 'The steeple at Farmington / Stands glistening and Haddam shines and sways' (*CP*, p. 533).

The completion and delimitation of Being come with death, with *my* death, for we cannot think authentically about the deaths of others. Heidegger had written much about this in *Being and Time*, and he thought about it in relation to poetry in essays written between 1947 and 1952, when Stevens' not dissimilar meditations were in progress and when he was saying he would like to read Heidegger. Only on the subject of care, on the necessity of speaking heavily and with radical plainness of being and ending, might he have found in the German a weight as of stones he chose not to lift.

But perhaps, after all, Stevens did know something about *Being and Time*. Perhaps it was knowing about it that sent him looking, in his seventies, for news of what that Swiss philosopher might have to say about his supreme poet. Heidegger wrestled with ideas we all wrestle with: the potentiality of no more being able to be there, he remarks, is the inmost, one might say the own-most, potentiality. We have many ways of estranging death; for example, we say, 'Everybody dies', or 'one dies'. So we conceal our own 'being-toward-death'; yet death is the 'end' of Being, of *Dasein* – and the means by which it becomes a whole. To estrange it, to make it a mere fact of experience, is to make it inauthentic. Being understands its own death authentically not by avoiding that dread out of which courage must come but by accepting it as essential to Being's everydayness, which otherwise conceals the fact that the end is imminent at every moment. There must be a 'running forward in thought' to the potentiality of death.

Only where there is language is there world, says Heidegger; and only where there is language is there this running in thought, this authentication of death. It is the homecoming that calls for the great elegy; it is 'learning at home to become at home', as Heidegger says of the Hölderlin elegy.[21] 'All full poets are poets of homecoming,' he says. And he insists that Hölderlin's elegy is not *about* homecoming; it *is* homecoming. Stevens knew this, whether he learned it from Heidegger or not. He knew the truth of many of Heidegger's assertions, for example, about the nature of change in art. 'The works are no longer the same as they once were. It is they themselves, to be sure, that we encounter ... but they themselves are gone by.'[22] The work of art 'opens up a world and at the same time sets his world back again on earth'.[23] The perpetuation of such truth is the task of an impossible philosopher's man or hero. Stevens' poet works in the fading light; the 'he' of the late poems has to make his homecoming, has to depend on his interpreters to make it for themselves and understand that it is impermanent. The advent of the Supreme Poet, who would stop all this, is like the return of the god. Heidegger's most impressive meditation on this coming event is in the lecture on Rilke, '*Wozu Dichter?*' (1946). The time is completely destitute; the gods will return only when the time is free. Poets in such a destitute time must 'sense the trace of the fugitive gods' and, in dark night, utter the holy. Of this night Hölderlin is the poet. Is Rilke such a poet? Certainly he came to understand the destitution of the time, a time when even the trace of the holy has become unrecognizable, and there is lacking 'the unconcealedness of the nature of pain, death and love'.[24] Certainly he understood the need for 'unshieldedness' and the need to 'read the word "death" without negation'. But it is not certain that he attained the full poetic vocation or spoke for the coming world era, as Hölderlin did.

The long, dark essay on Rilke is finally beyond the scope of Stevens. But Stevens knew that language makes a world of the earth and includes death in that world; he knew that it effects the unconcealment of the earth, that this is the poet's task in a time of destitution and seclusion. He could imagine a vocation for a supreme poet. Sometimes he could speak or chant of these things majestically enough, but in the last poems he would not dress the poet in singing robes. The poet is, mostly, at home and old, shambling, shabby, and human. He does not say ' "I am the greatness of the new-found night" ' (*OP*, p. 93). But he accepts that what one knows 'of a single spot / Is what one knows of the universe' (*OP*, p. 99). His Ulysses strives to come home; he seeks a new youth 'in the substance of his region' (*OP*, p. 118), in its commonness, like that of the great river in Connecticut, which one comes to 'before one comes to the first black cataracts' (*CP*, p. 533) of the other, Stygian river.

It should be added that the 'he', the poet, of some of the last poems, can be a 'spirit without a foyer' and search among the fortuities he perceives for 'that serene he had always been approaching / As toward an absolute foyer . . .' (*OP*, p. 112). It is a different version of the running-toward-death, and Heidegger would have approved of that 'serene', for Hölderlin used the word and his glossator turned it over many times in his mind. Is this ordered serenity too easy? When we climb a mountain 'Vermont throws itself together' (*OP*, p. 115); Vermont does the work, provided, of course, that we climb the mountain. It is not quite easy, but it is of the essence that it is also not quite difficult. The greatest image of the being at the threshold of death is, I suppose, 'Of Mere Being', a poem that is also, one may be sure, very late. It contains a foreign song and a foreign bird. There is dread in it. Heidegger, I dare say, would have admired it, but there is no reason to suppose that he would have been less severe on Stevens than on Rilke.

So one forces them together, Hölderlin–Heidegger in Freiburg or Fribourg, and Stevens in Hartford. But Stevens always draws back, as if to examine a binding or to keep some distance between himself and a mad poet or a very difficult philosopher. 'Philosophical validity', he assured a correspondent in 1952, was no concern of his; 'recently', he added, 'I have been fitted into too many philosophic frames' (L, p. 753). Perhaps the Heidegger frame would have pleased him better than most; for one thing, Heidegger's thought is very different from any that Stevens was accustomed to think of as philosophical. But Stevens would have drawn back. Not to find a copy of *Existence and Being* was, in a way, to draw back, to seek Heidegger instead in Paris, where his bookseller knew the kind of book he liked, and it would arrive like something exotic. Then again, there was a crucial difference of origin: Stevens was an American in America, Heidegger a German in Germany (not Switzerland), all life long. Part of this difference is reflected in varying styles of solemnity, in the fact that Heidegger is wholly without irony, while Stevens always has it within call.

There was an affinity between the ways in which they felt the world and understood poetry; between the truths they disclosed in the night of destitution by dwelling poetically in – that is, by saving – their worlds. Stevens had something of the quality that made Heidegger describe Hölderlin as himself having that third eye he attributed to Oedipus; he was virtually talking about it in the last lines of 'The Auroras':

> he meditates a whole,
> The full of fortune and the full of fate,
> As if he lived all lives, that he might know. . . .   (*CP*. p. 420)

But few could have refused more obstinately the fate of Hölderlin. For Stevens the world was by no means always a haggling of wind and weather or even of an *unheimlich* 'serene'. It was often, perhaps daily, a place of ease, of 'Berlioz and roses' if that happened to be 'the current combination at home' (L, p. 505), of postcards from Cuba, tea from Ceylon – fortuities of earth that solace us and make a world, or, like the Tal Coat painting that hung in his house in these years, an angel of reality. Such, too, though more elegant and more ornate, were the finely printed books of Mr Hammer, a Viennese 'without a foyer' but now growing accustomed to the reality of Kentucky, whence he might send surrogate angels to Connecticut. There dwelt the poet, watching the shining of the commonplace (occasionally, a distant palm, an unclassifiable, fire-fangled bird) and, for the most part, easy among his splendid books, though soon to die.

9

Secrets and Narrative Sequence

This lecture is probably the most arduous in the book. The subject is itself difficult, and the occasion was a Chicago conference on 'Narrative: The Illusion of Sequence', which may sound dry but was about as grand, and also as interesting, as academic critics ever experience. My paper was immediately under moderately friendly attack from the late Paul de Man, but among the less contentious speakers were Paul Ricoeur, Hayden White, Jacques Derrida and Roy Schafer, the admirable psychoanalyst who wants to simplify the jargon of his trade, which is also concerned with narratives, though of a different sort. My lecture could be called aridly academic, but I include it as a reminder that in the Seventies I spent much time devotedly doing this kind of thing.

In the conduct of an invented story there are, no doubt, certain proprieties to be observed for the sake of clearness and effect.

Joseph Conrad, *Under Western Eyes*

> Lucinda can't read poetry. She's good,
> Sort of, at novels, though. The words, you know,
> Don't sort of get in like Lucinda's way.
> And then the story, well, you know, about
> Real people, fall in love, like that, and all.
> Sort of makes you think, Lucinda thinks.
>
> George Khairallah, 'Our Latest Master of the Arts'[1]

The proprieties to be observed for the sake of clearness and effect are what enable Lucinda to get on sort of better with novels than with poetry. They ensure that words don't get in the way of story and characters ('real people') – characters, for example, by falling in love, are what enable the story to continue. 'And all' is sequence, also closure: plot, in short. These are the things that make Lucinda think; these are the things that are admitted (unlike words, which remain in perpetual quarantine) to Lucinda's consciousness; and what she is good at understanding is their message.

We are all rather more like Lucinda than we care to believe, always wishing words away. First we look for story – events sequentially related (possessing, shall we say, an irreducible minimum of 'connexity'). And sequence goes nowhere without his *Doppelgänger* or shadow, causality. Moreover, if there are represented persons acting, we suppose them to be enacting an action, as Aristotle almost, though not quite, remarked; and we suppose them to have 'certain qualities of thought and character' (*dianoia* and *ethos*), the two causes of action – as Aristotle really did remark (*Poetics*, 49b36).

Hence the first questions we like to ask resemble those of Keats: 'What leaf-fring'd legend ... What men or gods are these? What maidens loth? ... To what green altar ...?' There seems to be a *mythos*; these persons are acting, they seem to be trying to do something or to stop somebody else from doing it (the maidens are 'loth'), and they are heading somewhere. The *mythos* appears to have the usual relation to *ethos* and *dianoia*. But Keats, and we after him, are unable to discover the plot because the arrangement of the events (*synthesis tón pragmatón*) is not such as to allow us. Still, it must have some bearing upon our world, a world in which, as our experience suggests, there is evidence of sequence and cause; too much wine is followed by burning foreheads and parching tongues, sexual excitement is not perpetual and may be followed by sadness. Since matters appear to be otherwise on the urn, we are obliged to think that the contrast is the point of the story, for unless it has something to do with our normal expectations and beliefs, it can have no point. It lacks a quality we expect in imitations of our world, where heads ache and one may be disgusted. What it lacks is intelligible sequence, and this lack or absence must be the most important thing about it. That the young man will never stop singing, never kiss, implies a world in which the tree will never be bare nor maidens' beauty fade. Nothing in this sequenceless paradise has *character* – the ash, as Yeats put it, on a burnt stick. This utter eventlessness, this *nunc stans*, 'teases us out of thought', which is not quite 'sort of makes [us] think'. We are nevertheless anxious that it should *say* something to us. What it says, we say, is that even in our world, the familiar world of chance and choice, it is an important though not self-evident fact that beauty is truth and truth beauty. The importance of the story on the urn, then, is that in its very difference it can tell us, by intruding into our sequence of scandal and outrage, intimations not obvious but comforting. We have, in the end, made it say something that suits us.[2]

I've been teasing Keats's poem into thought, into parable. Even if the *mythos* is incomplete and the characters so far above breathing human passion that we can infer very little about *ethos* or *dianoia*, we make them all relevant to a world in which we behave as if causes operated and matters came to an end. If the story on the urn does not observe the proprieties, we shall none the less consider it strictly in relation to those proprieties; and that will enable it to *say* something to us. Of course the poem encourages us to do these things by ending with the sort of message that seems possible and proper.

Obviously our task, and the author's, will be easier with a completed action, as Aristotle, with his talk of failure and success and of the progressive exposure of the agents' *ethos* and *pathos*, would agree. And since we are not here to talk about immobile urns, I shall hereafter consider only invented stories in which the proprieties (as to connexity, closure, and character) are better observed. The first thing to say, I think, is that stories of this kind have frequently, perhaps to all intents and purposes always, properties that are not immediately and obviously related to the proprieties I have mentioned. This might seem self-evident; we are always asking questions of well-formed narratives that are not altogether unlike those put by the poet to his urn – questions about the persons acting, questions about cause, questions about what the story *says*. And although we are all very good readers, we argue about the answers, even if we agree that the story under discussion observes the proprieties. This is partly because most of the stories we care to discuss in this way have properties not so directly under the control of propriety. Good readers may conspire to ignore these properties; but they are relevant to my main theme, which is the conflict between narrative sequence (or whatever it is that creates the 'illusion of narrative sequence') and what I shall loosely, but with pregnant intention, call 'secrets'.

Consider first the rather obvious point that a story is always subject to interpretation. Stories as we know them begin as interpretations. They grow and change on the blank of the pages. There is some truth in the theory of iconotropy; if we doubt the evidence that it happened in remote antiquity, we shall not trouble to deny that it happened in later versions of myth, in folk etymologies, in daily gossip, and perhaps even in daily newspapers. Creative distortion of this kind is indeed so familiar as to need no more words. So is the practice of deliberate, conscious narrative revision, whether in narrative midrash or by historians. There is a perpetual *aggiornamento* of the sense. Interference with the original project may begin at the beginning; as Edward Said might say, its authority is subject to primordial molestation.[3] We take this for granted in some matters, as New Testament critics assume that the parables had been distorted not only by the appended interpretations but even in their substance, before they were written down. Consequently the world divides between those who seek to restore something authentic but lost and those who conclude that the nature of parable, and perhaps of narrative in general, is to be 'open' – open, that is, to penetration by interpretation. They are, in Paul Ricoeur's formula, models for the redescription of the world; they will change endlessly since the world is endlessly capable of being redescribed. And this is a way of saying that they must always have their secrets.

The capacity of narrative to submit to the desires of this or that mind without giving up secret potential may be crudely represented as a dialogue between story and interpretation. This dialogue begins when the author puts pen to paper and it continues through every reading that is not merely submissive. In this sense we can see without too much difficulty that all narrative, in the writing and the reading, has something in common with the continuous modification of text that takes place in a psychoanalytical process (which may tempt us to relate secrets to the condensations and displacements of dreams) or in the distortions induced in historical narrative by metahistorical considerations.

All that I leave to Roy Schafer[4] and Hayden White. My immediate purpose is to make acceptable a simple proposition: we may like to think, for our purposes, of narrative as the product of two intertwined processes, the presentation of a fable and its progressive interpretation (which of course alters it). The first process tends toward clarity and propriety ('refined common sense'), the second toward secrecy, toward distortions which cover secrets. The proposition is not altogether alien to the now classic *fabula/sujet* distinction. A test for connexity (an important aspect of propriety) is that one can accurately infer the fable (which is not to say it ever had an independent anterior existence). The *sujet* is what became of the fable when interpretation distorted its pristine, sequential propriety (and not only by dislocating its order of presentation, though the power to do so provides occasions for unobvious interpretations of a kind sequence cannot afford).

I do not know whether there is a minimum acceptable measure of narrativity. (On whom should we conduct acceptability tests? Wyndham Lewis's cabdriver? Philippe Sollers? The president of the MLA?) What seems reasonable, however, is the proposition that there will always be some inbuilt interpretation, that it will increase as respect for propriety decreases, and that it will produce distortions, secrets to be enquired into by later interpretation. Even in a detective story which has the maximum degree of specialized 'hermeneutic' organization, one can always find significant concentrations of interpretable material that has nothing to do with clues and solutions and that can, if we choose, be read rather than simply discarded, though propriety recommends the latter course.[5] In the kinds of narrative upon which we conventionally place a higher value, the case against propriety is much stronger; there is much more material that is less manifestly under the control of authority, less easily subordinated to 'clearness and effect', more palpably the enemy of order, of interpretative consensus, of message. It represents a fortunate collapse of authority (authors have authority, property rights; but they poach their own game and thereby set a precedent to all interpreters).

Whatever the comforts of sequence, connexity (I agree that we cannot do without them), it cannot be argued that the text which exhibits them will do nothing but contribute to them; some of it will be indifferent or even hostile to sequentiality. And although perhaps generated from some unproblematic ur-text, these nonsequential elements may grow unruly enough to be disturbing, even to the author.

Such was the case with Conrad, to whom I shall return in a moment. He was certainly aware of the conflict between the proprieties and the mutinous text of interpretation. There is no doubt that sequence, *ethos*, and *dianoia* minister to comfort and confirm our notions of what life is like (notions that may have been derived from narrative in the first place) and perhaps even constitute a sort of secular viaticum, bearing intimately upon one's private eschatology, the sense of one's own life and its closure. Such are their comforts, and sometimes we want them badly enough to wish away what has to come with them: the treacherous text, with its displacements and condensations, its debauched significances and unofficial complicities. Because the authors may themselves be alarmed by these phenomena (but also because they need to please), we may enter into collusion with them and treat all the evidence of insubordinate text as mere disposable noise or use the evidence selectively, when it can be adapted to strengthen the façade of propriety.

Secrets, in short, are at odds with sequence, which is considered as an aspect of propriety; and a passion for sequence may result in the suppression of the secret. But it is there, and one way we can find the secret is to look out for evidence of suppression, which will sometimes tell us where the suppressed secret is located. It must be admitted that we rarely read in this way, for it seems unnatural; and when we do we are uncomfortably aware of the difference between what we are doing and what the *ordinary reader* not only does but seems to have been meant to do. To read a novel expecting the satisfactions of closure and the receipt of a message is what most people find enough to do; they are easier with this method because it resembles the one that works for ordinary acts of communication. In this way the gap is closed between what is sent and what is received, which is why it seems to many people perverse to deny the author possession of an authentic and normative sense of what he has said. Authors, indeed, however keenly aware of other possibilities, are often anxious to help readers behave as they wish to; they 'foreground' sequence and message. This cannot be done without backgrounding something, and indeed it is not uncommon for large parts of a novel to go virtually unread; the less manifest portions of its text (its secrets) tend to remain secret, tend to resist all but abnormally attentive scrutiny, reading so minute,

intense, and slow that it seems to run counter to one's 'natural' sense
of what a novel is, a sense which one feels to have behind it the history
and sociology of the genre. That history has ensured that most readers
under-read, and the authors in turn tend to condone under-reading
because success depends upon it; there is public demand for narrative
statements that can be agreed with, for problems rationally soluble.
By the same token the authors are often suspicious of over-readers,
usually members of a special academic class that has the time to pry
into secrets. Joyce said he had written a book to keep the professors
busy; but James would not have said so, nor would Conrad, in whom
the struggle between propriety and secrecy is especially intense, nor
Robbe-Grillet, who claims to write for the man in the street. This
measure of collusion between novelist and public (his de facto contract
or gentleman's agreement is with *la cour et la ville* not with *l'école*)
helps one to see why the secrets are so easily overlooked and why –
given that the problems only begin when the secrets are noticed – we
have hardly, even now, found decent ways to speak of these matters.

If anybody thinks this is an exaggerated account of the matter, let
him reflect that Forster's *A Passage to India* had a very unusual success
on publication and gave rise to lively arguments about its account of
Indian life and politics; yet it was a good many years before anybody
noticed that it had secrets. What is more, I spend much of my time
among learned men who were devoted colleagues and friends of Forster
and who know *Passage* well, but they never seem to talk about its
secrets, only about its message and what, in their view, is wrong with
that message.

It is time, however, to consider a single text in more detail, and I shall
henceforth be talking about *Under Western Eyes*. This novel was not,
in 1911 or I think since, what could be called a popular success, though
it offers a decent measure of connexity and closure (falling off a
little, it must be allowed, from the highest standards of propriety). Its
political and psychological messages are gratifyingly complex; one can
engage in an enlightened critical conversation about *ethos* and *dianoia*
without talking about much else and so pass for an intelligent professional giving an effective 'reading'. Indeed that, until recently at any
rate, was what the normal institutional game consisted of. Nor is it

without interest; but the game is conducted within a very limited set of rules, in the establishment of which the author as well as the institution has played a part. Under these rules it is not obligatory to talk of secrets. There are handier, more tangible or manageable mysteries.

Under Western Eyes wants to allow this game to be played, but it also gives due notice that a different game is possible; it indicates, by various signs, that there are other matters that might be considered and that, though ignorable, they are detectable, given the right kind of attention. So it is a suitable text for my purpose, which is to consider the survival of secrecy in a narrative that pays a lot of attention to the proprieties which, according to its narrator, should be observed 'for the sake of clearness and effect'. Conrad took a high view of art and a low view of his public, which is why writing fiction seems to have been a continual cause of misery to him. It forced him into a situation sometimes reflected in his characters, a *dédoublement*. There is one writer who labours to save the 'dense' reader (one equipped, so to speak, with only Western eyes) from confusion, disappointment, and worry; and another dedicated to interpretation, to secrets, though at the same time he fears them as enemies of order, sequence, and message. There must be a strict repression of all that contests the supremacy of these features, 'else novel-writing becomes a mere debauch of the imagination', as Conrad told Mrs Garnett, who was worried about the 'self-imposed limitation' of the method employed in *Under Western Eyes*.[6]

I am already operating, and will continue to operate, a crude distinction in the readership, actual or potential, of *Under Western Eyes*. There is a larger public which Conrad, although he despised it, wanted to read his book. To some extent he abrogates authority (which the common reader values highly) by interfering as usual with the 'normal' sequence of the story and by installing an unreliable narrator; all narrators are unreliable, but some are more expressly so than others;[7] the more unreliable they are, the more they can say that seems irrelevant to, or destructive of, the proprieties. They break down the conventional relationship between sequential narrative and history-likeness, with its arbitrary imposition of truth; they complicate the message. They are more or less bound to bore or antagonize the simpler reader, who feels that he has been left outside and cannot, without pains he is unwilling to take, gain access on his own terms, the observance of a due sequaciousness being one, and another the manifest presence of authority, so that he need not reason why. Some such explanation will suffice for the cold public reception of *Under Western Eyes*; it has not grown much warmer in these days, for all that the book is now regarded as a classic.

Saying what is a classic is the business of a second group of readers, the professionally initiate. They perform other tasks, of course. One is finding things out, in the manner of Eloise Knapp Hay and Norman Sherry. And I hope we should all rather know than be ignorant of what they tell us; it is a first principle of literary criticism that no principle should stand which prevents our being concerned with what stimulates our unaffected interest – for example, in what Conrad, when he was not writing *Under Western Eyes*, thought about Russia, Slav 'mysticism', and Dostoevsky; or what Conrad originally planned to write, what he took to be the point of what he did write, and what, having written it, he cut. What he saw with his Eastern eyes is a legitimate subject of concern, though at present we are concerned with what he wrote in *Under Western Eyes*. And other members of this group assume the responsibility of saying what that was and how it is most profitable for us to think about it.

There are a great many books on Conrad, and I shall mention few of them. Albert Guerard's *Conrad the Novelist*, though it appeared in 1958, still seems to be a standard work, and not surprisingly, for it is a perceptive and resourceful book.[8] But it is characteristically uninterested in narrative secrets. On *Under Western Eyes* it makes plain that the author's first interest is in the psychopathology of Razumov; and it would have been possible to quote Conrad in defence of this preference. Razumov, the loner, the man of independent reason undermined by the shocks of Russian despotism and anarchy, is 'psychologically . . . fuller' than Lord Jim (p. 232). The design of the story (*synthesis tón pragmatón*) is commended because Razumov is enabled to keep quiet during his long period on the rack of guilt and fear, but to confess when every threat to his security has been removed. 'It would be hard to conceive a plot more successfully combining dramatic suspense and psycho-moral significance.' *Mythos, ethos, dianoia*: all present and sound.

Even the dislocated narrative sequence is said to have some advantages: by concealing what a more straightforward rendering of the fable would have revealed, it enables us to observe Razumov in Geneva before we find out that he has accepted employment as a spy for Mikulin. Such are the rewards of entrusting the narration to an observer who is not only limited and prejudiced but pretends to neither omniscience nor omnicommunicativeness. But these rewards are obtained at a cost, for the old language teacher 'creates unnecessary obstacles by raising the question of authority' (p. 248). He is a clumsy device for ensuring fair play to the Russians by reminding us that their actions are being reported through a rather 'dense' medium. On the other hand, first person narration, in the extended form here employed, gives 'eyewitness credibility and the authority of spoken voice' (p. 249).

Here is a contradiction, interesting though perhaps only apparent. Authority doesn't normally 'raise the question of authority'. They have it very oft that have it not. Yet there is a sense in which Conrad does both claim and renounce authority. Having it makes for clearness and effect; Conrad admired Trollope.[9] Not having it is to risk a debauch of the imagination. The contradiction of the critic replicates a conflict in the author. Writing under conditions even more agonizing than usual, Conrad said that 'following the psychology of Mr Razumov' was 'like working in hell'. The point to remember is that following the psychology required him to do many other things at the same time, or it would not have been so hellish. When a critic devoted to clearness and effect argued that *Chance* should be cut by half, Conrad replied sarcastically that yes, given a certain method, it 'might have been written out on a cigarette paper'.[10] Clearness and effect he sought, out of need, and desire too; but there was also the pursuit of interpretations. Hence the doubling I spoke of. In the hell of composition we see one writer committed to authority, another involved in debauch.

What is the critic to say when confronted with the evidence of debauch committed behind the back of authority? Guerard is not like Lucinda, the words do get in his way to some extent. Early in the book Razumov sees the phantom of Haldin lying in the snow. He tramples over it. Gaining from this act an intuition of Russia's 'sacred inertia', he decides to give Haldin up to the police. The phantom crops up from time to time in the course of the novel but can always be disposed of by reference to the psychological difficulties arising from the first hallucination. Or can it? When Razumov and Sophia Antonovna, in the garden of the exiles' villa at Geneva, are discussing whether there will be any tea left for her indoors, Razumov remarks that she might be lucky enough to find there 'the cold ghost of tea'. Guerard finds this odd and describes it as 'mildly obsessive'. So it is, but fortunately it can be got rid of, psychologized as 'hallucination, psychic symbol, or shorthand notice of anxiety'. In such ways are the ghosts and phantoms subjected to the needs of clearness and effect, buried in the psychology. I shall dig them out in a minute or two.

There are other ways of exorcizing secrets. Near the end of the book Razumov says he had been in a position to steal Natalia's soul. Guerard speaks of the Dostoevskian power of this moment of diabolism but is anxious to be rid of it, for it does not comply with what Roy Schafer might call his 'guiding fiction', his interpretation principle. Guerard dismisses Razumov's remark by arguing that Conrad, here, writing for the first time in Razumov's person, 'returned imaginatively' to his original plan for the novel, in which Razumov was to marry Natalia, so stealing her soul. The diabolism is, therefore, an irrelevant intrusion, a fault, a vestigial survival. Also near the end of the book, Razumov has the notion that the old language teacher is the devil. Of this second diabolistic conjecture Guerard says nothing, which is the more usual way of dealing with these awkwardnesses.

To attend to what complies with the proprieties, and by one means or another to eliminate from consideration whatever does not, is a time-honoured and perfectly respectable way of reading novels, especially when it is quite a task (as it often is in Conrad) to establish within proper bounds all the tricks and deviations which interfere with one's view of the fable. It is therefore not surprising that good readers, sensing that there is more going on than they have accounted for, show signs of strain. Guerard admires *Under Western Eyes* but admits that, having such a narrator, it lacks 'the rich connotative effects and subtly disturbing rhythms of *Lord Jim*' (p. 252). On the other hand, this 'self-effacing and more rational prose has the great merit of not interfering with the drama of ideas or with the drama of betrayal and redemption'. *Under Western Eyes*, that is to say, is unsubtle but clear and effective.

This is an extraordinary notion, and for a good critic to hold it is evidence of a strong though uneasy desire not to let the words get in the way – it is, after all, a refined version of Lucinda's view of the matter. To an eye undimmed by, or awakened from, the proprieties, this novel positively flaunts the 'irrationality' of its prose. It becomes 'readable' in the way Guerard wants it to be only when, by every possible means, attention to its secrets is repressed. Guerard's psychologizing of the phantom and his exorcism of the devil are of a piece with his decision that the prose is self-effacing and rational, lacking in resonance and connotation.

If you're looking out for this kind of thing, you find it almost anywhere. Eloise Knapp Hay, for example, rightly asks why Razumov's cover story, during the preparations for his visit to Geneva, should include an eye disease and a visit to an oculist (so far as simple plotting goes, any non-ocular meeting-place would have done just as well; indeed, no specification of this sort was, strictly, needed at all).[11] What Hay, having noticed this, makes of it is that Razumov, during these visits, is being commissioned 'to use his own eyes to spy for the state' (p. 294), and she mentions the young man's earlier discomfort at the stares of the goggle-eyed general who interviewed him on the night he betrayed Haldin. But to leave it at that simple allegorical level is precisely to refuse the kind of covert invitation of which this text has so many. Another of Hay's interesting observations is that behind the description of Russia as 'a monstrous blank page awaiting the record of an inconceivable history', there may lie an observation of Mickiewicz's to the effect that Russia was 'a page prepared for writing' – an alarming thought, since one could not know that the devil would not cover the page before God did (pp. 287–8). But she is content to observe that in Conrad 'the question is posed differently', without allusion to God and the devil. Here again, properly interested in the relation of Conrad's figure to its presumable source, she omits to ask what that relation is doing in the book and what it may have to do with the elements of diabolism. So too, she quotes the famous letter to Cunninghame Graham, in which Conrad says that to serve a national ideal, however much suffering it may cause, is better than to serve the shadow of an eloquence that is dead, a mere phantom (p. 20). We may think of Conrad as painfully finding out in the writing of *Under*

Western Eyes what the novel was; he did so by writing it, black on white, as if it were Russia, and by meditating on eyes, phantoms, and devils, as surely as by deciding to cut all the American material from the final version; it was Russia he was writing on.

The secrets to which these words and ideas are an index have no direct relation to the main business of the plot; as some analysts would say, they are not kernels but catalysts or, as Seymour Chatman calls them, 'satellites'. But they form associations of their own, nonsequential, secret invitations to interpretation rather than appeals to a consensus. They inhabit a world in which relationships are not arranged according to some agreed system but remain occult or of questionable shape. There is a relatively clean, well-lit plot – rectangular like the room in which its climax occurs, almost without shadow, having, like Switzerland, no horizons, for they are cut off by crude and impassable barriers like the Jura, by conventional closure.

Such a plot may be suitable for the citizens of a tedious democracy, either Switzerland, where they sit colourlessly uncouth, drinking beer out of glittering glasses, obvious in an obvious light, or England, which has made its bargain with fate, so much liberty for so much cash, knowing also that it is entitled to the obvious. Such a nation deserves novels like the view of Geneva on which Razumov turns his back in contempt, finding it 'odious – oppressively odious – in its unsuggestive finish; the very perfection of mediocrity attained at last after centuries of toil and culture'. But this novel contains another plot, misty, full of phantoms, of which the passage about the blank page of Russia forms a part, as would be manifest if anybody considered it in relation to the large number of allusions (they even look, when one is looking for them, obtrusive) to blackness and whiteness, paper and ink, snow and shadow – and to writing itself.

These are secrets from which, by a curious process of collusion, we avert our attention. It was a welcome surprise to find in an excellent paper by Avrom Fleishman proof that an effort of attention is after all possible.[12] Fleishman observes that the 'artlessness' of the narrator is not a guarantee of factuality so much as a hint that the text is extremely artful; he sorts out the interrelations between the various documentary sources the old man is supposed to be using, notes the hints of falsification and omission, and emphasizes the abnormal interest of the novel in the acts and arts of writing, as when Razumov, prompted to write by Laspara, composes his first (Russian) spy report in the shadow of the statue of the (Genevan) writer Rousseau. He also argues that the novel moves out of writing into speech, as indeed it does: the inspiration mentioned in the last off-key conversation between the narrator and Sophia is drawn in with the breath, Razumov is no longer a writer but a beloved speaker. Fleishman draws back finally (perhaps needlessly) from his own proposal that the book suggests an 'ultimate despair of written language, and of the art of fiction . . .'

And indeed it is obvious that *Under Western Eyes* (rather than any character in it) is obsessed with writing and also with deafness – deafness not only of the ears but of the eyes (Ivanovitch seems to speak from his eyes; Sophia Antonovna seems to receive 'the sound of his voice into her pupils instead of her ears'; at the grand climax the narrator is blinded by his own amazement, but the slamming of a door restores his sight). There is a hint that we may, though we probably won't, read for more than mere evidence of Razumov's psychological condition. If we are willing to do so, we shall find over the plot the shadow of a secret that has resisted being made altogether otherwise than it is for the sake of readers who want the work to be throughout like beer in a glittering glass. I have been giving instances of subtler, more learned modes of inattention; even good readers find means to dispose of the evidence rather than work upon it. It would be easy to give more: for example, the explanation of all the souls and phantoms of the text as part of a refutation, or parody, of *Crime and Punishment*. This can be used to sterilize larger portions of Conrad's text. I do not mean to argue that no such observations ought to be made. Like the psychological and political readings, they belong squarely to a tradition of ordinary reading that may be perfectly intelligent; a person might run his life in accordance with what he concluded from such readings, as Lawrence claimed he might do from his reading of *Anna Karenina*. I object only to their use as means to purge secrets from the text.

Let me now give one or two more detailed instances of the way in which this novel advertises and conceals its secrets. As the story of Razumov's treachery reaches its crisis, the narrator pauses to note that his job is 'not in truth the writing in the narrative form a précis of a strange human document, but the rendering . . . of the moral conditions ruling over a large portion of this earth's surface; conditions not easily to be understood, much less discovered in the limits of a story, till some key-word is found; a word that could stand at the back of all the words covering the pages, a word which, if not truth itself, may perchance hold truth enough to help the moral discovery which should be the object of every tale'. He stops, scans Razumov's journal, then takes up his pen again, ready to set down 'black on white'. Then he says that the key word is 'cynicism'.

Even in a novel so benignly disingenuous from the preface on (but perhaps it is not benign; in a sense it hates its readers), this passage is remarkable. Playing the role of straight narrator, the old man repeatedly veers close to the position of his occult double. 'A large portion of the earth's surface' is a periphrasis easily divested of its originating notion, Russia; the case is more general. He sees that the point of the narrative is not solely or primarily psychological but wanders away from the insight to speak of 'moral conditions'. He speaks of a key word; pauses, as it were, unwittingly speaks one of the key words of the book he is in ('black on white'), then lapses into the obvious or irrelevant 'cynicism'. For a real secret he substitutes a pseudosecret, though in doing so he cannot help telling the attentive reader that there is a secret there. Readers as 'dense' as he himself is will be happy with 'cynicism'. They will get on with sequence while the double busies himself with secrets and key words such as 'soul', 'eyes', and 'black and white'. Indications that these words have a special function are various. They occur with quite abnormal frequency; they are used in such a way as to distort the plausibility of narrative and especially of dialogue. Some instances may be explained away as evidence of Razumov's stressed condition ('what I need is not a lot of haunting phantoms that I could walk through' is the kind of remark that certainly suggests stress of some kind). But in others it is simply astonishing that anybody capable of reading could fail to observe the gross distortions in what they think of as 'self-effacing and rational prose'.

Let us look at a continuous passage; it is ripped from the midst of a longer one, so one must allow for an even greater measure of eccentric insistence in the context of the whole: 'We shall get some tea,' says Ivanovitch, leading Razumov to his mistress's drawing room. They cross a black-and-white tessellated floor. Ivanovitch's hat, black but shiny, stands outside the drawing room, which is 'haunted, it is said, by evoked ghosts, and frequented, it is supposed, by fugitive revolutionists'. (We may remember that the villa itself 'might well have been haunted in traditional style by some doleful, groaning, futile ghost of a middle-class order'.) The white paint of the panels is cracked. Ivanovitch, from behind his dark spectacles, speaks of the true light of femininity. His mistress has brilliant eyes in a death's-head face, they gleam white but their pupils are black. Ivanovitch speaks as if from his invisible eyes. The lady 'ghoulishly' eats the cakes Ivanovitch brought in his hat. Razumov gives a moment's thought to Tekla, the *dame de compagnie*: 'Have they terrified her out of her senses with ghosts, or simply have they only been beating her?' He is aware of having to come to terms with phantoms, with the ghastly. His interlocutors appear to understand nothing of what he says; Ivanovitch is as if deaf. The purpose of the revolutionary movement, it seems, is to 'spiritualise discontent', and the lady declares herself, in matters of politics, a 'supernaturalist'. She can see Razumov's soul with her 'shiny eyes'. What does she see? asks Razumov. 'Some sort of phantom in my image? . . . For, I suppose, a soul when it is seen is just that. A vain thing. There are phantoms of the living as well as of the dead.' He then tells them he has seen a phantom. Soon he leaves, passing the top hat, 'black and glossy in all that crude whiteness', and looks at the chequered floor below.

I'll pause there and admit that this is a very partial account of Razumov's visit, meant to bring out what a 'normal' reading largely ignores. The easiest thing to notice is the unidiomatic quality of the writing. 'Haunted . . . by evoked ghosts'; 'Have they terrified her out of her senses with ghosts, or simply have they only been beating her?'; 'Some sort of phantom in my image?' How are we to explain these oddities? I suppose the 'evoked ghosts' might be put down to Conrad thinking in French; possibly also 'simply have they only been beating her'; but however they got there we are, I think, obliged to read them, not wish them away. Both the remark about Tekla's scared appearance (was it caused by evoked ghosts?) and the character of the phantom the second-sighted lady might see in Razumov are, one might have thought, almost intolerably odd if one is reading this as a sequence-advancing, psychology-investigating dialogue. But our reading may be so sequence-connected that we can screen them out by thinking of psychology rather than the words. Conrad helps us to psychologize them out of the way by making Razumov enter into a dangerous, though censored, account of his encounter with Haldin's phantom. But only our recollections of anarchists of the period, their flirting with the occult and with feminism, can explain the interest in seeing souls coming to terms with phantoms; unless we decide, as we ought, that the emphasis on eyes and seeing is otherwise, and occultly, related to the virtually uncontrolled dispersion of souls, spirits, phantoms, ghosts, ghouls, and so forth. Here, against the repetitive black and white (against ink on paper, against the page we are *seeing*) are crowded the evidences of things unseen and the huge variety of eyes that may or may not see them. It is not an easy thing to talk about such a constellation of irrational figures, but it must somehow be done if we are to read secrets as well as sequence – to avoid attributing all these phenomena to Razumov's 'nervous exhaustion'.

What I ask you to believe is that such oddities are not merely local; they are, perhaps, the very 'spirit' of the novel. If one follows Razumov a little way from the encounter just described, one finds him talking to Tekla with her striped cat and terrified eyes and then with Sophia Antonovna, whose black eyes and white hair are mentioned almost as often as she is. It is in this interview that the ghost of tea occurs. Razumov has just mentioned that his mind is a murky medium in which Haldin appears as a featureless shadow. He adds that Haldin is now beyond the reach of feminine influence, except possibly that of the spiritualist lady. 'Formerly the dead were allowed to rest, but now it seems they are at the beck and call of a crazy old harridan.' 'Let us hope,' says Sophia humorously, 'that she will make an effort and conjure up some tea for us.' The figure arises naturally from the talk about the spiritualist lady. But it continues. 'There has been tea up there . . . If you hurry . . . instead of wasting your time with such an unsatisfactory sceptical person as myself, you may find the ghost of it – the cold ghost of it – still lingering . . .' And two pages later Razumov again tells her that she risks missing 'the mere ghost of that tea'. In her reply Sophia uses the figure yet again. Then they speak of ghouls, ogres, vampires. She denies that she is a materialist; she is described as Mephistophelian. Finally Razumov tells the story of his escape; it is in truth the story of Haldin, gliding from Razumov's room as if he were a phantom, at midnight; the flame gutters as he passes. She listens but as if with her eyes not her ears – with her black impenetrable eyes glowing under the white hair. At one point Sophia tells him to 'wait until you have trodden every particle of yourself under your own feet . . . you've got to trample down every particle of your own feelings'. These are words private to Razumov, not possible to her; only he, and perhaps Councillor Mikulin, knows about that trampling. Are we inclined to seek, in the body of the plot, a reason why Sophia should use such an expression? No, for any notion that she had access to secret police information about Razumov would extravagantly spoil the plot. No; here an expression private to Razumov (if we stick to conventional characterization) – evidence as to his peculiar psychological state – has bled into the texture of the book and attached itself to Sophia. I wonder if anything quite like it can be found in the English novel till Virginia Woolf. Note, too, the repetition ('trodden' . . . 'trample'): it is an indication that we are to pause and take note of it.

I have mentioned elsewhere[13] the oddity of Natalia Haldin's remark – that when she went to the villa she didn't at first see a soul, but then Tekla came in, and she *did* see a soul. Perhaps Conrad was not aware that the idiomatic expression 'I didn't see a soul' is incapable of a positive transformation. That doesn't matter; 'seeing a soul' is another important key phase. The oddity of the expression is a way of directing attention to it; it must not be swept away by talk of Conrad's English. So with the other key words, the repetitions – four ghosts of tea are surely beyond a joke. The frequency with which 'soul', 'ghost', and related words are used has not altogether escaped attention; but if one reflects that they occur (if one allows not only 'spirit' but 'inspired') well over a hundred times in the novel (sometimes in grotesquely thick concentrations), besides several ghostly apparitions, people appearing as if they had risen from the ground, and so on, it becomes obvious that the attention has not been very sustained. Of course, all these usages are somehow related to the appearance of Haldin's phantom in the plots of action and psychology; but they must not be totally subsumed in them. Indeed, on any reasonably minute and careful reading they cannot be, for they distort the dialogue and are incompatible with any psychology that could be thought appropriate to

Razumov, who is always sane. Nor should one forget the frequency of associated key words. I have counted well over sixty references to eyes – the eyes of all the principal characters are incessantly mentioned or described – and to seeing. Black on white occurs twenty-four times expressly and many more less directly – in references to snow and darkness, light in dark rooms, and, as I have said, ink on paper. All this adds up to a quantitatively quite large body of text which on the face of it contributes nothing to sequence – clogs it, indeed.

It would be to inflict even more laborious reports on you to specify at any greater length the character of the 'secret' material in *Under Western Eyes*. My purpose is to supplement the 'straight' reading, which irons out such considerable quantities of text. Conrad, when he began the book, called it *Razumov*; but when it was done (on the last page of the manuscript, in fact) he changed the title to *Under Western Eyes*. He had found out what he was doing. Most readers silently restore the old title, being readier to think about Razumov than about eyes. They want something clearly seen, a message to be apprehended with civilized ease. Let us look at the underside of one more scene, Razumov's confession to Natalia.

Razumov's face is pale, his eyes dark. The inner room is dark by contrast with the well-lit anteroom; Mrs Haldin's face is white against the undefined dark mass of her chair. Razumov has been writing and stopped to come and talk, so entering the writing, the black on white, of the narrator. He is safe; the phantom on the snow has been walked over, though the phantom's mother is white as a ghost. Natalia enters, like a ghost ('her presence . . . was as unforeseen as the apparition of her brother had been', with a pun on two senses of 'apparition').[14] She had done the same in the garden of the villa; she 'had been haunting him'. They stand in the rectangular box of a room with its white paper and lack of shadows. They are trapped, we might say, in a rational plot – the narrator has them captive 'within the boundaries of his eyes'. Razumov says that he was born clear-eyed but has seen apparitions. Natalia's eyes are trustful, as always. She says that her brother's soul is in Razumov, reason benignly possessed by spirit. There they stand, boxed in a Western room, brought out of a 'confused immensity' for the benefit of Western eyes. They do not see the old man. Natalia removes her veil. Her eyes are lustrous; he listens, as if to music rather than speech. She explains that her mother expects to *see* her dead son. 'It will end by her seeing him.' 'That is very possible,' says Razumov. 'That will be the end. Her spirit will depart.' He speaks of the phantoms of the dead. Natalia's veil lies on the floor between them. 'Why are you looking at me like this . . .? I need . . . to see . . .' He begins the confession: more phantoms. The old man intervenes; Razumov stands with the veil at his feet, 'intensely black in the white crudity of the light'. He seems to vanish. He goes home and writes more in his journal. In its pages, we are told of eyes, phantoms, his temptation to steal Natalia's soul. Was the old Englishman the devil ('I was possessed')? Natalia has saved him; she is an apparition ('suddenly you stood before me'), and the old man a 'disappointed devil'. He wraps the writing in the veil.

At midnight (when spirits walk) he runs down the stairs into the storm, the rain enveloping him like a veil. Later, deafened, he again runs into the storm, which has transformed the dull civility of Geneva. Lightning blinds him; he 'puts his arm over his eyes to recover his sight'; he wanders into a drift of mist, walking 'in a phantom world'.

This is of course psychological disclosure, but if it is *only* that it is full of irrelevant information, of redundancies, of what, if its business consists of sequence and psychology, is a feebly bloated rhetoric. I have spoken of secrets; but they are all but blatantly advertised. The book has a semblance of Geneva, but in the end it yields to Russia, misty, spiritual, its significance occulted; it is without horizon, only by trickery and collusion got into a square, well-lit box. The writing of the book, the covering of the monstrous blank page, is a work of 'strange mystic arrogance'; it gives the Western eye its box, its civilized mediocrity, but keeps its secrets also. It is a controlled 'debauch'; we may ignore this aspect if we choose and read it as Genevans or Englishmen would read it. It is a question of the form of attention we choose to bestow; of our willingness to see that in reading according to restricted codes we disregard as noise what, if read differently, patiently, would make another and rarer kind of sense. And the text, almost with 'cynicism', tells us what is there, confident that we shall ignore it.

'The illogicality of its attitude, the arbitrariness of its conclusions, the frequency of the exceptional, should present no difficulty to the student of many grammars . . . There is a generosity in its ardour of speech which removes it as far as possible from common loquacity; and it is ever too disconnected to be classed as eloquence.' I adapt these words from the passage near the beginning of the book in which the old language teacher speaks of the Russian character and the Russian use of language. He apologizes for the digression, which we should know is not a digression, exactly as we know it is not 'idle to inquire' why Razumov should have left his written record. He is telling us (or rather the double is telling us, ventriloquially) that a large part of what he says is precisely what we are not willing to attend to. He, who claims a professional mistrust of words, is talking about the book he is in, the black on white. He is necessary; for, as Razumov remarks, 'there may be truth in every manner of speaking. What if that absurd saying [that he himself might be a 'chosen instrument of Providence'] were true in its essence?' What if the old Englishman should be the father of lies?

It seems to be the case that there is in this book a 'manner of speaking' that is horizonless, misty. Is there some great idea that unites all the key words, the language with which the text is obsessed? One could make shift to discover such a truth, perhaps. Black on white is the manuscript or the book; the reading of black on white (including the seeing into its soul or spirit) is a hearing with the eyes of what is said rather than written, since it is not seen. It is in the veil that covered Natalia's eyes that the manuscript is wrapped. The secrets of the book are phantoms, inexplicably appearing, ignored, trampled down, turned into lies by the father of lies, a diabolical narrator. For the reading of such a book we have the wrong kind of eyes. It despises its Genevan readers, with their requirements of brightness and obvious structure, their detached, informed interest in alien 'mystery'.

And at this point why should we not add some biographical evidence? Conrad was in one of his greatest crises as he turned *Razumov* into *Under Western Eyes* and had a severe breakdown when he finished the book. Part of the trouble was poverty; not enough people read his books. They were not sufficiently obvious. So this book provides an accurate prophecy of its own reception which is the reception of all such works; like the language teacher, like Lucinda, we distrust words, think it better to ignore them if they seem wild or misty. And like the language teacher, we are surprised at the book's end, which is the ending of another story than the one he had seemed to be in charge of. The actual black on white defeats the narrator's attempt to achieve parsimony of sequence, squareness, limit. It seems that a god and a devil wrote simultaneously, another *dédoublement* if you like, and one that, somehow, the good reader must emulate; for if he does not he will, by concurring in the illusions of limit and authority, deny the god (the hidden god of secrets) his due. Thus may a novel complain against the common-sense way we read it, though this is the kind of reading it seems also to solicit by appearing to respect the proprieties and to aim at 'clearness and effect'.

IO

Botticelli Recovered

This was the first of three René Wellek Library lectures, given at the University of California at Irvine in 1983. I wrote it at a time when there was a general interest, and much dispute, about the nature of canons, arguments about why works of art and artists dropped out of or into these mysterious containers. The present piece takes Botticelli as an instance – there are many others – of an artist once highly valued, then disregarded, and then restored, sometimes with enthusiasm, sometimes even with veneration, to the notice and respect of those who care for such matters. It was an attractive idea to do some amateur art history before going on, in the next chapter, to think about a fairly secure member of the literary canon, namely Hamlet.

My interest in the life and work of Herbert Horne had preceded the writing of this piece, and was acquired from the late Ian Fletcher, at the time the supreme authority on the 'decadent' poets of the late nineteenth century. I was also indebted to the Warburg Institute, to the late Ernst Gombrich and to Joe Trapp, himself an animated catalogue of that extraordinary library, and the dedicatee of the lectures when they appeared as Forms of Attention *in 1985 (University of Chicago Press).*

Habent sua fata libelli, and so do paintings. The works of Botticelli were ignored for centuries; indeed it has been said, by the historian who has described with most authority the circumstances of his resurrection, that 'probably no other great painter, so far, has endured so long a period of neglect' as Botticelli.[1] He died, as Michael Levey puts it, 'at an awkward moment for his reputation'; but many artists have done that, and risen again much more promptly than Botticelli. He

182

was already, it seems, sinking from his zenith in the last years of his life, probably because by comparison with Leonardo and Michelangelo he was old-fashioned, even deliberately archaistic. Vasari, upon whom continuance of fame so much depended, took an evolutionary view of the art of painting, and although his Life of Botticelli did something to preserve at least the name of the artist, he could not have thought him comparable with the very great men of the next generation, and the biography is defective and perfunctory. Botticelli's frescoes in the Sistine Chapel were overshadowed by their great neighbours, and when they were noticed at all it was mostly by way of unfavourable comparison. Fuseli was not exceptional in criticizing their 'puerile ostentation'.[2] The Dante illustrations could not be admired until Dante himself again came to be so, and indeed they had to wait some time even after that event. In short, the oblivion into which this painter fell soon after his death was so close to being total that one might suppose it could be dissipated only by some extraordinary development in the history of taste.

And that is what occurred. The *Primavera* and *The Birth of Venus* emerged from obscurity and were hung, in 1815, in the Uffizi.[3] The side walls of the Sistine Chapel began to be noticed, even by some admired. In 1836 Alexis-François Rio published *De la poésie chrétienne*, a book containing passages in praise of the Sistine frescoes; it was translated into English in 1854, and Levey thinks it induced Ruskin to look for the first time at Botticelli. (One unpredictable consequence of his doing so was the painter's important appearance in *A la recherche du temps perdu*.) Meanwhile interest in Botticelli grew faster than accurate knowledge of him, and a collection might contain ' "Botticellis" by all sorts of people – but none by Botticelli.'[4] Among the painters, Burne-Jones was an admirer in the early Sixties. Conventional opinion was still easily shocked by the intrusion of pagan themes into Quattrocento painting; but the advocacy of Burne-Jones and, later, of Rossetti encouraged the avant-garde.

There persisted, in the Sixties, a widely shared opinion which must seem surprising to us, that Botticelli limited his appeal by preferring ugly women. A solid history of painting published in that decade described these women as 'coarse and altogether without beauty'.[5] The first Englishman to find a way of correcting this view was Swinburne in

PIECES OF MY MIND

1868. What had hitherto been called clumsiness was now transformed
into a 'faint and almost painful grace', and those ugly faces took on a
'somewhat lean and fleshless beauty, worn down it seems by some
sickness or natural trouble'.[6] Botticelli's archaisms, his unnaturally sad
Madonnas, were no longer faults. Fitted into a later historical tradition,
and a modern programme for painting, he was on the way to joining
the list of artists who had a special relevance to the modern world. Of
this tradition Mario Praz was later to write much of the history in his
book *The Romantic Agony*.

In 1870 Walter Pater published his famous essay, later reprinted
with little change in *The Renaissance* (1873).[7] Though it coincided
with, and in considerable measure caused, the great vogue of Botticelli,
Pater's essay is cautious enough to remember the familiar strictures.
'People have begun to find out the charm of Botticelli's work', he says,
and 'his name, little known in the last century, is quietly becoming
important.' Nevertheless Botticelli is still 'a secondary painter', and
needs a certain amount of justification. There are Madonnas, Pater
admits, who might seem 'peevish-looking' – they conform 'to no
acknowledged type of beauty'. It could even be said that there is
'something in them mean and abject . . . for the abstract lines of the
faces have little nobleness . . . and the colour is wan'. He sees these
Madonnas as detached, uninvolved in their role, like the 'Madonna of
the Magnificat', to whom 'the high cold words' of that canticle mean
little. Nor do the pagan Venuses escape this strangeness. 'Botticelli's
interest,' says Pater, 'is neither in the untempered goodness of
Angelico's saints, nor the untempered evil of Orcagna's *Inferno*, but
with [*sic*] men and women, in their mixed and uncertain condition,
always attractive, clothed sometimes by passion with a character of
loveliness and energy, but saddened perpetually by the shadow upon
them of the great things from which they shrink.'[8]

Yet *The Birth of Venus* reminds him of Ingres, which makes it
modern; and there is also in this painter a strong Greek feeling, as of
the modern world's first look back at the forms of antiquity. Moreover,
the visionary quality of Botticelli significantly resembles that of Dante;
and finally, he is a true manifestation of the wonderful early Renaissance. In a sense all these claims may be resolved into one, the claim
to modernity. The modern includes a new appropriation of Greek art,

184

of Dante, of the newly valued Quattrocento. All that disparate history comes together here, which is why one can find in Botticelli a modern 'sentiment of ineffable melancholy'. His goddess of pleasure, 'the depositary of a great power over the lives of men', is modern in that manner, and the Madonnas are modern in being saddened rather than pleased at what is happening to them. And so Botticelli, who depicted 'the shadow of death in the grey flesh and wan flowers' in a representation of Venus, becomes a modern painter.

Released at last from his historical oubliette, he was celebrated as new, as unacademic, as having affinities with the Japanese art that was now pouring into Paris and London by the tea chest. The cult was the subject of jokes in *Punch* and in *Patience*. Cheap reproductions abounded. But although he grew popular he made on the art of the period an impression that would last into a later modernism:

> Her present image floats into the mind –
> Did Quattrocento finger fashion it,
> Hollow of cheek as if it drank the wind
> And took a mess of shadows for its meat?

Now firmly established in his new setting, Botticelli was accorded a position of eminence from which he was unlikely ever to be completely dislodged. He owed his promotion not to scholars but to artists and other persons of modern sensibility, whose ideas of history were more passionate than accurate, and whose connoisseurship was, as I have said, far from exact. At this stage exact knowledge had no part to play. Opinion, to some extent informed, required, at this modern moment, a certain kind of early Renaissance art; Botticelli, along with some contemporaries – though first among them – provided it. Enthusiasm counted for more than research, opinion for more than knowledge.

I shall now give some account of a man born about the time of the great Botticelli revival, and strongly influenced by Pater as well as by Morris. His part, therefore, was rather to reinforce and secure than to establish Botticelli's fame. Herbert Horne's is not a famous name, and he was denied even a brief entry in the British *Dictionary of National Biography*. Most of our information about his life has been assembled by Ian Fletcher, upon whose published and unpublished work I here to a considerable extent depend.[9] Born in 1864, Horne was pretty exactly the contemporary of Yeats and Arthur Symons. Like them, he studied at no university, but he had very early acquired an expert knowledge of several arts. He was also a precocious and successful collector. Soon he became a follower of Pater. At eighteen he went to study design with the architect and designer A. H. Mackmurdo, founder of the Century Guild, which was dedicated to the unification of the arts. Horne became co-editor, with Mackmurdo, of the journal called *The Century Guild Hobby Horse*, which tried to bring on this unification by publishing new poetry along with articles of artistic and antiquarian interest. Horne himself was painter, bookbinder, architect and designer, an authority on furniture and ancient musical instruments, a remarkable collector of English eighteenth-century painting, and a poet.

Horne seems to have been a rather chilly and disagreeable man – if we are to believe Arthur Symons, a surly, even sinister figure, a successful but dispassionate womanizer, and a secret homosexual. An unpublished poem, reported by Fletcher, speaks of the poet (aged about twenty) as containing in his person 'the torrid and the frigid interwove', a combination reflecting his conviction that 'the poetic nature is the marriage of Heaven and Hell'. The line about the torrid and the frigid recurs in a half-amorous set of letters now in the library of the Warburg Institute, and Fritz Saxl took it as the key to the whole character of Horne, whom he greatly admired. From these letters we may also learn that in 1885 Horne was working at 'verse, painting, designing down to drainpipes', and also painting on a settle an allegorical panel with the Tree of Knowledge and Death in a thornless rose bush. He expresses an admiration for *Parsifal*, though not for *The Ring*, the former perhaps suiting better with a certain rather vague religiosity in the poetry he was writing. With considerably more animation he professes himself keen on the music halls, wishing some rich patron would rent him a stall at the Gaiety.

This ambition will seem odd or vulgar only to people unfamiliar with the preoccupations of artists and aesthetes at this period. Horne was always serious about the arts, and very nearly supreme among them was the art of the dance. His interest in the Gaiety and in the Alhambra was by no means entirely a matter for lusty hours of leisure.

Of course, one object was to pick up the dancing girls; but there is something distinctive about the aesthetics of such activities. The poet Ernest Dowson was grateful to Horne for taking the risk of publishing his poem '*Non sum qualis eram*' in *The Hobby Horse*; and he respected him as the benefactor of Lionel Johnson, and the host of the Rhymers' Club, established in January 1891; but he found him so formidable that he was uneasy about dining alone with him.[10] I mention this to provide some context for Dowson's account of a meeting with Horne and his great friend the artist Selwyn Image (Slade Professor of the History of Art at Oxford) at the back door of the Alhambra on a doubtless chilly night in January 1890. They introduced Dowson to 'several trivial choryphées'. 'There was something grotesque', he goes on 'in the juxtaposition. Horne very erect & slim & aesthetic – and Image the most dignified man in London, a sort of cross in appearance between a secular abbé and Baudelaire, with a manner de 18me siècle – waiting in a back passage to be escort to ballet girls . . . I confess, this danseuse-worship escapes me!!'[11]

But here Dowson, not his friends, is out of step. He holds himself immune to 'danseuse-worship', which was, among his peers, an important cult at the time. The dance was associated with the Mass as well as with the poetic image, and from Loïe Fuller and Jane Avril to Nini Patte-en-l'air, dancers were adored; respectable clergymen as well as artists and professors waited for dancing girls in back alleys, since the ritual required it.[12] The cult was by no means unrelated to that of Botticelli's enigmatic Venuses. (I do not know whether E. H. Gombrich's conjecture that the central figure of the *Primavera* – identified by most, though not all, commentators as Venus – is 'dancing with a slow halting step' had any antecedent in the Nineties.)[13] At all events, a quantity of poetry was dedicated to the dance and to dancers; there were many set pieces on Javanese and other exotic dancers, especially by Arthur Symons, and many on Salome. Out of this movement, and after great transformations, came the dances and dancers of Yeats and Eliot. Waiting in that back alley, Horne was doing nothing out of character for a Nineties artist, a painter of settles, an admirer of *Parsifal*, a lover of Botticelli.

Yeats, like most people who knew him, had reservations about Horne and Image (whom Horne, facetiously no doubt, described as 'the gem of this dim age'); he thought them 'typical figures of transition, doing as an achievement of learning and exquisite taste what their predecessors did in careless abundance'; but he admired Horne, too, for his 'conscious deliberate craft'. Like Saxl after him, he praised the church Horne built near Marble Arch on the model of the cathedral at Pietrasanta in Tuscany (it was destroyed by bombing, like most of Horne's buildings in London). And he credited Horne with 'what I must lack always, scholarship'; he was one of those, said Yeats, who helped to teach him that 'violent energy, which is like a fire of straw, consumes in a few minutes the nervous vitality, and is useless in the arts'.[14] Yeats is writing with the aid of hindsight, knowing of Horne's later achievements, patient and monumental; the burning of damp faggots was, as it turned out, more suited to the work Horne was born to do than any display of genius that burns itself out.

However, for the time being he went on with other tasks, painting settles, cretonnes, fenders, harpsichords; designing and binding books (he published a study of bookbinding in 1894); working as an architect; editing Jacobean plays and Herrick; collecting paintings; writing poems. When Verlaine paid his famous visit to London and Oxford it was Horne who helped Symons to look after him; he was right in the middle of contemporary poetry. His own slim volume, *Diversi Colores*, with his own typography and design, was published in 1891, the year of the Rhymers; it has forty-odd pages of poems strongly influenced by Campion, Herrick, and madrigal verse, with some fairly warm liturgical pieces and some cool love poems. On this evidence Horne was but a small poet; and Ian Fletcher makes only small claims for the verse that remains in manuscript. It is absolutely of its historical moment. Horne was a gifted minor artist at the centre of his world. At his house in Fitzroy Street artists of all kinds gathered: Fletcher lists Dowson and Johnson, Sturge Moore, Yeats, Sickert, Walter Crane, Augustus John, Oscar Wilde, Arthur Symons, Arnold Dolmetsch (who built the harpsichord Horne decorated), and Roger Fry.

But this phase of his life was ending. He grew more and more interested in antiquarian matters, and the files of *The Hobby Horse* show it. He became an authority on the restoration of old buildings, on book illustration, on fifteenth-century woodcuts. He added to his remarkable collection; as Fletcher remarks, the building of it with such slender resources must have required 'a certain ruthlessness and detachment'.[15] He quarrelled with Mackmurdo; *The Hobby Horse* died; and the aesthetic phase was over. Horne grew more and more interested in Italian art. He began to spend much time in Florence, and published a scholarly article on Uccello, but his main interest was Botticelli.

In 1908 he sold a considerable part of his English collection to Edward Marsh; most of it is now in the National Gallery in London. Horne used the proceeds to buy and restore an old palazzo in Florence, acquired in 1912. On his death in 1916 he left Casa Horne to the city of Florence, with provision for its upkeep; but the endowment was spent on unsuccessful investments. The Museo Horne may still be visited, though the most important of its contents have been moved to the Uffizi Gallery.

During these years in Florence Horne applied himself with remarkable dedication to the writing of a long book on Botticelli, and a second volume on the *scuola*; until very recently this second volume was supposed never to have been written, but I am told by Professor Fletcher that it has been found in the Museo Horne. Its publication will be an event of importance. Long before he moved to Florence, Horne, as Yeats tells us, was 'learned in Botticelli' and 'had begun to boast that when he wrote of him there would be no literature, all would be but learning'.[16] And Horne's *Alessandro Filipepi called Sandro Botticelli, Painter of Florence* (1908) might seem to justify that claim. It is regarded by modern art historians as one of the finest books ever written about a Renaissance painter; Sir John Pope-Hennessy, in his preface to the facsimile reprint of 1980, says that it 'has stood the test of time better than almost any other book about art history', and that 'all subsequent Botticelli scholarship depends' on Horne's.[17] Fritz Saxl admired it for its austerity, for Horne's unweaving of the frigid from the torrid; for, says Saxl, he writes 'accurately and disinterestedly in a frigid style which almost obliterates the personality of the author'. To such self-discipline, to the suppression of that 'torrid' streak, we owe, according to Saxl, 'an unimpeachable piece of historical scholarship'.[18]

It would be unreasonable to expect such a book to be very 'torrid'; it is primarily concerned with fact, with correct attribution and description, with offering the world an authentic Botticelli instead of the apocryphal figure it had come so much to admire. Such work demands a proper coolness of manner. Its power derives mostly from pertinacity of research – few documents have been added to those unearthed by Horne in his tireless quest through the Florentine archives – and from a habitual accuracy of eye. And Arthur Symons remarked that when Horne 'sat down to write something dry and hard came into the words'.[19] Yet I cannot think the book quite as frigid as Saxl and others have found it.

As to its design and typography it is, as one would expect of a work by Horne, an object of beauty – a book which could not have been as it is had there not been that movement in the visual arts and crafts in which Horne had been apprenticed and played a part. And the prose of the book has a sort of pedantic vivacity, a modernist archaism, that seems very much the proper style for the man; an 'aesthetic' style, but qualified by a pride in accurate learning. Of course, Horne is conscious of an intention to correct the notions that had grown up with, and fed, the taste for Botticelli. He is quite hard on Pater, a main contention of whose essay 'turns on the mistaken attribution to Sandro of the Palmieri altarpiece';[20] and he explains those 'peevish-looking Madonnas' who conform 'to no acknowledged type or obvious type of beauty' as 'school-pictures . . . in which the imitators of Botticelli exaggerate his mannerisms',[21] but which have come to be regarded as typical of the master himself. Indeed, Horne suggests that it was the resemblance between such pictures and the fashionable second-rate art of Burne-Jones that ensured their popularity. However, Pater had some excuse; Horne also explains that in 1870, when the essay appeared, 'Botticelli was nominally represented at the National Gallery by three Madonnas of his school, two of them being "Tondi", and the only genuine works by him then in the collections, passed under the names of Masaccio . . . and Filippino Lippi. . . . No wonder the attendant angels depress their heads so naively'.[22] And Pater, with all his errors, wrote what Horne regards as 'still the subtlest and most suggestive appreciation of Botticelli, in a personal way, which has yet been written',[23] a work therefore intimately related to 'the peculiarly English cult of Botticelli, which now [in the 1880s] became a distinctive trait of a phase of thought and taste, or of what passed for such, as odd and extravagant as any of our odd and extravagant time'.[24] Pater is one of the two dedicatees of Horne's book. Its main purpose, he assures us, is the accumulation of information, but especially connoisseurship. We may think it in some sense also the tribute of a sardonic personality, now matured, to the affectations and enthusiasms of his formative years; a rejection of the nonsense, of the false modernity, in terms which nevertheless accept the rightness of the valuation put upon Botticelli in 'our odd and extravagant time', and pay to the achievement of those years the compliment not only of the dedication to Pater, but also the greater one of a style that still acknowledges Pater. Like Yeats's, Horne's prose always remembers that master, conscious as it is of its own elegance and exactness, conscious too of its possession (proper also to the true though not the phantom Botticelli) of an *aria virile* to which Pater's could lay no claim.

Again and again we find, in this work supposed uniformly severe and scholarly, traces of Paterian taste and manner. Of the *Adoration of the Magi* Horne writes that it is the driest and most naturalistic of the works: 'nowhere is Botticelli's peculiar temperament obtruded into the painting; its grave and reasonable beauty nowhere disturbed by those "bizzarie", that "strangeness in the proportion", by which such works as the "Spring" and the "Calumny" are distinguished'.[25] More strikingly, he says of the *Primavera* that 'in no picture which possesses the sentiment of beauty at all in the same degree, are there so many forms and traits so far removed from the accepted ideas of beauty . . . In conception antique, solemn, religious; in expression modern, as it then was, Florentine, bizarre, fantastic . . . He derives the subject matter of his picture wholly from antiquity; but of Greek or Roman sculpture, or painting, he knows little or nothing; nothing, at any rate, that can hinder or distort his vision. And so just that which chilled or destroyed Post-Raphaelite art, served only in Botticelli to quicken his vision of the world around him.'[26] It seems doubtful that the insight could have found just this expression if Pater had not come beforehand. The same may be said of Horne's account of the picture of St Augustine in the Ognissanti, which takes up Pater's observation of Botticelli's 'Dantesque' quality and gives it precision, at the same time emphasizing what Pater did not understand, the *aria virile* thought by his contemporaries to be the painter's distinctive trait: 'We, at the present day, are apt to think that "undercurrent of original sentiment" which runs through his works, and even the exaggeration of that sentiment in the many works of his school which pass under his name, as the distinguishing character of Botticelli's manner; but for the Florentines of his own day this forcible, this Dantesque air, which in the fresco of St Augustine is first clearly shown, this *aria virile* as the Florentines themselves called it, was that which distinguished his work, from the work of his disciples and contemporaries'.[27] Horne will even ask tentatively whether the secret of the painter's greatness may not be that the modern view of him – as a visionary painter – and the contemporary view, which admired his virility, might be 'from their several standpoints, equally true'.[28] But then the historian in Horne prevails. When restorations have reduced the original force of a painting by inserting passages that are sweeter, or 'prettified', as in the 'Tondo of the Magnificat', he is sure that the 'misfortune ... has contributed not a little to the extraordinary popularity of the picture'.[29] When Pater finds in that painting the bizarre interest of a heretical Virgin, he may be credited with 'an exquisite personal revery' but he has also done some harm to the truth.[30] Similarly, the 'cadaverous' colour, as Pater called it, of *The Birth of Venus* is entirely the consequence of the deterioration of the pigment.[31]

It cannot be doubted that when it came to a choice between 'that modernity of sentiment and interpretation which is apt to distort our perception',[32] and the historical fact, Horne consciously chose the latter. If Ruskin finds 'strangeness and gloom' pervasive in Botticelli's work, that is only because the *aria virile* would seem so to 'a critic who, in reality, took as his criterion in all questions of painting, the refined and gentle art of the English landscape painters, and the English Pre-Raphaelites'.[33]

It is interesting to watch Horne at his business of tracing the emergence, in Botticelli's manner, of the virile air. He is no mere archivist, and can command that air himself, as in his vivacious and pure-styled account of the Pazzi conspiracy to assassinate Lorenzo de' Medici in 1478. His excuse for dwelling on the event was that, after the failure of the plot, Botticelli was commissioned, in accordance with custom, to make effigies of the condemned or executed conspirators. He put them in a fresco above the door of the old Dogana, but after a more successful coup some years later they were destroyed. However, the need, in these works, to emulate the naturalism of Andrea da Castagno, who had done the like before him, gave Botticelli a new 'rugged power'[34] which thenceforth showed up in his other work, first in the *St Augustine* of 1480; the Sistine frescoes, painted before 1482, show it fully. To the expression of this conjecture Horne brings a rugged power of his own, in sharp contrast to the period prose he had left behind him.

All the same, he sees Botticelli as growing increasingly mannered and nervous as his fame was eclipsed by the new school and his line of life crossed by that of Savonarola; he reverts more and more, 'not only in method, but in design and sentiment, to that tradition of Giottesque painting, from which he had so largely derived his art'.[35] And here, perhaps, is another excuse for those who, during the revival, got Botticelli wrong. There is an element of truth, after all, in both Ruskin and Pater; Botticelli has his 'discordant traits', his bizarrerie, his 'amatorious sweetness', and his archaisms.[36] In any case they played a part in restoring to our attention what Horne is willing to call 'the supreme accomplishment of modern art'.[37]

It might be reasonable, then, to characterize Horne's effort as an attempt to modify what had become the stock responses of modernity to this painter without completely denying his affinity to the relatively ignorant enthusiasts who preceded him; he wished to give to languid revery an exactness of registration, a precision that it lacked, though he did not wish altogether to disperse its achievement. If he held it at a critical distance, he also mistrusted the more pretentious minuteness of academic art history. If the aesthetes exaggerated Botticelli's sense of 'loss or displacement',[38] the professors could be nastily vainglorious: 'Professor Schmarsow has informed us exactly which of the figures of the Popes [in the Sistine frescoes] were painted by Melozzo; but as I am unable to follow the arguments of the egregious Professor, not having studied in the Academy of Lagado, I must leave his conclusions undiscussed'.[39]

And it is true, after all, that the professors had little or nothing to do with the revival of Botticelli. It was the work of opinion, never to be observed without its shadow, ignorance. And it was Horne, no professor – he had never studied in any academy whatsoever – who did most to reinforce opinion with knowledge, and so give to his subject, not immunity to future loss of regard, but certainly a new standing, a new attitude in the flow of time.

Aby Warburg, born in 1866, was Horne's junior by two years, and also a child of the decade that made Botticelli's revival an accomplished fact. His origins were very different; the son of a Hamburg banker, he was destined to be head of the firm, but he became a scholar instead, and a remarkable one. E. H. Gombrich's admirable 'intellectual biography' of Warburg[40] gives one a rather intimate view of an education that was wholly different from any that could be got, then or now, in Britain or the United States, and certainly a world away from the quite informal training of Horne. Warburg was the pupil of great men now largely forgotten – of Hermann Usener, remembered perhaps because of the phrase 'momentary deity', and the championship of Ernst Cassirer; of Karl Lamprecht, Anton Springer, Carl Justi; and of that August Schmarsow who inadvertently irritated Horne.[41]

Most of Warburg's teachers assumed that the findings of modern science ought to be applied to the humanities. They were affected, one way or another, by Hegel, but also by evolutionary theory, and by the tenacity of the primitive – the manifestations, in the life of an evolved civilization, of images or of behaviour that originate in some residual or atavistic layer of the individual mind or of the race, or simply of civilization. Lamprecht, whom Gombrich describes as the most influential of Warburg's masters, divided cultural history into five periods, each a further displacement of the primitive 'symbolic'; and Springer was interested in the ways in which the Middle Ages and the Renaissance looked at classical antiquity. It was he who called this the study of 'das Nachleben des Antike', an expression later strongly associated with Warburg.

Usener's quest for 'spiritual traces of vanished times' in later cultural epochs,[42] and the many other rather similar kinds of research in the latter half of the century, may suggest a quite different variety of *fin-de-siècle* preoccupation than those of Horne and his circle. These scholars were concerned with the construction of theories intended to have great explanatory power. One naturally thinks of a much greater man, Freud (though Warburg himself did not care to do so) as one concerned also with the relation of the primitive, and of primitive symbols, to civilization. I shall return briefly to Freud and his relevance to these questions in my third lecture; here I mention him only as a name more familiar than the others who sought something like total historical explanations, though they looked primarily to art for their evidence of symbolic survival.

Warburg himself sketches systems in his notebooks, but the pattern of the interests underlying them is clear and persistent; he rarely allowed his theoretical speculations to escape from his notes, and he was pained by the difficulty of reconciling them with his observations. As Gombrich delicately explains, Warburg's psychological constitution was such that he must have been especially interested in the idea that history demonstrates a progress from an archaic state of terror, and that symbols or images proper to that early state may recur under civilized conditions, but purged of their original dionysiac horror.[43] This lifelong sufferer from anxiety therefore had a personal motive for studying not only the survival of antique forms, but also the evolved conditions under which they might later manifest themselves. Springer had taught him that just as the historian has always to interpret the past from his own historically limited position, so too 'the object of interpretation – in the case of art – is itself a reinterpretation of some earlier source'.[44] Warburg accordingly combined a perpetual interest in the recurrent transformations of ancient symbols with minute research into the social and pictorial circumstances of their reappearances. He did not forget what Lamprecht had taught him – that all artefacts are evidence; and he knew that there was nothing in the history of thought – whether of art, religion, magic, or science – that was in principle irrelevant to his enquiries.

Like most ambitious thinkers, he used other men's thoughts and systems of ideas as stimulants rather than as schemes he might or might not adopt; he was not looking for something ready-made, but for hints, for the stimulus that might give rise to a brainwave of his own. The 'afterlife of antiquity' became his own subject – not in the old manner, the manner of Winckelmann, who thought of the classical influence as calm and idealizing, but instead as the memory of what had been tamed and put to human use. Images which had their origin in archaic terror, he believed, would recur in more reassuring contexts; they would then encapsulate the mentality of another epoch.

'God dwells in detail' was a motto of Warburg's;[45] but his observation of detail, his choice of interests, depended upon a larger need for a theory that would accumulate symbolic recurrence in changing historical conditions. After the First World War he spent six years in an asylum; on his return to work in 1924 he was still looking for a theory of transindividual memory. He found help in the doctrines of Richard Semon,[46] which concerned engrams or memory traces in the individual, and he extended this notion so that he could think of recurrent forms and symbols as engrams or traces in the memory of a culture. Artists make contact with these mnemic energies, and the history of art can be seen as a history of reinterpretations, updatings of these symbols, in the course of which they are purged of their original ecstasy and terror. In this way, he said, 'humanity's holdings in suffering become the possessions of the humane'.[47] He could, for example, compare Manet's *Déjeuner sur l'herbe* with the sarcophagus that, through Renaissance intermediaries, is its source, and call Manet's picture the transformation of a 'phobic engram'.[48]

Such ideas have a practical value quite apart from any interest they may have as theories; they provide methods of studying detail, and of choosing which details to study. In 1893 Warburg wrote his thesis on Botticelli's *Birth of Venus* and *Spring*. How did Botticelli and his patrons imagine the antique? To answer these questions calls for detailed knowledge of such matters as the relations between artists, patrons, and humanists. Warburg provided some of the answers, especially with respect to the literary sources of these paintings, and though there are many rival proposals for the programmes of the works, this early study of Warburg continues to be cited and, usually, endorsed.[49]

On the face of it, nothing could less resemble the essay of Pater, or even the assured connoisseurship of Horne, than this piece of German art history. Yet Warburg certainly had, in common with Horne, a fastidious dislike for the new vulgar cult of the Quattrocento and especially of Botticelli – indeed, for all that Horne meant to exclude when he told Yeats there would be in his book on Botticelli 'no literature'. And perhaps they had something more positive in common.

Warburg observed in the running female figure of the *Primavera*, the breeze blowing her dress against her body, a specific classical motif – an instance of the *Nachleben* of an antique form, which also constituted a sort of emancipation from the stiff northern fashions of contemporary Florentine taste. The literary source of the poem – Ovid, as mediated by the contemporary poet Poliziano – offers a similar modern version of the antique; but the visual image has a special suggestiveness. The female figure with agitated drapery, as it some-times occurs in late fifteenth-century art, was named by Leonardo the 'Nympha', and Warburg borrowed the word.[50] Long before, Hippolyte Taine had singled out for admiration a figure in Ghirlandaio's fresco of the nativity of St John the Baptist in Santa Maria Novella. 'In the "Nativity of the Virgin" the girl in a silk skirt, who comes in on a visit, is the plain demure young lady of good condition; in the "Nativity of St John" another, standing, is a medieval duchess; near her the servant bringing in fruits, in statuesque drapery, has the impulse, the vivacity and force of an antique nymph, the two ages and the two orders of beauty thus meeting and uniting in the simplicity of the same true sentiment.'[51] But Taine goes on to admit that such pictures, though interesting, lack skill, lack action and colour, belonging as they do to the dawn or first light of the Renaissance. Warburg did not feel the need to make these Vasari-inspired concessions; Ghirlandaio's Nympha interested him so much that he projected a study of the motif.

In a partly facetious correspondence of Warburg's with a friend equally interested in the Nympha, she is compared with Salome, who danced 'with her death-dealing charm in front of the licentious tetrarch', and also with Judith. 'There was', as Gombrich says, 'some-thing in the figure which struck the two students of art as the embodi-ment of passion'; and although Gombrich finds an explanation for this enthusiasm in the resemblances between the Nympha and the 'new woman' of Warburg's own time, and the call for less restricted move-ment in sport and in dancing, he also affirms that 'none of Warburg's published writings bears the stamp of the *fin de siècle* and of the fashionable Renaissance cult of those years to anything like the same degree as this abortive plan'. The Nympha, whether in Botticelli or in Ghirlandaio, was an embodiment of Renaissance 'paganism', an 'eruption of primitive emotion through the crust of Christian self-control', or perhaps an instance of their being made 'compatible', a word borrowed by Warburg from Herbert Spencer.[52]

'Have I encountered her before?' Is she a memory reaching back over 'one and a half millennia'? Is the Nympha the Maenad, or a trace of that figure erupting in the art of the Quattrocento as Salome into that of the *fin de siècle*? Warburg is undoubtedly thinking of her in a manner for which, much later, he was to find concrete terms in Semon; she is the reinterpretation of an engram, harnessing the energy of the old image, civilizing it. She represents the way in which antique forms may be modern. By understanding Botticelli's communion with the past we are afforded an understanding of our own.

So, in his very different way, Warburg too was fascinated by the dancing Salome; for him as for Yeats, such a figure represented the survival into modernity of images perpetuated in a process of memory that transcended the individual. What marks the difference between the self-educated poet and the scholar of many seminars and libraries is partly a matter of tone, but more of the type of intellectual system that each, according to his formation, chose. Warburg's explanations tend to have a scientific character, as his training required; Yeats preferred magic.

Over the years Warburg built a large, interdisciplinary, and idiosyncratic library, at first housed in the Institute at Hamburg. He called it an 'observation post for cultural history'. Anything that had some bearing on the *Nachleben* ought to be there.[53] For the study of detail and recurrence he used large screens, on which one could arrange images and study their mnemic interrelations; these screens he would carry across Europe in trains, a rich man's instruments for the study of cultural memory traces, a service to Mnemosyne, whose name was to give him the title of his last projected book. On such screens one might see the relation between Judith and an ancient female headhunter and also the sublimated image of a girl carrying a basket of fruit; she might be the Nympha as the Hora of Autumn, or Rachel at the well, in Botticelli's Vatican fresco. More playfully, perhaps, one connects a maenad with a female golfer. Gombrich illustrates the Nympha screen: a tondo by Filippo Lippi, examples of the classical origin of blown veils, an early Christian ivory, a photograph of an Italian peasant with a head basket, debased nymphs on travel posters. Warburg called the screen *Das Märchen vom Fraulein Schnellbring* – another jest, but he also associated her with manic states, in himself and in cultural history.[54]

It is easy to see that his work was both facilitated and constrained by his own psychology, and he pursued it passionately without ever fully justifying his method. Gombrich remarks that it is impossible to tell where 'the metaphor of survival ends and where a belief in the independent life of these entities [the archaic symbols] begins'.[55] But perhaps it is never simple to distinguish between the systematic expression of beliefs, and needs or drives more obscure, for which such systems may serve as metaphors.

The study of the *Nachleben* has taken new forms, though they are recognizably in the Warburg tradition, and testify to the continuance of his passion for detail, his cult of Mnemosyne. He was himself unusually aware that forgetting and mistaking were important parts of the action of memory. He pointed to the errors of the Florentine *camerata*, which sought to revive ancient music, misunderstood it, and so helped to make possible modern opera.[56] He knew that the pagan deities, which had survived in almost unrecognizable forms until restored to their old splendour and granted their original attributes in the Renaissance, were nevertheless not what they had been; their potency was altered, their place and play in the minds of later men was different; even an antique statue could not be looked on with ancient eyes. What is made of such things, he said, 'depends upon the subjective make-up of the late-born rather than on the objective character of the classical heritage. . . . Every age has the renaissance it deserves'.[57] He was none the less anxious to correct the misunderstandings of earlier scholars as to the true historical character of the Italian Renaissance, hoping no doubt that his own age deserved the truth.

His Institute, smuggled out of Nazi Germany, received in London, and now firmly established in Bloomsbury, had a history he could not possibly have foreseen, and work is done there that he could not have predicted. The language spoken in the corridors is no longer for the most part German, and the present director is the first to have English as his native language. But the library remains recognizably Warburg's, designed, as they say, to lead you not to the book you're looking for but to the one you need. The photographic collection still services Warburgian screens though I don't suppose the images thereon are thought of as engrams, and the familiar Warburg lecturing style still requires two projectors for the comparison of images. Over the door is written, in Greek characters, MNEMOSYNE.

'Of the general ideas to which I attach so much importance', wrote Warburg, 'it will perhaps be said or thought one day that there was at least one thing to be said for these erroneous schematisms, that they excited him to churn up individual facts which had been unknown before.'[58] About his having done much useful churning up of facts there is absolutely no argument; but much more than fact survives. It is perfectly possible to see in, for example, Panofsky's work on renaissance and renascence, and on the interplay of history and interpretation – on the *Nachleben*, as it were, of theories concerning the *Nachleben* – or in Gombrich's very different interest in memory and symbolism and his eye for the significant detail, transformations of recognizably Warburgian themes and precepts. When Sir Ernst recently told the American Academy of Arts and Science that the humanities were the memory of culture, he was, perhaps with deliberation, saying what his predecessor might have said on such an occasion. As we have seen, the interpretation of the Botticelli Venuses continues with many variations; but however they differ, they are all conscious of the tradition in which they have their place, and of Warburg's importance in its constitution. It is indeed inconceivable that such interpretation should ever come to a stop, or that it should not contain error, or that the mood of a later generation's understanding should exactly imitate that of its predecessors. If we have systems they will not be the systems of those predecessors. As Michael Podro says at the end of his study of the German art-historical tradition, 'no system, no systematic viewpoint could be regarded as identical with our thought and viewpoint. To make such an identification would be incompatible with the mind retaining its freedom'.[59] And yet there *is* continuity, there *is* a tradition.

Here then are two scholars, one of them bringing to the Quattrocento and especially to Botticelli all that he had learned from a largely German tradition of scholarship, the other discovering his admiration for the painter and his interest in Florentine history as he worked and played among the artists, poets, and dancers of *fin-de-siècle* London. Florence was the source and focus of their wholly independent enquiries; had there been no ignorant vogue of Botticelli it is hard to imagine that the two could ever have met or, indeed, wanted to meet.

But meet they did, and in Florence. Academic and amateur, each respected the other's scholarship, and Horne speaks of Warburg in tones very different from those in which he referred to that other German Quattrocento specialist, Schmarsow. They became friends, and when Warburg was not in Florence they corresponded. Then war divided them; but when Horne was dying in Florence in 1916 Warburg went to see him, citizen though he was of an enemy nation, and Warburg a patriotic German.

So these two scholarly lives improbably came together; but Horne's *Nachleben* has diverged very widely from Warburg's. Like its founder, the Museo Horne is little known, while Warburg's Institute, founded in Hamburg, flourishes transformed in Horne's native city, indeed in Bloomsbury, the scene of so much of Horne's activity; not a city or a quarter in which Warburg would ever have imagined it. Horne was not rich, and in any case would not have wanted to establish an academy; like his friend Berenson, he deeply distrusted German scholarship. All the two – Warburg and Horne – had in common were a belief that truth lived in detail, and a passion for the Quattrocento and especially for Botticelli – a painter of whom, had they been born a century earlier, they might never have heard or, if born half a century earlier, might not have considered worth more than a glance or a passing thought.

That they were both affected by a movement of taste over which they had no control, I hope I have shown. Horne, for all his strictures, polite or otherwise, on Pater, Ruskin, and the art of his youth, could not escape altogether from what he called 'literature'; his Botticelli may have the *aria virile* attributed to the painter by his tough Florentine contemporaries, but he is also the visionary, melancholy and some-times bizarre, whom Pater saw, or thought he saw. Warburg, though so much more remote from avant-garde myth and fashion, could not altogether avoid infection by the Romantic Agony, nor by the association of the dancer with the secret perfections of art that so dominated the aesthetic thought of his younger years. He too sought to be objective; but there is an important difference in the manner of his objectivity and Horne's. Warburg considered the significance of detail (of the Nymph's drapery or her flowers) against a background of cultural history that had no discernible limits; he needed, in principle, all knowledge to understand the cultural memory. Its archaic recurrences in an evolving civilization must be studied in science, magic, and religion, as well as in art. Behind him stood those powerful, schematizing professors. Horne's confidence in his own eye and his own mind must have seemed extraordinary to Warburg. He was not at all aware, so far as one can tell, of any difficulty to be faced in seeing his subject with a time-transcending eye. He has no interest in method; the archives are enough. And if we set aside, as of course we should not, the peculiar chill distinction of his prose, and his admirable conduct of a complicated narrative, we might think of his book as a work to be subsumed by other books, as the archives yield more information (though in fact they have yielded little; it does not take Pope-Hennessy long, in his preface to the new edition, to list the points on which Horne has been superseded or shown to have been wrong). There is behind Horne's work no such theory of art and culture as Warburg wanted, no symbolism, no doctrine of memory, whether literally or metaphorically intended. There is no myth to discount, except perhaps that of the independence of empirical observation from theory.

Botticelli became canonical not through scholarly effort but by chance, or rather by opinion. He was thereafter available to these two scholars, who accepted while wishing to inform that opinion, who were touched by the taste of their own time, but who brought to the task of converting opinion into knowledge methods and temperaments very diverse. In Horne's masterpiece there is little to discard, which may represent a failure of intellectual ambition. From Warburg there is a heritage not only of findings but of methods and attitudes; and these, as he knew, would need to be modified or even discarded, either because of discoverable faults or because it is in the nature of such things to be rejected, because new work may need new thinking about the whole huge subject, even if what must be seen anew is minute. What is left is a deposit of know-how, hints as to possible procedures, ways of deciding the true nature of problems. The relegation of 'theory' into partial oblivion may sometimes be slowed, in as much as powerful institutions can, up to a point, slow temporal change. But usually it is quick, and its use is primarily the consolidation of some work of art, perhaps only in explanation of why it *is* canonical, why it should call for repeated attempts at interpretation. There are what Donne grandly called 'unconcerning things, matters of fact', and Horne discovered a great many of them, as perhaps he did about the uncanonical members of the *scuola*. But they will not maintain the life of a work of art from one generation to another. Only interpretation can do that, and it may be as prone to error as the ignorant opinion that first brought Botticelli into question among the learned.

11

Cornelius and Voltemand

The frequency of doublings, of plot, character and language in Hamlet *had long been noticed, but it was while I was lecturing on the play at Columbia University in 1983 that I was struck by its almost obsessive interest in the figure called hendiadys, the expression of one through two. I listed many instances and wrote a draft of the part of this chapter that expressly deals with them. This I showed with modest pride to Edward Tayler, an excellent Shakespearian, who directed me to a recent article of George T. Wright, a brilliant study of hendiadys in Shakespeare that shows with statistics how deep was Shakespeare's interest in this device. Idiosyncratically used, hendiadys reaches a statistical peak in* Hamlet; *next in order of frequency are plays just before and after it. Hendiadys is rare before 1599, and falls away after it.*

Like anybody who thinks he has found something unnoticed by others, I was a little downcast by this discovery, but I went on with my essay, feeling that I was looking at the matter from a different angle and perhaps more rashly than Wright, whose work deservedly won the top prize of the year from the Modern Language Association of America. Here hendiadys is central, but considered not only as a rhetorical device given unusually heavy use but as one acute, almost pathological, instance of a more general habit of doubling, to be seen not only in Hamlet *but in many other works of Shakespeare. Whether everything I say here is beyond dispute I am not sure, and am still uneasy about the passage about Bushy's speech to the Queen in* Richard II. *Have I got it wrong in suspecting that Bushy, or Shakespeare, got it wrong? More might have been said about that. As to* Hamlet, *it might have been illuminating to compare the occurrences of hendiadys in all three contemporary texts of the play (Q1, Q2, F), a slow job but it would probably not have been a waste of time. But the aim of this chapter was to say something new about* Hamlet, *and to argue that despite the enormous size of the literature on the play it will always be possible to do so.*

We have seen Botticelli rescued from oblivion, or something like it, and at least begun to consider how it was done, and what the implications are of its having been done thus. I now turn to the almost opposite case of *Hamlet* – a work that from the first appears to have enjoyed great celebrity, and which, it is safe to say, could only be deprived of our esteem by some almost unimaginable revolution in taste.

It is true that attempts have been made to dislodge *Hamlet* from its eminent position in the secular canon. Voltaire, in the course of his long campaign against Shakespeare, said the play was without rule, *une pièce grossière et barbare*, that would in France be suitable only for peasants.[1] Obviously he took a wholly different view of the qualities honest men should venerate in art; and his view did not prevail. Had it done so, we should all be living in a completely different world, for so great a change in our ways of estimating value could not occur without an upheaval of even greater extent in culture and society. Tolstoy, who chose *King Lear* as his special target, was aware of the extent of his task, for he was attacking not only a grossly overvalued play but the corruption of a society which upheld that valuation, to the detriment of its members. Of *Hamlet*, he complained that the hero had no character at all, despite the encomia of the learned. Shakespeare idolatry was the creation, he believed, of the German Enlightenment, which he regarded as disastrously irreligious. To succeed in his assault he would have had to succeed with his own new religion, and contrive a future society the happier for not having Shakespeare or, for that matter, *Anna Karenina*. Another famous attack, Rymer's on *Othello*, was based on the critic's conviction that he knew exactly what a tragedy ought to be, as to both its form and its ethical purpose. Time demonstrated that he did not; that *Othello* was capable, as on the evidence of Gabriel Harvey *Hamlet* had been from the beginning, of pleasing the wiser sort.

That it did so by offering them the possibility of saying the most extraordinarily different things about it one can see from the history of *Hamlet* criticism. Conklin supplies the evidence for masculine and primitive, humane, gay and solemn, pensive and genteel, weighty and wild, cautious, coarse, heroic, weak, supersubtle, and delaying Hamlets. In 1778 the prince was naturalized German, and Goethe produced not only the 'flagrant impressionism' of his critique in *Wilhelm Meister* but some observations, possibly in the end more influential, on the partly occulted integrity and unity of the whole play, as distinct from the character.

Behind Goethe, and behind Friedrich Schlegel and Coleridge also, one may discern the loom of philosophical meditations proper to themselves and their time rather than to Shakespeare and his, and it is the mark of a powerful critic that one can do this. Such a critic will alter the current of traditional commentary by force, and that force is the product of a mind itself alienated from the commonplace by operations on a broader scale than normal criticism can or need attempt. The effect of such work is always to make the work under consideration look different, to alter its internal balances, to attend to what had been thought marginal as if it must be brought closer to the centre, even at the cost of losing what had hitherto seemed manifestly central.

Since we have no experience of a venerable text that ensures its own perpetuity, we may reasonably say that the medium in which it survives is commentary. All commentary on such texts varies from one generation to the next because it meets different needs; the need to go on talking is paramount, the need to do it rather differently is equally urgent, and not less so because the provision of commentary is a duty that has now devolved upon a particular profession, a profession which, at any rate until recently, has tended to judge the achievement of its members by their ability to say something new about canonical texts without defacing them. Respect for the plain sense is a very ancient restriction on wild interpretation, but the hermeneutical guidelines or *middot* of the early rabbis were not merely restrictive; they gave one useful tips about how to achieve new interpretations. If we were now to construct our own *middot*, one of them might well be: what has been thought marginal may belong more properly in the centre. Fifty years ago, 'character' was ousted from its central position (though not, I think, among ordinary readers and playgoers and, of course, not among actors), and there was a great deal of work on imagery and on the plays as poetry. It does not matter that much of this work is forgotten, or that we hear less about the Freudian Hamlet than the Lacanian – if, indeed, we now hear much of that. There must be new appraisals, and they will be possible only so long as new relations, new adjustments of centre and margin, are perceived in the play and given licit expression in commentary.

It may be that to be conscious of this state of affairs is to recognize an element of play in all commentary – as, indeed, the rabbis did, without for a moment supposing that what they were doing wasn't serious; the most serious thing in the world, in fact. I mention this because in what follows I am conscious that a sort of game is being played. *Hamlet* is not the Torah, but it can still permit or be patient of attentions that are, in a very restricted and 'ludic' sense, quasi-rabbinical.

I begin by reflecting, which seems the right word, on shadows and shows, on substance and its images, and on mirrors, in some earlier works of Shakespeare. Lucrece is troubled by shadows, and hopes Tarquin might be, in his turn. Hecuba in the Troy tapestry is a 'sad shadow' or reflection of Lucrece, a silent image of herself to which she can give speech. This is a deceptive doubling, for Lucrece's resemblance to Hecuba lies only in the fact that the rape was comparable to the fall of Troy, Hecuba's city treacherously penetrated. But Hecuba is an image of the ruin.

In Sonnet 37 the son is called the father's shadow, but is active when his father cannot be, and so has more substance than the father. The beloved, as seen in a dream, may be only a shadow; but his 'shadow shadows doth make bright' (43); and this collision of shadows, which produces a bright image, promotes in the next line a collision of 'forms' – 'How would thy shadow's form form happy show' – where the noun doubles the verb and produces a show, an appearance, a display, that is here, though not everywhere, 'happy'. There is no shadow without a substance, no show without a form that forms it. A beauty such as that of the youth must have many shadows, types of which it is the fulfilling antitype. 'What is your substance, whereof are you made / That millions of strange shadows on you tend?' (53). Those types may be Helen, or Adonis, or perhaps a rose ('Why should poor beauty indirectly seek / Roses of shadow, since his rose is true?' [67]), that is: actual roses are insubstantial, just phenomenal surrogates of the noumenal rose, the youth.

The relation between the substance and its representation as shadow or reflection or show is always a difficult one, and – as I have hinted – may tempt the poet or his critic into theological and philosophical complexities. The word 'show' itself is very slippery. Does the 'sweet virtue' of the youth answer his 'show' or is his beauty like that of Eve's apple, which was only an apparent good (93)? 'They that have power to hurt and will do none, / That do not do the thing they most do show' (94) is a celebrated difficulty, but at least the contrast between what appears and what is actually done is clear. And even in the Sonnets the world, which is a stage, is also a show ('this huge stage presenteth nought but shows' [15]). Shadow and substance, show and reality, are paired opposites. Together they express paradox, impossibility, *concordia discors* or *discordia concors*, something that, perhaps fascinatingly, comes between a lover and his desire: 'the master-mistress of my passion' (20). Sex is an emblem of these conjoined disjuncts, as we shall see.

In the theatre, itself the double of the world, its own Globe, Shakespeare early showed an interest in doubles. The comic tradition offered him twins, and in *Comedy of Errors* he doubled Plautus's doubles. *Two Gentlemen of Verona* has a pair of lovers, one faithful and the other not, together with a great deal of talk about shadow and substance. The treacherous Proteus asks Silvia, his friend's beloved, for her picture:

> For since the substance of your perfect self
> Is else devoted, I am but a shadow;
> And to your shadow will I make true love.

Julia, his own girl, happens to be eavesdropping on this scene, and remarks, aside, 'If 'twere a substance you would sure deceive it, / And make it but a shadow as I am'; and Silvia then answers Proteus: 'I am very loath to be your idol, sir, / But since your falsehood shall become you well / To worship shadows and adore false shapes . . .' she will let him have her picture (iv.2.123 ff). This beautiful little scene is a lot more complicated than it looks. Proteus rather drags in the shadow-substance opposition to say that Silvia's being sworn to Valentine reduces him to a condition in which he is fit only to love an image, not a substance. Julia remarks that if that shadow-image were a substance, the perfidy of Proteus would soon reduce it to a shadow anyway; this is what he has done to her, and she is in another sense a shadow, being in disguise as a boy, and so a shadow or false show of her substantial self. Silvia, perhaps noticing the word 'devoted', reflects that a shadow is an image and an image is an idol, a graven image, so that it is appropriate for the false Proteus to bow down before something equally false, like a false image of the true God. Of course everybody concerned is playing a part in a show, and indeed the two females are shows in another sense, for Silvia is a boy pretending to be a girl, a master-mistress, and Julia a boy pretending to be a girl pretending to be a boy.

Since all this doubling is very theatrical, we need not be surprised that it is not confined to comedy. *Titus Andronicus* shadows the Ovidian story of Tereus. Ovid's rapist is replaced in Shakespeare by two rapists, Demetrius and Chiron. The torment of Lavinia is double that of Ovid's Philomela, who had her tongue cut out to prevent her revealing the identity of her assailant; Lavinia also has her hands cut off to prevent her writing the names, writing being a double or shadow of speech, available to the shadow Lavinia but not to the substantial, oral Philomela. Thus the play invites us to emulate the crazy hero, and take 'false shadows for true substances' (iii.2.80). The figure is used repeatedly in the *Henry VI* plays, sometimes not very persuasively (Talbot as shadow of his substance, the troops, *I Henry VI* iii.5.45), sometimes perfunctorily, as when King Charles of France, reduced to the status of viceroy, will be but a shadow of his former self (*I Henry VI*, v.4.133 ff) or when (*II Henry VI*, i.1.13–14) an ambassador is the shadow of his king; but sometimes with more of the usual complexity, as when Clarence and Warwick in *III Henry VI* (iv.6) become the double shadow of King Henry, with the suggestion that, although the king must be the substance, it is the shadows who do the real work.

More or less simple variations on the theme crop up in other history plays (see, for instance, *King John* ii.1.496 ff), but the only occurrence I need to discuss here is the difficult one in *Richard II*. Bushy is consoling the Queen after the departure of Richard (ii.2.144 ff):

> Each substance of a grief hath twenty shadows,
> Which show like grief itself, but is not so;
> For sorrow's eyes, glazed with blinding tears,
> Divides one thing entire to many objects,
> Like perspectives, which rightly gaz'd upon
> Show nothing but confusion; ey'd awry
> Distinguish form; so your sweet Majesty
> Looking awry upon your lord's departure,
> Find shapes of grief, more than himself, to wail,
> Which, look'd on as it is, is nought but shadows
> Of what it is not.

Bushy's consolatory conceit is based on the optical trick called anamorphosis, which interested some sixteenth-century painters; a famous example is Holbein's picture *The French Ambassadors* (1533), in which between the feet of the two men there is an elliptical shape, without form when looked at from the front but, if eyed awry, representing a skull, a memento mori. Sometimes these formless shapes could be interpreted only by the use of prisms and lenses; over a century after Holbein, memorial portraits of Charles I were thus kept secret. Ordinary people were familiar with anamorphosis in the form of 'perspectives', double pictures, usually portraits, painted on the same ground in such a way that you saw one of them if you looked at the painting from one side and the other if you moved to the other side; from the front you saw only confusion. Shakespeare mentions these trick pictures more than once; see, for example, *Antony and Cleopatra* (ii.5.116–17), 'Though he be painted one way like a Gorgon / The other way's a Mars'. The most important use of the idea, as we shall see, is in *Twelfth Night*.

Bushy, then, is saying that the tearful eyes of the Queen are multiplying one substantial grief into many shadowy griefs, griefs of show. But, having launched thus into a figure from optics, he develops it: the Queen is like somebody looking at a perspective from the front ('rightly') and seeing nothing but a confusion of shapes or shadows, whereas from the side, eyeing it awry, she would see there was only one substantial figure, one grief. Unfortunately Bushy gets into a muddle, and says the Queen has been eyeing the object awry, and the conceit doesn't work out neatly, though the confusion seems not entirely inappropriate.

In the Deposition scene Richard sends for a looking-glass, and when he gets it, talks for a while like a sonnet; after studying his reflection he smashes the mirror: 'How soon my sorrow hath destroy'd my face,' he says, and Bolingbroke tells him 'The shadow of your sorrow hath destroy'd / The shadow of your face'. He knows the image in the glass was a shadow, and thinks he knows that the emotion, whether of rage or petulance, that caused Richard to break the mirror was the shadow thrown from a substantial sorrow, a false outward show of it. Richard takes some satisfaction in what Bolingbroke suggests, and glosses that suggestion in a way that makes it rather more sympathetic than was perhaps intended:

> 'Tis very true, my grief lies all within,
> And these external manners of laments
> Are merely shadows to the unseen grief
> That swells with silence in the tortur'd soul.
> There lies the substance ...   (iv.1.291 ff)

It is not always easy, when kings are concerned, to distinguish shadow and substance. Of the King's two bodies, which is substance and which shadow? Stripped of his 'additions' – 'unking'd', in Richard's word – Lear asks who can tell him what he is, and only the Fool can: 'Lear's shadow' (i.4.230–31). The robes of kings and magistrates, their additions, make a brave show, but they are the substance of their offices and powers. The king's two bodies, then, are substance to each other's shadow; and they are in a hermaphroditic union only death can end.

In theatres, mirrors of the world, but also elsewhere, as when the Lord Mayor sends his Show through London streets, what is put on is called a show. It might be simple ('some show to welcome us to town', *Taming of the Shrew* i.1.47) or spectacular, like the Show of Kings in

Macbeth, or the sort of parade you find in history plays, meant to please 'Those that come to see / Only a show or two' (*Henry VIII*, Prologue). Or it might be a dumbshow. Whatever it is, the purpose of it is to demonstrate and display, to give outward expression to sentiments or propositions which may or may not correspond to inward truth. The theatre is a scene of deception as well as of reflection, and actors are imperfect shadows in the show. Macbeth wants to put out the candle that throws the shadow of life, a walking shadow; the notion at once makes him think of an actor strutting and fretting in a show, and helping to tell an idiot tale, signifying nothing. Shakespeare seems not to have thought much of the profession; an actor was what Donne called 'an ordinary nothing', a shadow, the mere show of a substance. To Coriolanus all acting is hypocrisy, false show.

The theatre offered more doublings, all related to substance / shadow, stage and world. I have mentioned the twins of ancient comic tradition; but girl and boy twins were especially interesting as a kind of divided hermaphrodite. The simultaneous appearance of Viola and Sebastian at the end of *Twelfth Night* is thus greeted by Orsino: 'One face, one voice, one habit and two persons! / A natural perspective that is and is not!' (v.1.216–17). Bushy's optics are here imposed on Plato's hermaphrodite, and the metaphysical affirmation of the play ('"That that is is" ... for what is "that" but "that", and "is" but "is"?' [iv.2.19 ff]) is represented in an emblem that is also an optical illusion. Viola herself, the boy who is not boy but girl, not girl but boy ('I am not that I play', i.5.184; 'I am not what I am', iii.2.141), then finally, wearing truthful woman's weeds, to be girl though only in show, appeals to the taffeta taste of the period, to a sort of delight in erotic indeterminacies, fed by the theatre and its boy players, deplored by the preachers who cited the definiteness of the Law against these antinomian erosions of the borderline between one thing and another.[2] It is Feste as Sir Thopas who declares that that that is is, and the boy Viola who confutes him by being and not being at once, and by standing within the perspective with her twin brother, identical but distinct images.

Among Shakespeare's twins, by the way, we should probably count *A Midsummer Night's Dream* and *Romeo and Juliet*, comic and tragic variants of the Pyramus and Thisbe story. Since that story, reduced to farce, is also the theme of Bottom's play, the comedy is itself double, and antithetical, and its language reminds us that it is. 'Methinks I see these things with parted eye,' says Demetrius, 'When everything seems double.' 'So methinks,' replies Helena, 'And I have found Demetrius like a jewel, / Mine own and not mine own' (iv.1.189 ff). Earlier she had told Hermia that as girls they 'grew together / Like to a double cherry, seeming parted, / But yet an union in partition' (iii.2.208 ff), which is a highly characteristic Shakespearian state of affairs. The fairy kingdom doubles Athens, and the play itself is a shadow of the world's substance. As to the actors, 'the best in this kind are but shadows'. What is, and what is shown, are also an important pair in *Troilus and Cressida*, a play about truth and its shadow, opinion, in which heroes discover that glory is what you see only in the reflection of a steel gate, or of others' eyes, or hear in the reverberation of an arch, magnifying and distorting the shout of pride (iii.3.115 ff). Cressida, to the parted eye of Troilus, is at last split in two, a woman and a man's antithetical opinion of her (v.2.146). Even in *Julius Caesar*, where so much is done to ensure that one man should be but a man (*Antony and Cleopatra*, ii.6.19), there are two Cinnas, the politician and his shadow, the poet, twinning a hint in Plutarch with a hint in Suetonius, the mob, tyrannical as Caligula, killing the shadow because the substance is not at hand,[3] as the conspirators kill the mortal Caesar rather than his imperial substance, which is transmitted to the chilly but divine Augustus. *King Lear* twins follies, the King's and the Fool's, the King's and Poor Tom's, for Poor Tom is that mortal body, Lear's shadow. Edmund and Edgar are false, Regan and Goneril true doubles, like the boy who buttered the horse's hay and his sister who knapped the eels on the head. *Antony and Cleopatra* gives us Rome and Egypt as in a perspective, one rock hard, the other melting in its river. Cleopatra and Octavia are the pair, Voluptas and Virtus, between whom Hercules must choose; Antony's substance dissolves like a cloud dislimned, like shadow, a sky-show of the dragonish, the bearlike, the lionlike – no longer substance, only a passing show (iv.14.1 ff).

It certainly appears that Shakespeare's interest in these twins and divided pairs was exceptional. Spenser uses 'shadow', almost always, to mean 'shade'. It is true that he has his polarity, Una and Duessa, and that one is substance, two or many shadow; he has his twin

Florimells, true and false, his double-dealer Archimago. But although his poem is full of feigning and full of shows, Spenser does not make a linguistic issue of them. Donne was more like Shakespeare in this; he loved doubles and splittings, maps arbitrarily divided east and west, coins that not only have twin obverse and reverse but also bear the shadow of the king's face. He likes the baby doubles in lovers' eyes, and those alchemical conjunctions, replications *in vitro* of a cosmic hermaphroditism. But he chooses his illustrations to feed his transient conceits, he isn't obsessed with them; he hardly exceeds what might be expected of a learned and very witty poet in an age which, perhaps more than most, dwelt on favoured sets of opposites: nature and grace, action and contemplation, truth and opinion, the noumenal and the phenomenal. I do not think, however, that one can find anywhere else that passion for what John Carey, discussing Donne,[4] call 'joined opposites', which is so evident in Shakespeare, and which reaches a sort of climax in *The Phoenix and Turtle*.

Shakespeare's birds are doubled in their mutual flame; they loved 'as love in twain / Had the essence but in one; / Two distincts, division none'. They had the quality of transcendent singleness: 'Number there in love was slain', for one, the saying went, is no number. Thus, in them alone, the totally single self is mysteriously also another. 'Property' – the condition of being single to oneself – is appalled 'that the self was not the same'. The word *selfsame* is not unusual in Shakespeare, but here it is virtually a *hapax legomenon*, split into *self* and *same*, yet still the selfsame word and still one containing the notion of selfhood, property, in a novel combination with that of resemblance, which is inconsistent with identity. The scholastic terminology – 'property', 'distinction' as opposed to 'division', 'simple' contrasted with 'compounded' – is reinforced by ordinary language catachrestically twisted into antonymic conjunctions on the model of *selfsame*: 'either neither'. Alternatives are neutralized without being eliminated in this freakish linguistic optics; they form perspectives, weird shows of almost unimaginable substance.

Plato's hermaphrodite partook of the nature of both sexes but was cut in two, so that the self was not the same; and the divided parts strove to be one in the sense that the broken halves of a coin or of a symbol are one: 'two distincts, division none'. Within the distincts there is a principle of primal identity, of which we are aware when we look at the halves of an apple, or at twins, or lovers, or the Trinity; or at the phenomena, whether astronomical or rhetorical, that cause us to speak of *concordia discors* or of *discordia concors* in relation to conceits and stars. Neoplatonists and theologians could, by similar means, explain how love unites poverty and plenty, or word and flesh, undivided distincts and neither-eithers.

It is only because language submits to catachresis, or at any rate to metaphorical use and abuse that tend toward that condition, that we can speak at all of these tremendous metaphysical condensations. In *The Phoenix and Turtle* we encounter them in an extraordinarily pure, unqualified form, and we should not expect to find the like in poetry written first for the ear. Yet in the theatre there exist all the necessary conditions: it is remote but not asunder, distinct but not divided. The Globe is and is not the globe, it is a shadow of the globe; there is a theatre of the world that does and does not contain the world, 'a natural perspective, that is and is not'. It's liable always to the irruption of carnival, the opposite of Lenten reality, turning that reality into a play; as Belsey Bob bursts into the Mummers' Play talking like Sir Thopas in *Twelfth Night* but reversing his terms, saying 'That that is not'.[5] It is in the language of *Hamlet* that we may look for these conjunctures, perspectives, and condensations – for a vast expansion of that serious play given full concentrated expression in *The Phoenix and Turtle*, which was written, as it happens, about the same time as the tragedy.

As we know, attention was for a great while fixed on the character of the hero, at the cost of prolonged inattention to the language of the play as something more than evidence of character, and to those internal relations which are inexplicitly registered in the language. A blend of both sorts of attention may be found in Goethe, but a more decisive change in the conversation (to use Richard Rorty's expression for similar alterations of emphasis in philosophy) cannot be detected until much later, until some half a century ago. We may take 'conversation' in the sense – broader than ours but including it – which it still had in Shakespeare's time and beyond – 'the action of consorting or having dealings with others; living together, commerce', as the *OED* spells it out. It requires a substantial alteration in the habit of a community for such a change to be licensed, and the change is slowed by conservative persons who sometimes mistake the recent past for the entire tradition. To look closely not at the 'psychology' of Lady Macbeth but at the rhetoric of such expressions as 'what thou wouldst highly / That wouldst thou holily', and to give the entire text the sort of attention such examples demand, was the aim of L. C. Knights in his *How Many Children Had Lady Macbeth?*, a polemical pamphlet that over fifty years ago announced, though of course it could not of itself consolidate, the change of conversation. And quite independently of Knights, Wilson Knight urged upon us (with the powerful support of T. S. Eliot) an interpretative method that called for another sort of attention, the kind accorded to canonical books of which it is presupposed that all their parts are occultly interrelated – that they have a 'spatial' as well as a temporal mode. Also independently, scholars began to pay more attention to the formal rhetoric of Shakespeare, so that Lady Macbeth's 'highly-holily' might be cited as an instance of paronomasia, though of course that is only the first and most obvious thing to say about it in terms of rhetoric. The change in conversation may be expressed thus: the actual language of the play, its very texture, had been treated as a marginal matter, merely as the medium that enabled us to see more important things. Now it could be moved into the centre of our interest, and 'character' in consequence reduced to relative marginality.

I do not think it would be very useful, though it may well have been done, to list all the rhetorical figures found in *Hamlet:* lots of catachresis, plenty of turpiloquium (when words are 'wrung into a filthy sense'),[6] instances of attemperation ('so oft it chanceth in particular men'). This is archaeology. Let us use some of the old terms, but think rather of what it means to give to the holism of Wilson Knight and the poetic attentiveness of L. C. Knights the character of a modern analysis along the lines proposed by Roman Jakobson, who claimed that 'poetry sets off the structural elements of all the linguistic levels . . . everything becomes *significant, réciproque, converse, correspondant*';[7] that degree of intensity Jakobson gave to his reading of a sonnet cannot, of course, be matched in a study of *Hamlet*, but we can, as they say, 'foreground the utterance', and see what it tells us about the whole.

Broadly speaking, the central rhetorical device of *Hamlet* is doubling. This is partly an echo of the period rhetoric; we are familiar with it from the *Book of Common Prayer*, in which sixteenth-century English finds its own vernacular equivalent for a liturgy long entrusted to Latin, and needing some differentiation from ordinary language. 'We acknowledge and confess our manifold sins and wickednesses', runs the General Confession; it gets some of its effect from reduplication that mimes the multiple guilt of many sinners speaking together, and more, possibly, from the sense that to *acknowledge* is not quite the same as to *confess*, and that *sins* are theologically a bit more specific than *wickednesses*. In much the same way 'spare thou them, O God, which confess their faults, restore thou them that are penitent' reminds us of the Psalmist's *parallelismus membrorum*, yet within its doubling there is a slight discrepancy of sense, for to be spared and to be restored are not exactly the same thing, and even though it is harder to distinguish between being penitent and confessing, the second cannot occur without the first nor the first, properly, without the second, so that they are distincts without division; and even if they were not, even if they were identical in sense, their identity would be a contribution to the meaning of the whole, for as Hoskins remarks in his *Directions for Speech and Style* (a work exactly contemporary with *Hamlet*), 'in speech there is no repetition without importance'.[8]

Although *Hamlet* contains a good deal of rather expansive doubling along these lines, the most pregnant and interesting of its linguistic doublings is undoubtedly hendiadys. This is the figure which, as its name implies, expresses 'one through two', as when Virgil says *pateris libamus et auro*, 'we drink from cups and gold' instead of 'we drink from golden cups'. This figure occurs with remarkable frequency in *Hamlet*, and had not altogether escaped attention, but it seems significant of the changing nature of our conversation that the first systematic study of it did not appear until 1981. This was George T. Wright's 'Hendiadys and *Hamlet*' (*PMLA* 96, pp. 168 ff), an article that not only repairs the neglect of former commentary but is in its own right a brilliant piece of literary criticism. The trick at its simplest is to conjoin two distinct words in the expression of a single idea, as in 'ponderous and marble jaws'; but as the Virgilian example suggests, the combination may be much more forced than that, and the separateness of the conjoined ideas as important as their capacity for conjunction. 'Ponderous' and 'marble' could easily be distinct epithets alike appropriate to the 'jaws' of a sepulchre (in fact they emphasize that 'jaws' is also a figure: graves 'swallow' people and so have jaws, but really the jaws are heavy pieces of marble, etc.). But 'the perfume and suppliance of a minute' (Laertes describing Hamlet's courtship of Ophelia, i.3.9) is more complicated, because the suppliance – 'entertainment', 'passing the time' or such – has got itself scented by the perfume, and the perfume cannot work at all without the suppliance; 'the perfume of a minute' doesn't sound right, as 'ponderous jaws' or 'marble jaws' sound right. As Wright remarks, hendiadys can introduce unease and mystery by means of what Eliot called, in another connection, 'a perpetual slight alteration of language' – by deviations, by doing something other than we expect from words joined by 'and', by a sort of violation of the promise of simple parataxis. The effect is comparable to that of zeugma (an unexpected yoking: 'she left in a flood of tears and a sedan chair') where one verb syntactically serves two sentence ideas, so that the logical structure, like that of the metaphysical conceit, is close to that of a joke.

However, as Wright further remarks, hendiadys isn't funny; its conjunctions of distincts are apt to produce unease. And it had, as Wright definitively demonstrates, a peculiar fascination for Shakespeare in a period lasting for a few years after 1599. That is to say, it coincides, accidentally or not, with the company's move to the Globe, which tempts me to guess that the flag or emblem of the theatre, 'Hercules and his load', meaning the world, the theatre as the world, may itself be read as a hendiadys ('Hercules' load'). *Hamlet*, the most self-proclaiming theatrical of all the plays, also has far more instances of this trope than any other play – sixty-six by Wright's careful and conservative count, more than twice as many as *Othello*, the next tragedy and easily second to *Hamlet* in this respect.

Wright's criterion for hendiadys is a certain interplay between the parts, so that the figure takes far more explication than you might expect to have to provide. 'The sensible and true avouch / Of mine own eyes' (i.1.57) means something like 'the sensorily accurate testimony of my eyes to what I could not have believed on mere report', the first adjective modifying the second rather than modifying 'avouch'. Wright finds such instances of hendiadys exactly expressive of the 'deceptive linkings' characteristic of the play as a whole, and he makes a very good case for this view.

My only reservation is that in his scrupulous attempt to distinguish between hendiadys and other forms of doubling Wright tends to exclude the remainder from consideration, though they obviously have a lot to do with the tone and working of the play; it is possible even that there is a sort of hierarchy of doublets, with hendiadys as the most complex and the most central. At any rate, what is reflected at all levels is not just hendiadys but doubling. Cornelius and Voltemand are indistinguishable, distincts without division; one of them would have served very well. Rosencrantz and Guildenstern are a double cherry, a union in partition. The play-within-the-play is an uneasy double of *Hamlet*, and the dumbshow an imperfect shadow or show of the play-within-the-play. Whenever something can be doubled, it is: revenges and revengers, lawful espials, ghostly visitations. The chronography of Barnardo:

> Last night of all
> When you same star that's westward from the pole,
> Had made his course t'illume that part of heaven
> Where now it burns . . .   (i.1.38–41)

is doubled by Horatio's chronography at the end of the scene:

> But look, the morn in russet mantle clad
> Walks o'er the dew of yon high eastward hill   (i.1.171–2)

and these two flourishes enclose like parentheses the excursus of Marcellus on Christmas ('so hallow'd and so gracious is that time' [i.1.169]). Laertes, himself a shadow or show of Hamlet, has a double departure and is twice blessed by his father ('A double blessing is a double grace' [i.3.53]); and so forth. These compulsive duplications occur everywhere, and with varying effect. Sometimes they are simple, as when they underline the orotund vacuity of Polonius:

And thus do we of wisdom and of reach,
With windlasses and with assays of bias
By indirection find directions out.
So by my former lecture and advice
Shall you my son. You have me, have you not?   (ii.1.64–8)

(The effect is not unlike that of Othello's talk at the beginning of that play.) Or Ophelia's inadequacy:

... Th'expectancy and rose of the fair state,
The glass of fashion and the mould of form,
Th'observ'd of all observers, quite, quite down!
And I of ladies most deject and wretched,
That suck'd the music of his honey'd vows,
Now see that noble and most sovereign reason
Like sweet bells jangled out of tune and harsh,
That unmatch'd form and feature of blown youth
Blasted with ecstasy.   (iii.1.154–62)

Every line here save one contains doublets. Rosencrantz and Guildenstern dispose them in their courtier-like moments ('The single and peculiar life is bound / With all the strength and armour of the mind', etc. [iii.3.11 ff]); but so does Hamlet in his soliloquies. These doublings, which of course include the strangest and most figurative of doublings, hendiadys, are simply the habit of the play.

Before we consider more of them in detail, it will be convenient to have some central principle of doubling in mind. It may be said that the play is deeply concerned with two main sorts of doubling. One is the doubling of theatre and world, the theatre as mirror in which actors are shadows or reflections and, when they play the parts of actors, shadows of shadows. The other great doubling is marriage, and marriage in the peculiarly intense and maximally intimate form of incest.

The funeral of a king, and the marriage of his widow to another king, his brother, is a doubling that prompts Hamlet's sour joke about doubling the wedding breakfast with the funeral feast; the unnatural temporal proximity of these functions reflects the physical proximity of incestuous marriage. Two persons becoming one is a form of thrift in which the self ceases to be the same, and what ought to be distinct is not divided. When Hamlet says, in bidding the King goodbye, 'Farewell, dear mother', the King corrects him: 'Thy loving father, Hamlet'. But Hamlet knows what he is saying, his logic is the logic of two-as-one: 'My mother. Father and mother is man and wife, man and wife is one flesh; so my mother' (iv.3.52–4). He disallows distinction where there is no division: marriage, and especially incestuous marriage, this particular beast with two backs, is a kind of hermaphroditism, or, if the catachresis is permitted, a social hendiadys containing mystery and unease, displaying a one that seems concordant but is not so, or is too much so, the kinship of aunt-mother and uncle-father being excessive; one might speak, even more disgustingly, of aunt-father and uncle-mother. Pondering this kinship relation, Hamlet also calls his mother her 'husband's brother's wife' (iii.4.14), which, accurate as it is, stresses the position of the marriage outside the permitted degrees of consanguinity, though at the same time it represents the compound relation as a horribly single one. Hamlet's first line, 'A little more than kin and less than kind' (i.2.65) is almost a textbook paronomasia; it depends upon the resemblance of one word to another. 'Kin' and 'kind' are an imperfect doublet, related phonetically, orthographically, and semantically, yet also distinct in all these ways, and represented as antithetical, thus stressing the horrible disparities implied by so close and profane a union.

Incest is equivocal (husband-wife, brother-sister) and breeds equivocation ('my cousin Hamlet and my son . . . Our chiefest courtier, cousin and our son' [i.2.64, 117]); the repetition is not merely redundant, for it makes the usurpation of Claudius a multiple one ('think of us / As of a father') – the 'us' and 'our' are royal plurals. All these piled up doubles, whether hendiadys or not, must create a sense of oddness and uneasiness when seen in their context, the huge equivoques of the whole scheme. They can be ignored or treated as occult, as having to do with secrecy rather than sense (see iii.4.194), but it is proper enough, on occasion, to defy the defence mechanism by which we ordinarily suppress knowledge of them.

It would be impossible to list, let alone discuss, all the doublings of this text, so here is a list drawn from the first 180 lines of the play, with some comment.

a) *You tremble and look pale.* (ordinary language)

b) I might not this believe
Without *the sensible and true avouch*
Of mine own eyes. (hendiadys: see above) (approved by Wright)

c) . . . in *the gross and scope of my opinion* (hendiadys: 'full extent')
(Wright)

d) *Strict and most observant watch* (close and observant; but close to
'strictly observant', 'strictly kept', and so a near-hendiadys)

e) . . . *ratified by law and heraldry* (hendiadys, according to Wright
– 'heraldic law'; but not much more so than 'Strict and most
observant')

f) *by the same cov'nant / And carriage of the article* (hendiadys;
glossed by Arden editor as 'purport of the article'; the agreement
as carried out [?])

g) *unimproved mettle, hot and full* (hendiadys: 'full of heat')

h) *food and diet* (simple duplication)

i) *post-haste and rummage* ('hurry and turmoil'; but a pair, surely, a
nonce-formation on the model of helter-skelter, hugger-mugger,
handy-dandy, hurly-burly; and a sort of hendiadys)

j) *high and palmy* (palmily high? highly palmy?)

k) *squeak and gibber* (a composite representation of the sound ghosts
make? a pair, not two distincts?)

l) *trains of fire and dews of blood* (parallelism of members)

m) *And even the like precurse of fear'd events*
As *harbingers preceding still the fates*
And *prologue* to the *omen* coming on
Have *heaven and earth* together demonstrated
Unto our *climatures and countrymen.* (highly repetitive: 'precurse',
'harbingers', 'prologue', 'omen' – and possibly also 'preceding' –
form a very redundant series, each doubling the others, and the
simple pair 'heaven and earth', partnered by the stranger conjunction 'climatures and countrymen', meaning something like 'the
inhabitants of our region', brings the sequence to a close)

n) *If thou hast any sound or use of voice* (uncertain as to the kind of
response that might be expected, neither 'sound' nor 'use of voice'
commits him to an expectation of human speech; the Ghost might

squeak and gibber; here again is a pair in the general ambience of hendiadys, without quite fitting acceptable definitions)

o) That may do *ease* to *you* and *grace* to *me* (here 'ease' and 'grace' is a double divided, shared out one each)

p) *Lofty and shrill sounding* throat ('lofty throat' would be a little forced; the second epithet glosses the first)

q) Th'*extravagant and erring* spirit ('extravagant' and 'erring' are an apparently exact double, but there are semantic undercurrents that hold them apart; cf. *Othello*, 'extravagant and wheeling stranger' [i.1.136] and 'For nature so preposterously to err' [i.3.62])

r) *So hallow'd and so gracious is that time* (holy because the means of grace)

Of the eighteen passages here listed, Wright allows as true instances of hendiadys only the three I have indicated. In a supplementary list of 'phrases that, if not hendiadys, are close, or odd' but which he felt he must, 'in the last analysis, reject', he includes four more: *strict and most observant, hot and full, food and diet*, and *post-haste and rummage*. It would be a task of some delicacy to grade the hundreds of doubles in the language of *Hamlet*, to measure their oddity and their closeness to the oddest and sovereign figure of hendiadys. What is certain is that the cumulative effect is very intense and also very various. If the garrulous doublings of Polonius are on the whole comic, the same cannot be said of the doubled language of i.5. There, the Ghost says he must render himself up to 'sulph'rous and tormenting flames'; he must have his foul crimes 'burnt and purg'd away'. His full story, if he told it, would not only harrow Hamlet's soul but also freeze his blood; it would make his hair, which is at once knotted and combined (like the words used to describe it) both part and stand on end. However, he cannot unfold his tale to ears of flesh and blood. His murder was both foul and most unnatural, and his murderer a man both incestuous and adulterous. The poison employed courses through the gates (or wider streets) of his body, but also through its alleys, curdling the thin, therefore wholesome, blood, and covering him with a vile, that was also a loathsome, crust. His bed became a couch for luxury *and* damned incest – a hendiadys of sorts, the incest being luxurious makes it doubly damnable, the luxury being incestuous makes it more luxurious. Hamlet replies with a flurry of doublets: 'trivial fond records', 'youth and observation' (a classic hendiadys), 'the book and volume' of his brain. Meeting his friends again, he urges them twice to pursue their business and desires; Horatio joins in, remarking on Hamlet's 'wild and whirling words', which is paronomasia as well as doubling; and then, after all the excitement, the doublets dwindle to the commonplace but basic 'heaven and earth', 'grace and mercy', 'love and friending'.

Before those words are spoken, we have had one of those passages of rapid dialogue – no time for doubling – which sometimes vary the rhythms of this incomparable poem; and there are other long moments during which doubling, by its mere absence, helps in the establishment of a different tone. One such passage is the prose conversation between Hamlet and the newly arrived Rosencrantz and Guildenstern in ii.2; as we have seen, the spy-sycophants are perfectly capable of courtly duplication and duplicity ('Heaven makes our presence and our practices / Pleasant and helpful to him' [ii.2.38–9]); but in response to Hamlet's unaffected greeting they drop what in them is a courtly device, and the candour of the conversation in which Hamlet discovers their mission is reinforced. The more effective, then, is the doubling in the famous speech 'I have of late . . . lost all my mirth, forgone all custom of exercise' (ii.2.295 ff), and Hamlet's allusion, as the conversation ends, to 'fashion and ceremony', and to his 'uncle-father and aunt-mother' (ii.2.368 ff).

Such instances, and the doublings of Polonius, more art than matter, make it impossible to speak of the device as if it had a single purpose. It isn't, for example, the case that it is always excluded from prose scenes. Hamlet's prose when he speaks of the players is very receptive of doubles: he calls the actors 'the abstract and brief chronicles of the time' ([ii.2.520]: Wright, preferring to read 'abstracts' with F1 and Q1, classifies this as hendiadys). He later says they will show 'the very age and body of the time his form and pressure' ([iii.2.23–4]: 'age . . . time' is hendiadys for Wright); they should not strut and bellow, but they should 'suit the action to the word' (iii.2.17) – a pairing too often, in his view, parted. Not surprisingly, then, the Player's account of Priam has him falling at the 'whiff and wind' of Pyrrhus's sword (ii.2.469); and, not surprisingly, the soliloquy that concludes this remarkable scene begins as it means to continue: 'O what a rogue and peasant slave am I' (ii.2.544). We shall hear of fiction and dream, motive and cue, of a speaker dull and muddy-mettled. He had a father 'Upon whose property and most dear life / A damn'd defeat was made' (the appalling of property). He is 'pigeon-liver'd' and 'lacks gall' (the second expression explaining the first, since pigeons were thought to have livers without gall). He unpacks his heart with words like a whore, and curses like a drab. However, he has a plot which will serve the single yet double purpose of testing king and Ghost – each of whom is a king, and each of whom is his father.

Here as elsewhere it is the variety of effect that gives the poetry its character. The mechanical doublets of Ophelia (expectancy and rose, glass of fashion, mould of form, observed and observer, deject and wretched, jangled, out of tune, etc.) contrast vividly with the powerful, anxious hendiadys in the King's speech immediately following:

> There's something in his soul
> O'er which his melancholy sits on brood,
> And I do doubt the hatch and the disclose
> Will be some danger . . .   (iii.i.166 ff)

This has to be glossed as 'that which will be disclosed when it hatches' or in some equally unsatisfactory way; it is a very good example of the linguistic disturbance this form of doubling entails, an image of the anxieties that the play broods over. A simple double like the Queen's exclamation at the death of Polonius, 'O what a rash and bloody deed is this!' (iii.4.27) may begin a train of very complex ones: 'A bloody deed, / Almost as bad, good mother, / As kill a king and marry with his brother' (28–9), where 'good' seems to stand antithetically to 'bad' but is yoked, with ironic conventionality, and in Hamlet's view inappropriately, with 'mother'; where 'kill' and 'marry' form a wicked pair, and where the rhyme of 'mother' and 'brother' mimes the too rich rhyme of incest. The Closet scene, indeed, is full of such conundrums, far too many to mention: form and cause, scourge and minister, sense and secrecy. Hamlet's final soliloquy, 'How all occasions . . .' (iv.4.32 ff), anomalous as its position certainly is, nevertheless forms a kind of coda, recapitulating the theme thus: good and market, sleep and feed, before and after, capability and godlike reason, bestial oblivion and craven scruple, mass and charge, fantasy and trick, tomb and continent, delicate and tender, mortal and unsure. The crux at i.54 ('Rightly to be great / Is not to stir without great argument, / But greatly to find quarrel in a straw / When honour's at the stake') turns on the question of whether 'not' should properly be 'not not', one not doing the work of two, two negatives in a single mutual flame.

This, then, is a play in which self is sometimes joined with, sometimes divided from, same; opposites are conjoined and similars separated. Why is Horatio both familiar and a stranger? Why are we to be troubled with the question whether the Ghost is honest or not? Why should Hamlet double his abuse of woman, and berate Ophelia as he does his mother? Why, having persuaded her of her guilt, turned her eyes into her very soul, does he double his condemnations? Having cleft her heart in twain, why does he repeat his lecture on abstinence? Why is he doubly mad or not mad at all? A shadow of the actor who is himself but a shadow? Why, in short, is the play so often like a pair of twins, a divided hermaphrodite? The restoration of the primal hermaphrodite, according to Aristophanes in the *Symposium*, is attempted by the divided halves when, their private parts moved around to the front, they make the beast with two backs, when, in the rank sweat of an enseamed bed they reunite, touch, as *The Winter's Tale* expresses it, forbiddenly.

We can say, at any rate, that in the year or so that was occupied by the writing of *Hamlet, The Phoenix and Turtle*, and *Twelfth Night*, Shakespeare not only developed his taste for doublets, including the incestuous doublet of hendiadys – a development for which much in his earlier practice has prepared us – but took to extraordinary lengths his interest in twinning, male and female, in the self and the same, the self that is not the same. There are the great antithetical doublings of the social life, Carnival and Lent and all the other traditional opposites that make unions – one and number, knowledge and opinion, noumena and phenomena, substance and shadow; and they are reflected in the language of poetry as rhyme (either-neither, mother-brother) or assonance, or pun or hendiadys. Thematically they may emerge as the perspective of twins, or the one flesh of marriage and incest. Together, these things make a mirror of a world that is one, but built on a principle of opposition in all its structures.

Of that opposition, substance-and-shadow is a primeval figure. In folklore, to lose one's shadow is to be castrated or made infertile. In some languages, the same word does duty for 'soul' and 'shadow',[9] so that images and reflections are also projections of the soul. Mirrors are not to be broken; in times of mourning they are covered. In Lacan's *stade du miroir* we have our modern version of such spiritual disasters.

One's image or double may also be a rival, as son of father; the act of doubling is itself a reflex of the oedipal theme. Sisters may be the doubles of brothers; Narcissus mistook his reflection for his sister. The Duke in *Twelfth Night* thinks of Sebastian and Viola as a perspective, two in one, and Antonio says that a cleft apple is not more twin than they, but they are distinct also, and opposed; Viola thinks her brother a spirit 'come to fright us' (v.1.236). Shakespeare's twins Hamnet and Judith were born in 1585; Hamnet died in 1596, the year of the twin plays *Romeo and Juliet* and *A Midsummer Night's Dream*.

It has been argued by a follower of D. W. Winnicott that a twin may take the place of more usual transitional objects but may be a poor substitute, being too like the mother, animate; so that the move from inner to outer reality is impeded – there may be difficulty in achieving the required decathexis.[10] However that may be, there are fantasy twins as well as real ones. Hamlet's hypercathexis on his father has often been noticed; the true father was the substance of his shadow, and the defeat of his 'property' left Hamlet not with that substance but with its evil replacement, the shadow-king, shadow-husband, and shadow-father, Claudius. His mother splits in two; wife to both 'this' and 'this', her self is no longer the same, and Hamlet is appalled in the name of Property. In the catachresis of *The Phoenix and Turtle* and the perspective of *Twelfth Night*, we may see a concentrated version of that multilevel doubling and twinning that *Hamlet* expands to its full theatrical dimensions in the Globe, which is itself the shadow of the world's substance.

These remarks about *Hamlet* imply certain assumptions. Different as they are from the great bulk of past commentary, they have something in common with the way critics nowadays often talk. The main line of approach is rhetorical; not that I have sought to specify all the varieties of trope, merely using instances here and there, and not seeking, as Wright's admirable study sought, to distinguish sharply between hendiadys and other forms of doubling, or to study the many types of paronomasia to be found in the text. The assumption is, of course, that I might look anywhere in the play (in the 'world of the play', as we not inaccurately say) for resemblances suggested by my guiding idea, and that here, as Henry James remarked in another connection, 'relations stop nowhere'. Here they will sometimes appear to subsist between the obvious and the far-fetched, or, to be more generous to myself, between the manifest and the latent.

Assumptions of that sort are characteristically made about canonical texts, texts that share with the sacred at least this quality: that however a particular epoch or a particular community may define a proper mode of attention or a licit area of interest, there will always be something else and something different to say. There is, of course, room for dissent within the agreement that the last word cannot be said, but it is hard to suppose that there can be progress ensured by the testing of hypotheses; all we are sure about is that the inadequacies of earlier exposition become astonishingly obvious to later expositors, that there can be no simple and perpetual consensus as to the proper way to join the shadow of comment to the substance of the play. And this is what it means to call a book canonical. The game is in a sense the same one that Goethe and Coleridge played, but the rules change, and we know it is the same game only by reason of family resemblance: all grant to the text something like omnisignificance, all have canons of interpretation that are permissive rather than restrictive. Relations must appear to stop somewhere, and some views as to where they ought to stop are stricter than others, though they are views that are themselves mere opinions and not the certainties that they are sometimes taken for. Above all, the reason why friend and foe are both able to do as they wish, and to recognize that in the end their discourses are of the same sort, is that *Hamlet* is unshakably canonical – the dislodgement of such a work from canonical status would certainly involve the dislodgement of those discourses, of whatever party. In short, the only rule common to all interpretation games, the sole family resemblance between them, is that the canonical work, so endlessly discussed, must be assumed to have permanent value and, which is really the same thing, perpetual modernity.

As I was writing this, a man told me his dream. He dreamed that, being overweight, he dieted and became slender, feeling that in doing so he had acquired an entirely new personality. Then, in his new body, he had a dream within the dream, and in this inner dream he saw himself as he had been originally – much fatter, but somehow more at home in his ampler shape. Still dreaming, the sleeper decided to act on this hint, and resume his former, bulkier shape. On waking he found he had done so; he awoke and found it truth. He had, in the outer dream, reduced himself to a shadow of his former self, and in the inner regained his substance.

This reminded me not only that Hamlet, young and fit at the beginning of the play is, at the end of it, after his lapse in time and passion, fat and thirty, but also that his play is a fiction, a dream of passion, in which there are dreams within dreams, and mirror on mirror mirrored is all the show. Moreover, the conversations of interpreters are shadows or images, fat or thin, and not matters of substance, except that where there is shadow there must be substance, and a light on it; so the end of all this shadowy talk is after all to keep a real and valued object in being. That, to offer one more hendiadys, is my sense of the play and duty of interpretation.

1 2

The Plain Sense of Things

A meditation that starts from the beautiful Stevens poem quoted at the outset, this essay was written in 1984 as a contribution to a conference on midrash *at the Hebrew University in Jerusalem. It first appeared in a collection of much more learned papers than mine, edited by Geoffrey Hartman and Sanford Budick and called* Midrash and Literature *(1986). Once again it tries to stretch questions of biblical interpretation to cover other sorts, and in doing so it relies on authorities that have not always gone unchallenged. But once again it seemed worth a try, even though the effort probably exposes one to learned criticism; one can never know enough to avoid that entirely.*

My title is taken from a poem by Wallace Stevens:

> After the leaves have fallen, we return
> To a plain sense of things. It is as if
> We had come to the end of the imagination,
> Inanimate in an inert savoir.
>
> It is difficult even to choose the adjective
> For this blank cold, this sadness without cause.
> The great structure has become a minor house.
> No turban walks across the lessened floors.
>
> The greenhouse never so badly needed paint.
> The chimney is fifty years old and slants to one side.
> A fantastic effort has failed, a repetition
> In a repetitiousness of men and flies.

> Yet the absence of the imagination had
> Itself to be imagined. The great pond,
> The plain sense of it, without reflections, leaves,
> Mud, water like dirty glass, expressing silence
>
> Of a sort, silence of a rat come out to see,
> The great pond and its waste of lilies, all this
> Had to be imagined as an inevitable knowledge,
> Required, as a necessity requires.

This is a late poem by Stevens, but it continues a meditation that began much earlier. In its own very idiosyncratic way that meditation echoes a central theme of modern philosophy. The plain sense is itself metaphorical; there is no escape from metaphor; univocity in language is no more than a dream. The position is familiar, and the interest of Stevens' poem is that he is not so much affirming it as suggesting the movement of mind that accompanies its consideration. He is especially conscious of the extraordinary effort required even to imagine, to find language for, the plain sense of things and hold the language there for the briefest moment: worth trying, he seems to say, but impossible, this attempt to behold 'nothing that is not there and the nothing that is'. To make the attempt, he said in the earlier poem I have just quoted ('The Snow Man'), is 'to have a mind of winter' (*CP*, p. 9). Only such a mind, a snowman's mind, could attend to the frozen trees without adding to them some increment of language, of humanity, even if that increment is misery.

Such a moment, of unattainable absolute zero, is anyway only to be imagined as a phase in a cyclical process. Language, always metaphorical, falsifies the icy diagram, corrupts by enriching the plain sense, which can only be thus corruptly or distortedly expressed. 'Not to have is the beginning of desire' ('Notes toward a Supreme Fiction', *CP*, p. 382); and so metaphor, like spring, adorns the icy diagram; only when that desire is satisfied do we grow tired of summer lushness and welcome the fall and winter again. So the plain sense continually suffers change, and if it did not it would grow rigid and absurd. It must change, or it will simply belong 'to our more vestigial states of mind' ('Notes', *CP*, p. 392). But change is inevitable anyway, since the effort we make to attend to plain sense itself takes away the plainness. That this is the case may distress philosophers who want to be able to distinguish the literal from the metaphorical, but it is nevertheless a source of poetry: 'Winter and spring, cold copulars, embrace, / And forth the particulars of rapture come' ('Notes', *CP*, p. 392). The imagination's commentary is a part of the text as we know it – that is, distorted by metaphor, by secondary elaboration. This is what Stevens means when he speaks of the effect of the gaiety of language on the natives of poverty ('L'Esthetique du Mal'): the games, fictions, metaphors which accommodate the plain sense to human need. Without such 'makings', as he calls them, the world is just 'waste and welter' ('The Planet on the Table', *CP*, p. 532). And the makings are themselves part of a reality more largely conceived, of a whole which is not merely or not always poor; the words of the world are the life of the world.

In the poem at the opening of this essay there is a winter, a due season, a world stripped of imaginative additions, so cold that it resists our adjectives. The summer world made by our imagination is now a ruin; the effort has ended in failure. So, difficult though it may be, one tries to find an adjective for blankness, a tropeless cold. But to say 'no turban' is to introduce a turban, something exotic, a gift of imagination; the floors, though lessened, are still fully there; the structure is still a house. Imagination wants a decrepit greenhouse, a tottering chimney; blankness itself becomes a pond, and the pond has lilies and a rat. 'The absence of the imagination had / Itself to be imagined.' The pond has reflections, leaves, mud, as real a pond as imagination at the best of times could imagine. All these things have to be added to the plain sense if we want it; it is not to be had without comment, without poetry.

It may seem that I have begun this essay at a great distance from any topic that might be thought appropriate to the occasion of its writing, for I was asked to write about the Jewish interpretative practice of *midrash* and its relation – if any – to the interpretation of poetry more generally. In poetry there is often a plain sense and also senses less plain: we might risk saying, a sense corresponding to *peshat*, and others corresponding to *midrash*. But we know that *midrash* and *peshat* are also an intrinsic plural; that the play, might one say even the gaiety, of the one is required to give a human sense to the inaccessible mystery of the other. And it is on the other instances of this collaboration that I shall be expatiating. So it seems sensible enough to begin with a poet who saw so well the relations between plain sense and human need – saw it not as a philosopher or a hermeneutician, but rather as his own major man might, though the major man would understand wholly the supreme fiction in which plain sense and trope, truth and fiction, are finally apprehended as a unity, and the world stops. (Stevens sometimes thought of this major man as a rabbi.) For him the kind of poetry Eliot said he wanted would be a part, but only a part, of poetry: 'poetry standing in its own bare bones, or poetry so transparent that we should see not the poetry, but what we are meant to see through the poetry'.[1] Note that in speaking of this impossible nakedness or transparency the poet has to imagine a skeleton and a window. The most arduous effort to express the poetry of plain sense brings with it its own metaphors, its own distortions. There are, as Freud would have said, considerations of representability, there are secondary elaborations, there are fortuitous inessentials, days' residues; he might have agreed with Augustine that some things are there for the sake of the sense but not constitutive of the sense. And our only way to catch a glimpse of the sense is by attending to the inevitable distortions.

Northrop Frye remarks that the literal sense of a poem is the whole poem.[2] And the whole which constitutes the literal sense may not be a single poem; nor need that whole be the same for everybody. A canon may define the whole, and the same parts may figure in different canons. For Christian commentators the Psalms belong to a whole different from the whole to which they belong for Jewish commentators; they may agree that there are messianic psalms, but the plain sense of such psalms must be different for each, since the whole text of the Christian shows the fulfilment of the messianic promises. Herbert's poem 'The Holy Scriptures (II)' compares the separate texts of the Bible to a constellation, and remarks on the remote interactions of the verses:

> This verse marks that, and both do make a motion
> Unto a third, that ten leaves off doth lie . . .

But for some, though they might accept the principle, those ten leaves are not in their copies. The expression *Son of man* occurs in Psalms 8:4, and modern scholars agree that it means simply 'man', and that it ought not to be thought of in relation to the apocalyptic sense of the phrase in Daniel or the passages in the New Testament which seem to derive from Daniel. But, as John Barton says, the case would be different if the New Testament had happened to cite the passage from the psalm for christological purposes;[3] and in any case it seems unlikely that less scholarly Christians, coming upon these words or hearing them sung in church on the first day of the month, will quite exclude from their thoughts the resonances of New Testament usage.

So the whole, by which the sense of the part is to be determined, varies between the religions and the canons. And there is a further extension of context, which, since it will recur in my argument, I shall mention now. The Roman Catholic Church affirms the authority of the magisterium over all interpretation, and the Church is the custodian of a Tradition; so that to the two parts of the Christian Bible one adds a third contextual element, and the whole that determines the plain sense of the part is thus extended.

However, we need not confine the question thus: for it is clear that different people at different times will form their own notions of the relations between parts, and between parts and wholes. For example, some will maintain that christological interpretations of Old Testament texts are valid only when they have been made in the New Testament; others, a great army of them over the centuries, think otherwise. And the language in which each person or party expresses the sense of the text will necessarily be figurative. The plain sense is not accessible to plain common sense. That is why it has been possible to say, 'The plain sense is hidden'. Luther believed that 'the Holy Spirit is the plainest writer and speaker in heaven and earth', but we may well sympathize with Erasmus, who wanted to know 'if it is all so plain, why have so many excellent men for so many centuries walked in darkness?'[4]

The expression *plain sense*, as I am using it, covers the overlapping ideas of literal sense, grammatical sense, and historical sense. It is also a usual translation of *peshat*. The most obvious indication that the plain sense is not a universal and unequivocal property of mankind is that it resists translation from one language into another. A well-known example is John Lyons' demonstration of the difficulty of finding a French equivalent for 'the cat sat on the mat'; the nouns are troublesome but the verb is worse, since English does not adjudicate between the senses, in French, of *s'assit, s'est assis(e), s'asseyait*.[5] I shall return to the cat in another connection, but the present point is that plain senses can be tricky to translate. Bruno Bettelheim laments that Freud's English translators alter his sense by refusing to use the word *soul*.[6] But the senses of that word in English are very different from those of its German cognate; *soul* would often be wrong in English. Bettelheim is especially bitter that the translators of the Standard Edition have smuggled in a new word, very technical sound-ing, to translate *Besetzung*, namely 'cathexis'. But would 'occupation' or 'investment' really do the work? And how should we deal with *Überbesetzung?* No doubt 'hypercathexis' gives a different idea, but it is probably closer to Freud's sense than 'overinvestment', and the same must be true of 'anticathexis'.

These minor discrepancies are perhaps emblematic of much larger ones. Psychoanalysis changed when it moved from the Viennese into other cultures, and it can never again be what it was in pre-war Europe; like other religions it was fissile even in its early stages, and different sects and individuals have always found different plain senses in the original deposits of doctrine. There are obvious parallels in Christianity. Jerome began it, offering *hebraica veritas*, and Greek truth also, but in Latin. Thereafter *logos* became *verbum*, and *verbum* became so firm a part of the theological tradition that when Erasmus, with good philological justification, translated *logos* as *sermo* he got into trouble; for *verbum* seemed to match the required plain sense as *sermo*, a surprising novelty, could not. On the other hand More attacked Tyndale for giving 'love' instead of 'charity' for *agape*; but now 'charity' has changed its contexts and 'love' is preferred.[7] The naïve desire of the New English Bible translators to provide plain-sense equivalents for the Hebrew of the Old Testament sometimes leads them into what can fairly be called mistranslation, as in their version of the rape of Dinah by Shechem (Genesis 34:3): 'But he remained true to Dinah.' The sense of the Hebrew *nefesh* is lost, though the King James version, which has 'And his soul clave unto Dinah', conveys, as Hammond observes, the intensity of Shechem's erotic feelings. '"Remained true" is exactly the wrong phrase since it implies fidelity and honour; the point of the story is that Shechem's lust is not fulfilled by one act of rape.'[8] No doubt this view could be disputed, since *nefesh*, according to the Lexicon, is a tremendously complicated word, and no translation could do it justice. But King James wins by not seeking a commonplace equivalent.

When whole systems of belief are involved, as in the case of the Bible they always are, the difficulties are multiplied. Christianity decided to reject Marcion and keep the Jewish Bible, and thenceforth the question of the nature of its relevance to a non-Jewish religion became a permanent problem, with much bearing on the matter of plain sense. If the Law was abrogated the relevance of the Old Testament lay primarily in its prefigurative relation to the New; it became, more or less, a repository of types. But it contained other elements not easily given up – moral instruction and a history of God's providence and promises. And from quite early times there was some resistance to the copious allegorizing of the Alexandrian tradition, some respect for the *sensus historicus*. The school of Antioch limited allegorical interpretation to the sort of thing licensed by Paul, for example in his reading of the story of the sons of Sarah and Hagar. Theodore of Mopsuestia sought to understand the Old Testament historically; for instance, he rejected the usual (and, in the circumstances, obvious) reading of the Suffering Servant in Isaiah 53. But Theodore was posthumously condemned, and the majority of Antiochenes were in any case less rigidly historicist, as D. S. Wallace-Hadrill explains.[9]

And yet, despite the success of allegory, the importance of the literal sense was habitually affirmed, most influentially by Augustine, a contemporary of Theodore but working in a different tradition. Augustine was a historian, and as an exegete he held that an understanding of historical reality must be the foundation of any attempt to provide spiritual interpretation. His emphasis on Jewish history as continuous with Christian was influential. But he also ruled that no interpretation should transgress against 'charity': any literal–historical sense that was inconsistent with virtuous conduct and the true faith should be treated figuratively. And he provided for the frequent occurrence of texts that appeared to have no particular Christian relevance;

they were there for the sake of the others, as ploughs have handles.[10] Thus the typical quality of the historical sense is maintained, and the position is as J. S. Preuss describes it: the plain sense of some of the Old Testament is edifying in itself, but the remainder has value only because it means something other than it seems to be saying; the literal, grammatical, and historical senses include what should not be figuratively interpreted and also what must be so interpreted. But that which is edifying is so only because it already conforms with the New Testament, and the unedifying has to be made edifying by figurative reading in New Testament terms. Thus the extended context determines the plain sense, which, in the case of the Old Testament, resides effectively in the text of the New. There was a Jewish or carnal sense, to which one might attribute more or less importance; but the true sense was Christian and spiritual, and that sense could be represented as the plain sense. The figurative becomes the literal.

So, although the warning that the *sensus historicus* must be the foundation of exegesis was frequently repeated, it appears that a really active concern for the historical sense of the Old Testament did not recur until the later years of the eleventh century, when it was in large part the result of intercourse between Jewish and Christian scholars. It was at that moment that *peshat* entered, or re-entered, Christian thought. Erwin Rosenthal has explained with great clarity the position of Jewish scholarship after Saadya Gaon; how the distinction between *peshat* and *derash* now grew sharper, how *peshat* served as a weapon against christological interpretations, and how Rashi, by his more correct understanding of the relation between the two, influenced not only his Jewish but his Christian contemporaries.[11] The conflict between extreme adherents of *peshat* and *derash*, between the literal sense and the tradition, the literal sense and the mystical kabbalistic sense, continued within the Jewish tradition. But meanwhile a new respect for the Hebrew text and the *sensus Judaicus* was once again altering the context of Christian interpretation.

Beryl Smalley established the influence of Jewish scholarship on the work of the Victorines.[12] Relations between Jewish and Christian scholars were never wholly cordial, but they were productive, for the 'Hebrew truth' of Jerome was now taken back into its own language. Hugh of St Victor had some Hebrew, and he consulted Jewish scholars and reported their interpretations. There was a new emphasis on the historical sense as Jews understood it. Hugh anticipated Aquinas in arguing that to be ignorant of the signs was to be ignorant of what they signified, and so of what the signified, itself a sign, signified. It will, however, be noticed that this formula does nothing to alter the position that a true understanding of the Jewish Bible depends upon and is subsequent to a true understanding of the New Testament; for the Jewish reading, though it accurately carries out the first stage of the process, the establishment of literal, grammatical, and historical sense, plays no part in the second, which is to determine what the signified signifies. The Jewish sense is still the carnal one, and preliminary to the spiritual reading.

It would seem that Jewish scholarship was bolder, in that it sometimes risked everything on the plain sense. Joseph Kara, early in the twelfth century, could remark that 'whosoever is ignorant of the literal meaning of the Scripture and inclines after a Midrash is like a drowning man who clutches at a straw to save himself'.[13] Masters of Haggadah may mock him, he says; but the enlightened will prefer the truth. Nevertheless, we are told, he himself frequently inclined after *midrash*. It was the next generation of Jewish scholars, contemporaries of Andrew of St Victor, the hero of Beryl Smalley's research, who installed the literal sense more firmly. Andrew ecumenically devised a dual method of interpretation, giving the Vulgate text with a Christian explanation, and the Hebrew text with a Jewish. The literal sense was that of the Jews. For example, on Isaiah 7:14–16, 'Behold, a virgin shall conceive', Andrew cites Rashi to the effect that the literal sense is this: the bride of the prophet will conceive a son to deliver Israel. Though he rejects this interpretation with some vehemence, Andrew allows it the title of the literal sense.[14] But Christians live by the spirit, and their reading of the passage, based on the *virgo* of the Vulgate, is the true if not the literal one.

In using the Jews, to quote Smalley, as 'a kind of telephone to the Old Testament',[15] Andrew naturally annoyed some contemporaries. He was accused of 'judaizing'. But judaizing gave a new turn to the speculation about literal sense and its relation to spiritual sense. Henceforth the argument of Hugh of St Victor, as restated and given authority by Aquinas, prevailed. The words mean one thing only; but that thing may be a sign of other things, and it is from those second-order things that the spiritual sense derives. The historical sense, the sense of the human author, is what he says; but there is a divine author whose intentions are other than his. 'Truly, the literal sense is that which the author intended; but the author of sacred Scripture is God, who comprehends in his *intellectus* all things at once.'[16] So the spiritual or symbolic or typical interpretation is more faithful to the *mens auctoris* than the literal; and regardless of what is properly to be called the literal sense, the true sense is to be found in the New Testament.

There were various attempts to resolve the ambiguities of this position, as when the extremely influential commentator Nicholas de Lyra also spoke of the literal sense itself as dual; the symbolic interpretation was to be regarded as the literal one if expressly approved by the New Testament (a partial return to the Antiochan doctrine). When God says of Solomon (I Chronicles II): 'I will be a father to him, and he will be like a son to me', the application to Solomon is literal; but because the author of the Epistle to the Hebrews uses the text to show that Christ is higher than the angels, it has a second literal sense, which is also mystical. Preuss thinks this is the 'first time . . . a New Testament reading of an Old Testament passage is dignified with the label "literal"'; though the general idea is of course not new.[17]

It seems, then, that throughout this period there grew up a desire to narrow the gap between the Christian and the literal sense. But since the literal sense could still be referred to the New Testament, some Jewish scholars now abandoned their own messianic interpretations and clove to the *sensus historicus*, in order to avoid any suggestion that might give support to the christological reading, for example of Psalm 2. Once again it is apparent that the Christians, however devoted to the *hebraica veritas*, could not be so bold as the Jews; for their interpretations were always subject to censorship by the custodians of an infallible tradition that was partly independent of Scripture. Of course Jewish interpreters had to steer a course between the fundamentalism of the Karaites and the allegories of the Kabbalah; but the institution controlling Christian interpretation was very powerful, and the authority of the tradition, which in some ways stood to the New Testament as the New Testament did to the Old, could be enforced by the Inquisition; these were not merely erudite arguments.

By the fifteenth century the matter of literal sense called for formal discussion, as in Jean Gerson's *De sensu litterali sacrae Scripturae* of 1414, which decided that the Church alone had the power to determine the literal sense. It derived its authority to do so from the promise of Christ in the New Testament; that is, the literal sense of the New Testament confers on the Church the right to declare the true sense of any text. Preuss comments on the importance and timeliness of this pronouncement. Heretics claimed that their doctrines were founded on the literal sense of Scripture; but if the literal sense is by definition the 'literal sense of the Church', and not anything more generally available, then merely to affirm a different sense from that of the Church was proof of heresy. 'The possibility of argument from Scripture against the *magisterium* is for the first time . . . programmatically and theoretically eliminated.'[18] There would no longer be any point in asking Jews about the plain sense of an Old Testament passage; that sense was first revealed through Christ and the apostles, then protected and studied by the Church, and subsequently enforceable with all manner of sanctions.

So the lines were drawn for the struggle between Luther's plain sense, his *sola scriptura*, and the authority of Rome, only possessor of the sense of Scripture. Luther was speaking no more than truth when he accused the Popes of setting themselves up as 'lords of Scripture'; that was exactly what they had done. Of the religious, political, and military consequences of this hermeneutic disagreement it is unnecessary to speak. Curiously enough, in our own time it is a Protestant hermeneutics that has insisted upon the necessity of understanding tradition as formative of the horizon from which we must seek some kind of encounter with ancient texts, denying at the same time any immediacy of access to those texts. It seems that Gerson and the Popes had grasped an important point, namely that all interpretation is validated in the end by a third force, and not by the unaided and unauthoritative study of isolated scholars; and they wished to be sure that the third force was the Church.

Luther, as a matter of fact, opposed enthusiastic reading also; as far as he could see Müntzer and the Pope were both arrogating to themselves an improper authority over Scripture. But in the next century the Council of Trent made equivocation and compromise impossible by giving renewed emphasis to tradition and authority. The subsequent history of the Catholic view was determined by the Tridentine decisions.

It seems reasonable to conclude this brief anthology of disputes about plain sense by glancing at some exegetical problems which had to be settled at the time of Catholic Modernism. The intellectual atmosphere of the late nineteenth century, including the success over a generation or so of Darwinism and, perhaps even more threatening, the achievement and the fame of German Protestant biblical scholarship, made both Authority and Tradition subject to question. There arose within the Church scholars who thought the official position needed revision. An early hint of the new kind of hermeneutic understanding recommended to the Church is to be found in the work of the Tübingen Catholic theologian Johann Evangelist von Kuhn. He agreed with the Protestants that the Bible is privileged over all other documents, but said that they failed to understand this: Tradition, as distinct from traditions, is the preaching and consciousness of the Church *in the present moment*. 'Tradition is the *kerygma* of the present; Scripture, the *kerygma* of the past, is the *doctrina*-source of the present.'[19]

This new formulation places the sense of Scripture firmly in the here and now; it denies that application can be divorced from understanding. A related idea, very characteristic of its time, is that religion has undergone an evolutionary development, and that the old texts and forms might be thought of as types of later doctrine, an idea prevalent in the thought of the period, and given expression in literature (by Hawthorne, for instance) as well as in Catholic theology (by Newman, who said that 'the earlier prophecies are pregnant texts out of which the succeeding announcements grow; they are types').[20]

Such views were condemned in 1870, but a generation later they appeared again in a rather different form with Modernism proper. Its proponents favoured Tradition over Scripture, seeing Tradition as a process of inspired development. The reflex of the Church, inevitably conservative, was to retreat to a scriptural position. This is not surprising; it must have been rather horrifying to hear Von Hügel, a man of impeccable piety (Yeats praised him because he accepted the miracles of the saints and honoured sanctity) proclaiming that even if the Gospel narratives were unrelated to historical events they would still be true as 'creations of the imagination' – a position not really very far from that of some modern Protestants. The English convert George Tyrrell was shocked to find in the Roman Church the sort of bible religion he had thought he was leaving behind. He believed that God was he First Cause, and so the author of Scripture only in the sense that he was the author of everything. He was aware of the difficulty of steering a course between the two positions, one holding that the deposit was perpetually valid, the other that doctrine developed progressively. Here again is the hermeneutic problem about original and applied sense. Tyrrell failed to solve it and was disgraced. In France Alfred Loisy expressed similar views and with more force, remarking in a very modern manner that a book absolutely true for all times would be unintelligible at all times; he too saw the danger of reading back a modern idea of religion into the Scriptures. Caught between these positions, he too fell foul of the Church and was excommunicated.[21]

The plain sense of Scripture, as of anything else, is a hermeneutical question, and we have seen how different are the hermeneutics of Augustine, the medieval Jewish scholars, Gerson, and Loisy. One concept that was rigorously developed was that of the role of authority, the institutional power to validate or to invalidate by reference to Tradition; but when Tyrrell and Loisy were purged authority was acting as it were politically, for to the outsider it might have seemed that they were trying to give the idea of Tradition new force. Their proposals, like those of von Kuhn, offered the Church a plausible modern hermeneutic, with an acceptable view of the relation between the origin and the here and now; but the idea of development, though supported by the whole history of dogma, was too frightening.

Modernism was revived in a modern form in the 1940s and partly endorsed by Vatican II. The principal effect has been to allow Catholic scholars to engage in the sort of historical research formerly associated with Protestant scholarship; and this may seem belated, for elsewhere there is a strong shift away from the objectivist assumptions of that scholarship and toward a newer hermeneutics. It is now often maintained that the plain sense, if there is one, must be of the here and now rather than of the origin.

One thing is sure: the body of presuppositions which determines our notions of the plain sense is always changing, and so is the concept of the validating authority. As the new canonical criticism demonstrates, there are new ways of establishing relevant contexts, and new extratextual authorities, like the idea of canon in this case. And a hermeneutics that allowed for possibilities of change and adaptation might have suited the Church, as the defender of Tradition, very well, as – or so it appears – the Jewish tradition has accommodated change and adaptation without sacrificing the original deposit. What the Modernists saw was that if Tradition entailed change, there was a need for a theory of interpretation which could close the widening gap between doctrine and text and require newly licensed plain senses. In practice the means has always been available; the dogma of the Assumption of the Virgin, promulgated in 1950, depends on Tradition and not on Scripture, and on a tradition that can only with difficulty be traced back as far as the fourth century. It would have been particularly surprising to St Mark. But if we think of Tradition as the third part of the Catholic canonical context it is possible to suppose that the Assumption is part of the plain sense of the whole; and, after all, assumptions occur in both the other parts.

My purpose has been to suggest that the plain sense of things is always dependent on the understanding of larger wholes and on changing custom and authority. So it must change; it is never naked, but, as the poet says, it always wears some fictive covering. Time itself changes it, however much authority may resist. It must, of course, do so. And it cannot do so if it fails to preserve its foundation text; and, short of keeping that text out of unauthorized hands, it cannot prevent readers from making their imaginative additions to the icy diagram.

Finally, the plain sense depends in larger measure on the imaginative activity of interpreters. This is variously constrained, by authority or hermeneutic rules or assumptions, but it is necessary if the text is to have any communicable sense at all. Given plausible rules and a firm structure of authority, change may not be violent. One recalls Raphael Loewe's magisterial essay on 'The "Plain" Meaning of Scripture in Early Jewish Exegesis'.[22] The word *peshat* itself is metaphorical; its plain senses have to do with flattening, extending, and derivatively with simplicity and innocence and lack of learning, with the popular, the read-once-only, the clear, the generally accepted, the current, and so on; but the central sense, Loewe maintains, is authority. It is used to describe readings by no means literal, and applications 'entirely arbitrary'. Loewe concludes that the best translation of the word, at any rate up to the end of the period of the Talmuds and the midrashim, is 'authoritative teaching', which covers both traditional teaching and teaching given by a particular rabbi of acknowledged authority. And, says Loewe, 'the conventional distinction between *peshat* and *derash* must be jettisoned'. In times later than those of which Loewe speaks, the identification of *peshat* with plain sense became firmer, with important results. But its historical association with authority, and its inescapable association with *derash*, point clearly enough to the conclusion that our minds are not very well adapted to the perception of texts in themselves; we necessarily provide them with contexts, some of them imposed by authority and tradition, some by the need to make sense of them in a different world.

It is possible for some philosophers of language to speak of a 'zero context' – to maintain that 'for every sentence the literal meaning of the sentence can be construed as the meaning it has independent of any context whatever'. In expressing his dissent from this opinion, John Searle argues that the meaning even of 'the cat sat on the mat' depends upon 'background assumptions'; there is, he believes, 'no constant set of assumptions that determine the notion of literal meaning'.[23] Some of these assumptions are silently at work when we make the statement about the cat. Its plain sense depends, among other things, on the assumption that the cat and the mat are within the gravitational field of the earth; and Searle is able to fit out the sentence with speculative contexts which give it quite other senses. But this fascinating sentence invites other potentially interesting considerations. For example: the sentence is felt as somehow infantile, as belonging to a reading primer, perhaps; it owes its memorability to a triple rhyme – a phonetic bond which solicits our attention to the code rather than the message. That the procedures are metaphoric rather than metonymic gives the sentence a poetic quality and more potential intertext (so long as we have it in the original language). There is the further consideration that the sentence must almost always have a citational quality – Lyons and Searle both cite it as an example, and I have cited them citing it. Since it lives in such rarefied contexts its simplicity is certainly bogus, and its use variously coloured by pedantry and archness. It has no plain sense; it merely serves as a lay figure, like the poet's icy diagram, his lake with its shadows, rats, and lilies.

And that takes me back to the imaginary zero context where I began. There is no 'inert savoir'; to speak as if there were is already to speak 'as if'. Metaphor begins to remodel the plain sense as soon as we begin to think or to speak about it. If Stevens is right in saying that the words of the world are the life of the world, then metaphor runs in the world's blood, as if *derash* and *peshat* were the red and the white corpuscles, intrinsically plural.

I have taken most of my examples from exegesis as practised in religions which maintained over very long periods an extreme venera-tion for their sacred texts, and which certainly abhorred the idea of deliberate interference or distortion. The place of rule-governed imagination was clearly established in *midrash*. In the Christian tra-dition, with its basic belief that the sense of the Jewish Bible must be sought in another book, there is a quite different imaginative challenge. All such result in *Entstellung*, not *Darstellung*. Among the thousands of commentators there have been literalists of the imagination and also extravagant poets. But all have in their measure to be creators, even if they wish to imagine themselves at the end of imagination when the lake is still, without reflections; there may be silence, but it is silence of a sort, never zero silence.

13

Mixed Feelings

This was the third of four Northcliffe lectures given at University College London in 1988. The lectures look back to the literature and society of the Thirties, the period when I was first taking an interest in such matters. Among other things, this talk argues that posterity has been wrong to ignore the work of Edward Upward, who now, in his tenth decade, remains a writer of exceptional originality. Indeed the literature of that age is too easily neglected or derided; for example, the work of Chrisopher Caudwell is much more interesting than you would guess from the dismissive attitudes of more recent Marxists. The relative neglect of some of the writers of the period may be in part attributable to the eminence of W. H. Auden, who figures more largely in the next chapter.

The crisis that engaged the minds and spirits of the bourgeois writers of the Thirties appeared to them to be unique; and in one respect at least it was so, for I do not think that any English writers before them – or since – have felt as they did about inequality and the absence of respect and affection between classes. There was an evident need for something more than fellow-feeling, more than progressive reform. It was not merely that they began to attend to the plight of the poor. They applied themselves to a need much more overwhelming – the inevitability of vast historical change, of revolution and war, of which poverty and class hatred were the social signs. Conscience was reinforced by intellect, and the desire to love one's fellow humans by fear.

Because of all this the Thirties offer us what we are not sure how to handle: a literature of conscience that is also a literature of fear, and sometimes of a certain pleasure in the fear, even of a wish to be clever about the fear and the pleasure.

> These years have seen a boom in sorrow;
> The presses of idleness issued more despair
>   And it was honoured;
> Gross Hunger took on more hands every month,
> Erecting here and everywhere his vast
>   Unnecessary workshops;
> Europe grew anxious about her health,
> Combines tottered, credits froze,
> And business shivered in a banker's winter . . .[1]

The years of slump see a boom in sorrow, despair is inflated as when too much money is printed, Hunger becomes an industrialist, a mass employer, when the normal mass employers are closing their factories and yards. These are conceited inversions – perhaps we might think them just a little too smart. But in the world of 1936 they were (and are) very telling. And this was one of the voices we listened to; it was Auden who found and formed the right period style. There were others who warned us of our spiritual desolation. Eliot was calling us 'decent godless people' whose only monument would be 'the asphalt road / And a thousand lost golf balls'.[2] Ezra Pound blamed the bankers, 'news control and perverted publicity', and tried to sell his economic panacea.[3] John Strachey proved to the large Left Book Club readership that Communism was both desirable and inevitable. But a poet might believe that to be so, yet express, along with the excitement and alarm attending such a belief, a sense that the compound aura of feeling around it included also nostalgia and regret. It was hard to imagine the poetry of the future, and the poetry of the present had to deal with the particular sorrows and threats of the present, which required the sacrifice of much of the past to the necessities of history and conscience.

To understand what it felt like to be in this position we must first see that these writers were not simply experiencing one of those intermittent stirrings of conscience which had afflicted the intelligent bourgeoisie in the past, much as it does today. There really is a qualitative difference between these types of conscientious attention to social evils. Throughout the nineteenth century the attention of the well-to-do was at random intervals drawn to the existence of intolerable social conditions, and the harsh measures used to mitigate their consequences. When the crime rate increased greatly after the French Revolution those in power blamed the libertinism of that revolution, and took repressive countermeasures. But liberals blamed instead the policies of the government itself. 'Our progress towards the minimum of endurable privation', wrote William Maginn in 1830, 'has been as rapid as the most inveterate enemy of England could desire'. Prison turned occasional thieves into professional criminals; bankruptcy was common; and the principal remedy for these ills was emigration, either voluntary or compulsory, with consequent depletion of the labour force. The responsibility for social ills was firmly placed on the poor themselves.[4] The *Morning Chronicle* could startle its readers into a momentary awareness that the cities were really 'horrible muckheaps', as William Morris called them; Dickens could urge his readers to understand that rich and poor were of one body, that the diseases of the slums were not obliged to spare the middle classes. Thackeray expressed his dismay at learning how people had to live in slums not five minutes away from his own Garrick Club. Mayhew's *Life and Labour of the London Poor* (1861–2) placed a lot of evidence, some of it horrible, some of it curious, before the public; and *The Economist* condemned his work as 'an encouragement to communism'.[5] But horror soon gave way to renewed indifference, and the problems were again left to the heroic charitable organizations, until the next wave of interest. These periodic alarms about the condition of England continued well into the twentieth century, and they still go on. The uproar caused by the television play *Cathy Come Home* was typical: Tony Garnett told me that a year after its showing, when the urgent calls for action had subsided, the number of people in Cathy's position had greatly increased. No doubt it is now much larger.

Between these periodic awakenings many middle-class people appeared to resume their old view of poverty as inevitable or self-inflicted. The poor (the proletariat, as they began about this time to be called) were an anonymous unwashed mass, to be feared, despised, and disciplined. The severity with which they were treated by those forced into contact with them went far beyond what was needed to punish or even merely exploit them, as for example in heavy fines for lateness at work, and the prohibition of singing in factories.[6]

Most people rarely came into contact with the poor except in their capacity as servants. Engels, who had told the world about the lives of workers in Manchester, was impressed by the arrangements which made it unnecessary for the well-to-do ever to see the conditions under which those workers lived; the roads which carried them from their suburbs to their businesses were driven through the working-class districts in such a way that they did not need to pass through the mean streets. And he observed that 'the middle classes have more in common with every other nation in the world than with the proletariat which lives on their own doorsteps'.[7] Not the least remarkable aspect of this situation was the docility of the working class. Engels saw that Chartism was simply too deferential in its manners, too gentle, to achieve its objectives. But he believed that the next slump in the cycle would inevitably produce a qualitative change, a change which entailed revolution; deference would stop, the attention of the middle class would no longer be switched on and off at convenient intervals; the bourgeoisie would be involved in a world-historical process, and not merely taking a look at the problem when it chose to do so.

He was wrong, of course, and his mistake was repeated in the Thirties, when capitalism was once again in its death throes, and history had again brought about that qualitative change which precedes revolution. But deference was again triumphing over tendencies to militancy. The conditions of the poor were perhaps not very different. The city was still the great image of social division, often not much changed from the previous century when Walter Bagehot, in a famous conceit that would nowadays qualify him as a Postmodernist, compared it to a newspaper: 'everything is there, and everything is disconnected';[8] wealth and poverty, virtue and scandal, all in the same place. In the nineteenth century there was a popular song called 'I can't find Brummagem' and in the twentieth the middle-class poet Louis MacNeice, exiled there for a time, called it 'a sprawling inkblot', lived on its genteel south side, and escaped by car whenever he could, leaving behind his 'unresponsive' and 'undernourished' students; as they made the prison-like lecture-rooms resound to the verses of Homer recited in Midland accents they seemed as different from the 'clean-cut working man' of his fantasy as they were from Oxford undergraduates.[9] And 'up in the industrial district on the north side of Birmingham the air was a muddy pond and the voices of those who expected nothing a chorus of frogs for ever resenting and accepting the *status quo* of stagnation'.[10]

The calm or resignation of the proletariat in these pre-revolutionary times continued to puzzle middle-class left-wingers, and their puzzlement is a measure of the frightful task they set themselves when they proposed to breach the class frontier. I think again of Edmund Wilson's novel, in which the narrator begins to explain Marxism to his working-class mistress but soon gives up, seeing that she can't believe it has anything to do with her and the way of life she knows and he doesn't. I myself lived through most of the Thirties in a small town in the Isle of Man which had very high seasonal unemployment. Poor children were easily identified because they wore clogs, issued free by the municipality to the children of the unemployed. These children were despised but also feared by those of us, not all that much richer, who wore boots or shoes, were brought up not to be rough like the clog-wearers, and threatened with their fate if naughty. There was some grumbling about the bosses when times were particularly hard, and even, at a moment of extreme poverty, a successful general strike. But for the most part the interests of working-class people didn't extend far beyond their own kind and their own problems. There was a good deal of gaiety and gossip, since within these limits everybody knew everybody else, or if not, knew her cousin. There was no great envy or dislike of the gentry, indeed there was a measure of respect (one was always being told to behave like a gentleman). Animosity was reserved largely for those who were a rung lower, the wearers of clogs. I don't remember any talk of revolution and the word 'bourgeoisie' wasn't used; nor, for that matter, was 'proletariat'.

All this tended to reduce the possibility of concerted proletarian action; it was just the sort of thing the infatuated bourgeois intellectual couldn't know about. There was another consideration tending to reduce that possibility, no doubt less surprising to us than to people in the Thirties, few of whom will have known about it anyway (which illustrates the difference between living in a period and knowing about it later). It is this: people who had work were better off than ever before; real wages rose throughout the decade, and the gap between those in work and the unemployed steadily widened. It was no easier then than now to feel the misfortunes of others; and as one motored down the new asphalt roads to the ball-strewn golf course the unfortunate, like Engel's slum-dwellers, were nowhere to be seen, and were remembered, if at all, only for their feckless refusal to prosper. Yet there was a myriad of them, out of sight, not only of the poor but of the crippled. More than two-and-a-half million men were drawing pensions for disabilities sustained in the still quite recent war. These were carefully apportioned: 16s. for a whole right arm, 14s. for an arm missing below the elbow, and so on. These men tended to show up only on Armistice Day. And if you had £5 a week, poverty and privation were remote considerations. If you were a 'rentier poet' with £500 a year you thought about them only because of a deliberate and educated act of conscience. And once committed to this course you might feel compassion, beyond necessity no doubt, for almost the whole population; manual workers earned about £3 a week, and 88 per cent of the population had less than £250 a year.[11] It is true that a family like my own managed fairly well on £3, and people lived with enviable style on £5. But the bourgeois poets could hardly be expected to know that.

The point is that consciousness of the need and the possibility of action was to a very considerable extent an affair of the middle-class conscience. And it is surely to the credit of the intellectual left, now somewhat despised for *naïveté*, that they were so moved, that they came to believe that they must do something about the whole system that in their view made poverty and war equally inevitable. When they joined the Communist Party, or fellow-travelled, they were not climbing on to a bandwagon; even in the days of its greatest pre-war success, the great days of the Left Book Club, before the German–Soviet Pact, the Party had only a few thousand members. Ordinary people only began to worry about world politics in 1938, with the frantic trench-digging in Hyde Park, and the barrage balloons, so weird then, soon to be so familiar. Moreover the events of 1939, including the introduction of conscription, made political argument an irrelevance, especially for nineteen-year-olds like myself. Even those who had said they would not fight in a capitalist–imperialist war quietly went along. The rhetoric of the coming proletarian revolution was no longer much heard.

As I've suggested, it had always been in some degree ignorant. The proletariat wasn't the beautiful, doomed, unlucky, but potentially irresistible body fantasized by the bourgeois Communist sympathizer, transferring his sense of what it meant to be outcast, alienated, *maudit*, to the worker. The proletariat was a strange tribe, and it might be lovable. In fact intellectuals invented Mass Observation to find how the workers lived and behaved, much as if they were a 'primitive' tribe and the Observers anthropologists willing to learn a new language in return for knowledge of an alien culture. They observed such events as the Silver Jubilee celebrations of George V and the coronation of George VI, and they observed perfectly ordinary, arbitrarily chosen days like 12 May 1937. They wanted to know what people did in dance halls, bathrooms, and pubs. They developed the fashionable genre of reportage, and they unwittingly established techniques of market research that are still too much with us. Their motives were excellent; they wished to learn about and possibly love the unknown, the Other.

The poets looked at the proletariat less methodically, more speculatively than the Mass Observers. Tending to repeat one another, they were, for example, astonished at the degree to which the poor seemed to depend for comfort on the cinema – not Russian films or John Grierson's, but Hollywood's.

> Enter the dream-house, brothers and sisters, leaving
> Your debts asleep, your history at the door;
> This is the home for heroes, and this loving
> Darkness a fur you can afford . . .
>
> Bathed in this common source, you gape incurious
> At what your active hours have willed –
> Sleepwalking on that silver wall, the furious
> Sick shapes and pregnant fancies of your world.[12]

How did Cecil Day-Lewis know this? He didn't; he assumed it must be so. And where did George Barker find the word 'marvellous' used as he uses it in these lines?

> I encountered the crowd returning from amusements,
> The Bournemouth Pavilion, or the marvellous gardens,
>
> The Palace of Solace, the Empyrean Cinema . . .[13]

Here 'marvellous' means, roughly, 'not marvellous', or 'what ordinary people ignorantly think marvellous', and Barker of course got it from Auden ('long marvellous letters', etc.). It may also have been Auden who first put it about that cinemas were a pathetic kind of solace for the poor: 'bowers of bliss / Where thousands are holding hands', 'Gaumont theatres / Where fancy plays on hunger to produce / The noble robber, ideal of boys.'[14] It didn't matter if you used the cinema yourself as a means of escape, as MacNeice and his wife did, four or five times a week, in Birmingham, going

solely for entertainment and never for value, holding hands like a shopgirl with her boy-friend. The organist would come up through the floor, a purple spotlight on his brilliantined head, and play us the 'Londonderry Air' and bow and go back to the tomb. Then the stars would return and the huge Cupid's bows of their mouths would swallow up everybody's troubles – there were no more offices or factories or shops, no more bosses or foremen, no more unemployment and no more employment, no more danger of disease or babies, nothing but bliss in a celluloid world where the roses are always red and the Danube is always blue.[15]

You can tell from the tone that it was all the other people in the cinema who were experiencing this bogus solace and not the MacNeices, who were there with them, but not of them, almost nightly, being entertained, not seeking value where only the others could be deluded into thinking they might find it.

Such, it was supposed, were the compensations of terribly restricted lives. Here another poet describes how those poor lives are lived:

> The greengrocer's cart, the haggling to save a halfpenny,
> On the boiled orange or the Argus-eyes potato;
> The fecund red-elbowed women with their baskets,
>   And their humourless menfolk.

These will never hold aces or travel farther
Than a tram will take them. And their summum bonum
The threepenny double which comes up by a head,
   Unlimited bitter.[16]

Those lines come from a long poem, desperate, indignant, compassion-
ate; but it certainly makes the poor keep their distance. The Horatian
stanza is itself a mark of detachment, even of retreat. Then there is the
learned little joke about the potatoes, the patronizing *summum bonum*,
the women so very unlike our own ('fecund red-elbowed') and their
men, so very unlike us ('humourless'). The workers' Cockaigne is
defined by a bet won with a derisory stake, and a gutter flowing with
beer. The poem is saying to the poor what Upward's hero said to his
girl: 'How ugly you are!' But it is also trying to add, 'This is what we
must learn to love'. Those fashionable definite articles (the cart, the
haggling, the orange, the potato, the women, the threepenny double),
also from Auden (neatly labelled by David Trotter, who calls them
articles of 'unfulfilled specificity'[17]), mean *ex uno disce omnes*: from
these types you will understand the collective whole. I don't know
about boiled oranges, which sound exotic, but the proximity of this
one to the obviously substandard potato suggests that it represents the
exoticism of a poverty we do not, at this stage anyway, share.

   Kenneth Allott's poem goes on to tell us that the poet lies in bed
thinking of these things, hearing the water knocking in the pipes, or
perhaps it is his own heart; while outside the 'necessary' light awakens
'the seasons and cities'. The light is necessary as Auden's lovers are
necessary, part of the going on of a world from which the poet
contemplates his detachment. 'The moon is usual. . . . The planets rush
towards Lyra in the lion's charge . . . And tomorrow comes. It's a
world. It's a way.'[18] The usual is given cosmic scope, yet we don't
belong to it. Mere rags of it as we are, we cannot fail to join the
universe; yet to make a point of our having to do so also sets us apart,
just as we are apart from the red-elbowed women and the humourless
men whom we must also somehow join. To know the ordinary other
one is forced to be extraordinary, which makes it difficult to join the
ordinary. The poetry emerges as at once cool and distraught, and so
much in the fashion and dialect of the time that to see its value requires

a patient effort of historical understanding. Given that, we may read it not exactly as it was but with a supplement of later sympathy which shows it to be struggling for a cathexis unwillingly willed. It is an attempt to do as Auden's sages taught – to renounce 'what our vanity has chosen', to pursue 'understanding with patience like a sex'.

The sheer difficulty of pursuing understanding like a sex was coldly described by George Orwell as both moral and technical.

Books about ordinary people behaving in an ordinary manner are extremely rare [he said], because they can only be written by someone who is capable of standing both inside and outside the ordinary man, as Joyce for instance stands inside and outside Bloom; but this involves admitting to yourself that you *are* an ordinary person for nine-tenths of the time, which is exactly what no intellectual ever wants to do.[19]

But, even if being a writer is to be truly extraordinary only one-tenth of the time, you are a writer when you are writing, and so extraordinary, even when writing about the ordinary, the necessary, the usual; and Joyce would serve equally well as evidence in support of this truism. Orwell himself was compelled to behave in an extraordinary way, to be a writer of pastoral, by the excitements of those early days in Barcelona, intimations of proletarian triumph which for a moment induced even in Auden a sense of solidarity with the workers. Orwell's essay 'Looking back on the Spanish War' ends with a poem about an Italian militiaman, 'his battered face / Purer than any woman's', and about a handshake that is as much between classes as between men:

> The strong hand and the subtle hand
> Whose palms are only able
> To meet within the sound of guns . . .[20]

So to Orwell himself it seemed that the writer must search for and love an ordinary wisdom different from his own (the Italian soldier 'was born knowing what I had learned / Out of books and slowly'); and there is no inaccuracy here in using the word 'love' and no difficulty in understanding what it was that Orwell loved – a person who stood for a class:

a fierce, pathetic, innocent face . . . which I only saw for a minute or two . . .
He symbolizes for me the flower of the European working class, harried by
the police of all countries, the people who fill the mass graves of the Spanish
battlefields and are now, to the tune of several millions, rotting in forced-
labour camps.

He is one soldier but all that as well:

> . . . the thing I saw in your face
> No power can disinherit:
> No bomb that ever burst
> Shatters the crystal spirit.

Orwell didn't often write like that; but that he did so on this occasion
shows the special quality of the intellectual's attitude to the worker,
however difficult it was to articulate. It isn't the slight ache of conscience over breakfast; it isn't anything Morris or Ruskin or Shaw
would have felt. It is also very different from that 'aesthetic' form of
socialism to which Wilde gave his blessing, a socialism that did not
seek the handclasp of subtle with strong, but hoped by a redistribution
of income and property to avoid such contacts altogether. 'The chief
advantage of Socialism is undoubtedly the fact that Socialism would
relieve us from that necessity of living for others which, in the present
condition of things, presses so hard on nearly everybody.' Hideous
poverty, hideous ugliness, hideous starvation, says Wilde, tempt one
to try to ameliorate things, which always makes them worse. Despite
its facetious tone, Wilde's essay encapsulates some of the stronger
motives of English parlour socialism. The sentiments of the Thirties
writers were different because they wanted, or tried to want, that
handclasp with the unknown and innocent oppressed.

It is part of the story that the wish to love was accompanied by its
opposite, an uneasy desire to withdraw, a repugnance like that of
Upward's hero. Stephen Spender explained that in the end he finally
had no real choice but to prefer his own aesthetic individualism to the
'historically correct position'.

To believe that my individual freedom could gain strength from my seeking to identify myself with 'progressive' forces was different from believing that my life must become an instrument of means decided upon by political leaders. I came to see that within the struggle for a juster world there is a further struggle between the individual who cares for long-term values and those who are willing to use any and every means to gain their political ends – even good ends. Within even a good social cause, there is a duty to fight for the pre-eminence of individual conscience ... the individual must not be swallowed up by the concept of social man.[21]

Spender is thinking of the disillusioning tactics of the Party in those years, but the word that keeps on recurring is 'individual', and the sacrifice that is refused is the sacrifice of individuality, of the subtle hand; once the position is clearly understood, the writer, unless he is as totally committed as Caudwell or Upward, simply backs away from proletarianization; the sacrifice is too appalling, he feels he would have nothing left to work with or indeed to love with.

So most of the middle-class writers did fall away from active leftist politics as the decade drew towards its end. But the record of their affair with the workers is an honourable one, and we shouldn't allow stock responses about pink or pansy poets to usurp our judgement. They had mixed feelings, but, as Auden remarked, poetry 'might be defined as the clear expression of mixed feelings',[22] which could very well consist of a consciousness of extraordinary novelty and deep anxieties about loving the unknown.

A clear expression of similarly mixed feelings is Edward Upward's *The Spiral Ascent*, a trilogy of novels long meditated and completed only in 1977. It has won less attention than it deserves, perhaps because it came so late, perhaps because it was easy to deplore Upward's departure from the manner of his admired early story 'The Railway Accident', which, as Isherwood records in *Lions and Shadows*, was one of the Mortmere fantasies devised by Upward and Isherwood in their time at Cambridge. There is also a change of manner from Upward's early novel *Journey to the Border* (1938). Samuel Hynes, in one of his rare mistaken judgements, says that 'the tension between his imagination and his political ideology shrivelled his natural gifts, and left him an arid, unimaginative and unreadable realist'.[23] In fact

Upward did feel he had to achieve a new socialist simplicity of style, but he believed he could do so without ceasing to be an artist; for 'an artist cannot give his best to a political cause if in his art he is a politician first and an artist second'. Of course it was difficult to hold this position, and indeed holding it is a principal subject of his book. He could not altogether abandon the style of fantasy which came naturally to him as a writer; but, although it is true that the first volume of the trilogy represents a willed socialist realism, Upward can justifiably claim that in the rest of the work he was moving to something richer – not the old Balzac bottles with new wine in them, but what he calls 'new forms'. He admits that he found this progress easier after he became disillusioned with politics – 'the Party, I was able to see, was becoming un-Marxist' – and when he left the Party in 1948 he was in a position to abandon the strict canons of socialist realism, or to transform that kind of realism in very remarkable ways.[24]

Upward's hero is a middle-class, public-school poet, sure of his vocation but full of what Caudwell would have described as an anarchistic hatred of his own class, of the 'poshocrats' as he always calls them. The early scenes report with remarkable directness some naïve conversations between this poet, who is a straight version of Upward himself, and his friend, who is Isherwood. ' "I've realized lately that I'm against the plus-foured plutocracy, and for the cockneys and lower orders," ' says the Isherwood character. ' "I'm for them too," Alan said. "But I haven't your courage. I am afraid they will despise me. How did you do it?" "By behaving naturally. They are rather proud of their gentlemanly friend." ' These lower orders are contrasted with the guests at the big holiday hotel, blazered young men and confidently striding girls. 'In their dress, their voices, their every minutest gesture and facial movement, they represented for Alan what he loathed more than anything else in the world: they were the loyal young supporters of that power . . . which despised the living poets and the truth.' Not long after this, however, Alan goes to bed with one of the confidently striding girls; she is about to be married but clearly enjoys her bourgeois irresponsibility. The theorists were always saying that all socialist realism need do to discredit the bourgeoisie is to show it as it actually is.

As one reads these early pages it is difficult to avoid the thought that this very deliberate attempt to invent a Communist style of writing merely proves that the new style is bound to be mistaken for bad writing by the unreconstructed bourgeoisie. However, Upward, even in this first volume, confounds this judgement by doing some good bourgeois writing, too. Certainly the effect is original, and it seems to me that the value of the whole is enhanced by the intrusion of this highly accented unproletarian rhetoric into flat grey stretches of candid socialist realism. In the representation of natural objects for instance, Upward cannot prevent himself from writing well in an older style: 'Then the miniature waves detaching themselves from the spent breaker and scarcely having the power of individual motion: these flopped on the sand with pause and dip like the rolling of a metal ellipse, or like the movement of the genitals of a naked male runner.' For all its ideological assertiveness, its continual worrying about how to mix solitary art and comradely Party business, Upward's book is always *written*, always organized, and always true to the sort of self-consciousness that is supposed to be the privilege of the privileged. In that degree it is pastoral, but it does not acquiesce in the fate of the poor. And if it was true, as Upward believed in 1937, that only a Marxist or near-Marxist attitude could produce good writing,[25] it was equally true, and just as well understood by him, that only good *writers* could produce good writing, and that, because of their traditional habits of mind and of work, good writers would have their difficulties with Communism, and find it hard to avoid pastoral attitudes to the workers.

Here Alan and his friends are watching some workers at a dance: '"What is it that makes them so fine?" . . . "It can't be just sex." "No. Perhaps it's beauty, eh?" "Then it's because they're *living*." "Yes, that's partly it. But there's more to it than that . . . I've got it . . . It's because they're doomed." "Boy, I believe you're right." "It's because in ten to fifteen years' time all these girls will be prematurely middle-aged and ugly. And they're dancing now in defiance of the inevitable rot which will come upon them." "Yes, that's it."' Later this insight is developed: it isn't only the young women who are doomed; the men are just as fine and they're doomed, too. '"What makes people vile is being comfortably off. That's why most of the hotel visitors are so poisonous. They are the wicked, the devils. Only the doomed are good, and we must be on their side always."' His friend agrees. '"Our duty is to live among the doomed, and in our poetry we must record and celebrate what they are."' And then Alan names the price to be paid for choosing the noble and rejecting the vile: '"We ourselves, in our own way, are doomed too . . . We shall always be misfits, not properly belonging to any social class. We shall never settle down anywhere. We must walk the earth. We must descend into hell."'

There is often a certain quasi-religious fervour in Upward, but rarely to the degree that in this passage he attributes to himself as a young man: first to be like the disciples and walk the earth, homeless and without possessions; then to be like Christ and harrow hell. It seems to be weirdly excessive, absolutely dated, yet because rather than in spite of that, it sounds right. It would be as well to add that there is present also a hint of self-irony, a suggestion of reserve. And we can't grasp the full sense of these opening pages until their material reappears, splendidly transformed, at the close of the trilogy, 760 pages later.

What follows it more immediately is Alan's going to bed with his girl poshocrat, and then contemplating suicide. He understands that a commitment to Communism could save him, but fears the effect of such a move on his writing. His poetry had failed hitherto because it wasn't, for want of such commitment, rooted in life and reality. To have any hope of writing well he must join the Party. But he must not do so simply in order to be able to write poetry. And in any case Party work might prevent his writing. Finally he joins because there is no tolerable alternative.

When Alan meets the workers at the local branch he is struck by the drabness of the habitat and the beauty of the inhabitants: 'From their eyes, bleared or bright or set in undernourished faces marked with skin disease, there looked out the life of the future.' They were finer than the well-dressed men and women from the hotel, more beautiful than the well-kept girl he had fallen in love with in the last days of his bourgeois life. He must work with these people, distribute pamphlets, turn up at meetings; he must also write, but there could be no compromise with bohemianism or liberal anarchism. Shunning bourgeois romance, he takes up with Elsie, who is plain and has not 'the look of a lady'; when he marries her he is quite expressly 'marrying the party'. She is thus a perfect emblem of the sexualized politics I've been trying to explain.

There is no salvation outside the Party, but we are not allowed to forget that its routine apocalyptic certainties, ritual condemnations, and repetitive propaganda can be tedious. Nevertheless the faith, as expounded in Alan's 'dusty stable loft', will prevail, and it is a great thing to be living at this hour of crisis, 'qualitatively different from former periodic crises'. The hour which should have struck in 1917 – when the clock was stopped by the interventions of democratic socialism, by a Labour Party which was merely an instrument of capitalism – that hour is now at hand.

Writing after the event, Upward must have been conscious of historical ironies. The Labour Party ceased to be the servile instrument of capital when Moscow, in the interest of the Popular Front, suddenly said it wasn't. The confident assertion that 'Communism was the only force in the world which was uncompromisingly on the side of the doomed and against them who wanted to keep them doomed' must surely have acquired an ironical ring after the Stalinist purges became common knowledge. But at this stage Alan is keeping faith with a pure Communism that can cohabit with poetry. He is aware of a tension between them, but that tension is exactly what must be resolved by faith and works.

The beauty of Upward's slowly developing design is that such conflicts are registered and reconciled, as perhaps they only could be reconciled, in a work of art. It may be that in this respect it stands alone. Some of Upward's younger contemporaries thought their duty to be the writing of articles and pamphlets or poems about those who excelled all others at the making of driving-belts, thereby violating their sense of what poetry really was. Upward finds a way of putting in all the pedestrian detail and giving it a relation to the whole work (a criterion of value despised, I'm afraid, by modern Marxists). Alan finishes his long poem after many years of work, and his poem is Upward's novel, with all its longueurs and embarrassments. Here is a hero who is disgusted by Party rhetoric, by the stereotyped gesture, even by the infidelity of its leaders to Marxist Leninism; yet when he is expelled from the Party he falls ill with the sickness of the excommunicated.

Upward calls his trilogy 'a dialectical triad' – the political and the poetic as dialectical opposites, with a synthesis at the end, following the 'spiral ascent'. The final volume represents the synthesis. Alan is no longer described in the third person; the narrator is now 'I'. He has withdrawn into bourgeois security, but in finishing the book he simultaneously finishes his poem, so that they share a beautiful coda, the effect of which is to synthesize poetry and Communism.

To express admiration for such refined structures and transformations is to use measures devised for the sort of writing which advocates of the proletarian novel reject. However, they are the measures appropriate to such skill and originality. Anybody who wants quick assurances that these are the proper terms of praise might look at a recent short story of Upward's, called 'At the Ferry Inn', which appeared in 1985.[26] It recounts a single incident and is seemingly a quite flat and over-detailed piece of slightly disguised autobiography. On inspection, however, it is not that at all. A poet called Walter Selwyn, quite obviously Auden, pays a visit to his old friend Arnold Olney, that is Upward, on the Isle of Wight, where Upward happens to live. They have been estranged for forty years (perhaps since Auden's departure to the United States in 1939). The ferry will bring Selwyn over for a day before he returns to New York. The arrival of the ferry is described with much detail. Among its passengers Olney observes a young man, 'tall, broad-hipped, sloping-shouldered', his hair thick and yellow, his cheeks plump and smooth-skinned. It is as if only a week or two has passed since their last meeting.

Olney (Upward) has had a dream about his friend in which he met him at the ferry, remembering at the same time Auden's sonnet 'just as his dream foretold' – which, though he doesn't say so, contains the lines 'at each meeting, he was forced to learn, / The same misunderstanding would arise . . .' 'How well Auden's sonnet gets the inconsequent feeling of dream', thinks Olney. In the dream the poet's face is 'saggingly old'. Also in the dream Olney accepts a suitcase from a stranger, and places it on the steps of a bank.

The friends drink at the Ferry Inn, with a group of hostile blue-blazered poshocrats at the bar. Perhaps they overheard Olney telling his friend about the bomb in the dream, and the interpretation offered by Selwyn, which is that the bomb stands for the dreamer's guilt for so many years of political activism. 'You were loyal for longer than the rest of us', says the poet, 'to the "clever hopes", as Auden afterwards called them, that we all fell for in the nineteen thirties, but your book has brilliantly rejected them at last.' He has been reading the final volume of *The Spiral Ascent* (which actually came out four years after Auden's death). The author of that book protests that he was 'deconverted' not from Communism but from Stalinism. But the poet insists on congratulating him for having understood that he must put his trust not in politicians but in artists. 'Art', he says, quoting Baudelaire in an Anglo-American French accent, 'is the best testimony human beings can give of their dignity.' By now they sense the growing disapproval of the blazered poshocrats; but the author nevertheless affirms his confidence in Leninist Marxism as a force in a world of deepening capitalist crisis; the coming revolution must prevent nuclear war. The poet now says that a proletarian revolution was never a clever hope, adding that poets didn't save a single Jew from the gas chambers. Whereupon he departs to the lavatory, leaving his host to reflect on the hostility of the yachtsmen, but also to remember that, had he not known the poet, he 'would never have known how marvellous human life at its best could be'. After a long wait he goes in search of his friend, fearing that he might have fallen ill or been beaten up. But he has gone, and Olney can only glimpse him on the disappearing ferry, his face 'even more saggingly and horrifyingly old' than it had been in the dream. Was the poet offended? No; he had waved cheerfully, the estrangement was over, though they could never meet again.

It is a complex tale, dream within dream; here is a dreamlike double Auden, quoting himself as if he were another poet, the old poet quoting the young one, of whom he no longer approves; here is Upward's paranoid vision of middle-class manners. The inn of the outer dream is the womb towards which, on such occasions, there is a retreat. The poet's face is old in the dream, young in the dreamed reality. There is a synthesis of old aspirations and old conflicts, the clever hopes raised above cleverness, the Thirties as the low dishonest decade of the defector, the very poet who had, in that time, shown how marvellous human life could be. Reportage and fantasy are reconciled. Baudelaire was right; but so, too, was Marx; and so too was Kafka in his union of world and dream.

Upward is sometimes called naïve, or even ignorant, but to join that chorus is to accept the myth which, as I've said, is partly the creation of

Orwell, though it also owes much to political opponents like Wyndham Lewis. From Lewis we get an antithetical view of Thirties politics, as well as of human dignity. He doesn't want to love the proletariat – the peons, the *Massenmenschen* – and he does not love those who wish to love them; they earn his contempt and disgust as bad artists. If Lewis wasn't interested in peons he wasn't interested, either, in bourgeois individuals. His characters tend to be types, humours, even marionettes.

The Thirties pamphleteering of Lewis, 'that lonely old volcano of the right' as Auden almost affectionately called him,[27] is pretty well forgotten, but *Hitler* (1931), *Left Wings over Europe* (1936), and *Count Your Dead* (1937) were of some importance in their day. Lewis's latest biographer calls *Hitler* 'scantily researched and hastily written' – he hadn't even read *Mein Kampf* – but it was less a plug for Hitler than an expression of his hatred of Weimar, homosexuality, and the English writers who liked both.[28] Its contempt for the masses is so virulent that the Marxist critic Fredric Jameson, by ingenious dialectical manœuvres, can argue that its 'oppositional stance' puts the book finally on the side of the revolution.[29] Nobody except biographers and historians would want to read it now, and even Lewis's belated recantations, *The Jews, are they Human?* and *The Hitler Cult* (both 1939) have no interest; but *The Revenge for Love* is sometimes called the finest political novel of its time.

Lewis's novel appeared in 1937, at a time when left-wing writers were most deeply involved in the Republican cause, and it was read as an anti-Communist manifesto. So in a way it was; but Communism is for Lewis but one fraud in a world of frauds. To be a Communist is to be either a hired hand or a victim. What makes Lewis's position idiosyncratic is that he sees the sordor of the world of Communism as analogous to that of bogus art. Day-Lewis's confession that he felt small when he saw a Communist is repeatedly and derisively cited as evidence that a fake will always feel small when confronted with the real thing, however ugly. Lewis's Communist agent, Percy Hardcaster, is not a political idealist but a technician: 'There is a *technique* of the general strike, of agitation, of the *coup d'état*. Those are technical problems. Once you begin *acting* instead of merely talking, you become a technician.' Hardcaster accepts as part of his business both the beatings he suffers and the amateurish stupidity of his middle-class associates, just as the real artist, Lewis, accepts the rough treatment he gets from frauds and philistines, and the amateurish pseudo-artists that surround him. Communism and the business of forging paintings have exactly the same moral status.

So Percy gets some ironical respect because he is a professional; the real villains are the middle-class intellectuals. In fact they are the only real Communists because Communism is a fraud and only frauds would profess to believe in it; Percy at least isn't a fraud, nor are the worker-Communists, who are in it for what they can get. The workman, when he becomes a Communist,

regards it as just another job – a jolly sight better paid than any he can get out of the bosses. And when he makes himself into a Communist he brings with him all his working-class cynicism, all his underdog cowardice and disbelief in everything and everybody . . . That is why Marx insisted on the necessity of his *hatred* being exploited.

When a middle-class intellectual argues that his purpose is to free the workers from such moral bondage, he is given an unsavoury account of proletarian manners and told derisively, 'It is with *that* that you have got to make your Communism rhyme.' The person who wants to free the workers is, significantly, a painter of abstracts. 'Don't you ever see anything – except *abstractions*? Like your pictures! But you are dealing with men and women of flesh and blood. A mob of treacherous idiots! That's what you're doing – who snigger up their sleeves at you for the sucker you are . . .'[30]

Here, then, is the opposition, in the form of a book about Spain which consigns the Republican cause to the hands of mercenaries, dupes, and frauds, and is especially hard on worker-loving pink artists of the sort I've been praising. But Lewis's contempt for them, and for the workers, is really only a special case of his disgust with the human world in general. His novel has two central emblems: a grotesque dwarf and a malignantly howling baby. They stand for what forces Lewis into his role as Enemy – the repulsiveness of human generation, of a race malformed, bitter, and loathsome. Much the same spirit informs his hatred of homosexuality (which he rather oddly supposed to be a consequence of the unfairness to men of bourgeois marriage laws[31]) – like Communism it was a fraudulent cult, but he saw these cults as having the malignant, distorted energy of the dwarf and the baby. Admirers of Lewis tend, I think, to smoothe him out, to ignore the deeper sources of his disgust, as I think Julian Symons does in his introduction to the 1962 edition of *The Revenge for Love*. He treats the book as a justified attack on 'parlour Communists' and on 'the liberal myth about Communist behaviour', a myth we can all now see through because we know 'about the honeycomb of deceit and treachery that marked every Communist Party in the Stalinist era'. Symons reports with irony Lewis's expressed hope that 'his book would some day be read as a novel, with its politics forgotten'; in his view it earns its status as one of the three great political novels of the century (the others being *The Middle of the Journey* (1947) and *Darkness at Noon* (1940)) precisely because of the energy with which it exposed the liberal myth.[32] These are all remarkable books, I admit, but their value cannot be dependent on the myth that they are good because they expose a myth. It is not enough to have seen through something, and Lewis knew that, was aware that opinions quite different from his own could be incorporated in works of art. Upward's achievement, for instance, seems to me quite untouched by Lewis's polemic. And both his novel and Lewis's have what is more important than a critique of political attitudes in a past age: they surprise us by their own complexity, and by the force with which they violate commonplace perceptions, whether out of hatred for the self-seeking, deformed, brutal, and rank-scented mass of humanity, or out of love for the doomed and a desire to redeem them.

There are other myths as unacceptable as the one Symons is glad to have seen demolished. There is the myth of the uncorrupted classless artist facing alone the plebeian mob, its slippery tribunes and its deluded soft collaborators, the phoney artists and the sentimental intellectuals. And whether or no we accept Lewis in this Coriolanus pose – some do and some do not – it seems that his indictment of the intellectual left has to a large extent prevailed. There is a willingness to believe that the work of these writers was founded on ignorance (Orwell's repeated charge) or on bad faith and stupidity (Lewis's repeated charge). And there is an implication that to reject the politics of the bourgeois left of the Thirties implies the necessity to reject its art.

Which accounts for our over-willingness to accept harsh judgements, sometimes made by the writers themselves, of a literature that might still, if we could escape from this myth, strike us as bold and troubling.

I don't hope to show that these writers were never deluded, never silly; nor that their courtship of the proletariat did not lead them into difficulties and out of their depths. But we should not allow our opinion of their politics to serve as a judgement on their art. Indeed one only has to say so out loud for the point to be over-obvious. If I were referring to the great moderns of the previous generation – to Yeats, Pound, Eliot – the remark would be thought a truism; yet that elementary wisdom doesn't at present come into play when we are talking about the Thirties. Perhaps the difficulty is that we are still in some ways close to the writers of the Thirties, some of them still alive, so that it is in that measure harder to think about them without confusing history and value, without allowing our disillusion with their politics to colour our reading of their work – something we manage quite easily to avoid when thinking of more distant times.

And yet that doesn't seem a happy or adequate answer; the Thirties were the decade of the Fascism we allow for as well as of the socialism that embarrasses our judgements. I am clearly not yet done with this subject, and will return to it in the next chapter, when I shall have time to say something about the most important and controversial of all these writers, W. H. Auden.

14

Eros, Builder of Cities

The title of this, the fourth of the Northcliffe lectures, comes from the closing lines of Auden's great elegy for Freud:

> *One rational voice is dumb. Over his grave*
> *The household of Impulse mourns one dearly loved:*
> *Sad is Eros, builder of cities,*
> *And weeping anarchic Aphrodite.*

Reporting MacNeice, I spoke of Stephen Spender's vulcanite desk and Wyndham Lewis portrait as a story denied by Isaiah Berlin, and I dutifully noted his remark. But Spender himself later told me the story was perfectly true. One shouldn't put too much trust in the conflicting reminiscences of survivors. I daresay my remarks about Goronwy Rees, another survivor of my acquaintance, may sound too acerbic for the occasion, but this occasion merely remembered others that had shaped my attitude.

The chapter ends with a defence of 'the English Auden', the poet as he was in his youth, the poet whom he came to dislike or distrust. I included in the lecture a guess that having made such brilliant use of Anthony Collett's book The Changing Face of England *when the cheap edition of 1923 came his way, he turned to it again years later in his poem 'In Praise of Limestone'. Now I know that he was looking for another copy of Collett in 1947, and he presumably found one, for it affected that splendid poem. This information may be found in Edward Mendelson's* The Later Auden *(1999). Mendelson and I have an ancient quarrel about the early Auden, perhaps particularly about 'Spain', which I take some notice of in this chapter. This inveterate difference of opinion does nothing to reduce my admiration for Mendelson as scholar and executor of the Auden estate; he has managed the poet's* Nachleben *with extraordinary generosity and skill.*

The poet's debts to Collett's book are also recorded by the second of the major living Auden authorities, namely John Fuller, in his W. H. Auden: A Commentary *(1998). Auden, as Janet Adam Smith once noticed, had a habit of hoarding phrases for future use, and he was greatly taken with Collett's book, which is full of such treasures. Except in this connection it seems to be forgotten – another injustice, for it has exceptional power and distinction. No doubt its geology has dated, but that is appropriate enough, as if Collett's book were miming what it describes, the perpetual mutability of the English scene. What should have preserved it was the power and felicity of its prose. But I suspect that Collett's politics, miles to the right of the modern Conservative Party, would be the most important obstacle to a revival.*

One of the chief difficulties of writers compelled by conscience or desire to cross the frontier of class was simply habit, an attachment to their own way of life. An Upward might teach himself to hate that way of life, but even he could not altogether forfeit the inheritance of bourgeois manners and education; and others, though convinced that it must be sacrificed, could not bring themselves to despise it, or to abandon it in what they took to be its last days. The inheritance included certain attitudes very much at variance with the straight-faced and solemn courtship rituals with which they approached the proletariat. They were clever and cliquish, weaned on private jokes and teases which could take a nightmarish turn, as in 'Paid on Both Sides' (1930) and *The Orators* (1933) (both strongly affected by Upward's earlier manner). And they naturally teased one another; and might be expected to comment on what sometimes seemed false or strained in the poses struck in public by friends.

In his posthumous autobiography *The Strings are False* (1965) Louis MacNeice, who was perfectly capable of teasing himself, teased his friends for talking too much about 'barricades' and the like – he might have added 'struggle' and 'history' or even 'love'. There was Stephen Spender, moving forward from liberalism to Communism in a chic apartment with a vulcanite desk and a Wyndham Lewis painting over the fireplace.[1] There was – to focus for a moment on an interesting minor figure in MacNeice's circle – an impassioned Welshman, haranguing a group of writers as if from the pulpit, but not with the object of instructing them in the old ways of virtue; for his message was that in future they must take their orders from the proletariat, lay down their personalities, and become the trumpets of the people, the working class in whom lay all hope of victory in the struggle. The meeting over, the exhausted speaker demanded, and was given, oysters at Prunier's, where oysters were very expensive.

This speaker was Goronwy Rees, not a writer of importance but a figure of some interest to students of bourgeois life and love, and also Oxford, in the Thirties. I say a word about him here because I want at the end of this chapter to distinguish rather sharply between the genuine article and the reproduction, closely associated though they were in the Thirties, as no doubt at other times. MacNeice, who knew him well and liked to take him to rugby internationals at Twickenham, says he would have made 'a wonderful travelling salesman',[2] but he became a Fellow of All Souls instead. Oxford had attached to him that almost irremovable label 'brilliant', and he was famous for charm. By the time I came to know and for a time to work with him the admired black curls were white, but a fair share of folly and misfortune had not quite extinguished the brilliance or the other qualities for which he became well known. I see that there is at present an argument in progress as to whether Rees was ever signed up by the KGB; later it might have been a question rather of the CIA. But it would be a pity if it came to be thought that his association with spies was the only interesting thing about him.

The son of a Welsh preacher, he tells us he had not wanted to go to Oxford, seeing it as the opposite of what he took to be the just order of things; but he soon changed his mind, and congratulated himself on avoiding the corruptions of Cambridge, a university he held responsible not only for the treason of his friends Burgess and MacLean (and doubtless Blunt, about whom Rees remained silent), but for the homosexuality then rampant at Oxford, which he attributed at least in part to the unwise importation from Cambridge of the teachings of G. E. Moore and E. M. Forster. In those days, one gathers, Oxford was a male society, recruited largely from the public schools, and it

seems that homosexuality was flaunted as a class marker. The young
Welshman found it all very strange, and wondered how it had come
about that two universities, one preaching and the other practising
corruption, should provide the nation with its rulers as well as with its
spies. Nevertheless he quickly joined this decadent society.

However, as the Twenties turned into the Thirties, there was a
change of moral climate. For the kind of life Oxford had offered one
had now to go to Berlin. Politics, to which nobody had hitherto paid
much attention, now became important. In 1931 Rees, already a
socialist, became a Prize Fellow of All Souls, with £300 a year, a bed
and board. 'It only slightly marred my enjoyment of it', he writes, 'that
an unemployed family in South Wales lived on 30/- a week.' Shortly
afterwards he was asked to dinner by Felix Frankfurter, and so met 'the
most brilliant undergraduate of his day at Cambridge', Guy Burgess.[3]

Rees justly commends the ruling class of the time for its easy acceptance of a brilliant outsider, even if Welsh, Wesleyan, and heterosexual.
And he gives as good an explanation as anybody of how the aesthet-
icism of the Twenties was transformed into the gay Communism of
the Thirties. The change was a change of interest rather than of class
feeling. And, however easy his acceptance, it is hard to think of
Rees as being fully incorporated. Capable of wildness, he was quiet
compared with Burgess. He wrote prose of dignified precision, totally
lacking in the virtuoso excess of Auden or of his friend Henry Green,
famous for his extremely idle and luxurious way of life as an undergraduate. He was loyal to the sect he had joined and kept Burgess's
secret for sixteen years, revealing it only when Burgess had decamped,
but doing so, with ridiculous indiscretion, through that trumpet of the
proletariat, the Sunday *People*.

For this performance he got into terrible trouble, and it will doubtless
be for his minor role in the Burgess and Blunt affairs, though possibly
also for other vagaries, indiscretions, and brilliances, that he will be
remembered. But he is also interesting as a charming *métèque*, a
talented mimic, a curiosity; very attractive, serious much of the time,
unafraid of the *louche* but also of 'big houses where things are done
properly'. That phrase comes from Elizabeth Bowen's novel of 1938,
The Death of the Heart, which is widely and correctly believed to
contain a portrait of Rees as a young man. The society represented in

the novel has more elegance than conscience: 'The most we can hope for,' says one character, 'is to go on getting away with it till the others get it away from us.' 'These days,' says another, 'there's something dreadful about talk; people's convictions keep bobbing to the surface, making them flush.' Should one try to earn the respect of the workers (feudalism) or simply pay them for what they do (cash nexus)? In this milieu Eddy seems in a way innocent, like the girl Portia (also a portrait of a well-known and still living writer), who, though a relation, is regarded as of a lower class than the family. However, we are instructed that in such a milieu innocents are forced to be disingenuous: 'the system of our affections is too corrupt for them; so they blunder and cheat and betray.' When Portia runs away it is the perfect servant, Matchett, feudal fossil and ethical norm – her name conventionally reduced to deny her both gender and baptism – who goes after the girl. Matchett's values are not corrupt because she is not involved in that system of affections. Eddy, who partly is, cannot be found at the critical moment, and is therefore, though rather oddly, described by the family as 'a scab'; meanwhile they get on with their dinner.

Eddy is an illustration of Orwell's argument that there can't be lower-class intellectuals because as soon as they become intellectuals they are forced to live in a world very different from their own; and sometimes, we might add, in a system of affections which induces them to blunder and cheat and betray. This was simply an acute form of the problem everybody had when habit or self-interest attached them firmly to a way of life which conscience insisted they should give up; acute because, having but recently arrived at that way of life, one finds it necessary, like some of the other inhabitants, to denounce it in order to be comfortable in it. This could expose one to teasing, as MacNeice, who would never have teased his more important friend Blunt, teased Rees. His revivalist performance at the writers' political gathering was a calculated regression to a nonconformist origin; MacNeice, whose origin was prelatical, couldn't possibly have made such a speech with a straight face. But the lapse was partly redeemed by the amusing request for oysters.

MacNeice wasn't always amused, but he was always conscious of the irony of professing commitment to a cause of which the success would be measured by the degree to which it destroyed the way of life he enjoyed. He was willing to call himself a snob; he liked pleasant places to live, wine, poetry, upper-class women, Greek and Latin classics, in-jokes, and Twickenham better than boiled oranges and Argus-eyed potatoes, and he was reluctant to give them up though sure that they must be given up. Poetry may be sometimes flippant, sometimes sad; but it should always be a civilized admission of this necessity. Minor poet though we may think him, MacNeice – like other poets called minor – did something new, wrote a new poetry of departure, entirely different in tone from the freakish nostalgia of Auden's 'good-bye to the house with its wallpaper red / Good-bye to the sheets on the warm double bed . . .'[4] Writing *Autumn Journal* in the aftermath of the fall of Barcelona and the German occupation of Prague, MacNeice feels that more than a sort of comfortable candour is called for, but he is determined not to risk dishonesty. It is because he has the technical resource to be honest that *Autumn Journal* survives as a sensitive record of the failures and successes of a class response to what now seemed a terminal threat. Even in its rehearsal of stock themes I've already mentioned it shows an intelligent blend of sympathy and self-interest.

> August is nearly over, the people
>   Back from holiday are tanned
> With blistered thumbs and a wallet of snaps and a little
>   *Joie de vivre* which is contraband;
> Whose stamina is enough to face the annual
>   Wait for the annual spree,
> Whose memories are stamped with specks of sunshine
>   Like faded *fleurs de lys*.
> Now the till and the typewriter call the fingers,
>   The workman gathers his tools
> For the eight-hour day but, after, the solace
>   Of films or football pools
> Or of the gossip or cuddle, the moments of self-glory
>   Or self-indulgence, blinkers on the eye of doubt,
> The blue smoke rising and the brown lace sinking
>   In the empty glass of stout.

Everything in this passage about duties and pleasures suggests a sympathetic wish that everybody could be as fortunate as the poet, so that one becomes almost too aware of a note of self-congratulation: *our* sprees are more frequent, *our* work less mechanical, *our* consolations more genuine than films and football pools; what *we* do when we cuddle is not called cuddling, and *our* conversation is not just gossip, though we can have that, too. Also we can compare the foam of the Guinness (in *your* glass, not ours, of course) to brown lace. We deplore these contrasts as the result of

> an entirely lost and daft
> System that gives a few at fancy prices
>   Their fancy lives
> While ninety-nine in the hundred who never attend the banquet
>   Must wash the grease of ages off the knives.

But in spite of this knowledge,

>   habit makes me
> Think victory for one implies another's defeat,
> That freedom means the power to order, and that in order
>   To preserve the values dear to the élite
> The élite must remain a few. It is so hard to imagine
>   A world where the many would have their chance without
> A fall in the intellectual standard of living
>   And nothing left that the highbrow cared about.

'Which fears', he continues resolutely, 'must be suppressed.' But the effect of the poem derives from the relaxed way in which it declines to suppress them, though without making too much fuss about the refusal. Neither his personal troubles, delicately alluded to in the poem, nor his purely intellectual complicity with the unwanted revolution, can really prevent this civilized poet from being himself as he waits, somewhat incredulously, for the gun butt to rap on the door.[5] The mind will not follow the heart: 'My sympathies are on the Left. On paper and in the soul. But not in my heart or my guts . . . With my heart and my guts I lament the passing of class.'[6] One could think but not feel the unthinkable.

And that is something we should be able to understand, as we struggle to imagine nuclear winter and carry on as pleasantly as possible with our lives. The war images were different in the Thirties, more thrillingly apocalyptic (Auden's crumbling flood, Empson's forest fire ripening the cones), but they were inevitably based on the recent world conflict, with some imaginative trimmings. At the time of the Spanish Civil War there were great numbers of men around who had fought in France or elsewhere less than twenty years before, and even some who were young enough to fight in the war that was coming: it was expected to be like the Somme, plus aerial bombardment with gas, electric rays, civilian panic.[7] But even after Guernica it smacked for most people of fiction, and the left-wing poets sometimes felt that they were almost alone in their awareness of the historical situation, so that the demands on them were felt as much greater than those to which poets are accustomed, and of a different sort. 'It is quite easy to prove that we are in the first peculiar crisis of civilization,' wrote Geoffrey Grigson, 'and if poets say that rather often now in a good many different ways, is there a fact for us which is more important?'[8] And looking back at those times from a distance of many years, Stephen Spender stressed the isolation of the poets who thought so:

if a small but vociferous and talented minority of what were called 'the intellectuals' (this was the decade in which this term began to be widely used and abused) were almost hypnotically aware of the Nazi nightmare, the vast majority of people – and the government and members of the ruling class – seemed determined to ignore or deny it. One had the sense of belonging to a small group who could see terrible things which no one else saw.[9]

To have that sense was of course to be cut off from the proletariat all over again. The keener one's awareness of imminent war and proletarian revolution, the greater one's difference from the mass of people. It is MacNeice's serious but unimpassioned, rather nostalgic understanding of this that gives *Autumn Journal* some of its value. Others felt they must do something more positive than he – write articles and pamphlets, go to Spain. In the end most came to see that their actions were of small importance, that Spender's 'Who live beneath the shadow of a war, / What can I do that matters?' was the wrong question – a natural, even admirable mistake, rather like the mistake of the Party itself in sending young writers to be killed in Spain. Auden, Day-Lewis, and MacNeice, each in his own way, came to understand this. And, as I said in the previous chapter, Spender, much better informed politically than the others, was forced to conclude that political action in the real world – political action on the only possible side – would be a worse affront to his conscience than abstention. Loyalty to Moscow meant telling lies. It was a simple but decisive consideration.

These were not the first poets to lose faith in a pure revolutionary cause – to become rather desolately aware of the discrepancy between ideals of social justice and the world of political power. Comparisons would, I think, suggest that this group came rather well out of the experience. Such failures are more valuable than some successes. Whether or not Auden was right to believe in the end that poetry can make nothing happen, it must be true that there can be poetry about the sort of thing that poetry cannot make happen, and about that failure. Here it might be useful to compare *The Borderers* and Spender's *Trial of a Judge*, neither work satisfactory to its author yet central to his development. Wordsworth withheld his play from publication for almost half a century; Spender has in recent years given his extensive revision. Of the original version he seems to accept MacNeice's opinion, that he had intended to express the weakness of liberalism and the necessity of Communism, but that this intention was 'sabotaged by Spender's unconscious integrity; the Liberal judge, his example of what-not-to-be, walked away with one's sympathy'.[10] The play shows that the Judge is wrong when he says with quiet conviction, 'My truth will win', and that his enemy Hummeldorf is equally wrong when he states that 'Abstract justice is nonsense'. Although the Judge dies in a 'vacuum of misery' he redeems Hummeldorf; in some sense his truth *has* won, despite the power of the state to erase or deform the record of its victory. The play has obvious faults, but it is not a fault that it fails to make the political point mentioned by MacNeice. At the crisis there is nothing the Judge can do except suffer, yet the idea of Justice survives him, whether or not it is to be identified with the hopes of the Communist prisoners.

In the same year, 1938, Rex Warner published his novel *The*

Professor, a book that deserves to live, not as another tragedy of liberalism or another indictment of Fascism, but as a study of abstract justice. The hindsight of the narrator can assure us that the Professor, summoned to power as his country is about to capitulate to Fascism, is quite unfitted for politics, believing as he does 'not only in the existence but in the efficacy of a power more human, liberal, and kindly than an organization of metal'. Some future civilization, the narrator allows, may judge the Professor not to have been entirely without value. However, in his own day he is totally defeated by the tricks of the Fascists, the follies of non-Communist labour leaders, and the treachery of a beloved mistress. Possibly his most important encounter is with a philosophical cobbler, who wants nothing to do with economic improvement, the amelioration of poverty, or the cure of disease, holding that infinite human wretchedness is the true ground of love. This rather remarkable passage seems to offer a more abstract version of that love of the poor for their doomed wretchedness so notable in Upward.

In Warner's novel, classrooms, parks, and streets are merely sets before which long serious debates are staged; though sometimes they are invested with a dreamlike terror which reminds one of his earlier book *The Wild Goose Chase* (1937), as well as of Kafka and Upward. These settings seem exactly suited to the impossible logic of the discussions: book-burning, torture, and rape seem to happen in a dream, but when such dreams invade the waking world the existence of justice is signalled only by its absence, and that of love by its present impossibility. This stately, wretchedly noble book, I'm glad to say, is not wholly forgotten. It could not have been written at any other moment, but it still touches the conscience; it expresses very well our interest in justice and our sense of its inaccessibility; and its severity is a reproach to our habit of dismissing books merely because we think their surface ideologies dated.

We do this the more readily when the books in question are so obviously caught up in a slightly embarrassing historical moment, especially when that moment was one of a crisis supremely important in detail and implication to writers conscientiously seeking a direct engagement we know by hindsight to have been unavailable – in the present case, with the immediate issues of poverty, war, and revolution. We know what happened, and cannot re-experience the excitements and terrors of the time, or be assailed in conscience by that set of facts; such reconstructions are impossible even to the most laborious of historians. Instead of smothering ourselves with futile historical fact we rely on convenient mythical formulations to make that past accessible. The myth of the Thirties as a 'low dishonest decade'[11] began to circulate before the decade was over, and, as I said earlier, the influential voice of Orwell helped to give it permanence: its most celebrated writers were a pink clique, a pansy left, enfeebled by a gutless inability to surrender their class privileges. They may have wished to violate frontiers, transgress, defamiliarize the idea of class; but they were too ill-educated and too self-indulgent to do so.

Orwell was a transgressor, a violator of the frontiers of class, including its rhetorical frontier, the one that divided the mandarin from the demotic. One can imagine what he might have said about Rees in Prunier's, and one knows what he said about Auden. Orwell had made many painful enquiries; he knew what it was to be poor, and what it meant to fight and be wounded. These writers who talked a lot but did no first-hand research were not really artists, not really men, not really alive. He thought of them as a transient historical phenomenon. The great writers of the preceding generation hadn't been at public schools or English universities; they had not been Communists; most of them had not even been English. But now the English had swarmed out of their educational reserves and temporarily taken over. The times forbade them to go in for what would have suited them best, 'art for art's sake'. 'Between 1935 and 1939 the Communist Party had an almost irresistible attraction for any writer under forty.' So these young writers joined the Party, or came close to doing so, in much the same way as the previous generation had tended to join the church. They were quite right in their belief that '*laissez-faire* capitalism was finished' but quite wrong to think they must therefore throw in their lot with Stalin. Not to perceive that the Russian Communism then available was nothing more than an instrument of Soviet foreign policy testified to a degree of stupidity possible only to an intellectual or an ignorant working-man. They felt the need of a cause, something to take the place of patriotism, honour, and the like; but they were too ignorant to find a true one. They had no notion of what life was like in countries less fortunate than their own, in police states; for 'cultured' middle-class life in England had 'reached a depth of softness at which a public-school education – five years in a lukewarm bath of snobbery – can actually be looked back on as an eventful period'. Here he is hitting out at Cyril Connolly and his opinion that Eton was an experience after which the rest of life must be something of an anti-climax.

The stick Orwell used to beat these softies in *Inside the Whale* (1940) was, unexpectedly, Henry Miller. Miller wrote strong demotic prose, was, on his own account, heterosexually virile to an unusual degree, and didn't give a damn about the fate of the world. This endeared him to Orwell, who did care about the fate of the world but attached great importance to being demotic and uncommitted. Marxism, he said, could easily prove that 'Bourgeois liberty of thought' is an illusion; yet without that illusive liberty 'the creative powers wither away'. Hence the folly of the pink writers in choosing a faith which required its surrender. But it has been part of my argument that these writers were well aware of the difficulty; Upward gives lengthy testimony to the agonies it caused, and the others all came to see that their honest choice was precisely the bourgeois illusion, if illusion it was. Orwell's attack really comes down to saying that they were ignorant, cowardly, and self-regarding, and it is true that they were less tough and less knowing than he was; but they had their own peculiar understanding of their problems and the cost of their solution. They were not quite the half-hearted, the gullible, the gutless Thirties poets of the myth.[12]

The greatest of these poets, Auden, made his own solid contribution to the myth. Arriving in New York on the day Barcelona fell, and failing to go back home when the European war began, he seemed to have declared for bourgeois liberty, however illusive; but that was only the beginning. I agree with Barbara Everett that his move to the United States – hardly the result of a solemn decision – resulted from what he himself diagnosed as a perpetual 'desire for separation', and that it was, at worst, a 'graceless' act.[13] I vaguely remember thinking at the time that he and Isherwood were quite right to make themselves safe, whether or no that was their intention, and I still think this a sensible view of the matter. Anyway, Auden's more substantial contribution to the myth of his own early failure was his wilful and, as I believe, imperceptive renunciation of his own work, his implied denunciation of himself as liar, fraud, or dupe.

Despite some quite strongly expressed views to the contrary, Auden remains at the centre of our thinking about the Thirties, and it will not seem inappropriate if I conclude this chapter by discussing him at slightly greater length than I have so far. I will begin by mentioning one of the more celebrated instances of his meddlings and recantations, the 'Prologue' to *Look, Stranger!* (a title I may be alone in preferring to Auden's own choice, *On This Island*, for it sets him at a distance from this island, affords those panoramic views of what he did not know and meant to find out). I have for fifty years thought the 'Prologue' a great poem and I don't suppose anything could induce me to change my view at this stage, though I admit that believing it to be so may have affected my notion of what one sort of great poem should be like. But Auden himself was very unhappy with it, messed it about, and later dropped it altogether from his canon.

Edward Mendelson, who probably knows more about Auden than anybody else does, and certainly a lot more than I do, has always championed the poet's decisions in such cases, and he does so here, calling the 'Prologue', along with some other poems, 'deeply self-contradictory or inauthentic'. He points to May 1932, the month in which the poem was written, as the moment of a major change in Auden's manner; a switch 'from clinical distance to didactic exhortation'. His admiration of the final lines of the poem is muted; here they are:

In bar, in netted chicken-farm, in lighthouse,
Standing on these impoverished constricting acres,
The ladies and gentlemen apart, too much alone,

Consider the years of the measured world begun,
The barren spiritual marriage of stone and water.
Yet, O, at this very moment of our hopeless sigh

When inland they are thinking their thoughts but are watching these
    islands.
As children in Chester look to Moel Fammau to decide
On picnics by the clearness or withdrawal of her treeless crown,

Some possible dream, long coiled in the ammonite's slumber,
In uncurling, prepared to lay on our talk and kindness
Its military silence, its surgeon's idea of pain;

And out of the Future into actual History,
As when Merlin, tamer of horses, and his lords to whom
Stonehenge was still a thought, the Pillars past

And into the undared ocean swung north their prow,
Drives through the night and star-concealing dawn,
For the virgin roadsteads of our hearts an unwavering keel.[14]

'Splendid as the rhetoric is,' says Mendelson, '– and the retention of
the verb *drives* until the end is splendid indeed – it leaves some
doubts . . .' For instance, 'Merlin, tamer of horses' is inappropriate,
since, if Merlin follows Dante's Ulysses beyond the Pillars of Hercules,
his fate should be that of Ulysses, not millennium but disaster.
Mendelson catalogues faults and loosenesses elsewhere in the poem,
and Auden's thefts from Anthony Collett's book *The Changing Face of
England* (1926, cheap edition May 1932, the very month of the poem)
are, it is implied, further evidence of opportunism and inauthenticity.[15]

It is likely enough that Auden himself would have accepted these
criticisms, but they seem misplaced all the same. The poem isn't truly
didactic, for it doesn't teach – it prophesies, with a reminiscence of
John of Gaunt. In the Newton passage condemned by Mendelson,
Love (that now vast impersonal force, the Eros that builds cities and
reforms societies) is addressed like this:

Here too on our little reef display your power,
This fortress perched on the edge of the Atlantic scarp,
The mole between all Europe and the exile-crowded sea;

And make us as Newton was, who in his garden watching
The apple falling towards England, became aware
Between himself and her of an eternal tie.

This is surely a very just conceit. England is little, a reef, a fortress, a
mole; it is seen, like everything else in the poem, from a height, a

distance; on one side Europe threatens, on the other the sea (enriched by the epithet 'exile-crowded', which makes it a nowhere full of anxious transients, in contrast to our home, our known and loved bit of territory, the garden in which, if anywhere, we walk in peace). It is to this small spot, a rock sticking out of the ocean, that gravity impelled the apple of Newton, thus demonstrating that the power which maintains the constellations is a perfect figure for the way we perceive, in our tiny habitat, the operation of another cosmic force, here called Love, which also moves the sun and the other stars.

As for the debt to Collett, it was noticed long ago in a review of *Look, Stranger!* by Janet Adam Smith, who attributed it, admiringly, to Auden's sensible habit of hoarding phrases.[16] Collett's book is already a hoard of phrases, and, given the sort of book it is, a poet of Auden's cast, with a passion for panoramic views and long historical perspectives, would have been mad not to use it. Its very title – *The Changing Face of England* – is exact for the period; but to see how apt the book was we need to observe that the changes Collett talks about are large-scale – geological, ethological, philological, and this is what enabled Auden to project his sense of catastrophic political change on to the scale of those vast but slower upheavals that change our coast, our rivers, and our language. It is a magnificent book, now of course out of date; changes Collett describes as occurring have now occurred, and his patriotic musings on race would certainly be called racist. But he has real grandeur and real point. What, to mention the most famous borrowing, could better illustrate the relation of England to the continent as one of unity in separation than the remark Auden brilliantly stole for the great chorus in *The Dog beneath the Skin*?[17] There Collett's observation that the North Sea 'is still so shallow that if St Paul's was planted anywhere between the Dutch and English coasts the golden cross would shine above the water' is repeated with no more modification than Shakespeare would make to suitable bits of Plutarch. And Collett, in this modern version of the *Mutability Cantos*, dwells on the instability of what may seem fixed boundaries, the land liquefied by the sea, the sea as it were solidified by the land, the apparently eternal boundaries always in flux. A poet who likes to look on this island like the hawk or the helmeted airman could hardly do better than use Collett as a chart, showing the immemorial cliffs that are yet so new in geological time that solidity cannot be expected of them – 'Like the moulting crab they need time before their surface hardens' – and then closing in on the curled ammonites as the poet had done on the cigarette-end smouldering in a garden border. Auden, remembered the ammonites, was grateful to learn about the Sugarloaf standing sentinel over Abergavenny and the children in Chester scanning the summit of Moel Fammau to judge the weather prospects. Years later he must have thought of Collett when he wrote 'In Praise of Limestone'; and perhaps when he used the Welsh word 'nant' to mean a brook or burn. Collett's book offered him language that was already on the way to being poetry, a view and a love of England close to his own, the cosmic force intensely felt in one's own garden yet known as universal; and a certainty that change is the law of the world.

That is why Merlin (a Trojan, therefore a proto-Briton) turns *north* from the Pillars, not south like Dante's Ulysses (a Greek) and finds not destruction but England, when England was not yet even a thought. The ancient possible dream will arrive in the same way to transform the impoverished constricting acres. Auden quite enjoys telling us it won't be comfortable, that it's no use raising a shout, that our talk and kindness will have to be laid away because they existed only for 'ten persons'. It was for this kind of talk – 'its military silence, its surgeon's idea of pain' – that some admired him and some, like Orwell, thought him too ready to speak of what he didn't understand. But now, I think, we can see that it has its own accuracy. This is how it feels to contemplate a future, long prefigured by history, and now imminent, over which you have no control and from which you can expect no comfort save that of conscience and compliance. It will be a catastrophe, but of the sort Auden would later have called a eucatastrophe.

So that last sentence of the poem isn't to be dismissed as mere rhetoric, however splendid. It celebrates, with the aid of its extended simile and the mythic charge it carries, an improbable, even a painful victory for goodness, for history as impersonal and alarming but ultimately benign – a victory as epoch-making as the one Auden celebrated almost thirty years later in the poem 'Hammerfest', when he spoke eucatastrophically of

> . . . that preglacial Actium when the huge
> Archaic shrubs went down before the scented flowers,
> And earth was won for color . . .[18]

But that palaeobotanical victory happened, and the voyages of the Trojan Merlin and the possible dream didn't, so that, when Auden decided that 'nothing is lovely,/Not even poetry, which is not the case',[19] he concluded that such poems as the 'Prologue' were mendacious as well as useless. Certainly the 'Prologue' did not reduce the crowd of exiles, hasten the millennium, or even, in all probability, win recruits for the Party. Its usefulness, if it has any, is as a prophecy of love and its attendant terror.

Something of the sort may be said also of *Spain, 1937*. We all remember Orwell's sneer at 'the conscious acceptance of guilt in the necessary murder' – it could only have been written by a person to whom murder is at most a *word* – but fewer recall that he also described the poem as 'one of the few decent things that have been written about the Spanish war'. Stephen Spender, who thinks it a rare attempt on Auden's part to write a poem with the formal structure of the dialectic, feels that it expresses 'an attitude which for a few weeks or months he felt intellectually forced to adopt, but which he never truly felt'.[20] Mendelson accepts the poet's own judgement, which is that, like 'September 1, 1939', it is 'infected with incurable dishonesty' – a dishonesty which, according to Mendelson, lies in its 'implicit claim to have joined the realm of the private will to that of the public good, when in fact the union had been made through the force of rhetoric alone'. This distrust of 'rhetoric' – after all the only instrument available for the purpose – the critic has inherited from the poet, and he gives the word a very restricted sense, associating it, I suppose, with propaganda. However, he allows that neither *Spain* nor 'September 1, 1939' is simply 'public and didactic', calling them 'equivocal',[21] as indeed they are. Sometimes I find it hard to believe that Auden could have so badly misunderstood his own poems unless it was from a simple desire to escape the memory of what it had been like to write them. Anyway, I believe that both Spender and Mendelson, despite their closeness to the poet and his work, are wrong about *Spain*.

In 1937 the Spanish Civil War seemed to have simplified the great historical issues by offering a plain though painful choice; as Spender expressed it, an individual could believe that his own action or failure to act 'could lead to the winning or losing of [that war], could even decide whether or not the Second World War was going to take place'.[22] The government seemed not to care much, even when British ships were bombed, and it might have seemed that the masses went on with their 'dreams of freedom'[23] and did not bother about the other dream uncurling from the ammonite, the tidal wave that would soon breach 'the dykes of our content'[24] – the satisfactions of the middle class, or of the poor content with the pools, the odd cuddle, the bitter beer, and the annual baring of flesh 'beside the undiscriminating sea'.[25] If Auden came to think it wrong or hopeless to write poems intended to move some parts of that large public, it is not difficult to understand why he went on to join the party of his detractors and deplore his own past.

But *Spain* is not a marching song or a recruiting poster; it is an attempt to express what it feels like to confront a great historical crisis. At bottom such crises have elements in common, and in this respect Auden's poem resembles Marvell's 'Horatian Ode' – indeed in my view it is our best political poem except for Marvell's. Both deal with the great work of time and its ruin with individual will and its relation to historical forces. Both have wit and magniloquence, and both are, in Mendelson's word, 'equivocal'. As the execution of Charles (which divides Marvell's poem in half) divides one age from another – however much one might regret the past and hesitate before the unknown future – so Spain divides history and concentrates attention on today and its 'struggle'. 'Tomorrow, *perhaps*, the future . . .' The skewed detail, its oddity and force, may strike us as too much of their period, but the strong build of the poem supports them, as Marvell's supports his puns and conceits.

Auden came to hate the last stanza most of all:

> The stars are dead; the animals will not look:
> We are left alone with our day, and the time is short and
>   History to the defeated
> May say Alas but cannot help or pardon—[26]

and yet it seems to me exactly right. Heaven and earth leave us to our moment; choice is necessary, failure irredeemable. When he said this was 'unforgiveable', Auden had changed his mind about history and redemption; but that cannot hurt the poem, which ends with a remark as clear-sighted and as urgent as that which ends Marvell's poem: 'The same arts that did gain / A power, must it maintain'; 'History to the defeated / May say Alas but cannot help or pardon'. The ideas are ancient, the politics modern; and so too with the individual poetic response.

So *Spain* does deal with what is the case, even if the poet came to see it as a reflection of an uneasy or shaming interlude in his intellectual life. There is the past, wittily sketched as a history of instruments – the counting-frame, the cathedral, the dynamo – and a future less clearly definable; there is Life, an evolutionary force that once operated independently, as when it established 'the robin's plucky canton', but whose action now depends on human decision. Life is now boldly identified with Spain, which at this critical moment offers itself to human choice. Henceforth the forces of life, like Marvell's 'ancient rights', will 'hold or break / As men are strong or weak'. They tell you to choose, not what to choose. The whole of history, evolutionary as well as cultural, culminates at this moment, and in Spain – a figure for crisis and necessary choice, a reef or mole between past and future. We have always projected our individual crises on to history, so Spain is caught up in a typology, and it is the nature of typologies to transcend history; because we all at times have to make more or less desperate choices, the urgency of that Spanish moment does not disappear with the moment itself. It becomes part of our mythical habit. It is this validity of type, as well as its magniloquence and wit, that preserves Auden's poem.

My brief doesn't require me to argue that Auden was never glib or false; as he said later, he was always a British Pharisee,[27] not as other men were, and lacking the sense other men might have that they needed at least to seem consistent in their opinions, or to give plausible reasons for changing them. Auden, I think, never really bothered to do that, and there is good reason not to accept his Thirties poetry at his own valuation. It was written under conditions of considerable intellectual discomfort, at a time when, in Spender's phrase, there was a real compulsion 'to make some choice outside the entanglements of our private life'.[28] The effort to do that enabled Auden to discover an appropriate magniloquence, something that was to recur very rarely in his work over the following thirty years, because he falsely equated it with falsity.

Auden once said of Kipling that poem after poem of his deals with encirclement, danger, and fear, 'vague menacing shapes which can be kept away by incessant action but can never be finally overcome'.[29] There is something of Auden himself in this description. He feared encirclement – Spain and Thirties politics, each in its way, were something of the kind; they invaded the mind from all points of the compass; and, lacking Kipling's ability to build bulwarks, Auden simply – or not so simply – withdrew. There was poetry in the being afraid of encirclement and in the departure from the ring as well; in the attempt to be on the side of Eros, builder of cities, as well as in the abandonment of Eros in favour of Agape.

I began this chapter with some words on a minor figure, Goronwy Rees, who was part of the network of acquaintance that included both the poets and the spies who trafficked more or less lovingly between upper-class life and the politics of proletarian revolution; and I have ended it by discussing a major poet who belonged to the same connection. I did so because I hoped the differences between the two might be instructive. The terms of abuse and the terms of the myth can hardly fit both cases. When Auden talks about 'the struggle' he is engaged in one, and writing a poetry which, with all its virtuosity, is a poetry of struggle. This is not done by bullying other writers into accepting the virtue, beauty, and power of the proletariat. If we can't tell the difference between these responses it may be that we no longer understand the peculiar stimuli which produced them, both the honourable and the not so honourable. They were apocalyptic, or at least sham apocalyptic, and, as I remarked earlier, our apocalyptic sympathies are probably exhausted now that apocalypse, which used to be a moment, has become an epoch, not a threat of Armageddon so much as a permanent migraine. The modern Irish poets know something about struggle, and the entanglements of private and public life, but we are dulled. On the left, it seems to me, thinking grows more and more rarefied and academic, less and less intimate, or desirous of intimacy, with the life of the people, with the threat of encirclement, with crisis as a condition more than merely notional. It takes an Upward, a lonely old warrior never not to be committed, never not aware of the need for action, to speak now of CND as then, long ago, he spoke of the Party, as a shield against the last destructive assaults of a dying capitalism.

I don't of course mean that one has to join some group or party in order to apprehend what is valuable in Thirties bourgeois literature, and to allow for the distortions caused by historical myths of convenience. The effort required is critical and historical; if we make it we may come to honour what is too often calumniated without much examination – a literature that is often splendid in the moment of its enforced engagement with the almost unthinkable Other – across the frontier, almost cut off, encircled, but capable of fineness even in its moment of withdrawal.

What I have been trying to tell is, in its way, a love-story, almost a story of forbidden love. If asked to define that huge word I will not repeat my reference to the Eros of Freud, or to Caudwell's amorous economics, but simply repeat a definition of love Auden himself once gave: 'intensity of attention'.[30] He might well have been thinking of the uneasy passion with which he looked at 'the defeated and disfigured',[31] or at Spain, or at his friends' encircled lives.

15

Memory

This chapter derives from one of four lectures on autobiography delivered at Yale University in 1994. A much shorter version of it appeared in Index on Censorship, *January 2001, an issue that had memory as its theme.*

The pages on 'forgetting' are older, having been written around 1988. If they served any particular occasion I have, appropriately, forgotten what it was. On reflection I thought the interest of the topic would excuse the somewhat inchoate character of these pages, and for the same reason I appended a set of notes I seem to have made when contemplating an extension of the piece. I have not tidied them up, hoping that in their present form they may be as suggestive as they must have seemed at the time.

Whether it is a question of a single person, or a multitude of persons falsely represented by the self-biographer (selves-biographer?) as one, there is no avoiding the question of memory, as Augustine was the first to understand. We are warned that he used the term in a much wider sense than we do. For him it was the very instrument of personal continuity, the basis of self-identity, and 'the stomach of the mind.'[1] And it was also the means of access to grace. Since his narrative is of a delayed self-opening to grace, memory is in every sense the basis of it. The importance of Augustine's placing God and his actions in the human memory is that it situates God 'at the very foundations of the person', it 'finds him at the very root of memory'; and it does so without resorting to the Platonic notion of prenatal knowledge. We can search to know ourselves because we have an innate disposition to understand ourselves; we look within for the means to progress to self-knowledge, and that means is, like God, to be found in the memory. The path to above is through within.[2] So, as Charles Taylor remarks, 'in Augustine's doctrine, the intimacy of self-presence is, as it were, hallowed, with immensely far-reaching consequences for the whole of Western culture'; as Augustine expresses it, God is 'the power which begets life in my mind and in the innermost recesses of my thinking'[3] which makes it possible for me to know what I seek and ultimately what I am.

Memory also offers the clue to the way the world at large functions, for the world is also fallen into materiality and sense, so that its redemption must be a matter of history, of a cosmic memory. One sees why Augustine follows his autobiographcal narrative with the philosophical enquiry into memory that occupies the tenth book of the *Confessions*. Here are some of the famous words:

I come to the fields and vast palaces of memory, where are the treasuries of all kinds of objects brought in by sense perception. Hidden there is whatever we think about, a process which may increase or diminish or in some way alter the deliverance of the senses and whatever else has been deposited and placed on reserve and has not been swallowed up and buried in oblivion. When I am in this storehouse, I ask that it produce what I want to recall, and immediately certain things come out; some require a longer search, and have to be drawn out as it were from more recondite receptacles. Some memories pour out to crowd the mind, and when one is searching and asking for something quite different, leap forward into the centre as if saying, 'Surely we are what you want?' With the hand of my heart I chase them away from the face of my memory until what I want is freed of mist and emerges from its hiding places. Other memories come before me on demand with ease and without any confusion in their order. Memories of earlier events give way to those which followed, and as they pass are stored away available for retrieval when I want them. And that is what happens when I recount a narrative from memory. (X.viii)

This is a simple model, basically rather like a library, and it does distinguish easy access books from books on reserve. However, the books interact. What the senses have collected and stored is modified by association with 'whatever we think about'. Some items come easily, even too easily, so some must be waved away. Some are deep in the stacks or in special collections. The section that follows describes a sort of cataloguing system, in which acquisitions are organized according to the sense that introduced each of them: sight, sound, smell, taste, touch. Access to these resources enables one to enjoy and compare images of the world: 'I distinguish the odour of lilies from that of violets without smelling anything at all' (X.viii). And in these halls of memory 'I meet myself and recall what I am, what I have done, and when and where and how I was affected when I did it'; moreover, with those recollections other images less immediate to that self-meeting may in their turn be blended and combined.

Augustine's meeting of himself reminds us once more that in a sense all autobiographers take on the properties of doubles, acquiring a sort of personal ambiguity; it is worth inserting here an observation of Jean Starobinski's:

The difference established by autobiographical reflection is . . . twofold: it is both a temporal difference and a difference of identity. The personal reference (the first person, the 'I') remains constant. This constancy is ambiguous, for the narrator then was different from what he is today. But how could he fail to see himself in the other person he once was? How could he refuse to accept responsibility for his errors? . . . The invariant pronoun is the vector, as it were, of this permanent responsibility: the first person is the basis both of present reflection and the multiplicity of bygone states. Changes of identity are indicated by *verbal* and *attributive* elements.

Starobinski goes on to describe these indications, by which it is possible to treat the first person as 'a quasi-third person'. One, available in French, is to use the aorist tense to assign 'a certain coefficient of otherness to the first person'.[4] There are others more generally available for the description of such self-encounters.

To see what Augustine meant by self-exploration amid the contents of memory one needs to reflect that it is not merely sensory images that are collected and combined. Ideas are stored in the memory before one has learnt them. As in Plato's *Meno*, though with the important difference that Augustine doesn't admit prenatal knowledge, learning is remembering. Similarly stored, part of the original deposit, are 'the affections of my mind'. Thus the rememberer can identify affective experiences when he or she has them later; but as preserved in the memory and reported to the enquirer, they may differ strangely from what they were as primordial experience; and here the doubling effect is obvious: 'I can be far from glad in remembering myself to have been glad, and far from sad when I recall my past sadness. Without fear I remember how at a particular time I was afraid . . . I remember with joy a sadness that has passed and with sadness a lost joy' (X.xiv).

This is far from all that should be said about Augustine's *memoria*, but here it will be enough to add only one or two points of importance. First, forgetfulness is treated as a feature of memory: 'memory retains forgetfulness . . . So it is there lest we forget what, when present, makes us forget' (X.xv). I must remember forgetfulness, even though it destroys what I remember. One further point: how is it possible to aspire, as everybody does, to a felicity which, though we have the idea of it, we have never actually experienced? We have no memory, in the ordinary sense of the word, of any earlier happiness on which to model such hopes. Yet where else can they come from, if not from memory? The notion of happiness must be there, put there by some prior agency, innate. God, too, is in the memory, but by his own intervention, to be found there perhaps very late, when fascination with his creation gives way to love of him. Here comes the requirement of continence, a degree of abnegation, achievable only by grace. *Da quod iubes*. God must give the continence he commands. Only then will he be found, and the enquiring spirit enabled to meet itself.

From this remarkable passage we can derive the idea of a necessary doubleness, and also the notion that the experience as remembered is not, affectively, of the same quality as the experience itself; or, as one almost needs to say, the experience as remembered is not the same as the experience remembered. Here is another aspect of difference in doubleness. A pain recalled is recognized as a pain, yet it may be recalled with pleasure; a past joy can be remembered with intense sadness (a point perhaps remembered by Dante, in a famous passage, as well as by Wordsworth). Augustine is sure, as many of his successors have been, that what memory celebrates is not, in tone or significance, identical with the actual moment remembered. For, as he remarks in

Book XI. xviii, meditating on past and future, 'the memory produces not the actual events which have passed away but words conceived from images of them, which they fixed in the mind like imprints as they passed through the senses . . . when I am recollecting and telling my story, I am looking on its image in present time . . .' This image belongs to what he calls 'the present of things past'. Other memories have worked on the image – and Augustine here anticipates the Freudian *Nachtraglichkeit*, or deferred action[5]; forgetfulness affects memories, of course, but memories can do the work of forgetfulness by modifying the original deposit, which is further changed when the product of time and much reworking must suffer a translation into language.

For Augustine any such translation must be a fall. Language, in its nature successive, is part of the fallen world, the world of time. He sets the word against the Word; the Word belongs to the simultaneous present, the *nunc stans*, of eternity. It came and dwelt among us, but the words it spoke in human language, in time, dropped, syllable by syllable, into the past. The general idea is echoed by Rousseau when he says that 'the supreme intelligence has no need to reason. For it there exist neither premises nor consequences nor even propositions. It is purely intuitive. It sees both what is and what can be. All truths are for it but a single idea, all places but a single point, all times but a single moment'.[6] An autobiographer learns that he is in his own way simulating that integrity.

In a famous passage (XI. xxviii) Augustine speaks of reciting a psalm. Before he begins to do so he has an expectation directed toward a whole. Verse by verse, as he recites, it passes into memory; so there is a blend of memory and expectation. But his attention is on the present, through which the future passes into the past. As he goes on, memory expands and expectation diminishes until the whole psalm has been said, and all is in the memory. The same action occurs in the life of the individual person, 'where all actions are parts of a whole, and also of the total history of the "sons of men" (Psalms 30:20) where all human lives are but parts'. So one's life, in this respect like all other lives, passes into memory and has a typical near-completeness which, so long as we remain alive, we can seek in the memory; always remembering that when we report it in words we have in some measure to undo that completeness, both because we are using words, and because memory always entails forgetting.

Although he stresses certain dualisms in the action of memory Augustine does not doubt the continuous individuality of the 'I' which is doing the remembering and the forgetting. Nevertheless he sees his life, and the life of all the fallen, as a collection of scattered fragments. But he is far from wanting to represent the memory-image and his own report of it as such; for in achieving closure, totality, it has taken on a kind of intemporality, it imitates the eternal Word. His story is in fact of the unification of those fragments by his conversion, the terminus of his narrative, the conquest of division. So in this matter of frag-mentation and dispersal of the self you could say he is aware of the problems of memory and subjectivity, but not that he would have recognized his problem as expressed in the language of Nietzsche or that he could have accepted the rhetorical and formal solutions offered by Barthes or Valéry in the *Cahiers*. Augustine recognizes fragmen-tation but his whole drift is to mend it. He is thus antithetical to these writers, and also to Henry Adams, who expressly wanted to deny the illusion of unity in his life, to bring it back 'from unity to multiplicity'. This is the counter-Augustinian trend in modern autobiography. But the Augustinian strain remains strong.

Our modern assumptions about memory are likely to derive in large part from traditions unavailable to St Augustine, as his are unavailable to us in the full philosophical context to which they originally belonged. We are likely to refer more directly to the Freudian tradition. In a recent paper called 'Freud and the Uses of Forgetting' the psychoanalyst Adam Phillips begins by remarking that 'People come for psychoanalytic treat-ment because they are remembering in a way that does not free them to forget'. Symptoms are involuntary and disguised memories of desire, unsuccessful attempts at self-cure. Those memories need to be forgotten, but desire, for Freud, is unforgettable. Repression is simply a way of seeming to get rid of things by keeping them. There is no cure for memory, though we try to use it to forget with, as in screen memories – devices designed to enable us to forget memories of a forbidden desire. Psychoanalysis attempts a cure by inducing the kind of remem-bering that makes forgetting possible. The only certain cure is death.

Here are paradoxes on remembering and forgetting that represent the two as a doublet and in that respect are faintly reminiscent of Augustine's; but the differences are at least as marked. Phillips can think of the logic of Freud's psychoanalytical process as being the reverse of what we take to be the autobiographer's: 'Either the most significant bits of one's past are unconscious, and only available in the compromised form of symptoms and dreams: or the past is released through interpretation into oblivion.' Forgetting is the only way to remember; remembering is the only way to achieve benign forgetting. The product of analysis is not autobiography but evacuation. And Phillips finds in the analyst's ideal state of 'free-floating' or 'evenly suspended attention' a parallel use of forgetting; the analyst must learn not to mind not having things in mind, he works by not trying to remember. This is not, to most people's way of thinking, at all like the practice of attentive reading (though it is sometimes held to be the correct practice, as in the writings of André Green and some others[7]).

So the concept of memory offered by psychoanalysis is at first sight hostile to the truth of autobiography. What we profess to remember is what we have devised to protect us from the truth; and this will be the case even when, or perhaps especially when, the attempt to hide nothing is exceptionally strenuous and well advertised, as with Rousseau. The concept of *Nachtraglichkeit* explains how a past is recovered in a distorted form; a childhood memory becomes a trauma, a trauma not directly associated with a 'real' childhood memory. Memory invents a past. Its reworkings defend us against the appalling timelessness of the unconscious. What we remember we may remember because we are forgetting in the wrong way; our remembering then takes the form of repetition, of acting out. If the analyst cures this repetition by fostering 'the work of remembering' he is not doing it because the memories thus elicited are valuable, but because he wants to dispose of them as bad for the patient, as what he needs to forget.

Here the timeless is not, as in Augustine, eternity, but the unconscious, and we struggle against its forces, using substitute memories, writing about what ought to be disposed of precisely because of its inauthentic link to the unconscious. There are deposited anterior memories, and Augustine had those, but his were related to felicity and to God, not to incest and murder. Augustine needs access to the timeless, but our need is rather to forget it as totally as possible. We achieve access to its contents by the dual imaginative activity of the transference, but we do so with the object not of verifying them but of destroying them: to remember them, or even seem to do so, is a stratagem to relinquish or dispose of them. But Augustine needed them alive, because he sought the timeless for reasons having nothing to do with destruction; he wished to account for his life as a whole, given shape, like the psalm, made so by the action of memory and the timelessness into which it passes when it is finished.

There seems little doubt that the dominant myth of autobiography is still Augustinian rather than Freudian. Of course it may be that all autobiography is in Freudian terms defensive or resistant, that to totalize, to close, to advertise a psychic structure that cannot on a strict view be authentic, is false and evasive. But it seems to be true that what excites many writers is to achieve some measure or simulacrum of closure, and thus a substitute timelessness; they seek it, sense it, even when, like Ruskin or Henry James, they cannot finish the book, even when, like James once again, they eschew all devices of presentation that signal closure; even when they revise and revise over years, seeking a truth and a plenitude that the mere passage of time continually erodes. Rousseau is in hot pursuit of a closure to be achieved by leaving nothing out, by inserting, and then later supplementing, innumerable bits of truth and leaving the reader to make them a whole. Tolstoy got over being impressed by the *Confessions* when he decided that far from demonstrating the love of truth Rousseau lied and believed his lies,[8] which of course made him incapable of the truth to which he claimed to aspire. Rousseau himself admits that he left things out – from very pure motives – and occasionally made things up. Nabokov's artful autobiography is full of elegantly rendered and various detail, but, as he once remarks, what gives such a work its formal value is thematic repetition. He illustrates the point with an anecdote of a general who amused him as a little boy by playing tricks with matches. Years later this general turns up, dressed like a peasant in a sheepskin coat. He stops the boy's father, now in flight from the Bolsheviks, and asks him for a light. While hoping that the general also escaped Soviet imprisonment, Nabokov adds: 'but that was not the point. What pleases me is the evolution of the match theme . . .

The following of such thematic designs through one's life should be, I think, the true purpose of autobiography.'[9] It is a way of offering the reader the possibility of closing the book for him. And readers, animated by the same myth, will certainly help; they will find some way to totalize even the episodic, unreflective Cellini, for instance; for certainly one derives from his autobiography a powerful impression of its writer as a single person, a vertical man, and of the book itself as simple and single.

This is a point taken up by John Sturrock in the conclusion to a book that studies autobiography from Augustine to Michel Leiris, his greatly favoured model for modern biography. Sturrock allows for the changes modern literary theory has brought to our understanding of autobiography as a genre in which truthfulness is a problem differently seen, where the relation with fiction is differently understood, and so on. But he makes a plea on behalf of the Common Reader, who, however limited as to theory, is capable of deriving so much pleasure from the reading of autobiography. There is, says Sturrock, 'an urge to autobiography within any individual, seeking expression at every level from the loosely and ephemerally conversational to the enduringly artistic. And following on from that, we may suppose that there are drives and thematic configurations whose combination in a text is specific to autobiography . . .'[10] These configurations are supplied by the author and understood, possibly on occasion supplied, by the reader, each knows the rules of the game. Of course this common knowledge is of the sort Barthes used to call 'endoxal', and those who, like Plato, reject *doxa* as an enemy of the truth will have nothing to do with it.

Sturrock is especially interested in the phenomenon, so often repeated in autobiography as to be endoxically recognizable, of what he calls the 'turn' – the point of epiphany or conversion, seen as the moment when the person under description individuates or selves himself, as it were, finds the point from which all can be seen to cohere, and so achieves a kind of closure. This moment is easily detectable in Augustine or Newman, but is present in some form virtually everywhere. It draws on or constitutes the memory of a deviance, often apparently quite slight, from some norm of experience or behaviour, a deviance that makes the writer, in his own eyes at any rate, worth writing about as a single person. In the process he cannot avoid providing relevant material on what he takes himself to be deviating from, so that autobiography appeals to our notions of normality as well as to our interest in the myriad possible deviancies; and to our interest also in wholeness, a quality we seek when recounting to ourselves our own lives. Everybody takes these things for granted, and if they want confirmations they will look for their best expression not in the narratives of analysands, which require a different and specialized form of attention, but in the works of people who understand the conditions of art: say, in poets, such as Wordsworth. For to communicate persuasively the experience of the turn it is necessary to practise an art.

Various kinds of memory are subject to various sorts of classification, but we are familiar, largely on the evidence of works of art, with the idea that there is a rough, recognizable distinction between two kinds of memory, roughly voluntary and involuntary. Proust and Beckett alike sought explanations of these phenomena in Bergson; Beckett's little book on Proust is a youthful exploration, somewhat affected in manner, of the Proustian version, and he doubtless had in mind the relevant pages of Joyce. The psychological study of memory has grown more refined, and an adhesion to Bergson dates the adherents as merely Modernist. But perhaps it does not greatly matter where the philosophizing comes from; when de Man and Derrida discourse on memory they have nothing to say about the unfashionable Bergson, yet they sometimes seem to be talking about approximately the same things. Those 'turns', those hinges or fulcra on which a whole narrative depends and which justify the very existence of the narrative, are a very conspicuous, very 'placed', treatment of involuntary movements of consciousness momentarily present in some more accessible area of the memory, brought, as Augustine might have said, from special collections to open shelves, and then displayed against a background of simpler recollection. Now, their subtly fine bindings gleaming against the drab covers of commonplace recollections, they stand out, and seem worth recounting. Though they are the sort of thing that can, perhaps does, occur to everybody, these privileged moments are not easy to put into words; they are not only what the author is really about but also a test of whether he ought to be an author.

Instances of the largely secular 'turn' are Rousseau's 'illumination' on the road to Vincennes (Starobinski remarks that it is hard to believe he did not have Augustine in mind[11]) and his decision not to return to Geneva when the gate was closed against him. Sturrock mentions these contingencies as having 'a determinant role in his story' as if, like Wordsworth later, he were having vows made for him.[12] There is Mill's crisis and the moment of its Wordsworthian solution; Newman's Sicilian experience; Mark Rutherford's finding a copy of *The Lyrical Ballads* and comparing the experience to Paul's on the way to Damascus;[13] Henry Adams's slightly ironic epiphany, induced by the dynamo in his twenty-fifth chapter. Even Gibbon, who would hardly admit that his life was dictated by external agency or involuntary choice, speaks of the discovery at Lausanne of his statue in the block of marble; he meant that an educational process had revealed what was already there – stored, as Augustine would say, in the memory – the figure of a historian of great gifts. The discovery changed nothing, as he insists; yet it takes its place in his narrative as a critical moment, an emblematic moment.[14]

Here I will borrow from Barrett J. Mandel a neat little illustration from Edmund Gosse's *Father and Son*. The author describes it as one of the many 'trifling things' that make up a life, but still 'a landmark'. The boy's fundamentalist father wanted him to decline an invitation to a party, and suggested that he pray for guidance from the Lord as to whether he should go. Asked what the Lord's answer was, the boy, well knowing his father's confidence that God's response would favour his own view, nevertheless replied, 'The Lord says I may go to the Browns.' The father 'gazed at me in speechless horror' and left the room, 'slamming the door'. Mandel admires this and calls it genuine autobiography, but adds that the writer Gosse knows more about the father and his thoughts than the boy Gosse can have done, and for that reason is able to pinpoint this moment as one of significant rebellion, a type of such resistance, and set it in a larger context that explains why it was significant, a landmark and not a trifle; by an author who wishes us to understand that he can now see how things hang together in a larger view of his remembered life. It is the mature, hindsighted record of an important stage in the widening gulf between father and son, part of a narrative designed to chart that process. We allow without demur that Gosse could not possibly be remembering his father's precise words; we already know, from our own memories, the nature of the relation of such a moment to truth and memory. As Mandel expresses it, the author is saying to the reader: ' "My life was as this tale I am telling".'[15] This is a satisfying formula, and it implies a claim that in this form (as this tale) it will have power to indicate landmarks and confer meaning on what would otherwise be mnemonic trifles.

We can add that an episode of this sort could have been worked over, told and retold to the author himself and perhaps to others; as the memory of a memory, of many memories perhaps, it acquires those associations of which Augustine speaks. To give this degree of centrality, of totality, to a memory, or to 'thematize' in the way recommended by Nabokov, is to seek to confer on the narrative a power to eliminate the restrictions of time; to institute its own laws of causality, to endow it with totality by invoking what Yeats called 'the artifice of eternity'. Much autobiography presumes to imitate that power.

Wordsworth also offers an account of his life as 'this tale I am telling', though he might have accepted both the ultimate relation of time-dispersed elements to eternity, as adumbrated by Augustine, and the apparent triviality of some of the scattered episodes in themselves. As de Man remarked, it is impossible for anglophone lovers of poetry – or autobiography – to accept the rule that excludes verse from consideration as autobiography (doubtless a lingering notion, with a long history, that poetry is lying). No doubt Wordsworth was not clear about many things – how much ordinary biography ought to be included in what was after all a preliminary poem, a prelude, how to bring the account to a satisfactory end, how far the philosophical poetry demanded by Coleridge should appear in this place rather than in the even more spacious, cathedral-like structure he planned. We know that the spectacular Snowdon passage was early designed for the climax[16] and perhaps find it hollow and in a forced relationship to what precedes it. And we can agree to say of Wordsworth what Rousseau said of himself, that he was 'painting the state of his soul twice, once as it was and once at the moment of the description'.[17] Yet we do think of *The Prelude* as aspiring to or even achieving some sort of provisional totality; it represents the growth of a poet's mind, and gives many indications that whatever boons the future might provide, that growth was complete, that it was accomplished with many significant vicissitudes between birth and the time of writing. As revisions and expansions follow, the sources grow more remote: the 'spots of time' were in the two-book *Prelude* of 1798, and persist in the more diffuse versions that we think of as 1805 and 1850, versions which have a little more to say about the growing inaccessibility of the spots of time. The pattern changes. It changes because the self-knowledge sought by the autobiographer grows more complex.

In the passage Wordsworth added in 1802 to the Preface of 1800 he has a dscussion of Prose and Poetry, claiming that they are virtually identical: 'They both speak by the same organs . . . their affections are kindred, almost identical, not necessarily differing even in degree . . . the same human blood circulates through the veins of them both.'[18] Poetry, he maintained, should speak the language of men. And so he comes to discuss the relation between men and poets (in his case, an autobiographical poet). The words are celebrated:

He is a man speaking to men: a man, it is true, endued with more lively sensibility, more enthusiasm and tenderness, who has a greater knowledge of human nature, and a more comprehensive soul, than are supposed to be common among mankind; a man pleased with his own passions and volitions, and who rejoices more than other men in the spirit of life that is in him; delighted to contemplate similar volitions and passions as manifested in the goings on of the universe . . .[19]

The poet is to ordinary people as poetry is to prose, but poetry and prose are kindred, and such is the affinity that his verse must be sometimes prosaic. His own difference from ordinary men is a difference only of degree; and sometimes that difference works in favour of men and against poets. But the difference of degree remains enormous; and it is calculated by the power and purpose of giving pleasure. We understand, from the passage I quoted, all that is needed for the provision of pleasure: sensibility, liveliness, enthusiasm, tenderness, pleasure in oneself and one's passions, joy, delight; in fact powers of the sort Yeats would call 'self-delighting'. We know about this precarious joy, so memorably evoked in 'Resolution and Independence', and unique to the poet, or the great poet. It is the task of the poet-autobiographer, and perhaps of all autobiographers, to acknowledge, like Wordsworth, the relation of joy – or whatever strikes him as his own singularity – to 'the naked and native dignity of man' and 'the elementary principle of pleasure'.

Wordsworth talks about 'joy in widest commonalty spread', but must strive to show in his own life its distinctive lines of force, its swellings and fadings. It is of course his main theme, and it always marks a difference from what he rather revealingly calls (ii. 405) 'common minds'. That is the business of *The Prelude*, and in some form it is the business of all autobiography. Having reverently celebrated his own endowment with genius, he is thinking of it when he declares that 'Points have we all of us within our souls / Where all stand single'; but he must add that 'each man is a memory to himself . . . there's not a man / That lives who hath not had his godlike hours . . .' (iii. 187–192). Godlike hours are hours remembered, by everybody, though it is the work of the self-delighting poet to record them. The 'uniformitarian' strain in Wordsworth is as essential to his self-understanding and self-valuation as the conviction that he stands single.

'Not used / To make a *present* joy the matter of my song' (i. 55–6): the plan of this autobiographical poem is to range from the origin, through the refinement, loss and recovery, by the action of memory, of the primal distinguishing joy, the gift that called the author to be 'a dedicated spirit'. One remarkable thing about Wordsworth is that such scenes as the theft of the boat or the bird, which for Augustine would have been testimonies of shame and unregeneracy, become part of the necessary and benign education of the spirit; he is more like Rousseau when he says 'Though mean / My object, and inglorious, yet the end / Was not ignoble' (i. 339–41), and he congratulates himself (very splendidly, it must be said) on having acquired from 'discordant elements' 'one society' (i. 354–5), and a 'calm existence' (360).

Certain elements in this exercise in self-distinguishing are worth further mention. Like Rousseau, Wordsworth is aware of the double consciousness all autobiographers must contend with. Childhood days have 'self-presence' in his mind (ii. 30–32); but more generally it is the present consciousness that speaks of a remote past recreated, remembered sometimes without his being able to give simple reasons for the memory. The most memorable of these memories, I suppose, are those spots of time: the gibbet, the girl with the pitcher, the bleak music of an old stone wall. These are the memories that count, and they count because the language that expresses their freight of emotion is, so to speak, adequately inadequate: it cannot verbalize what was not verbal, and so devotes itself to mystery and even discomfort. Wordsworth is sometimes in a corner, as with the lines on the crossing of the Alps, when it seems that as he was writing he was expecting some grand climax; but he cannot find it while remaining faithful to the recall of the original experience, and so goes off instead into a Coleridgean apostrophe to Imagination. Or, speaking of having seen a 'froward Brook' tamed in a garden, he admits that he did not then respond to it as he does now: moreover that he can now see that the brook was an allegory of himself, tamed by the forms imposed on the powers of life and true anamnesis by the light of common day (iv. 40–55).

There are other escapes; one of the great things about Wordsworth, as with Augustine, is that one sees them as constituents of that calm society he could, at the end of this story, with pained rejoicing, detect in himself. There are displacements: of the Annette Vallon episode on to 'Vaudracour and Julia', and, more nobly and splendidly, of the poet himself on to the boy of Winander, the old soldier, the blind beggar in *The Prelude*, the Old Cumberland Beggar and the Leech-gatherer. These are doubles, and have all the eeriness of doubles. They bear premonitions of loss, of privations to which the only defensive response (in normal life) must be stoic, though there is another answer, the poem. For loss, and these insistent premonitions of further loss, he needs consolation, a word that occurs, in company with a 'strength' that endures, as early as *The Prelude* (1805), iii. 108–9. Yet the fulcrum, the moment of illumination, comes a little later, when, after a night of dancing, he moves through 'a common dawn' and recognizes, although making no vows, that nevertheless 'vows were then made for me'; that henceforth he would be, 'else sinning greatly, / A dedicated spirit. On I walked / In blessedness, which even yet remains' (iv. 337–45).

This *kind* of experience, here so delicately rendered, recurs in most autobiographies, always as a claim to distinction, to the stigma of individuality, of election, though as a rule far less distinguished. For in the end what distinguishes is not the experience itself but the force and authority of the language claiming it. The religious tone is unmistakable, the sense of involuntary vocation, calmly accepted; the boldness and pathos of that 'even yet remains'. It is, we say, pure Wordsworth; and we say the same again, a little later, of the meeting with the soldier. The poet arrives in a receptive mood, in a solitude that encourages contact from 'some distant region of my soul' – images modified by association with 'a consciousness of animal delight', as if the scheme of Augustine was working here, the contents of deep memory passing through, and modified by, more accessible memories of what the senses deliver; and then, suddenly, the emblematic figure encountered on the road, the discharged soldier, still, almost silent except for murmurs of complaint, until on request he tells his tale; and the poet moves, with a 'tall / And ghastly figure', a strange double, at his side, towards a labourer's house where the man can shelter. As they walk the soldier speaks:

> solemn and sublime
> He might have seemed, but that in all he said
> There was a strange half-absence, and a tone
> Of weakness and indifference, as of one
> Remembering the importance of his theme
> But feeling it no longer.

This has real psychological force – a projection that works, even discharging the radical panic of autobiography, the forgetting why it is important – so that the poet can pass on 'with quiet heart' (*The Prelude*, 1805, iv, 504). And we recall that 'The Discharged Soldier' was an independent poem, only later worked into *The Prelude*, and roughly contemporary with *The Ruined Cottage*, in which the 'aged man' who tells the sad tale of Margaret can end by saying 'I turned away / And walked along my road in happiness' (524–5; Gill, p. 44). These anecdotes are purgative. To provide authentic accounts of the passions of others was, as Wordsworth remarked in the 1802 'Preface', a distinguishing mark of the poet; and we understand these doubles as testimony to that distinction as well as to all that the poet must have in common with widow and vagrant before these transferences of pain or anxiety can work. They speak for the poet himself; we can infer that their place in an autobiography is owed entirely to that creative force, though we may feel we have to seek an explanation of why this autobiography deals with the memory of guilt and sorrow by such displacements. The word 'dream' occurs in both passages, and they are like dreams in their reinterpretations of memory; they also represent some kind of absolution. They have dealt successfully with some profound remembered anxiety. So it is with other passages, such as that of the drowned man in Book V, an image of terror that the nine-year-old poet, as memory represents him, can see as beautiful.

The pattern of the poem is made up of such moments, and of reminders that at this or that stage – say in the Cambridge years – the gift, 'the morning gladness', was still active – and may, at four and thirty, still be so (vi. 55–60). The hope recurs in the woods at Lake Como (end of vi); in the dead child spared the 'distress and guilt' of the world (vii. 395ff), in the instructive sightless eyes of the beggar (vii. 610ff) and the shepherd, alarming doppelgänger, looming hugely with his dog, 'His sheep like Greenland bears'; but it is radiant in the setting sun, an allegory of mist and light, an image of that which penetrates and magnifies the mere reports of the senses and keeps the poet's face 'towards the truth' (viii. 397 ff). Some memories become 'divine', he says, 'only now', as he writes about the weight and shapes of London (viii. 710) he hardly knows what to do with them ('Alas, I feel that I am trifling' (iii. 706–7)), as if only now they came near to making the kind of sense he wants. Tears now start into his eyes, though they did not do so on the remembered occasion in France when they might have been appropriate (ix. 273ff). As for Vaudracour, his fate was to be silent – a fate Wordsworth could not contemplate in his own person, so wished it on to his surrogate; the fictive hero suffered for the poet, as so many others have done.

Like Augustine's story, this narrative features two Helpers, contributors to his preservation or restoration. They were his sister – he apologizes for giving her insufficient attention in 'this biographic verse' (xiii. 341), and Coleridge; the 'spots of time' passage was written when they were around. Now, by their help, he can call himself 'A meditative, oft a suffering Man', but he at once adds, 'And yet, I trust, with undiminished powers' (xiii. 126–7). The helpers are again admitted at the very end of the poem. Once more, in the Snowdon passage, light has penetrated the mist. There have not been many other named persons in this autobiography; it has been an intensive investigation of one mind, that which displays, against a background of common humanity, a splendid singularity.

The Prelude is the greatest and most original of English autobiographies, but it is so not because Wordsworth's intention is so different from most others. What we see particularly clearly in his prose is his desire to break through the assumptions and habits controlling or limiting normal introspection, as they limit poetry. The forces that break through, and enable deeper self-examination, are all anterior in origin to the formation of customary and habitual behaviour, shades of the prison-house; they are deep in the memory and hard to reach because of the distracting mist and clamour of ordinary life. But the memory, for a time at any rate, is accessible, its records can be reached, brought up from the deep store. It is not surprising that Wordsworth used the Platonic trope of anamnesis, for, as Augustine also knew, the memory contains what seems not to have been put into it by the senses. Probably many vocations are discovered by some such process. These deep, vertiginous mnemonic plunges most of us know about from literature rather than from ourselves – not because we are denied them, but because they have to be given appropriate expression or enactment.

16

Forgetting

These tentative remarks address what seems to be the neglected or forgotten importance of forgetting in hermeneutic processes. There is no need to speak of its obvious place in the preservation and updating of historical records, its precedence in all processes of recovery from the written past. Nor need we remind ourselves that for Plato writing was an agent in the destruction of memory, a practice which is in itself an ally of forgetfulness; nor of the importance to him of un-forgetting, anamnesia.

There have been some ambitious attempts – for example Aby War-burg's – to describe the operation of a transindividual memory, of anamnesic eruptions or recurrent 'engrams' in the history of images and symbols, in what he thought of as a cultural memory – an enterprise which must, in however negative a manner, take account of what seems to have been the repression as well as of the sudden recollection of the image, when, for instance, the Maenad bursts into quattrocento painting as the Nympha.[1] But remembering is more interesting than forgetting, its shadow or double, and it is with remembering that the emphasis of investigators always seems to lie unless we disturb it. We remember memory but forget forgetting. I suppose there is no reason to wonder at this inclusion of forgetting among that which, for whatever cause, is forgotten.

It will probably be agreed that in the reception of literature, of art in general, all depends upon the kind and form of attention solicited and given. We are familiar with certain difficult varieties of attention, which require the dissolution of lazy expectations; that is to say, people are ready to suppress, or repress, convenient assumptions or conventions in the interest of, say, deconstructive rigour and veracity.

What may escape us is the part played by such suppressions or repressions in the constructive acts of attention we must make in far less exacting circumstances: for example, when we comply with the dramatic invitation known as recognition.

'Great thing of us forgot!' says Albany, and no wonder the line is largely forgotten, for most directors omit it (*King Lear*, v.3.237), though it stands in both Quarto and Folio texts of the play, and must have been intended for performance. You will remember that Albany has been busy. Regan has been poisoned. There has been a chivalric duel, in which Edgar has mortally wounded Edmund. Edgar has also given a quite lengthy Wotan-like narration of his doings throughout the play, as well as a fairly detailed account of his father's death. Albany himself has just had news of his wife Goneril's suicide. His response to all these unsettling events is appropriately firm, but we must suppose a degree of mnemic overload, and until Kent comes in looking for the old king, now technically his prisoner, Albany has simply forgotten about Lear, his liege lord and the eponymous hero, and also about the king's daughter Cordelia, the captive Queen of France, though in fact it was only two hundred lines earlier (v.3.45ff) that Edmund informed him of his sending them both off to prison. In that interim, say a quarter-hour of stage-time, the murder of Cordelia is added to all the other deaths.

With so much going on it seems quite likely that the audience has also forgotten the great thing. Its attention has been fully stretched by a succession of relatively little things, minor deaths and recognitions; the playwright could count on this, and save the great recognition till the last, where it would benefit from the shocking remembrance of what has previously seemed unforgettable.

Shakespeare apparently saw no harm in drawing attention to the stratagem. Now we see that we have been deceived – have deceived ourselves – into thinking of the recognitions so far (the deaths of the villains, called trifles, or judgements of the heavens, the happy heartbreak of Gloucester) as giving the right note for the end. And when the note is struck (the mad, weak old king has, astonishingly, killed his man, and comes in with the one beloved daughter, dead, whether he recognizes it or not) we learn that this, and not what preceded it, is what can be thought the promised end, or at least an image of that horror. This recognition is both familiar and difficult, both terrible and memorable, as it might not have been had we not been involved in an almost ludicrous social act of oblivion, an oblivion that it is for us if anybody, and certainly not for the text, to feel ashamed of.

That forgetting is essential to recognition is perhaps implied by Aristotle, but, like the entire question, so far as I know, it is largely repressed in later theory, especially if one takes 'recognition' in a wider context than the dramatic. Barthes, however, wrote in *S/Z* (section xciii) of 'classic' texts that seem replete with meaning but reserve an ultimate, unexpected meaning which he calls *reconnaissance*, recognition, 'the signifier of the inexpressible, not of the unexpressed'. He is generalizing the issue by speaking, as it were, of the unconscious of texts, but implicitly acknowledging the sort of effect given by the end of *Lear*, though the shock there arises in a more complicated manner from the illusion that the inexpressible is deliberately brought near to expression. The apparent recognitions experienced earlier now seem substitutes, evasions; they must be worked through before the true recognition comes, which only after that exercise in sloughing off can be felt as real, a beast in a jungle; that earlier work is rewarded not by the vision we might have for many reasons expected, of a father and daughter, a king and queen, at last reconciled and honoured, but by an end, or an image of it, that we recognize as dismaying and, or as we might prefer to say, more sanative, more cathartic.

We begin to understand that what Terence Cave calls 'the scandal of recognition' is related to the scandal of forgetting.[2] After we have, like Albany, dealt with death and its repetitions (which touch us not with pity) we at last have what the repetitions left out: the inexpressible is expressed, the repressed returns.

Peter Brooks speaks of plot in general as 'the syntax of a certain way of speaking our understanding of the world'. 'The desire of the text (the desire of reading),' he says, 'is hence desire for the end, but desire for the end reached only through the at least minimally complicated detour, the intentional deviance . . . which is the plot of narrative . . . Repetition toward recognition constitutes the truth of the narrative text.' But it does so deviously: the middle of a plot is 'a state of error: wandering and misinterpretation'.[3] In the end we have to be returned, like Pip in *Great Expectations* as he recognizes and accepts Magwitch, to the great thing of us forgot. Plot, it is implied, is, up to the point of recognition, a way of forgetting, of being induced to forget the end by the interest offered by the devious path towards it. Without that interested forgetting there will be no ultimate recognition, no gift of truth for error, of life and death for fiction.

Brooks has an explicitly psychoanalytic model, and quotes appositely from Freud's characterization of the dynamics of transference: 'The unconscious impulses do not want to be remembered in the way treatment desires them to be, but endeavour to reproduce themselves in accordance with the timelessness of the unconscious and its capacity for hallucination.' This is plot short of recognition. The analysand tells a story that isn't good enough, lacking the true memory of (forgetting) a desire that must become present in the conditions of transference. Recognition, when it comes, has to be a full remembering, an end of forgetting that is no longer partial and delusive.

The business of plotting depends technically upon the assumption that we can be induced to mistake contingencies for absolutes and deviances for ends, a point made, along with others relevant to this issue, by Muriel Spark in her allegory *Not to Disturb* (1971). The end being assured, the plotting seems to the author merely a matter of 'vulgar chronology', and whatever seems to the reader likely to disturb that end (which, since most novels, though not this one, are in the past tense, has already happened) can be quite brutally arranged or eliminated. They are feints merely, the purpose of which is to delay recognition of a predestined and memorable truth – to enhance the really relevant recognition. We are trained to be docile about these devices, which make us forget the true course of the fiction. This is demonstrated by the ease with which we overlook or forget authorial error, committed, if for no other reason, because authors are also readers, and so schooled in the oblivion of plots.

Here one should try to estimate the relevance of quite casual forgetting in novels, instances in which, as so often in life, the thing of us forgot is apparently not a great thing. They can occur even when the promise of narrative pleasure depends upon an apparently exact fidelity to shared notions of plausibility. There are faults in the clockwork of *Tom Jones*. Tolstoy muddled some of his dates in *War and*

Peace. Dickens, working from part to part and aware of the chances of amnesia, had to keep memoranda on the ages of his characters and the relations between them; on details such as the state of the tides at the time of Magwitch's capture; and on various loose ends in his developing narrative that he hoped eventually to tidy up. Careful scholarly reading – after all, an act of abnormally close attention – has revealed that he still forgot about some things – for instance the dog Diogenes in the final part of *Dombey and Son*. On one occasion, when he had to put something right by making last-minute additions to the proofs, he sent two alternative corrected versions, each offering a different solution to the difficulty.

There is presumably no limit to such plot improvisations, when error can be purged by the invention of new deviances. Lister, the butler-author in Spark's novel, explains and demonstrates that the necessary adjustments can be made quite painlessly. For Lister, we are told admiringly, pertains, which means that he knows how to deal with the merely contingent: 'Lister can adjust whatever it is. Lister never disparates, he symmetrises.' As between 'events that arise from and those that merely follow after each other' he believes that 'those that arise are preferable', and arranges them accordingly; they are, after all, merely part of the delusive progress towards the end.

The ease with which Lister contrives to do so much more than merely list suggests something about the disposability of much plot material. There has to be provision for forgetting in the pre-recognitive phases, as a necessary preparation for the remembering of the recognition. The plot cannot be so tightly made that one can't make innumerable insertions and changes, and in any case it is, as Brooks says, a place of error (or, as Mrs Spark suggests, quoting Webster, it is like life, 'a mist of error'). Some errors, apparently insignificant, can be left to look after themselves, that is, to be forgotten; others, potentially more memorable, and therefore liable to raise the wrong kind of question, may require adjustments. In Part VIII (Chapter 22) of *David Copperfield* Dickens memorably introduced the grotesque Miss Mowcher, probably intending to use her later as an accomplice of Steerforth's in arranging the elopement of Em'ly. However, a chiropodist named Mrs Hill wrote protesting that Miss Mowcher was a recognizable and offensive portrait of her; whereupon Dickens apologized and promised to correct this false impression 'in the natural progress and current of the story', a bit of Listerian pertaining and symmetrizing being called for. He first tried to do it in Part X, where it proved too difficult. When Miss Mowcher does reappear in Part XI, it is clear that Dickens had failed where Lister might have succeeded, for she is quite transformed in character, and now useless to her author as a conspirator of Steerforth's. I don't know how many readers spotted this quite gross inconsistency, but the likelihood is that most did not remember well enough, or feel strongly enough, to complain; or that they were used to disparities which might in due course be symmetrized, but could easily be forgotten if they weren't.

Incidentally, at one point in the same novel the words 'Mr Dick was partial to gingerbread' were misread by the compositor and set as 'Mr Dick was partial to going abroad'. This potentially productive error was picked up in proof, but if it had not been, Dickens could either have written into the story a trip to Boulogne, or simply decided to rely once more on the charity of common forgetfulness in his reader, taking the risk that he or she wouldn't want, as we say, 'to make something of it'. For we have always to be deciding, as we read, whether to make something of it or let it go: 'forget it'.[4]

Again, to this day Dickens's editors have to decide what to do about the sometimes quite substantial portions of his writing that had to be cut at the last minute when a part was overlength, and which nobody has really missed. Would anybody have guessed that there was a version of the ending of Great Expectations other than the one imposed on Dickens by Bulwer Lytton? Like his friend Forster, we think of the original ending as a more pertinent recognition, but Lytton thought this pertinence was what the contemporary reader would prefer to repress. And the original ending of King Lear was withheld from the stage for almost two centuries, as if it were obscene, as if recognitions could be too scandalous to pertain.

More mysterious and suggestive instances of error and forgetfulness are found in Ford Madox Ford's novel The Good Soldier, a book constructed with such careful virtuosity that we are tempted to suppose that these slips of memory are themselves part of the design. The book has been devotedly scrutinized. The bold dislocations of chronology which give the work much of its force – Ford's quest for 'exhaustion of aspects', as against mere sequence, mere despised 'story' – must certainly have taxed the author's memory and his ingenuity to some degree. Then again he introduced certain potentially disruptive changes, as we know from the publication of the first part of the book in *BLAST* shortly before the beginning of the First World War. Ford became obsessed with the date of 4 August, and his attempt to make as many of the crucially disastrous events occur on that date put the complicated scheme of the book under some strain.

All the same, it does seem extraordinary that he should let his narrator speak of the girl Nancy as dead, at a time when we know she is in the same house as he, mad but alive. And that is only the oddest of several apparent blunders. By the time Leonora reveals to Dowell, the narrator, the fact of the girl's madness, he has already alluded to it four times. It almost seems as though there are two coexistent plots, in one of which Dowell knows about Nancy's fate from the time he starts writing, and in one of which he doesn't. Again, the apparently veracious statement that Nancy's mother is dead turns out to be greatly exaggerated. The striking of Maisie by Leonora cannot have happened on the day the Dowells and the Ashburnhams met; and so forth.[5]

One explanation is indeed that Ford intended his narrator Dowell – who, on his own admission, knows practically nothing in practically any sense of the verb, who has been described as a voyeur who sees nothing, who can plausibly be thought bad at deciding what to remember and what to forget, whether to make something of it or let it go – to be responsible for all the mistakes, so gaining all his configurational victories without incurring responsibility for the parts that don't really fit. If this was the game, the author could gamble without fear of losing – without bothering too much about accuracy. Dowell certainly does make mistakes which couldn't possibly be Ford's – about the DSO, about the feast of Corpus Christi – but these can be related to his nationality or his religion or his stupidity. And so his false reporting and melodramatic discoveries are made a part of his character as unreliable narrator.

Yet it is hard to believe that the elaborate narrative coups of this book are meant simply to contribute to so dull an end. It is manifestly more ambitious; the structure of the affair was what interested Ford, and its so to speak concentric implications in terms of the history of civilization and religion. It would surely have irritated him to learn that he had been writing an incredibly detailed psychological study of an uninteresting and imperceptive American. Rather we might say that he was experimenting, that his scheme was to avoid the kind of narrative where you have a long trail of manipulable contingencies followed by a recognitive ending. He was trying to employ the material of the recognition throughout; every climax in the book (usually a death, but sometimes more complex, like the scene over the Protest) is really of the stuff of endings, though neither the reader (at first reading) nor Dowell can fully know this.

At any rate it appears that this attempt to give what might be called recognitive status to every episode, or block of events – and so avoid what seems to go with the scandal of recognition, namely the scandal of forgetting – continues to involve spots of oblivion; also, of course, that it is not always possible to distinguish between willed and unwilled amnesia. Not far down the road from *The Good Soldier* lie the willed deceptions of Robbe-Grillet, in which nothing is forgotten, and where what is disappointed is precisely recognition; there are impossible-object novels, which, like Escher's drawings, confound you by showing that the mechanisms of recognition, and the forgetfulness on which they depend, are inherently limited; you can be shocked into the recognition that this is so. That is the game of fiction at an advanced level.

We should of course do well to remember what Paul Ricoeur has reminded us of, namely that this game cannot be played on all occasions; for instance, it has no part in a certain kind of historiography, and this sets history and fiction decisively apart. 'Historiography can exist without memory when it is driven by curiosity alone . . . But there are crimes that must not be forgotten, victims whose suffering cries less for vengeance than for narration. The will not to forget alone can prevent these crimes from ever occurring again.'[6] But in fictions none of Ricoeur's admonitions has force. 'Advanced' fictions of the sort I mentioned a moment ago are meant to expose the unexamined conventionality of our belief in the transparencies of realism. What is strange is that they continue to be thought of as experiments, even as oddities or sports. We do not, it seems, alter our basic expectations of fiction because we have read the novels and essays of Robbe-Grillet.

It used sometimes to be argued that the next stage in the history of the novel was always an anti-novel, which in turn became the novel that had to be countered with another anti-novel. But this seems not to be true. The structure of *The Sound and the Fury* still seems very unusual, and there is a long history of avant-garde fiction which never ceases, as it should on this theory, to be avant-garde. And what is remarkable about Ford's book is that it doesn't flaunt its breaches of convention; like James and Conrad he found quite enough to do within the horizon of ordinary expectation – just within it. And ordinary expectation is prepared both to remember and forget; it does not include recognition of faults in the fabric, sutures whether huge or tiny, whether flaunted or inadvertent.

I have not forgotten my point that there seems to be little serious theoretical discussion of forgetting in fiction or drama. Yet the matter cannot be too simple for investigation; it must have been overlooked. Even the psychologists seem to have little to say on the subject, always excepting Freud; unless I have missed something, they are understandably more interested in the positive issue of memory than in forgetting. Still, it may be worth saying what help I have found.

What are the ordinary uses of forgetting? Bartlett[7] in the Thirties demonstrated processes of recall that might have a bearing on the way in which we handle the large masses of detail that inevitably occur in a long novel. In the process of recall, he argues, we submit the material not only to our personal set of interests but to a set of interests amounting to conventions, which we accept as members of a society or culture. Sometimes the consequences are very strange, and the mechanisms of persistence and transformation can produce results remote from the original record. And although there is necessarily a good deal of simplification (of which forgetting is one of the instruments) there is also a curious persistence, well documented by Bartlett, of detail apparently irrelevant to the simplified or transformed scheme.

Different societies have different mnemonic conventions, and so remember (and forget) differently. Bartlett remarks that the narration of a series of events by an uneducated witness, or a witness from a different culture, can exasperate a magistrate by piling up what strikes him as totally irrelevant detail. I have noticed the same sort of thing in children when, for instance, they are telling you the story of a movie. Eliot simulates it in the unfinished narrative of his *Waste Land* pub scene ('Well, that Sunday Albert was at home, they had a hot gammon', etc.) Demands that the witness or reporter stick to the point are met with genuine incomprehension and confusion.

What Bartlett called the 'social control of remembering' must have as corollary a certain social control of forgetting.[8] Broadly speaking, we have a capacity, more or less common to the members of a group, to retain 'gists' at the cost of distorting or eliminating whatever, for lack of obvious relevance, is not regarded as gist, and if we try to fill in the missing detail it is likely to be erroneous or, to use the word of Philip Johnson-Laird, 'fuzzy'.[9] Whether or not we find this fuzziness a nuisance depends on our grouping. Bartlett's magistrate found the Swazi witness intolerably fuzzy. Johnson-Laird speaks of scientific investigators who are interested in the contrasts between gist and distortion. In the reading of fiction there is a similar distinction between gists and fuzz, a distinction hardly evident to the ordinarily attentive reader, whose choice of gists is in any case likely to be more conventional than that of the specialist.

There are of course specialists who regard gists as necessarily false or inauthentic; to select and arrange them is called 'thematization', and thought a bad thing. You might say that it is the fuzz that provides the gists on which deconstruction works. Its dislike of conventional gists is clear; they are the product of 'thematization'. I take it from Rodolphe Gasché that Derrida's main preoccupation here is philosophical, and part of his debate with phenomenology, especially with Husserl. For Husserl thematization was 'the articulate formulation of what was somehow already implicit in an unthematic, unthought, and unpredicated manner in the primary natural standpoint . . . Thematization objectifies the unthematized of the neutral standpoint in an articulate judgment', which is 'the factual existence of what it encounters in the real world around it'. Derrida opposes the notion that the unthematized can be reduced in this way. He 'questions the ultimate possibility of an *Endstiftung* through thematization'. Thus his attack on literary thematization is only an aspect of his general critique of phenomenological thematization.[10]

However, it is for literature the most important aspect. For Derrida the reductions we all habitually commit when we think about literary texts are falsifications; they simply and culpably forget the play of signifiers, just as structuralist criticism in its turn depends on an 'eidetic reduction' and forgets the specificity of the text. Thematic criticism ignores the undecidability of the texts it addresses.

This critique of thematization seems to be, finally, a critique of all criticism in so far as criticism can be practised. Thematization leads to totalization. Hence the attack on the Book, a false totality under 'the encyclopaedic protection of theology and of logocentrism against the disruption of writing'.[11] Some sort of 'doubling' commentary is, with severe reservations, allowed to be necessary; it should exist in dialectic relationship with the process of deconstruction. Presumably such commentary is obliged to practise what Nietzsche called 'the art of forgetting', essential because to live is to interpret; what it forgets is the limitless and unthematizable play of the text. Derrida more than once recalls Nietzsche's 'active forgetfulness', which is said to protect us from history, so enabling us to act and 'to make room for a new thing'. The question may be whether the philosophy of Derrida should not, like the philosophy to which he argues that literary criticism is historically enslaved, become part of that history which we should 'actively forget', in order not to lose that present which, as Nietzsche says, cannot be had without forgetfulness. There is then a kind of knowledge, doubtless mendacious but humanly useful, which is only to be had by forgetting.

Such is the kind of knowledge we ordinarily use when we read. We make tacit provisional treaties with the text and its world, agree that it has limits, accept the illusory fence around it. If this is reductive, then most of our dealings with any of the worlds we inhabit have to be reductive. We practise reductiveness in the world we physically inhabit, and usefully understand. We follow by these means, and could not do so if we hadn't internalized them. Of course that is also why we value that which defamiliarizes, makes us remember valuably what in the ordinary course of following we forget. It may be best – as perhaps Aristotle would have agreed – for the defamiliarization to enable us to remember what was already there at the outset, by a newly selected re-collection, a re-cognition, that will surprise us after a sequence of forgettings.

So much for the thematizations of ordinary reading, which enable us, by constructing theme and closure, to ignore what, within the horizon of our particular social memory, doesn't belong to following, and identify what does, whether what is being recounted is the story of *Middlemarch* or of last night's movie. Of course literary critics even of the more conventional sort, and especially those who believe in plurisignificance, try to do much more than that, though what they do will come under the same ban. They may discourse on the imagery of jewels in *Middlemarch* or discuss the rendering of a modern crisis in terms of a crisis in politics, religion, medicine, etc., that occurred forty years earlier than the time of writing; and they will introduce dozens of other considerations, all of which involve the organization of unitary themes into a totality; they might claim that as perceived by their interpretative society much that is fuzz to the ordinary reader can be regarded as gist. The deconstructive quest among the fuzz for what might be called un-gists, little giveaways, the end of some inconspicuous string that may be disentangled, is a kind of negative transformation of the more ancient practice, like the substitution of ubiquitous undecideabilities for the false ontological assumptions of the past. Yet the ungists have to be selected as not proper to be forgotten under the conditions of memory preferred by the society of deconstructors; and the selection is necessarily conditioned by an 'active forgetting'.

Even at a pre-deconstructive stage of critical theory the question as to social or institutional mnemonic horizons turns out to be quite complicated. Karlheinz Stierle, for instance, speaks of a level of reading that concerns itself with mimetic illusion, or 'quasi-pragmatic reception', and of a higher kind (practised by an obviously limited number of insiders) which he calls 'autoreferential', and an even more competent sect capable of receiving from a text its *Relevanzfigur*; this requires precisely what deconstruction would forbid, yet what is surely very common, a hierarchization of narrative elements. Other narratologists and reception theorists, having similar requirements, make similar assumptions; it takes competence to describe literary texts in terms of the transcendental model of Iser, or to move from surface to deep narrative structures by means of the process Chatman calls 'reading out'. Of course the acts these formulae attempt to account for are performed almost automatically, but they depend on an internalized competence which expresses itself by selection, by distinguishing between what gets the act together from what merits only the response 'forget it'. All such competences – one thinks of medical diagnosis – depend on 'active forgetting'.[12]

Although there are few direct treatments of forgetting in literary theory as such, there are allusions. Thus Percy Lubbock, writing so long ago that he could condemn literary criticism for 'its long indifference to . . . questions of theory', hovers a moment over the subject; Tolstoy, he says, forgot the main theme of *War and Peace*, but the reader can get round this difficulty by a practical piece of active forgetting, namely by skipping whenever he sees on the horizon another disquisition on the iniquities of Napoleonic historians.[13] Barthes approaches the issue more closely near the beginning of *S/Z*, affirming that given a plural text it is not a fault for a reader to forget a meaning:

To forget in relation to what? What is the sum of the text? Meanings may well be forgotten, but only if one has chosen to impose on the text a singular [i.e., non-plural] scrutiny. But reading does not consist in arresting the chain of systems, establishing a truth, a legally constituted text which accordingly institutes 'faults' in its reader. It consists rather in making these systems engage one another, not according to their finite limits but according to their plurality (which is something which has being, not something to be reckoned up): I pass, I articulate, I disconnect; I don't count. Forgetting the meaning is not something that calls for excuses, not an infelicitous fault in performance; it is a positive value, a way of affirming the irresponsibility of the text, the plurality of the systems (if I were to close the list of them I should, inevitably, be reconstituting a singular, theological, sense: it is precisely because I forget that I read).[14]

Here forgetting is a way of avoiding the myth of a single closed text, a way of liberating it for plural play, as when Barthes somewhere says that a reading of Proust is never repetitive because on each reading one skips different passages. The secret of this sort of reading is to take one 'lexie' at a time and consider it as crossed by multiple codes. In 'classic' texts tonal instabilities are produced by what is called 'fading'; by it the search for an origin or a meaning of that single lexie (selected, but mechanically, not like a 'theme') is frustrated. Most utterances in classic, as distinct from modern, *scriptible* texts, are attributed to a particular speaker, so that fading is important as a way of establishing the limited plurality allowed to the classic; the voice of the attribution 'is lost, as though it had leaked out through a hole in the discourse' (48–9).

This fading is taken from Lacan, who borrowed it from telecommunication jargon and converted it to psychoanalytical use in talking about 'the vanishing of the subject'.[15] It becomes an important constituent of Barthes's later distinction between *plaisir* and *jouissance*, for pleasure comes from continuity and *jouissance*, the greater and more complex experience, from discontinuity, interruption, loss, dismay. The value of modern texts lies in their duplicity: roughly, without the *plaisir* of the known and continuous, there is no *jouissance*, which is almost its antithesis, and even lacks a language.[16] Perhaps one could, without too much strain, associate *jouissance* with forgetting; it is continuity that calls for remembering.

There is here, no doubt, a certain indebtedness to the early Derrida, but Barthes's deployment of his codes makes explicit provision for the operations of 'social memory', whereas part of Derrida's purpose is to exclude them. What that memory occults by means of its hierarchical preferences and protections, its assumption of spurious presence and totality, its control of 'play', is to be negatived. It 'should have its place in a critical reading' as a means of avoiding the absurdity of a 'critical production' that can go anywhere and 'say almost anything', but it merely polices or facilitates the 'exorbitant' readings; the 'guard rail' readings of traditional criticism have rules, says Derrida, though it has not been possible to say what they are.[17]

This apparently contradictory attitude to traditional criticism – it is to be repressed or forgotten, but also remembered and used – has been quite trenchantly criticized, as by Robert Scholes and by John M. Ellis, who attributes its seeming embarrassment to a false identification of all 'traditional criticism' with 'Lansonism', the monolithic and dictatorial methods of literary history against which a Parisian revolt (with Barthes as its champion) was inevitable and commendable; Ellis sees no need for such a revolution in America, and believes that American disciples have sold, or are in danger of selling, a worthy inheritance for a mess of alien potage.[18] And surely it is true that there has been some simplification, that the representation of the traditional criticism depends upon a certain forgetfulness, the counterpart of that determination not to forget the same things.

That latter determination results in the preference for aporia over recognition, which depends on old-fashioned forgetting, or, if one prefers, on that fading which occults one signifying chain at the expense of others. Barthes's 'enigma' depends upon delays of recollection, on suppressions, imposed by his horizontal codes. No doubt the ease with which his analysis was accepted by old critics inspired a certain distrust in those for whom his licence of plurality still observed the restrictions of 'classic' texts, allowed too little 'play'; still, while preferring the *scriptible*, remembered the 'guard-rails' of the *lisible*. A more counter-intuitive anamnesis was preferred, and we may suppose that it was preferred because those old mental habits remain in thrall to logo-centrism, to myths of reference, to confusions about the relation of writing to themes and totalities, about voices and persons.

It may seem ironic that the person and voice of Derrida are so memorable; it is another contradiction, related to those acutely noted by Robert Scholes. And one more such occurs to me. If we have discovered that the entire 'ontotheological' tradition has involved a suppression of the truth in the interest of the myth of presence, what is this discovery but a recognition, and one of virtually apocalyptic force? It recovers the great thing of us forgot, hints at and allegorizes the promised ending.

I am nearing the end of these tentative speculations with as yet hardly a mention of Freud. His presence is simply too obvious, unforgettable; though it might be fitting to recall his perception that errors of memory beget fictions. For him the most remarkable kind of forgetting was infantile amnesia – we forget, he said, those 'childhood achievements' which 'exercise a determining development for the whole of . . . later life'. He was astonished that we should not be astonished by this amnesia, that we have to learn about our forgotten childhood achievements from others.[19] Barthes, by way of elaboration, remarked that the child of three years invents all at once the sentence, the story, and Oedipus:[20] that is to say, two totalitarian forms plus a complex of enigma, power, guilt and recognition of which, though we are oblivious of its origin and, except by studying others, its operation, we nevertheless suppose Freud's anamnesis to have established the recognizable truth.

Perhaps one can say that we seem to be, ontogenetically, so constituted that we have to forget much, and also remember much, including all that makes us, perhaps absurdly, try to hammer our lives and thoughts into a unity, a dubious totality. There is, if you like, a synergy of memory and forgetfulness, the thematic and the dispersed, the total and the fragment. Without memory and totality, no *plaisir*; without dispersity, dismay, mnemonic loss, no *jouissance*. That function of forgetfulness may be the great thing of us forgot, though it could not be so unless we remembered things less great.

NOTE (12.5.88)

I woke up with a contrapuntal series of verses in my head: first 'Alas, regardless of their doom / The little victims play; / No sense have they of ills to come, / Nor cares beyond today', – which is fairly accurate (should be 'care') but sounding along with these were the following: 'But sorrow's [blank] delights to trace / Its lineaments in another face' which is a version of Cowper's 'The Castaway': 'But misery still delights to trace / Its semblance in another's case'. A third tune, sounding simultaneously, was this: 'In vain they fought, in vain they bled, / They had no poet and are dead', which is a mangled version of Pope's translation of Horace, Odes iv. 9: '*Vixere fortes ante Agamemnona . . .*' (I remembered the Latin accurately but not the English: 'Vain was the chief's and sage's pride, / They had no poet and they died!'). This must have come in by association with the ('forgotten') lines from Cowper's poem: 'No poet wept him: but the page / Of narrative sincere, / That tells his name, his worth, his age, / Is wet with Anson's tear. / And tears by bards or heroes shed / Alike immortalize the dead.'

The fact that this complex of memories could probably be given a psychological explanation is not the point that occurred to me as I awoke. I thought: it is not strictly these words, and not even these rhythms, that are remembered, but a kind of tune, and each tune is peculiar to its poem as a whole though I could not, in most cases, remember the poems as wholes (Gray's, for instance, is much longer than I remembered, and I didn't associate the Horace paraphrase with Pope, or remember any other part of it). The suggestion is that the experience of a poem, the uniqueness of the tune, is dependent on its apprehension as a whole (Housman was 'given' the lines or rhythms which made his hair bristle, but they were already part of poems which had to be written; Valéry started within a rhythm for which he had to find words, as if to discover the context which made the rhythm interesting). That the scraps in my head also related to wholes larger than single poems does of course depend on my own associative constructions, and it may be relevant that my first acquaintance with all of them, including the Horace in Latin, goes back to my teens. For the provision of contexts for such involuntary exercises is part of cultural history. Yet the distinctiveness of the 'tunes' may be a cause of their memoration by a community of many persons; and though their copresence here is personal and as it were fortuitous, their necessary unity with the remaining lines of the poems from which they come is an argument for the substantial bounded unity of the poems.

NOTE (27.5.88)

Between Memory and History, ed. M. N. Bourguet, L. Valensi, N. Wachtel. (*History and Anthropology*, II,ii, October 1986). The destructuration of the group determines the destructuration of memory. Gaps are formed which are filled by a sort of bricolage. (R. Bastide, 'Mémoire collective et sociologie du bricolage', *L'année sociologique*, 1970) as quoted by Nathan Wachtel in Introduction, p. 215.) This kind of work founded by Maurice Halbwachs, a pupil of Bergson and disciple of Durkheim, in *Les Cadres sociaux de la mémoire*, 1924. '. . . individual recollections only exist and are localised in the past by linking up with the memory of others; one only ever remembers as a member of a social group. The singularity, the irreducible originality of personal recollections, are in fact produced by the criss-crossing of several series of memories which themselves correspond to the various groups to which we belong (family, friends, political party, social class, nation).' Even if you leave the group this remains true, since the forces are internalized. (212–13), since C16 nationalist history has enabled a common memory, now complicated by the move from narrative history to 'problem history' (218).

In 'Histoire littéraire et mémoire nationale' J-M Goulemot says the writing of literary history was part of monarchical propaganda for legitimation; it had the effect of making a national canon and replacing the study of rhetoric. (225 ff).

In 'The collapse of memory' M. Bozon and A-M Thiesse deal with collective failure of a social group as causing mass amnesia. The victims recall not a life-story but life in the old days, avoiding the pain of apprehending failure. In the process these northern French peasants mixed up two episodes of flight before the German army (1914, 1940); they telescope history (250–51). The memory of decline is also memory in decline.

Other contributions affirm the compliance of individual Jewish reminiscences with existing paradigms (L. Valensi, 'From sacred history to historical memory and back: the Jewish past,' 283 ff. (Jewish communities in Tunisia.) Also in N. Wachtel, 'Remember and never forget', 307–35, mostly Polish Jewish autobiography. Other studies of Mexican Indian versions of Spanish Conquest, and in African nations (e.g. urban painting in Zaire) – the relation of individual memory to the *imaginaire social*).

This approach could be applied to particular institutions such as our own. It could be argued that the change of paradigm mentioned by Goulemot (rhetoric to canon) has been reversed, so that the decay of canon is accompanied or even caused by the renascence of rhetoric. Consequently we are in the business of socially forgetting literature.

ON MISQUOTATION IN T. S. ELIOT
(21.7.88)

Misquotation: 'In some minds certain memories, both from reading and life, become charged with emotional significance. All these are used, so that intensity is gained at the expense of clarity.' (Eliot, in an unpublished lecture on *Ulysses*, given in 1933, and quoted by F.O.

Matthiessen, *The Achievement of T.S. Eliot*, 3rd ed (paperback), p. 56.) See note on p. 26 of F.K.'s *Selected Prose of T. S. Eliot*, 1975. (F.K.)

Ex, from F. K. 307 ff: 'I loved this woman in spite of my heart' (*The Changeling*, 5.3); correctly, 'in spite of her heart'.

'I that am of your blood' (*Changeling*, 5.3); correctly, 'I am that of your blood'.

Middleton's scene is obviously important – the climax of the play, and the point where Beatrice-J recognizes her corruption, and De Flores was originally speaking of his passion for her in spite of his knowledge of her corruption. Eliot's change unites them in corruption; he recognizes his own, but there is a memory of the original reading, in which it is hers. In the second misquotation there is a simpler explanation; the wrong version is much weaker, but still relates to family; the true version treats her imminent death as a surgical bleeding to restore the health of her family (thought of as a body diseased by her existence) and explains the next line: 'Let the common sewer take it from distinction' – which he quotes, in isolation from the preceding lines, in the essay on Massinger (1920) (F.K.156) – with great admiration ('that perpetual slight alteration of language') doubtless impressed by the unexpectedly abstract 'distinction' after the very concrete 'sewer', which continues the figure of bloodletting. It is 'the common sewer': 'common' here is opposed to 'distinction' but the expression 'common sewer' means 'a drain through which all or a large part of the sewage of a town passes, a main drain . . .' (*OED*, 2.) – a sense that probably came in, according to *OED*, with an act of 1606 relating to town drainage: this play is dated 1622, so the idea might have been quite strikingly new. Part of the pleasure is the double function of 'common', first as a rather up-to-date qualification of 'sewer', then, unexpectedly, as a contrast with 'distinction', generic word for persons of quality, as if the distinguished normally contribute no effluents to the sewer, but are now going to do so. How, given his sureness of choice and keenness of eye, did Eliot lose the connection with the preceding lines? He seems to have recalled it in isolation – yet another line from the same scene, accorded a kind of independence but in our view deprived of much of its force, yet in his mind joining some subterranean context; a kind of touchstone. In the Middleton essay of 1927 he quotes the passage at length from 'I that am (*sic*) . . .'

including the next remarkable figure, 'Beneath the stars, upon yon meteor / Ever hung my fate, 'mongst things corruptible'. Here again the contrast between the incorruptibility ('distinction') of the stars, and the meteor (De Flores) for meteors were supposed to be generated from the bowels of the earth, that is, in corruption. The dates of the passages are: 'I loved this woman . . .' 1917 (correctly, 1927, where he quotes several lines, doubtless with a copy before him: 'It is De Flores, in the end, to whom she belongs . . .' (Incidentally De Flores compares his pleasure in the prize of Beatrice's 'honour' to a drink, drained so that none is left for any other man to pledge him.) 'Let the common sewer' is quoted, without the preceding lines, in 1920, where it would be hard to say what was meant, and juxtaposed with a line from *Women Beware Women*, another Middleton play: 'Lust and forgetfulness have been amongst us' – but in context in 1927.

17

The Cambridge Connection

This essay was written for a series of talks given by various speakers at the London Festival Hall in January 2000. It is meant to be straightforward enough for a general audience with an interest but no professional familiarity with the subject of the series, which treated of modern literary criticism. The subject has of course been treated elsewhere in more intimate detail, but here what was wanted was a general account of the importance of the 'connection'.

No doubt to come from Cambridge and speak about the importance of Cambridge to modern literary criticism is to risk the accusation of parochialism; but the risk must be taken, for there is a real sense in which modern Anglophone criticism had its origins there in the years immediately after the Great War. This tradition of criticism flourished for quite a long time, probably reaching some sort of peak in the Fifties and Sixties.

Literary criticism in those days was a discipline that clearly interested a considerable non-specialist, non-academic, educated public. Respectable general publishers were glad to include literary criticism in their lists. I shall later say something about the way in which this public was created and sustained, and why the likes of Chatto & Windus and Routledge published so much of it, far more, indeed, than the university presses. Some professors found the abundance of such critical books alarming, though one remarked that the fashion reminded her of the nineteenth-century vogue for sermons, and would, in time, be as dead as they were.

The forecast was not far out. Immense quantities of criticism are still produced, but are now almost entirely academic and presuppose little or no interest in a wider educated public. Lionel Trilling, a fine, independent critic of what we must now call the old school, was always worried about keeping open the channels between the academy and the intelligentsia broadly conceived; he contemplated with dismay the decline of serious periodicals that discussed literature, as well as of other matters, politics and society, with that public in view. Writing of that kind has not wholly disappeared, but it has certainly diminished in quantity and perhaps in quality also. This is an age of theory, and theory is both difficult and usually not related to anything that meets the wider interest I speak of. Expansion and professionalization have meant that the *common* pursuit of true judgement, as Eliot, echoed by F. R. Leavis, called it, is a lot less common than it used to be.

The age of criticism, if one can call it that, can be dated, as I said, from the Cambridge of the years immediately after 1918. The idea of English literature as a proper form of academic study had hitherto not been countenanced at Oxbridge, and in institutions where it was accepted the methods employed, for example at University College London, and in the great northern universities, were based largely on Germanic philology and literary history. So it was, with some differences, in the American universities. The study of literature in one's own language seemed too easy, so Old and Middle English were conscripted to do the work of Greek and Latin grammar. One motive for the changes I'm about to describe was a new conviction that real literary criticism was not at all too easy; that it called for hard theoretical competence and high analytic intelligence as well as common sense.

The idea of the importance of literary criticism, considered as a necessary aspect of the national culture, was not in itself entirely novel, and the achievement of the great nineteenth-century reviewers was still remembered. Other Victorian bearers of this civilized tradition were Matthew Arnold and, to a slightly lesser degree, Leslie Stephen, and they provided an obvious contrast to modern Sunday newspaper reviewing. Note that these models were essentially non-academic, though products of the academy. Indeed one of the reasons why Stephen was admired was that he had given up a Cambridge fellowship on conscientious grounds and become something like a modern free-lance writer without sacrifice of scholarly standards and authority.

The new Cambridge critics wanted to foster the more valuable elements in the culture of their own time, so, despite wide differences of method and assumption, they shared some basic ethical assumptions with these predecessors.

The academics who sought to introduce a new style of literary study in Cambridge were, necessarily, not men who had been trained in 'English literature'. No such training was available, at any rate in Oxbridge. They had started out as classicists or historians or philosophers, though their educational experience was much wider than those descriptions might suggest, for they had benefited from the relative smallness and intimacy of the university and the accessible presence of some very impressive minds. I. A. Richards, reading History and later Moral Science, had access to Bertrand Russell and his pupil Wittgenstein (but he meant 'very little' to Richards), G. E. Moore and J. M. E. McTaggart among the philosophers. James Ward the psychologist was his teacher; without Charles Sherrington's neurology Richards' *Principles* would not have been possible.

Among his contemporaries and collaborators, the polymathic C. K. Ogden ('he was just unbelievable as an intelligence') was within his daily reach. 'In those days at Cambridge,' said Richards, 'you had no assigned reading', and he called the Moral Science courses 'the last word in philosophic savagery'. However, the audience at the Moral Science Club might include Russell and Moore and F. C. Bartlett, McTaggart and other neo-Hegelians; possibly Lowes Dickinson and Forster and Keynes as well. Moore was particularly important to Richards, but Ogden, as a contemporary and his collaborator on *The Meaning of Meaning*, a severe treatise on semantics, had perhaps a more direct influence, and so had Mansfield Forbes, a brilliant colleague who died young; he alone shared Richards' interest in matters of literary-critical theory and practice.

Richards took a first in 'Moral Science' and eventually eased his way, and spread his doctrines of philosophical and linguistic analysis, into the newly founded English School (the course was 'English Literature, Life and Thought'). The history of the foundation of that School, and later of the Faculty of English, has been told many times: the opposition of the classicists and others; the doubt as to whether such a course, shorn of the linguistic study that was demanded elsewhere, was sufficiently difficult to be called a discipline. All agree that Richards' was a dominant voice. But neither he nor his sympathizers had any real power in the university, for they were not recognized university teachers. Consequently they were unable to do much about the bureaucratic development of the new Faculty. Over the following years English at Cambridge remained distinctive, not very like the subject anywhere else, but it was not what Forbes and Richards wanted.

It is right and necessary to emphasize that in spite of the psychologistic element in such books as *The Principles of Literary Criticism* (1924) and the methodological novelty of its sequel *Practical Criticism* (1929), there was always a strong ethical component in Richards. He was interested of course in science, but believed that art of high quality was needed to supplement the cognitive achievements of the scientists. He expressly agreed with Matthew Arnold that poetry could do the work of religion (that it was 'a perfectly possible means of overcoming chaos'), but to achieve that end it was necessary to understand how poetry worked. 'I was interested in psychology . . . But my psychology came out of G. F. Stout . . . and William James's *The Principles of Psychology*. Those were the real formative things. Those and Sherrington's *Integrative Action of the Nervous System* to put the physiology into it. I was someone really saturated in psychology and neurology making up a book about the literary approaches.'

The display and explanation of this psychological machinery was largely confined to the early books – all the talk of equilibrium of impulse, the psychological justification of that high claim for poetry, yielded to the urgent necessity of *practical* criticism, the intense study of 'words on the page'. Richards spoke of its object thus: he intended 'to introduce a new kind of documentation to those who are interested in the contemporary state of culture, whether as critics, as philosophers, as psychologists, or merely as curious persons. Secondly, to provide a new technique for those who wish to discover for themselves what they think and feel about poetry, and why they should like or dislike it. Thirdly, to prepare the way for educational methods more efficient than those we use now in developing discrimination and the power to understand what we hear and read'. Of course he had opponents who believed that it was absurd to say that you needed to be taught to read your own language. But by means of his work on the Cambridge course he may be thought to have beaten them. Later, more successful opposition came from a resurgent Marxism, from younger critics like Raymond Williams who condemned Richards' notion of 'equilibrium' as entirely passive: according to Richards the desired effect of poetry was the achievement of a condition in which no further action was necessary, and, for Williams, this was to stop the process at just the point where it should have issued in political action. These are important objections. The fading of Richards' influence meant the end of the first age of the Cambridge connection. His methods gave way to a newer, anti-aesthetic style of criticism that is even today dominant in the academy.

To return to the Twenties: once there was a Faculty of English in existence, conditions grew harder for Richards and his colleagues, all of whom, as I've said, lacked regular appointments. And as the enterprise began to crumble, Richards considered new possibilities outside Cambridge. He was attracted by China and by the USA; it was as if having dedicated himself to the education of a handful of people in Cambridge he wanted to take on the education of the whole world. He devoted more and more time to Basic English, in the invention of which he had assisted Ogden. He remained a prolific writer about literature, but his influence on criticism waned. He continued to write poetry and climb mountains, and he was deeply respected in China as well as in the United States; but when he returned to Cambridge for his last years he felt himself to be rather irrelevant, now an outsider, and a victim of the well-known *froideur* of the Cambridge social climate. Still, he was an unignorable figure, and we have lost much by forgetting his example to the degree that we have.

Of course he belonged to a world now remote; he took little interest in Freud, and with Ogden decided against Saussure, two of the founding fathers of modern criticism. But we could do with a revival, not of the old psychologies and linguistics and semantics, but of the application of devoted intelligence to the actual texts of literature.

Practical Criticism is still a paper in the Cambridge English Tripos, and it has been imitated, with many variations, all over the Anglophone world. Richards' book, with its 'protocols' and lists of critical faults (inability to get the plain sense, stock responses, doctrinal adhesions, etc.) may now seem in some respects quaint, but in the course of assembling it he discovered a truth no less important today than in 1929. What he discovered, with surprise and some incredulity, was that people who had enjoyed what was assumed to be the best education available made absurdly elementary mistakes in writing about the poems he set before them. They missed the plain sense, were slaves to stock responses, judged poems in terms of their doctrinal assumptions, and so on. Such readers were, in spite of their paper qualifications, dangerously uneducated, manifestly ill-equipped to receive the psychic or neural benefits that poetry can offer, as well as being vulnerable to exploitation elsewhere.

Richards was not recommending very loose or licentious interpretation. He was hostile to what he later called 'omnipossibilism'; as he expressed the point much later, 'deep freedom in reading is made possible only by the widest surface conformities'. That is why 'deep reading' can be taught. Attention to surface conformities must precede and control imaginative interpretation.

The importance of this position for future criticism is obvious. Readers could be trained; they would, in consequence, be more balanced and valuable persons. Practical criticism, deep, informed attention to texts – texts, not doctrines – was to be of all intellectual disciplines the most rewarding. You could become very good at it, at the same time sharpening your sensibility, balancing your impulses, and receiving a modern substitute for the comforts of religion.

Such interpretative experiences need not be confined to the academy. The appearance of a non-academic criticism of superior quality was signalled by the opportune publication of Eliot's *The Sacred Wood* in 1920. Richards was in touch with Eliot, though they did not always agree. Richards wrote the first important critique of *The Waste Land*; and Trinity thought Eliot serious enough to give him honorary academic status as Clark Lecturer.

It can be seen, then, that the Twenties were alive with possibilities for a new criticism. It was not all Richardsian, but he was the principal academic figure. And soon the whole narrative was to take a new turn under the influence of Richards' extraordinary pupil, William Empson. Empson, born in 1906, was thirteen years junior to Richards. He had read mathematics at Magdalene but switched to English for Part Two of the Tripos and became Richards' pupil. Like his teacher, and partly because of his example, Empson spent many years of his life abroad, mostly in China and Japan, and he loyally proselytized for Basic English, lamenting its failure to the end, and perhaps unreasonably blaming Churchill for killing it by his sponsorship. Though sometimes critical of Richards and temperamentally quite unlike him, Empson remained devoted to his teacher, who was the dedicatee of *The Structure of Complex Words* (1951), the book Empson regarded as his major achievement.

Empson's first critical collection, *Seven Types of Ambiguity* (1930), is well known to have had its origin in undergraduate essays written for Richards, and so far as I know it is, considered as the work of a critical prodigy, without rival. It was very fortunate that there was a young person of genius at hand to show what high intelligence, combined with a measure of youthful irresponsibility, could achieve by using the method of close reading. Though Empson was always sure that what he was describing in his criticism had been part of the writer's intention, however broadly conceived, his primary interest was in the ingenuities possible to his own mind. In the opinion of many, he flouted Richards on the matter of omnipossibilism. But nobody who has experienced the exhilaration and daring of Empson's early books will regret this wickedness. *The Structure of Complex Words*, written when Empson, after a wonderfully adventurous career, had reached his forties, is probably – as he himself certainly believed – a greater achievement than *Seven Types* or its successor, *Some Versions of Pastoral* (1935), but it was less outrageously unexpected.

By the time I was an undergraduate in the late Thirties Empson's early books were in the hands of all young lecturers and the more enterprising students, though they were treated with some suspicion by their elders. It is safe to say that nobody had ever done this kind of thing before. To take a single example at random: here are some lines from a soliloquy of Claudius in the third act of *Hamlet*:

> May one be pardon'd and retain th'offence?
> In the corrupted currents of this world
> Offence's gilded hand may shove by justice,
> And oft 'tis seen the wicked prize itself
> Buys out the law, but 'tis not so above:

There is no shuffling, there the action lies
In his true nature, and we ourselves compell'd
Even to the teeth and forehead of our faults,
To give in evidence.   (III. iii. 56–64)

I would offer the following as a competent gloss in accordance with 'the widest possible conformities': Claudius asks, already knowing the answer, whether he can repent and still retain the benefits of his crime. 'Retain th'offence' is very compressed; a soliloquy of this sort is distinguished by its great alterations of pace, its constrictions as well as its expatiations (some of which, like 'teeth and forehead', are highly characteristic of the language of *Hamlet*). Claudius speaks of 'the corrupted currents of this world', and 'currents' is vague – it can mean the course of events, as in modern 'current affairs', but can also have a sense of 'flowing' or even 'sloping', 'having an inclination to fall'. A 'corrupted current' could be a sewer. Claudius, represented as a man of turbulent intelligence, does not develop this idea but instead presents an allegory so briefly sketched in that it almost avoids being identified as allegory: Offence, the crime, holds money in his hand and shoves by Justice – pushes him away. Then, relaxing into the literal, the speaker puts the matter thus: the gold obtained by the crime may be the bribe that ensures the offender's security. He contrasts this position with what obtains in the world above where 'There is no shuffling, there the action lies/In his true nature'. 'Shuffling' means underhand or equivocating conduct, here especially legal trickery (he moves from Justice to Law). The action (the prosecutor's case in court) lies – is sustainable, and a full confession is inevitable. 'Even to the teeth and forehead of our faults': the brow, the facial expression that can give a man away, is now associated with the teeth. The lines are usually taken to mean a hostile face-to-face confrontation, but the point is that the evidence of the accused amounts to a total confession; the teeth and brows will be ashamed not defiant. The fault is now an unconcealed shame; no mask or helmet can cover it. The violent, rapidly shifting metaphors of this wonderful passage prefigure the complexity of Shakespeare's later language. It is just the kind of thing that must, if literary criticism was to do the job proposed for it, be submitted to intensive close reading.

And this is what Empson gives it. He insists that the passage requires the reader to 'open his mind to' all the associations of the words. And he goes on to quote five lines of the speech, before commenting thus: [*Seven Types of Ambiguity*, Penguin ed., pp. 91–2]

You put your hand down the hole, feel at the rat's head and face (*forehead*) in an attempt to drag it out, and then (*teeth*) it bites back at you. 'God will force us to bring our faults out into the open, however much we struggle.' A *forehead*, besides being a target for blows, is used both for blushing and frowning. 'We will be ashamed and a little indignant at having to confess such things.' *Teeth*, besides being a weapon of offence, are used in making confessions, and it is a mark of contempt, I suppose for your weakness, even where you might seem most dangerous, that you are struck there. 'We must confess all in plain words, or God will give us the lie in our teeth.' Perhaps, too, the *forehead* covers the brain where the *fault* is planned, while the *teeth* are used (whether for talking or biting) in carrying it out, so that they stand for the will to sin and the act of sin respectively. Or, making a fair attempt to give *of* its grammatical meaning, so that the *teeth* and *forehead* are not *ours* but our *faults*'; 'We shall have to start giving evidence at the very bottom of our faults, and go right on up to the top where they are at their most striking and important.' *Teeth* are a naked part of the skeleton and the *forehead's* bone is near the surface; 'The Last Judgment will give little or no margin to the flesh; we shall have to go right down to bedrock in turning up our faults.'

This is all very fanciful and irrelevant, the reader may think. But what *is* relevant to these notes of the material for rhetoric, this poetry by physiological shorthand? All we are given is two parts of the body and the Day of Judgment; these have got to be associated by the imagination of the reader. There is no immediate meaning, and in spite of this there is an impression of urgency and practicality, and being in the clutches of an omnipotent ferret. Such an effect must rely, not perhaps on flashes of fancy in the directions I have indicated; I doubt if such occur in the normal reader; but on a sense that the words themselves, in such a context, include, as part of the way in which they are apprehended, the possibility of flashes of fancy in the directions I have indicated. The words are intended for the stage; they certainly convey something to an audience; and there is no time for them to convey anything more definite than this before the soliloquy has swept on to another effect of the same kind.

How did those rats get in? Empson hedges a bit, but it is clear that his notion of the range of association is much less restrictive than Richards', and his love of what he calls 'the great parades of association' (p. 93) amounts almost to an acceptance of 'omnipossibilism'.

And this was one important question raised by the criticism that flowed from Richards' pioneer work. The question was how to keep comment within bounds, to show respect for the widest possible conformities. It recurred in another development of the Richards tradition. He and his work became well known in America, perhaps principally through the work of Cleanth Brooks, but also because of Empson. Brooks was a Rhodes Scholar at the right time, and he got to know Richards and his work. He took his ideas to Vanderbilt, where they were welcomed by John Crowe Ransom, Robert Penn Warren and others. What came to be called the New Criticism was born, and it became a powerful educational influence through the successful Brooks–Warren anthology, *Understanding Poetry*. There were some doctrinal differences; Brooks was a Christian, and the movement was politically associated with Southern Agrarianism. It inherited from Eliot the historical hypothesis of a seventeenth-century dissociation of sensibility, and this belief had some effect on its criticism. But it was accepted that doctrine was not a primary issue, that poetry certainly should not be didactic, and that the mark of great poetry was that it reconciled impulses of 'extraordinary heterogeneity', as Richards claimed. The reconciliation was to be detected and experienced by intensive, accurate reading.

Brooks developed his own terminology (tension, paradox) and in due course the movement, settling down at Yale, acquired its own theorist and adjudicator, W. K. Wimsatt. One of the common principles was a refusal to regard literature as something proper to be discussed in terms of biography and literary history; Wimsatt wrote a famous article about the 'intentional fallacy', a complaint against the quest for meaning in the biography of the author.

Meanwhile the older school of literary historians and philologists vigorously opposed these innovators. The New Criticism won a great though not a lasting victory. There is something in the complaint that it led to a situation in which clever students could write Ph.D. theses without ever disturbing the dust in the library; and in the hands of less clever students it could be mechanical and tedious. Its dismissive attitudes to history and doctrine proved fatal in the end; a new, revived anti-aesthetic historicism meant the end of the New Criticism.

The question of the relations between poetry and belief (especially Christian belief) was a popular topic at the time. But although the purposes of Richards were always in a sense ethical (via psychology) the clause about 'doctrinal adhesion' liberated poetry from belief as ordinarily understood. Behind his views lay a sort of psychologistic humanism, but in principle you could, and should, adopt his methods whether you had a religious adherence or not. The Formalists of course disagreed among themselves as well as with other people, and indeed were thought by some to be too interested in literary theory, especially as formulated and contested by Wimsatt (who happened, incidentally, to be a Catholic, as was Allen Tate, a distinguished poet as well as a critic). The heyday of the New Criticism ended in the Sixties, even before the onset of a New New Criticism, and a resurgence of Marxist interests in a far more sophisticated form than was available in earlier times signalled the re-evaluation of doctrine. But it is remarkable, given the speed of change in this world, that the ideas formulated by Richards in the Twenties had their influence, however remote, in thousands of American classrooms as late as the Sixties. It is worth adding that the new regime had, and has, little time for 'close' criticism of the Brooksian sort, and that in the opinion of some it is time for close criticism to return, in whatever new theoretical guise, as necessary to the continuation of an interest in the text itself rather than in the text as one among many competing contemporary discourses to be studied by way of illustrating the conflicts of power and resistance to it in the historical period in question.

Meanwhile, back in Cambridge, another set of ideas, ultimately stemming from Richards, was in its own way emphasizing the ethical, but this way was so different that the new school would in the course of time virtually disown Richards. The central figure was F. R. Leavis, who entered the scene just as the English school was forming, in the immediate post-war years. Leavis was twenty-four and had seen service in France. Francis Mulhern, the admirable historian of *Scrutiny* (the journal that became the main vehicle for Leavis's ideas) points out that the change in ideas about English as a subject coincided with an alteration in the social structure of the university, for a new wave of teachers (and students) was recruited predominantly from the middle classes and below, including people who did not begin with classics and who had no claim on the status of scholar-gentleman. L. C. Knights, who actually started the journal, was a Tawney-inspired left-winger, inspired by a certainty that literary criticism was the instrument necessary for the true understanding of human values, and a confidence in the purgative social power of a 'critical minority'. Leavis's wife Q. D. Leavis, a fierce judge, and as a sociologist devoted to the example of R. S. Lynd and H. M. Lynd's *Middletown* books, was a formidable enemy of upper-class pretention in literature as well as in society.

Yet the programme of the group in its early years – not its later proclamation of an authoritative canon, not the uncertain left-wing politics – derived directly from Richards. A particular concern was the importance of affective in contrast to cognitive discourse, and the conviction that criticism was in fact the finest exercise of intellect. Of course this meant an end to the gentlemanly critical commentary of the likes of Quiller-Couch, the first King Edward VII Professor (though Leavis in his way remained loyal to that figurehead). The aim was once again ethical, and the stance was necessarily oppositional, for the group had almost no academic power, and indeed very often had no jobs, which is why Knights went off to Manchester and did not return to Cambridge for thirty or more years.

Leavis was a fine if harsh 'close critic' but he did not see that activity as an end in itself. He regarded his close colleagues and pupils as the nucleus of a new élite, even, as Mulhern puts it, 'a new *estate*: a compact, "disinterested" intelligentsia, united in commitment to "human values", whose function would be to watch over and guide the progress of society at large'. This was the programme of *Scrutiny*. Its intention was to save the culture, generally thought in those years, as in others, to be in trouble. Its enemies were not only bad critics, the London literary establishment, Bloomsbury, the Book Club, but advertising, mass production, the press, the cinema, the education system. The values they represented, the values of mass civilization, must be opposed by a minority devoted to the restoration of the values enshrined in the great Victorian periodicals and also in the culture of early seventeenth-century England, with its peasant communities and extraordinary vitality of language.

Scrutiny was therefore more than a journal of literary criticism, but literary criticism was a prime agent of culture. It took certain positions of Richards (the need for great art and poetry, indispensable to both individual and social well-being) and developed them in ways he had not foreseen. Internally, as often happens when groups of this kind form, there were quarrels, expulsions, increasingly charismatic attitudes on the part of the Leavises. But their pupils went out to the schools and made a great difference there. In Cambridge they always had the old enemies, but acquired new friends and disciples; interestingly, some of them later established themselves in ways that might not have pleased their teachers. I think of Karl Miller, who joined the hated London literary establishment (and even, once or twice, persuaded Leavis to write for him) and, in America, Marius Bewley, Richard Poirier and Norman Podhoretz, editor of the fiercely rightist *Commentary*; for the G.I. Bill visitors were attracted to the one combative, programmed centre of English studies in Cambridge. As Leavis remarked in his 'Retrospect' of *Scrutiny*, 'The research students and undergraduates who used . . . to meet at my house, which was very much a centre, did not suppose that they were meeting at an official centre of "Cambridge English", or one that was favoured by the official powers.'

Theories of history and society were essential to the programme. 'I have no doubt,' wrote Leavis, 'that [the training] will make the student a better literary critic, but the test of his having profited duly by his course of studies will be his handling of a historical or sociological work as much as his handling of a novel or a book of poems.' Literary 'tips' would be offered, and the books thus recommended duly read, but the whole scheme was much more than literary.

The journal ran from 1932 to 1953, and that was in itself a remarkable achievement; twenty years is a long life for any minority journal, and its demise left Leavis weary and rather disconsolate. It had been, and according to him could only have been, a Cambridge achievement. Its causes were, he said with some defiance, 'of great moment' and 'only at Cambridge could the idea of *Scrutiny* have taken shape, become a formidable life, and maintained the continuous living force that made it hated and effective'.

In 1963 the Cambridge University Press reissued the whole series with Leavis's 'Retrospect'. He still had a good many years of work before him – on Lawrence, on Dickens, even on Tolstoy, despite the disadvantage of Tolstoy's not having written in English. And the disciples were still active. But Richards, who had planted the seed, was no longer much admired, and Eliot, formerly a model, was set aside. Leavis's tone grew more acerbic, the prose more contorted. 'Leavisites' became less prominent in schools and universities. The New New Criticism, founded on Saussure and developed by Derrida and de Man and others, now proved more exciting. Marxist criticism thrived in some universities. The group at Downing had its day, as schools of criticism do, and then it died, leaving, one hopes, something of value to its successors.

It was curiously academic and somewhat parochial (only Cambridge would do) and at the same time anti-academic, in relation to the powers it opposed. It provided a good many of those books of critical essays I mentioned earlier. From the beginning it was embattled, which can be attractive, and political, and acrimonious, often beyond necessity. But much that was good in what we are calling 'the Cambridge connection' derives from Leavis and his school. (We needn't be surprised to learn from the 'Retrospect' that nobody in the university, though many outside it, bothered to commiserate with him on the demise of the journal.)

Despite the forces that gave it so different a shape and so different a destiny, that school derived ultimately from Richards. In the course of his long career he moved away from literary analysis into enterprises which, for good or ill, became less and less influential. At the end of his incessantly active life he was revered in Peking rather than in Cambridge, where little notice was taken of his later work. The *Scrutiny* school was convinced of the need for an oppositional cultural minority, whereas Richards was sure that the benefits of his methods were far more generally available, since the psychology involved was everyman's psychology and not dependent on the existence of a specially endowed and trained cult. Perhaps if he had stayed in Cambridge matters would have turned out differently, though I doubt if he could, in any case, have matched the moral fervour of Leavis. He would not have shared the strain of vehement anti-scientism that drove Leavis in his polemics, the most famous of which was the assault on C. P. Snow's 'two cultures'. And now even that fervour is lost, and with it what remained of Richards' influence on a wider public than Cambridge could provide.

In America his descendants, the New Critics, were rejected. Other critics of independently founded theoretical and interpretative ingenuity – Kenneth Burke, R. P. Blackmur, Yvor Winters – diversified the American critical scene. His English descendants narrowed and politicized their inheritance. Yet it would be impossible to write their histories without allusion to Richards, and to the *scherzando* adaptation of his first insights by Empson. To have done so much to make possible the achievements of Leavis and Empson, and to have given the New Critics the means to dominate American humanist education, was a great achievement. It is by no means Richards' only claim on our gratitude. But it justifies the inclusion in this series of a talk on the Cambridge Connection.

18

Literary Criticism: Old and New Styles

This was given as a lecture in Oxford on 14 February 2001 and published in the issue of Essays in Criticism *that appeared in April. It seemed to be one of the few occasions on which it would be proper to exploit one's age; I read the journal from its inception, and knew F. W. Bateson, who founded it. The talk was written when I was feeling mild irritation about certain excesses of 'the New Historicism' and meant to have a little fun at its expense. Some of my hearers were apparently disconcerted by my procedures, not least the dénouement. However, it was a reasonably festive occasion, and most agreed that a little not indecorous levity might well be allowed to qualify, for a moment, the professional gravity of dons.*

F. W. Bateson's *Essays in Criticism* is more or less exactly fifty years old, so this may be the moment for a nostalgic glance at some of its early numbers. The leading article in the first issue is the late John Holloway's 'Matthew Arnold and the Modern Dilemma'; possibly Bateson's editorial manifesto, 'The Function of Criticism at the Present Time', wasn't ready, for it appeared only in the third issue. The titles of the two essays seem to be gently insisting that the influence of the former Professor of Poetry was still being felt.

Holloway remarks that 'perhaps two of the most distinctive tenets of modern criticism are that poetry is an imaginative fusion, and that it fuses not few but many elements into a single complex with an organic unity'. This sentence in itself tells us how long a time is fifty years in the history of critical fashions. Expressions like 'imaginative fusion' and, especially, 'organic unity' are highly unlikely to occur in a modern critical context. And when Holloway states with approval that 'the crucial operation for Arnold is to distinguish major works from minor', he is endorsing a position now quite generally regarded as naïve and reprehensible. Nor would it now help his cause to quote Arnold in response to his critics: 'those who are insensitive to poetry . . . are likely to be insensitive to language as a general means of expression', though in the view of a few survivors that observation has not ceased to be apt.

Among the other contributors to that first volume there occur some unexpected names: L. A. G. Strong, for instance, and Montgomery Belgion and Middleton Murry. Unlike its contemporary, and for a year or two its rival, Scrutiny, Essays in Criticism had not, or not yet, divested itself of all relations with the critical world outside the universities, the London literary scene so often deplored by Dr Leavis. Belgion, who had been a regular contributor to T. S. Eliot's Criterion, is now forgotten, except, perhaps, as the author of an anti-Semitic review once wrongly attributed to Eliot. Murry was an active literary journalist and editor, close to, and from time to time at war with, both D. H. Lawrence and T. S. Eliot. The Problem of Style is still mentioned occasionally, which is remarkable enough for a critical work published in 1922, but it is Murry's marriage to Katherine Mansfield that brings him more often to notice. Strong was primarily a novelist, though he wrote a book about Joyce and taught for a while at Oxford, where Bateson probably met him. Few will regret that the appearance of such writers in Essays in Criticism was fugitive, but their rapid disappearance does hint at the increasingly academic orientation of literary criticism.

Bateson himself contributed an amusing refutation of an article by Leslie Hotson on Shakespeare's 'mortal moon' sonnet, in which he warned against 'the limitations of pure scholarship', and also the inaugural entry, on 'Comedy of Manners', in what was intended to be a cumulative Dictionary of Critical Terms. The general intention was that the journal would carry on indefinitely, scholarly enough and critical enough; and so it has, to the great credit of the founding editor and his successors.

As an aspiring youngish critic I shared the general excitement caused by this new venture; it promised to be the riposte to Scrutiny so many of us wanted, or at least a complement to it. Of course we did not then know that the days of *Scrutiny* were numbered – it expired in 1953, a rather unexpected event that enhanced the importance of Bateson's venture. There was in those days a general belief, now weirdly archaic, that literary criticism was extremely important, possibly the most important humanistic discipline, not only in the universities but also in the civilized world more generally. These were the times when reputable London publishers were actively soliciting books from young critics. Of course we shouldn't deny that *Scrutiny* had a large part in bringing about that state of affairs, but the eyes of the London scouts were now on *Essays in Criticism*. Naturally we all wanted to contribute, and I was very pleased with myself when, with my learned footnotes drastically trimmed, I made it into the second volume.

By that time the journal was already more decidedly academic. Those London bookmen and men of letters had disappeared by the second number, to be replaced largely by youngish English dons. Here was Ian Watt's celebrated essay on *Robinson Crusoe* and a piece, hardly less durable, by J. W. Saunders on 'The Stigma of Print', concerning the constraints on publication experienced by courtly authors in the Elizabethan period. The journal wasn't all that parochial, and there were essays by some eminent foreign practitioners: Ernst Curtius, Kenneth Burke, Marshall McLuhan, Hugh Kenner, Harry Levin, R. B. Heilman. But on the whole the contributors were keen young British academics.

Altogether it was an achievement that called for editorial flair and determination. 1951 was not a good time to start such a journal; paper was short and so was cash. It remained so; as late as the sixth volume we find Bateson complaining that he had to pay Robert Graves's agent twenty guineas for one of the lectures Graves delivered as Professor of Poetry – an outlandishly large sum, especially as Bateson was not accustomed to paying his contributors, who were quite eager to work for nothing. The eclectic character of his editing, mixing known and unknown authors, never allowing the journal to become cliquish, didn't suit everybody, nor did his conviction that criticism should be backed by scholarship, that is, scholarship short of pedantry. But many waited with unusual impatience for the next quarterly number.

Still, as one reads on, even though with a pleasure probably less easily available to more youthful readers, it's impossible not to feel that the whole effort looks dated: not dead, but dated. Certainly there was life in it, sometimes bad-tempered life, but then critical vitality has often been bad-tempered and sometimes unreasonable. Leavis was scathing. William Empson, newly returned from China, took a surly interest. His presence was important, but he came down heavily and sometimes too rudely on what he called the 'quaint rigour of the modern young', meaning their tendency to take moral positions of which he could not approve. No longer the prodigy he had been, yet still only in his forties, Empson sensed a wide generation gap and clearly thought it indicated a sad decline. In 1956, when he used the phrase I've quoted, *Seven Types of Ambiguity* was already a quarter of a century old, and had virtually no discernible successors apart from Empson's own books. An obvious explanation of this lack might be that nobody else was clever enough, but he preferred to attribute the decline of criticism to the growth of a malign neo-Christianity, occasionally and deplorably evident in *Essays in Criticism*. For his part Leavis deprecated the air of optimism that attended the arrival of the new periodical, expressing amazement that some people were prepared to believe the literary culture was in better shape than it had been twenty years before.

Still, I think we can say that despite the carping and the quarrels, despite the great variety of critical approaches that were becoming available – the American New Criticism, the Chicago Critics, the maverick Winters and the maverick Burke and the maverick Frye – there was still a fundamental consensus: literary criticism was extremely important; it could be taught; it was an influence for civilization and even for personal amendment. The claim to an Arnoldian inheritance was justified. Less explicitly, the meliorist impulse of the early I. A. Richards was still present. And in very diverse ways the cultural and educational claims for literary criticism, fostered by these critics, were upheld by such dedicated teachers and editors as Leavis and Bateson.

The way things have changed since then is in large part my subject, but I begin, for reasons that will, I hope, emerge, at a distance from it, with an anecdote about a twentieth-century composer. Richard Strauss, president of the Reichsmusikkammer, had a Jewish daughter-in-law, Alice, whose grandmother lived in Prague. Despite his many

Jewish connections, Strauss was by no means exempt from the charge of anti-Semitism, but he was also a man who loved and protected his family, demanding that all its members should be treated with the same consideration as he himself had a right to expect. He did enjoy many privileges, was on good terms with Goebbels and Goering, and even had access to Hitler; for the top Nazis were involved in musical politics to an extent inconceivable in a British government, taking sides in controversies about atonality and the programmes and plans of the nation's opera houses.

Strauss pulled various strings to get the grandmother away from Prague to Vienna, where, he believed, she would be safer. When he failed the old lady was sent to the concentration camp of Theresienstadt. Assuming that his fame, his position in German society and his personal appearance would be enough to ensure her release, Strauss had himself driven in a large car to the camp gates, where he announced to the SS guards 'I am the composer Richard Strauss.' What the guards said is not exactly known – presumably it was the equivalent of 'Is that so?' – and he was sent packing. His name, in this context, lacked power.[1]

This rebuff must have been a shock to a man commonly regarded as among the most celebrated of all living musicians. He seems to have had a quasi-magical confidence that when his name was uttered the gates of the camp would open. They did not open, and he was, in both senses, driven away. Curiously enough, when, years later, the victorious Americans arrived at his villa in Garmisch and gave him and his family twenty minutes to leave, he told them he was Richard Strauss, and they at once departed and left him in peace.

Names can have power, but not always. 'What cares these roarers for the name of king?' cries the Bosun in the opening scene of *The Tempest*. 'Heaven in my mouth / As if I did but only chew his name' says Angelo in *Measure for Measure* (ii.4.4–5), the original form of this statement having almost certainly been 'God in my mouth', before the law of 1606 forbade such language. The name of God connotes the power of God conveyed in the Eucharist, but Angelo, full of guilty desire, devalues or desecrates it, sacrilegiously reducing it to a useless piece of bread. When Richard II speaks of 'aged Gaunt' the old man indignantly accepts that as his proper name: he is named Gaunt and he *is* gaunt; Richard sneers at him as a sick man playing with his name, and Gaunt replies that the king seeks 'to kill my name in me' (ii. 1. 86) which is usually taken to mean that he has extinguished the Gaunt line by exiling Bolingbroke; but he also means that his own authority has departed – as Richard confirms when he gets angry and points out that it is he who has the power, including the power to behead the old man; and the power is related to his name:

> I had forgot myself, am I not king?
> Awake, thou coward majesty! thou sleepest.
> Is not the king's name twenty thousand names?
> Arm, arm, my name!   (iii.2.83–6)

Indeed Shakespeare more than once insists that the audience give some thought to the power of names. They have an obvious importance in recognition scenes, for example in the climactic, protracted interview between Marina and her father in *Pericles* v.1. He enquires insistently about her parentage and her kinsfolk. Then he asks for and obtains her name, which, she says, 'was given me by one that had some power / My father, and a king', the suggestion being that her name reflects his power. 'How, a king's daughter? / And call'd Marina?' Pericles now surely has evidence enough; if he accepted what Marina has said so far the business of recognition would already be at an end. But he goes on in a dazed way, asking why she is called Marina, wanting to know who was her mother. She replies by naming her nurse. Still incredulous, he asks where she was 'bred', and is circumstantially answered; finally she names her father as Pericles. She asks Pericles his name ('title') and he gives it; but it is only when she does name her mother correctly that he is ready to say he is convinced. In the related texts, Laurence Twine's *The Pattern of Painful Adventures* and George Wilkins's novel *The Painful Adventures*, names are also exchanged, as could hardly be avoided – they are as necessary in these circumstances as birthmarks – but that is all; there is no more fuss, no more redundant demands for proof. It is Shakespeare who draws the matter out and makes names agents of power and revelation.

When Coriolanus confronts Aufidius in his house, Plutarch has him say that at this stage he has nothing left but the name Coriolanus, won in battle from the people he now seeks as allies; but Plutarch says no more on that score, just giving Coriolanus a longish speech explaining that he understands he might not be welcome. But Shakespeare (*Coriolanus* v. 5) deals with the matter as if it were a long-drawn-out recognition scene. Aufidius demands the Roman's name; Coriolanus says Aufidius must name himself; Aufidius repeats his demand, 'What is thy name?', four times before Coriolanus offers, not his birth name but his 'surname' or *cognomen*, Coriolanus. 'Only that name remains'. At the end of the play Aufidius denies him even that stolen surname, calling him only 'Martius'; and that name is disallowed because of its relation to 'Mars': 'Name not the god, thou boy of tears!' (v.6.100). His *cognomen* was peculiar to him and it is lost; now even 'Martius' is rejected. He has lost both his significant names and is now insultingly called just 'boy'. He repeats the insult with furious dismay. The word 'name' echoes through this play, and I don't think we can avoid the conclusion that Shakespeare is playing a game, no doubt a serious game, about names and naming.[2] He has touched on it quite seriously before:

> what should be in that 'Caesar'?
> Why should that name be sounded more than yours?
> Write them together, yours is as fair a name;
> Sound them, it doth become the mouth as well;
> Weigh them, it is as heavy; conjure with 'em,
> 'Brutus' will start a spirit as soon as 'Caesar'.
>
> (i.2.142–7)

But it won't; Caesar proves to be the magically effective name. What Cassius is doing is raising a large issue (the belief that demons inhabit a world where names are important, are indeed inherent in the demon or spirit itself) and doing it in a sceptical manner that suits his suasive intentions. Indeed it seems that Shakespeare's interest in the story of Caesar arose partly from the fact that he took names seriously, or at least took seriously the thought that names could be serious matters; or was just interested in the idea. (The name 'Cinna' is a name of ill omen; it gets a poet treated as a politician, part of the joke being that in this play the poet is a feeble and ridiculous figure.) The fear that

Caesar might be named king and thereafter enjoy a limitless increase of power is one of Brutus's worries: 'He would be crown'd: / How that would change his nature, there's the question' (ii.1.12–13). And this is only an extension of more general interest in names: in *Two Gentlemen of Verona* a name is written down and torn up, wounded as if it were a person ('I throw thy name against the bruising stone's', (ii.2.108). Iago informs Othello that 'good name in man and woman ... Is the immediate jewel of their souls' (iii.3.155–6). This contradicts what he has recently been saying to Roderigo about reputation (ii.3.262–70), but here he is sanctimoniously proposing the conventional view.

One moment in *Coriolanus* (v.2) provides an oddly comic sidelight on the play's fascination with names. Menenius visits the Volscian camp outside Rome in order to persuade Coriolanus to abandon the siege and save Rome. He is stopped by sentries, and tells them his name. They reply that 'the virtue of your name / Is not here passable'. He insists, unable to believe his name will not prevail. Coriolanus himself then appears, but rejects his friend. The sentries tease Menenius as he departs: 'Now, sir, is your name Menenius? 'Tis a spell, you see, of much power'. Menenius has an impotent name, for the source of its power was not in the name itself but in the word of Coriolanus. No such embassy is mentioned by Plutarch. It is part of Shakespeare's game.

Can one find ways of making critical capital out of the juxtaposition, after a brief journey through the records, of Strauss at Theresienstadt and Menenius at the camp of the Volscians outside Rome? Typically, one would give the Strauss anecdote the position of privilege assigned to such anecdotes in the practice of the new historicists. For example: in 1831 the *American Baptist* magazine published an essay by a distinguished clergyman, the Reverend Francis Wayland, later president of Brown University. Discovering that his fifteen-month-old son was very self-willed, he set about to 'subdue' the child, withholding food and then offering it as a bribe for submission. With great difficulty he achieved his end; the child's disposition became 'mild and obedient', his will was broken – an effect the father hoped would persist through life. He would now kiss the father he had long shunned, indeed kiss anybody his father told him to.

Stephen Greenblatt uses this narrative as a way into *King Lear*.

The minister has used the same sort of love-test as Lear. Cordelia, withholding love, is deprived not of food but of her inheritance. Students of Elizabethan and Jacobean drama agree with such historians as Keith Thomas and Lawrence Stone in seeing Shakespeare's age as one which believed in the need for severe restraint on adolescence and early adulthood. The will must be curbed. The difference between the two cases turns on the age at which it was thought a suitable exercise of *patria potestas* to force the child into submission. What interests this new historian is the similarity between the cases, and their historical connection. Paternal power in the later case has been devolved from the state, domesticated; in the earlier it has evident political and public authority, but the situations are essentially similar. Greenblatt's argument allows for the cultural changes of 200 years, notably the triumph of Protestantism; but in a slightly modified form the love-test survives these changes. He ends his study with some poignancy, revealing that Wayland's tormented child was later to write a two-volume biography of his anxious father, whereas Lear 'dies looking on his daughter's lips for the words she never speaks'.[3]

This accomplished performance (here imitated by me) involves the use of anecdote, apparently come upon at random, in a fashion that is a mark of new historical writing. The initial incident recounted (for instance, the story of Wayland's successful manoeuvre) need not belong to the same period as the target work, if we can call it that – in this case *King Lear*. There can be a 200-year gap between instances which can't conceivably have been brought together before. In my example the gap between Strauss and Menenius is more than 300 years. All we have to do is fill it, for otherwise the preliminary anecdote will have no purpose. Some ingenuity is called for, and there is some explaining to do.

In defence of the method, it can be argued that the *petit récit*, the anecdote that apparently lies to the side of the main current of narrative history, can upset the conventional *grand récit* – in Greenblatt's words, 'puncture the historical *grand récit* into which it [is] inserted'. One can, as it were, roam backwards through history, always looking for counter-history, for what looks, to the conventional historian, either trivial or without relevance. In this way one may come upon connections not previously suspected.

The virtues of this procedure are celebrated in an essay to be found in a collaborative work of Greenblatt and Catherine Gallagher entitled *Practicing New Historicism* (2000). These authors argue that anecdotes which serve their purpose must be 'outlandish and irregular' if they are 'to preserve the radical strangeness of the past'. By the application of such unconsidered bits of archival information literary texts can be 'rubbed against the grain of received notions about their determinants'. And these counter-histories 'would be all the more exhilarating to launch if their destinations were as yet undetermined and their trajectories lay athwart the best traveled routes'. When you arrive you find that the anecdote may have bound 'history and counter-history, into a knot of conflicted interdependence' (p. 68). And thus 'literature's own dormant counter-historical life might be reanimated: possibilities cut short, imaginings left unrealized, projects half formulated, ambitions squelched, doubts, dissatisfactions, and longings half felt, might all be detected there' (p. 74).

This cult of the anecdote is intended to introduce into the writing of literary history some of the advantages enjoyed by dissident historians, historians of the apparently marginal, such as those of the *Annales* school, and to exploit the discoveries of Foucault which question the validity of existing accounts of political and cultural orders. Lurking behind this approach, which is certainly exciting in some ways, is an assumption – partly it seems traceable back to Herder – that 'poetry . . . is not the path to a transhistorical truth, whether psychoanalytic or deconstructive or purely formal, but the key to particular historically embedded social and psychological formations' (p. 7). The new history will not, like the outmoded 'close readings', 'build toward an intensified sense of wondering admiration, linked to the celebration of genius', but rather it will be 'skeptical, wary, demystifying, critical, and even adversarial'. However, in spite of all this, 'major works of art remain centrally important', though 'jostled now by an array of other texts and images' (p. 9).

I will return to the matter of 'the central importance' of works of art, merely mentioning that by no means all new-historical practitioners would accept it, and adding further that although we have to accept the word of these exceptionally able writers it is sometimes hard to see how they can hold that view against the weight of their theoretical position. Anecdotes, it seems, are best when wayward, when least obviously associated with the ordinary run of historical narrative. The argument for anecdote has the authority of Foucault's remarks on the illumination provided by 'that which is thrown out of official history, the "other" of power' (p. 70).

Joel Fineman, a critic who had close associations with the founders and sponsors of this 'intellectual posture', speaks of its 'characteristic air of reporting, haplessly, the discoveries it happened serendipitously to stumble upon in the course of undirected, idle rambles through the historical archives'.[4] Fineman provided a theory of the anecdote, and the hostility of his tone in this passage is only apparent, but it is worth quoting because it does indicate that the methodology can be as random as the anecdote it looks for. The plot of new historicism consists in establishing the substance of the anecdote as somehow, despite its apparent waywardness or seeming irrelevance, a source that illuminates or qualifies understanding of the complex culture of the time, especially as that has been described in their blinkered way by more conventional historians; and secondly, in finding a way of connecting the anecdote to some text of more central interest, whether that text is of the same period as the anecdote or not. Clearly the task is easier if anecdote and central text are roughly coeval, but more fun (and this, I repeat, *is* a kind of game) may be had if they are centuries apart.

Since I have been imitating or mimicking this 'intellectual posture', it may be thought right that I should provide some sort of historical thread connecting Strauss and Menenius. For instance, and here I borrow a point from Geoffrey Hartman, there is a distinction, formulated by Saussure, between ordinary nouns such as *table* and *chair* on the one hand, which point to a referent in the world of things, but rely on a *concept* of table and chair to signify; and on the other hand names, which are pure signifiers that have only a referent (the person indicated) and no concept or signified. The only kind of name that escapes pure signification is a nickname.[5] We may remember that in the dialogue between John of Gaunt and Richard II, which I mentioned earlier, the name of Gaunt is actually reduced to a nickname.

But this is a modern formulation and there is plenty of evidence that names were not usually thought of in this way, namely as pure signifiers. The *Cratylus* inaugurated the long debate about 'the correctness of names'; it is a matter some think can be determined by etymology, and Socrates does a lot of etymologizing himself, but doesn't accept the view of Cratylus that this is the right way to get at the natural meaning of names. However, he does not go on to assert that their meaning is merely conventional – that we willingly call somebody John or Peter without at all having to attribute to him some petrine or johannine essence. We are told that Cratylus finally refused to believe that anything stayed still long enough to be referred to, and, giving up words, confined himself to pointing. However, his earlier position, that names were of the nature of the named, was used by Christian cabbalists in support of their view that not only words but their letters could be put to magical use. Parallel Hebraic practices, equally extreme, are well known. Some words, replaced in writing by the Tetragrammaton, were so directly involved with the nature of their referent, in this case God, that they could not, without blasphemy, be spoken at all, and indeed the Tetragrammaton is specifically designed to be unspeakable.

The idea of *vis verborum* was strong among Platonists and related to magical efficacy, and so the orthodox felt a need to distinguish, in this matter of the power of words, between magic and religion. The power of the words spoken by the priest at the Eucharist (*hoc est corpus meum*) was not a magical power, though Thomas Aquinas held that transubstantiation could occur only if these words, along with *hic est calix sanguinis mei*, were spoken, with no others. Such a consecration is valid regardless of whether the priest is in mortal sin or a heretic, but it would be invalid if spoken in the vernacular. The reason why this was not magic was that God performs the validation, provides the power, as we might say. Magical spells, despite their resemblance to these sacred words, could not only be diabolic. A major difference, yet both sides depend on 'a theory of language according to which there is a real, not conventional, connection between words and what they connote'.[6] The matter was clearly of high importance at the time of the Reformation. The power of names was also detected in writings not in themselves magical or liturgical. The Bible offers a precedent: 'As his name is, so is he; Nabal is his name, his folly is to him' (1 Samuel 25: 25).

It is clear that the habit of seeking the nature of a name by etymology was commonplace from the Greeks to the Renaissance and much later. It could be ridiculed – *lucus a non lucendo* was originally a serious Stoic proposition; humanity had much corrupted the divine originals. Quintilian says *ludus* can mean 'school' because there is no playing there. The encyclopaedic and universally known Isidore of Seville was a notorious etymologizer. And, to abbreviate this excursus, one still hears people attempting to defend usage or explain sense by etymology.

All these instances call for a search for power within the word, and that search, taking different forms in different epochs, is an indication of a perpetual quest for such power. So we may say of names that when properly conferred and used they bestow power, as when Jacob was blessed and renamed Israel; and we note that Jacob's request that his opponent should give his name is refused. Names withheld may be powerful; names proclaimed may be powerful. They can be used as an exercise or demonstration of power or privilege, they can be wounded (as Hardy saw when he picked up Lucetta's 'poor wounded name' from *Two Gentlemen of Verona* for the title page of *Tess*). If they fail when used in an attempt to exercise power the consequence is ridicule and scorn.

The experience of Richard Strauss was the result of the same tradition that found out the emptiness of Menenius's claim, and both suffered political failures, presuming as they did on the delegated power of a great person or institution, Coriolanus or the Nazi party. Such power as the names possessed was easily nullified by the authority deputed to ignorant soldiers.

We have seen the quality of royalty drained away by a change of name. King Edward to Duke of Windsor is a change representing the disastrous loss of a power not inherent but conferred. A princess is painfully reduced when no longer a royal highness. New names, names of power, are continually created. We may say that there is much power in a name but that it is always, and always has been, an unstable commodity, its permanence at the mercy of the power that awarded it.

Offering an exercise in a modern critical mode, I have traced a connection between an anecdote, the story of Richard Strauss, and an apparently unrelated episode in a play of Shakespeare's. Such a procedure would have been inconceivable to the critics who wrote for

Bateson fifty years ago. Almost everything depends on the choice of the initial anecdote. The guards at Theresienstadt are not impressed by the name of Strauss. The Volscian sentries refuse to acknowledge the power of Menenius's name. The game consists in closing the gap between these moments, and the wider and less probable the gap the better the game.

I had another look at the early issues of *Essays in Criticism* to see if anybody had written about *Coriolanus*. Sure enough, there was in the fourth volume a piece by D. J. Enright called 'Coriolanus: Tragedy or Debate?'. Enright argued that although we hear a great deal of talk about Coriolanus we are not presented with 'a creature who is, at any remove, truly human and truly living'. The character of the hero remains 'shadowy'. Consequently the play suffers from 'low tension'. It has no 'tragic conflict' and 'evokes only intellectual curiosity'. Not only is it a 'success of an altogether lower order than *Macbeth*', it were best not to think of it as a tragedy at all, but as a debate. I. R. Browning, replying to Enright, emphasizes Shakespeare's alteration of Plutarch's Coriolanus, his substituting anger and hate for Plutarch's 'noble carelessness'; and he directs attention to the role of Volumnia, who 'made a man' of her son. Coriolanus performed his bloody deeds in order to be loved; like a child he seeks love and attention by making a nuisance of himself.

Professor Enright is a poet and critic who, in the following half-century, has put us all in his debt. The point of referring to this youthful essay is simply to show that it is a work of its moment, as it happens, by an admirer of Leavis. It does what Arnold said one should do, and puts one play in a lower rank than another, even denying it the honorific of tragedy. No young critic would write in this way nowadays. One might add a different point: that this critic was and is a poet of distinction and has little to say about the verse of *Coriolanus*, to which the expression 'low tension' has surely no relevance at all.

Browning, though his main interest is again in character, 'the truly human', etc., is perhaps more forward-looking; his emphasis on the hero's mother and the importance of anger is of interest to modern critics of a psychoanalytical bent. Volumnia is not a nourishing mother: 'Anger's my meat: I sup upon myself', she says (iv.2.50) and Coriolanus is a male version of her, committed to a 'phallic standing alone'. Blood is more beautiful than milk. And so on. I refer, inadequately, to a rather famous study by Janet Adelman,[7] a learned and ingenious feminist, who takes the argument about anger a good deal further than anybody, except perhaps Empson in his mood, would have ventured fifty years ago.

This is an image of what one might call the progress of criticism. Everybody knows that there has been a dash for interdisciplinarity – that literary criticism is now on terms of a sort with anthropology, linguistics, psychoanalysis, feminism, 'queer theory', certain varieties of philosophy – and the kinds of history, or counter-history, I have been talking about. This is a matter of fashion, partly, but it probably also represents a radical change. The remark of Matthew Arnold I quoted, at the outset, from Holloway's essay, implies a canon. The idea of canon is, in principle, abhorrent to the new criticism; though there may, in some important practitioners, be a vestigial respect for some great works of art, the general attitude appears to be, rather simply, that there are no criteria for such valuations, that they are merely an unreflective tribute to works we have been taught to admire.

However interesting we may find the best of modern criticism, it is certain that its achievements are won at a considerable cost. It has much broader interests than the criticism of fifty years ago, and the 'quaint rigour' of the young has taken a different and less pious form, but it has marked disadvantages: its principles actually prevent it from attending closely to the language of major works (in so far as that description is regarded as acceptable) – to the work itself, rather than to something more congenial, and to some more interesting, that can be put in its place. Nobody, I think, would want to go back; but it is reasonable to be apprehensive about the future, and the possibility that literature itself, let alone literary criticism, may not easily survive the onslaught of undisciplined interdisciplinarity. I don't think even Freddy Bateson could start a journal resembling *Essays in Criticism* today.

Perhaps I had better say, in conclusion, that the connection between Richard Strauss and Menenius seems to me to be quite illusory.

19

Shakespeare and Boito

This essay had its origin in my rather awed respect for Verdi's Otello, *which I first saw – repeatedly – at Covent Garden in the mid-Fifties, with Gré Brouwenstijn, Ramon Vinay and, not quite always, Tito Gobbi. Many years later I wrote programme notes for a new production at the Opera House, and was induced by Patrick Carnegy, then the dramaturge, to give a talk there about the relations between Shakespeare's play and the opera. However, the idea of saying something more coherent and original on the subject came up after a further lapse of time when Roger Parker, then the new professor of music at Cambridge, asked me to give a lecture on the subject. Professor Parker being a Verdi scholar of great distinction, I trembled and obeyed.*

I had of course long known and admired Joseph Kerman's famous essay in his Opera as Drama, *and I had read J. A. Hepokoski's short book on the opera, but there was more to be considered, and my brief would have been enormous if not artificially restricted. One consequence is that I say very little about* Falstaff, *though I don't doubt that detailed study of the libretto in relation to the play would continue to be rewarding. Another consequence is that I have more to say about Boito than Verdi. Finally it appeared that Boito, for all his great merits, had joined, whether voluntarily or not, the long line of persons who thought it necessary to tone down Shakespeare's play to protect the public. He was an intelligent censor, and could allow for the fact that Verdi could put the horror back, as he did in 'Era la notte' and elsewhere.*

The point of least resemblance between *Othello* and *Otello* comes at the very beginning of the story. Verdi's Otello enters grandly out of the storm, makes a terrific announcement generously sharing his victory with God, who arranged the storm. He is adored by everybody except Iago, who is sorry the general's ship didn't sink. Otello at once departs, and there follow general rejoicings and bonfires.

It took Boito and Verdi about five minutes to land Otello in Cyprus, whereas Shakespeare needed more like three-quarters of an hour. And he begins not with a storm and a triumph but in the gutter, in the dark, with obscenities instead of victory chants. Two soldiers, perhaps a bit drunk, certainly foul-mouthed, as soldiers may be at the end of the evening, are muttering together in a street in Venice. We don't know who they are but gather that one of them wants revenge on a superior officer who has passed him over for promotion, while the other wants the woman with whom that officer has apparently just eloped. The object of their dislike is a foreigner, a black man. The senior soldier is inciting the other to make a row outside the house of a senator, father of the absconded woman. They tell the old man, without euphemism, that his fair daughter has gone off with 'an extravagant and wheeling stranger', that she is at that moment making the beast with two backs, is being 'tupped' by 'an old black ram', or, alternatively, 'covered by a Barbary horse', along with other civilities of that sort. The old fellow, understandably shocked, bestirs himself and collects a gang of neighbours to disturb the couple on their first night together.

This interruption of the wedding night is a version of the charivari, the custom of making an angry row outside a bridal chamber with jeers and catcalls, banging of pots, dustbin lids and so on, to signify neighbourly disapproval of the marriage, as it might be because the woman's first husband is too recently dead, or because she is a known adulteress, or because there is an offensive disparity of age between the parties, or because the man is a stranger or of different race. This custom, ancient and at one time almost universal, is said to have died out in Europe only quite recently.

So the first we hear of the matter is this: the woman's father agrees with the soldiers that his daughter has secretly made a disgusting, impure marriage with a lascivious old black man. Remember that the audience knows nothing about Othello or Desdemona, who aren't historical figures like Antony and Cleopatra. Even their names are so far withheld. So we may be surprised to discover that the Moor, as he has been named by all – even by Desdemona – turns out to be a remarkably dignified general, confident, grandiloquent, and evidently honest, no longer a 'thicklips' on the make but an important servant of the state. He has even been on friendly terms with the senator whose daughter he has spirited away, so transgressing the social limits of that acquaintance: he could be accepted as a dinner-guest but certainly not as a son-in-law. But he successfully defends himself before the Senate and gets permission for his wife to go with him on his mission to Cyprus.

Not a word of this found a place in the opera, which omits Shakespeare's first act, save for the reminiscences in the love duet at the end of Verdi's. Boito, the librettist, said he regretted the cut, and one sees that it had to be done, but it was also costly. For a start, Desdemona's distressed father, the senator Brabantio, the elopement, the element of charivari, have all been lost. And the cuts involved some censorship, voluntary or not. I shall return to that subject.

The history of Shakespeare's play is in part the history of its censorship. It was written probably between 1602 and 1604, so we could now be celebrating its 400th anniversary, and it was published posthumously in two different versions. There are hundreds of variant readings; the later version has 160 lines not found in the earlier, and so on. Details of the relationship between the two texts is a perpetual editorial problem, though it now seems to be accepted that the second version may have been partly based on a revision by Shakespeare himself. In 1606 Parliament passed an Act to Restrain the Abuses of Players, the purpose of which was to curb profanity on the stage. It imposed a fine of £10, a considerable sum, for each offence. Thereafter there was no question of leaving in the text the fifty-two profanities that occur in the earlier version. A £520 fine would have been ruinous. It may well be that in returning to the text in order to eliminate the profanities, Shakespeare made other revisions, which would account for more of the discrepancies and additions, and also for a perceptible change of tone.

The interest of all this lies in the fact that the process of expurgating *Othello* began quite shortly after it was written, and I shall argue that it was still going on in Boito's version. The first word in the play is Roderigo's mild oath 'Tush', but Iago's first word, in line 4, is ''Sblood'. Although prudence required that it be cut, Roderigo's oath is just feeble, which suits him, but Iago's is technically blasphemous and clearly forbidden under the Act. Iago might be thought the character most prone to use this kind of language, but Othello himself several times says 'Zounds', which is just as bad as ''Sblood', and his profanity is duly and impartially purged. Since vulgar swearing represents a departure from Othello's usual lofty conversational style it serves to mark a loss of control, and I think the reviser, forced to cut the oath in iv.1.36 ('lie with her! 'Zounds, that's fulsome') felt the need to put something in its place, so he added some lines of distracted prose as the prelude to Othello's falling into a fit.

It must, however, be said that apart from banishing the plain profanities to satisfy the law, the later version showed little sign of squeamishness. It did nothing to diminish Iago's grossness and even added to what is already objectionable, for example Roderigo's description of Desdemona's elopement:

> Transported with no worse nor better guard
> But with a knave of common hire, a gondolier,
> To the gross clasps of a lascivious Moor . . .
> Tying her duty, beauty, wit and fortunes
> In an extravagant and wheeling stranger . . .   (i.1.124–36)

We shall have other examples of intrusions by the reviser that have an intensifying rather than an expurgatory function. But the real business of censoring *Othello* was not long delayed. As David Littlejohn remarks in an interesting essay on the point, '*Othello* is one of the most savagely and explicitly *sexual* good plays ever written',[1] and for that very reason it has a history of being disconcertingly difficult to handle. The acting companies of the post-Restoration period cut it heavily, though the introduction of female Desdemonas is said to have enhanced its erotic effect. The part of Othello needed attention from critics anxious about breaches of rhetorical decorum. 'Love and jealousy are no part of a soldier's character', says the critic Thomas Rymer, who thought the whole play ridiculous. Others tidied it up, giving corrective emphasis to Othello's soldierliness. He was not allowed to say, for instance, that housewives might make a skillet of his helm; that was indecorous (i.3.272).

Essentially, I think, they were all scared of the play and its unmistakably central topic, and I think they had a right to be. Later the decorum insisted upon was less of the rhetorical and more of the frankly moralistic variety. Dr Johnson was far from alone in finding in the language of the tragedy 'terms which a modern audience would not easily endure'. From early in the nineteenth century there were many editions expurgated for domestic use, yet there were still complaints about the 'palpable grossness and obscenity' of the play. *Othello*, it was said, 'is indeed a most replenished brothel of the vilest "goats and monkeys" of Shakespeare's brain' ... And, as the most celebrated of the expurgators, Thomas Bowdler, remarked, even if you eliminated all the indecent words there remained others which, though 'naturally innocent', acquired indecency by reason of context, so that, for example, the innocent word 'bolster' became 'grossly improper' in Iago's mouth: 'Damn them then, / If ever mortal eyes do see them bolster / More than their own' (iii.3.398–400). For 'tupped' or 'topped' there could obviously be no reprieve. Yet as the keen-eyed Bowdler recognized, if you were to cut on that scale, with 'bolster' having to go, along with such commonplace words as 'lie', the story could not be told at all.[2]

This difficulty is absolutely central to the reception of *Othello*. Of all the great tragedies it touches most intimately on a pathology into which most people – on the Freudian view, everybody – have some insight or experience, which is why Othello's masochistic and pornographic imaginings, so assiduously fostered by Iago, can seem at once so painful and so disgusting. Deprived of its sexual horror the play would be pointless, as Bowdler, who after all had a practised eye for obscenities, understood so well. There were plenty of sexually explicit plays – perverse, cruel, cynical – in the theatre of the early years of the seventeenth century, and they are still not forgotten – the works of Middleton, for instance, and Webster and Tourneur. But there is something about even the greatest and most deliberately shocking of them – say *The Changeling* or *The Revenger's Tragedy* or *The Duchess of Malfi* – that makes them seem always to refer, however thrillingly, to other people; *Othello* somehow has the air of being disturbingly about everybody.

Anybody wanting to see what a sexless *Othello* might look like should read Trollope's novel *He Knew He Was Right*. Written in 1869, it is roughly contemporary with *Don Carlos* and *Aida*. Trollope felt challenged by an article in some magazine that claimed a modern *Othello* was impossible, so he undertook to write one.[3] It is true that the moral collapse of his hero echoes that of Othello, but he was throughout under the crippling difficulty that the hero's wife, a well-born Victorian lady, could not conceivably have been accused of adultery; the cause of her husband's crazy conduct is an obviously innocent friendship. But his wife, as it happens named Emily, though beyond question faithful, was disobedient in obstinately maintaining a friendly relation with another man – incidentally a much older and presumably safer man, twice Cassio's age.

Only the private detective hired by the husband could even think adultery was in question, and he is an Iago whose everyday business is to suspect or assume sexual misconduct. The husband rightly suspects nothing of the kind. So here was a sexless *Othello*; no tupping, no nakedness in bed an hour together, whether or no meaning harm. The man collapses into melancholia because his wife will not give up an old friend.

Nevertheless the ground bass of the book, however faintly stated, is still pathological jealousy. Operating under impossible constraints, Trollope offers a Victorian *Othello*, virtually without sexual content; its absence is almost as conspicuous as its presence would have been. Perhaps only with the arrival of Salvini, whose Othello (in Italian) had a great success in London, did anything like the full eroticism of the play return; and it can't be insignificant that this revolutionary Othello was a celebrated warm-blooded Italian, an extravagant and wheeling stranger; it seems he actually went so far as to strike Desdemona when the text indicated that he should. Even so, it seems he had to cool it down a bit.[4]

Now, as I have already remarked, Boito has nothing about the elopement, no charivari, no extravagant and wheeling stranger, nothing about the Othello we heard about at the outset, with his stereotyped lechery, his sooty bosom, his reputation for sorcery; even his over-developed consciousness of his own worth, a subject on which his discourse impressed the Doge though not Brabantio. Iago's lost comment on his general's conceit of himself was not wholly off the point. And Othello's modesty had to be enacted, as he himself knew, and, as he says, he knows his cue without a prompter (i.2.83–4). But Boito didn't allow even a hint of bragging. So: a lot of leaving out had to be done, some choices had to be made.

Inevitably there are many things that may look dispensable to the eye of the abbreviator, yet add depth to the play. For example, the scene in the Senate, a shade improbable but full of bustle and movement concerning urgent affairs of state, preparations for war with the Turks, the arrival of rapidly changing intelligence reports: all that is important to the play, and so is the ending, which features not a kiss but more emergency arrangements, the disposal of Othello's property, a dispatch to the state, the torture of Iago. As elsewhere in Shakespeare, domestic tragedy may take place in a context of high politics. Othello is dead but the world carries on. Joseph Kerman remarks, oddly echoing Rymer, that Boito's Otello, despite some spectacular military gestures, is in the course of the opera cut down to a mere lover.[5] And in that missing Senate scene we also hear a motive that is as important to Shakespeare as the kiss is to Verdi: it is Brabantio's warning, 'Look to her, Moor, if thou hast eyes to see, / She has deceived her father, and may thee' (i.3.292–3). She has committed 'treason of the blood' (i.1.169) – and these are lines we should bring to mind when Iago reminds Othello of them (iii.3.206) and when Othello, suspecting that his wife is deceiving him, raves about his need to *see* his wife's adultery, to have 'ocular proof' (iii.3.360). Nothing in the opera could remind us of Brabantio's sullen remark, just as it has nothing that could give the faintest plausibility to Iago's contention that this marriage was 'betwixt an erring barbarian and a supersubtle Venetian' (i.3.355–6). Boito had no need of that idea.

So his choices are always reasonable, but almost always involve loss. What best served for opera he quickly included. Thus he chose to include the Willow Song (missing from the earlier version of the play) but chose not to include the remarkable speech in iv.3 added, in 1623, to Emilia's part and arguing for the sexual liberty of women:

> . . . I do think it is their husband's faults
> If wives do fall . . .
>   Let husbands know
> Their wives have sense like them; they see and smell,
> And have their palates both for sweet and sour
> As husbands have . . .
>   And have not we affections?[6]
> Desires for sport? And frailty, as men have?   (iv.3.86–101)

This proto-feminist meditation, either added to the second version or cut from the first, goes on for eighteen lines. It follows a rather chatty discussion between Emilia and Desdemona about the limits of female fidelity, and seriously reinforces it. Perhaps it was included to point up a contrast between the impeccably pure Desdemona and a woman of less rigid morality, of whom, as Iago her husband claims, there were many in Venice, where ladies 'let God see the pranks / They dare not show their husbands' (iii.3.302). Boito wasn't interested, and such a lack of interest may constitute a sort of unconscious or conscious censorship. Iago's contention that Emilia has cuckolded him with Othello might be thought by some to find support in these dialogues; but Boito had no time for that suspicion, either. As for Emilia, he rather diminishes her – she is reduced to a confidante, helps the plot along by surrendering a handkerchief, and receives an incomparably beautiful farewell. The play has a devastating moment when, after the murder, Emilia screams at Othello, calling him 'gull' and 'dolt', 'as ignorant as dirt' (v.2.163–4), but in the libretto, accurately but with more moderation, she merely calls him 'assassin'. Only a faint trace of her feminism remains, when she tells Iago she is his wife, not his slave. The absence of Bianca from the cast of the opera is another palpable loss; in the play she serves to qualify our respect for Cassio, whose habitual lyric enthusiasm for Desdemona is, in view of his attitude to Bianca, to be seen as qualified by a certain contemptuous libertinism. Finally, Boito, perhaps inevitably, ignores most of the terrible poetic games Shakespeare plays with the words 'honest', 'see' and 'think'.

So Boito, perhaps unavoidably, joined in the more or less universal business of censoring the play. Considered as literature, his libretto is, in a way, a doctored Victorian *Othello*, though he was far from being as

reticent or as timid as Trollope. However – and this is centrally important – he could depend on the power of the composer to supply effects
impossible to the librettist, and that is a matter I must shortly turn to.

Before I do I'd like to make a brief excursion about another force
that drives the play and the opera apart – the intractable, barely soluble,
demand of operatic translation. Here is an innocently exemplary tale.

Boito, when working on the libretto of *Falstaff*, came to the part of
The Merry Wives of Windsor where Mistress Quickly informs Falstaff
of Alice Ford's invitation to join her during her husband's absence
'between ten and eleven'. This time didn't suit Boito – probably not
because he thought it an unsuitable moment for a Windsor wife to be
merry, but because the expression translated awkwardly into Italian.
dalle dieci alle undici. So he altered the time of the assignation and
wrote *dalle due alle tre*, from two to three, a neat, cheeky phrase that
Verdi would use to excellent comic effect. Now suppose this phrase
has to be translated back into English, the language of the original, for
use in the opera. Shakespeare's 'between ten and eleven' still wouldn't
do. Nor would 'from two to three', for neither version fits Verdi's little
six-note phrase, very much part of the fabric of the opera. The English
National Opera's translator, Amanda Holden, rather brilliantly came
up with 'from eleven to twelve', which fits the music exactly, though
once more changing the time of the assignation, now, as originally,
before lunch. One wonders how translators into other languages have
solved this problem. It would be tempting to the modern French
translator to say 'de cinq à sept', but that doesn't fit, either.

That is a trivial example of the way translation can insist on a change
in the plot. In *Falstaff* it doesn't matter, for nobody's virtue is in danger
– the whole thing is a joke, as the final fugue insists. The story is a
variation on an old fabliau-type theme evidently as dear to Verdi and
Boito as to the English, who still love the baiting of Billy Bunter by his
classmates; he is greedy and a cheat, but his basic fault is his fatness.
So with Verdi, who refers to Falstaff in his letters as 'Big Belly' and
says he would like to see him 'soundly thrashed' (6 July 1889). His
punishment, ostensibly for lechery, is really for being fat, an abnormality that makes him ridiculous, not least because he makes improbable
claims concerning his sexual powers and comments along with everybody else on his paunch.

With *Othello* the case was different, the original being so grand and fearsome, certainly no joke. In terms of structure Boito, as all commentators agree, was deft as well as ambitious, for instance in changing the time of Desdemona's first appeal for Cassio so that she makes it when Otello is already suspicious, as well as in accepting such gifts as the drinking song for his *brindisi* and seizing on the material for all four splendid act endings – the opera is beautifully built, founded on much thought and research, and deeply respectful of its original. Both Boito and Verdi revered Shakespeare. I find impressive the way odd lines of *Othello* caught Boito's fancy and tempted him to use them even if he had to do so out of their original sense and context. Othello greets his wife in Cyprus with the splendidly conceited compliment 'O my fair warrior' (ii.1.180) but Boito writes *Mio superbo guerrier*, changing 'fair' to *superbo*, giving the words to Desdemona and paying the compliment to Othello. Boito wanted to keep the phrase but not the affectionate English joke; yet a trace of Shakespeare remained in his head and got into his book. Having the artist's natural distaste for critics, he picked up Iago's sardonic remark to Desdemona – 'I am nothing if not critical' (ii.1.119) – which occurs in a rather dull passage of badinage that he cut, and found a better place for it, when the tipsy Cassio urges Iago to join in the praise of Desdemona: *io non sono che un critico* – I'm nothing but a critic – not for him Cassio's poetic extravagances. This was amusing but also well judged, for in its new position the remark emphasizes the contrast between Iago's pretence of sardonic judiciousness and the excesses of the man he wants to establish in the role of Desdemona's lover.

The question may now arise, how direct was his knowledge of the tragedy? The singer Blanche Roosevelt, who knew Boito, said 'he reads Shakespeare very well in English'. Julian Budden said he had a 'smattering', William Weaver that his command was 'shaky'. James A. Hepokoski says in his book on the opera that Boito could 'struggle through English', and in his article on the genesis of the libretto that he could 'struggle through the original' – a far stronger claim, for the language of the play is not simple, even for native speakers.[7] Indeed it is agreed, and Hepokoski has liberally documented the point, that Boito's principal source was the French translation by François Victor

Hugo. The English editions owned by Boito were a flawed version by the German Shakespearian Delius, along with something called the Handy-Volume Shakespeare, apparently a popular series in the second half of the century, almost certainly bowdlerized, and a single-volume Chandos Classic edition dated 1883. It has been remarked that no two editions of this play are exactly alike, but certainly nobody who had to choose would choose any of these.[8] Apart from a few marginal corrections in the Delius, which Hepokoski declares to be merely philological, with no bearing on the libretto, there is not much sign of intimate contact with the English original.* Yet despite this dependence on the French translation, and despite the loss of so much material that seems central to the theme, I believe the opera to be almost as potent a pathological study as the play, and the question must be asked how this was achieved when so much of the play wasn't directly available. I have mentioned the lost obscenities of the opening scene. Another example, which I touched on earlier, would be the way the opera treats Othello's demand for ocular proof, and Iago's comment:

> Would you, the supervisor, grossly gape on,
> Behold her topp'd?
> It were a tedious difficulty, I think,
> To bring them to that prospect. Damn them then
> If ever mortal eyes do see them bolster
> More than their own . . .
> It is impossible you should see this
> Were they as prime as goats, as hot as monkeys,
> As salt as wolves in pride, and fools as gross
> As ignorance made drunk.   (iii.3.398–408)

The nearest Boito will approach to this is to have Iago ask Otello if he would like to see the lovers embracing (*Avvinti / Vederli forse?*)

---

* A small point: the operatic pronunciation of the heroine's name (Desdémona) presumably derives from Hugo, though there is a possibility that Boito was influenced by the 'Disdemona' of Giraldi Cinthio. Despite his enthusiasm for Shakespeare, Verdi presumably had no opinion on this matter. Later he had to ask Boito where the stress fell on the name 'Falstaff'.

which almost entirely forfeits Shakespeare's point. In Shakespeare's play Iago makes his disgusting observation three times over, as if to see how far he could go, to decide how deeply Othello was mired in his pornographic jealousy. Later we learn how deeply, when at a moment of deep distress, and in the presence of the embassy from Venice, he involuntarily cries out 'Goats and monkeys!' (iv.1.263).

Boito avoids all this, perhaps thinking it all a bit too much for a contemporary audience, perhaps uncertain of its demands on the composer. But when Iago goes on to tell the tale of his night in bed with Cassio it must have seemed the issue could not be evaded for ever; Boito included it and it fell to Verdi to provide the equivalent music. He succeeded:

> There are a kind of men
> So loose of soul that in their sleeps will mutter
> Their affairs – one of this kind is Cassio.
> In sleep I heard him say, 'Sweet Desdemona,
> Let us be wary, let us hide our loves.'
> And then, sir, he would grip and wring my hand,
> Cry 'O sweet creature!' and then kiss me hard
> As if he plucked up kisses by the roots
> That grew upon my lips, lay his leg o'er my thigh,
> And sigh, and kiss, and then cry 'Cursed fate
> That gave thee to the Moor!'   (iii.3.428–38)

In Boito's rendering of this we find the dream and the caution (*cauti vegliamo*) and the cursing of fate; but now the recipient of Cassio's kiss is specified as the image of Desdemona (*l'interno imago quasi baciando*) and there is no laying of leg on thigh. Boito was of course aware of these physical demonstrations, if only from Hugo; but he censored them as surely as an English editor. Yet they were important in that they gave Iago's blatant sexual temptations a new quality of perversity, and also in that they emphasized Othello's credulity. To leave all this out would be enfeebling, so it had to be included; the work must be done by music, and so the task fell to Verdi in *Era la notte*. That is music which leaves very little to be said about the evil of Iago, or the skill with which he goes to work in the dark, in the sewers, as it were, of jealousy. It's worth remarking that even in *Falstaff*, where cuckoldry is a joke, the point being its extreme improbability, Boito and Verdi provided an impassioned, uncomic, aria for the suspicious Ford (*E' sogno? O realtà?*). If they could not use all of Shakespeare's language in this scene they could count on supplying musically something of what had to be lost to the demands of decorum. Here the censorship is eerily, even beautifully, evaded.

One notices in particular the line *l'estasi del ciel m'innonda*, 'Heavenly ecstasy engulfs me', which Iago attributes to Cassio. It has no equivalent in the Shakespearian source passage, but I think we can say where it comes from. Reunited with Desdemona, Othello says in Shakespeare's ii.2: 'I cannot speak enough of this content; / It stops me here, it is too much of joy', which Hugo translated thus: *Je ne peux pas expliquer ce ravissement / Il m'étouffe, c'est trop de joie.* As Hepokoski notes, Boito underlined these words in his copy of Hugo. The rendering of 'content' by *ravissement* must surely be thought a mistranslation, partly justifying Otello's *la gioia m'innonda*, 'joy overwhelms me'. And this use of *estasi* makes the words more applicable to Cassio's supposed dream ecstasy than to the mood of Othello at that point – he is 'content', enormously pleased, but not about to have an orgasm. Content is not *ravissement* or ecstasy. So in using the word in a more suitably amorous situation Boito is remembering Hugo. And then, in *Era la notte*, he remembered Otello remembering Hugo, and wrote *l'estasi del ciel m'innonda*, 'heavenly ecstasy overwhelms me', in his fictitious account of Cassio's amorous fantasy. The echo, whether intended or not, creates a wicked irony – Otello's lawful pleasure corrupted by Iago and attributed to Cassio as Desdemona's lover, the language of his happiness conferred on its supposed destroyer. No wonder Verdi mistrusted French translators and spoke of the 'penal servitude of translating an opera from Italian into French, an even more arduous job than from French into Italian'.[9] Here, however, the interposition of Hugo's French, together with Boito's readiness to steal from one part of the play for the benefit of another, helped to make possible *Era la notte*.

That eerie music illustrates Verdi doing his job. If you'd said that the effect was Shakespearian he would have valued the compliment. However, the passage in the libretto he actually did call 'Shakespearian' was not this one but Iago's *Credo* near the beginning of Act 2.[10] Opinion is divided about this extraordinary piece. This Iago, who proclaims that his own wickedness is not unique but common to all men (*son scellerato perché son uomo*) seems to some very unlike Shakespeare's character, and he is also unlike the character as Verdi originally imagined it – nonchalant, gentlemanly, casual in manner – and this music is not what he had had in mind for Iago – nothing spectacular, mainly *parlando, mezza voce* 'apart from a few *éclats*' and a few necessarily (hypocritical) lyric moments.[11] And much of Iago's part fits this prescription, exceptions being the duet *Si pel ciel* that ends Act 2, where the reason is obvious, and the *Credo*.

Boito borrowed the ending of that declamation from a libretto he had intended for an opera by Ponchielli, so his representation of atheism and blasphemy was practised. The atheism is of a nineteenth-century type, unlike the Renaissance variety we associate with Marlowe, for instance, and altogether more solemn than Edmund's in *King Lear*, a part that had greatly interested Verdi. As I suggested, the aria is sometimes said to be a blot on the opera, though it has its defenders.[12] To me it seems that Verdi has here made Iago do all the things he had declared inapposite, for Iago proclaims at the top of his voice (no *mezza voce* here) his nihilistic belief in life as a godless progress from germ to worm, claiming to act from a set of well-established beliefs rather than from a disposition to vicious mischief. I suppose it could be said that there are in the midst of the rodomontade sinister little touches of gaiety, and there is a lyric spring in the voice, perhaps a gesture of satirical complicity, when Desdemona appears; she represents a world he has seen through, whose manners he can simulate, and which he hates as he hates himself.

Iago's need to be accepted for his own purposes by that world explains one of the mysteries, which is also one of the pleasures, of this opera – the lyric quality sometimes present in Iago's dealings with other characters. The need of music suitable for such interactions is something about which Boito and Verdi must have reached an understanding. They rejected the idea of Iago overhearing and commenting on the love duet in Act 1 – Satan observing the connubial happiness of Adam and Eve – one of those rather brilliant ideas that turn out to be no good; it would have altered the tone of the entire work. But they found other ways to merge Iago's voice with the mood and music of innocence.

Consider, for instance, an episode that comes after Iago has introduced the word and the idea of jealousy to Otello. He does so in a sinister arioso which, as Kerman points out, will provide the theme of the prelude to Act 3, so indicating in advance the subject of the conversation between Iago and Otello that follows.[13] Otello is already in torment when, offstage, the Cypriots start to sing the praises of Desdemona. Iago is already near the point of claiming he has evidence of Desdemona's guilt. He tells Otello to watch Desdemona carefully; and the Cypriots' music is punctuated by Iago's almost lyrical word of warning: *Vigilate*, be vigilant. It is sung almost sweetly as if in collusion with the peasant singers.

Their songs come to an end, and Otello has almost forgotten what Iago had been saying a few moments earlier: 'this song conquers me', he says, and repeats it: *Quel canto mi conquide*. Desdemona sings of joy, love and hope. Beauty and love in sweet harmony, comments Iago. And he remembers one of his lines in Shakespeare and promises to shatter that concord: 'O you are well tun'd now, but I'll set down / The pegs that make this music . . .' (ii.1.199–200). It is a music of which he himself has been, momentarily, and for his own purposes, a part. Then Desdemona starts to plead with Otello for Cassio's pardon; and the untuning begins.

The choral episode is sometimes dismissed as padding, but to me it seems well wrought. There is a continuum of pleasing music and Iago's commentary does not destroy the harmony but has its own place as a prelude to the discord that will follow the untuning of the strings. Iago understands the music perfectly; its pleasant harmony stands for what he thinks must be destroyed. And all this complies, in its own idiom, with the spirit of the original, just as the *brindisi* complies with its simpler source in the play.

So the processes of translation and re-imagining brought their own rewards; Shakespeare has nothing like these seminal, sinister lyric moments of Iago. But I may be better qualified to say what was lost than speculate on what was gained; so here, to end with, are two more instances of loss: first a patch of dialogue from Shakespeare's play, spoken by Iago and Cassio just before the drinking scene.

IAGO: Our general cast us thus early for the love of Desdemona – whom let us not therefore blame; he hath not yet made wanton the night with her, and she is sport for Jove.

CASSIO: She's a most exquisite lady.

IAGO: And I'll warrant her full of game.

CASSIO: Indeed she's a most fresh and delicate creature.

IAGO: What an eye she has! Methinks it sounds a parley to provocation.

CASSIO: An inviting eye, and yet methinks right modest.

IAGO: And when she speaks, is it not an alarum to love?

CASSIO: She is indeed perfection.

IAGO: Well, happiness to their sheets.   (ii.3.12–29)

This brilliant bit of writing Boito could not use. Cassio's civil rejection of Iago's cold bawdiness is lost. But Cassio, a little embarrassed and not in his usual mode of lyrical extravagance, which would here be inapposite, does rather well. As for Iago, this provocative coarseness is very much a part of his mental habit, on view once again when Othello arrives and asks about the disturbance. Iago answers with a gratuitously salacious simile: 'I do not know,' he says. Until the fighting started they had been 'friends all, but now, even now, / In quarter and in terms like bride and groom / Divesting them for bed' (ii.3.175–7). Boito won't have this: *Non so . . . qui tutti eran cortesi amici / Dinanzi, e giocondi* – 'here all were courteous friends before, and merry'. Another excellent piece of writing lost to the censor.

Despite the relative simplicity of its core narrative, *Othello* is a long play (second only to *Hamlet* in the canon) and of course it can afford divagations and digressions that would be out of place in opera, which cannot hope to convey every slightly ambiguous or contradictory verbal nuance. A striking instance in the play is the conversation between Desdemona and Emilia after Desdemona has been publicly shamed and struck. She is waiting in her bedroom for Othello, and is on the point of singing the Willow Song as Emilia helps her to undress:

EMILIA: Shall I go fetch your nightgown?

DESDEMONA: No, unpin me here.

This Ludovico is a proper man.

EMILIA: A very handsome man.

DESDEMONA: He speaks well.

EMILIA: I knew a lady in Venice would have walk'd barefoot to Palestine for a touch of his nether lip. (iv.3.32–9)

This was not Shakespeare doodling, but revising: there is nothing accidental about it; the passage was added in the second version.[14] That Desdemona should, at such a moment, speak admiringly, even if distractedly, of another man, has upset editors to this day, and some, including the most recent, transfer the line 'This Ludovico is a proper man' to Emilia; otherwise, they claim, it is 'out of character'.[15] Yet it is no stranger than Desdemona's reply when Emilia asks her how she is, after Othello has just humiliated her in the Brothel Scene: ' 'faith, half asleep' (iv.2.99). Boito and Verdi had no use for that, either. It's a loss; but in casting the accounts one must think also of the astonishing opening of the third act, so masterly, so far beyond the range of any merely spoken drama. It makes up for many lost ambiguities and obliquities.

Still, it is just such obliquities that give force to much of Shakespeare, and the instances I've quoted show him inserting just the kind of dialogue that confers ambiguity, and insists on complexity of response. Neither his education nor his trade would have equipped Boito to reproduce such bewilderments, and Verdi probably would not have wanted them, either, though he had grown, in his own way, splendidly complex. The wonder is that we have before us two works of genius on the same theme; that despite the obvious debt of the later to the earlier, and despite the intervention of a long tradition of censorship, they are generically so hugely different; and that they nevertheless have it in common that for all their mature skill and power, their very different kinds of beauty, they call, each in its own way, for our best, most educated efforts of understanding and yet touch, in the end, on the same reserves of primitive feeling.

373

SHORTER NOTICES

20

Raymond Carver

Raymond Carver was much taken with the idea that every writer creates a distinctive world: 'Every great or even very good writer makes the world over according to his own specifications . . . It is his world and no other.' The idea is hardly original but one sees why he liked it. Carver's world is something like a room in which the television is always on, unless you happen to be subjecting the neighbours to home movies. The ashtrays are overflowing. There may be an alcoholic, active or reformed, lying on the living-room sofa. Is he thinking about the pint of whiskey he has hidden under the cushions; or has he just got home from an exhausting AA meeting? He has a job he does not like and is not getting on too well with his wife, who may well be at work in a fast-food restaurant. If so he might just go along there and watch the male customers eyeing her shape. Living somewhere in the Pacific Northwest, he is probably thinking of moving house, perhaps just across the state line to Portland, a city often mentioned but never visited, or, more ambitiously and yet more hopelessly, to Alaska. However, he never does seem to move, and if he ever did find himself in Alaska he would still spend much time smoking on the sofa in front of the television. If he has children he cannot think them unmixed blessings. He knows he needs to love them but cannot bring himself to believe the pleasures of parenthood outweigh its pains.

He and his wife only rarely have neighbourly relations with other people; to be asked out to dinner is to face a small social crisis, in which all parties behave with a touchingly awkward, repetitive, unpractised courtesy. The kinds of thing they say on such occasions, as on all others, are recorded with bleak and dispassionate accuracy. Out in the inhospitable great world, not far away from the street where they live, are many pitilessly illuminated motels and gas stations, as aptly pictured on the jacket of this book, on which the photograph powerfully, inevitably, alludes to Edward Hopper. Whatever is going to happen around here is likely to be depressing – possibly just a marital argument, more seriously a fire in a neighbour's house, or the death of a child. Such happiness as can be expected must be looked for on fishing trips, and even fishing trips are likely to be ruined by the intrusion of a floating corpse. Yet some stories turn out to be funny in unexpected ways.

This latest Carver* is a miscellany containing five posthumously discovered stories, five early stories not previously collected, and some essays and reviews. Some of the essays are autobiographical. His father, also called Raymond, worked in sawmills, moved a lot, and drank a lot. Carver married young and also moved and drank a lot. He had an ambition to be a writer but his life was so disrupted by the need to make a little money and by the incessant demands of his children that he could never get far with a novel. He had to be content with short stories and poems, and in time came to prefer brevity. 'Get in, get out. Don't linger. Go on.' 'No tricks' is another piece of advice, picked up at a creative writing course, and studiously followed. The prohibition applies to terminal narrative twists, though sometimes he allows himself one, as in the story 'Vandals', in this last book. But it extends to more modern 'formal innovations' as well. They are not needed and they destroy the story's contact with the real: 'It's possible, in a poem or short story, to write about commonplace things and objects using commonplace but precise language, and to endow those things – a chair, a window curtain, a woman's earring – with immense, even startling power. It is possible to write a line of seemingly innocuous dialogue and have it send a chill along the reader's spine . . .'.

Carver came to be exceptionally good at short stories not only because he worked hard at them, but also because he listened to advice, especially from John Gardner but also, more remotely, from Hemingway, Chekhov and V. S. Pritchett. One of the things he learned was the need for arduous revision, draft after draft. Another lesson

---

* Raymond Carver, *Call Me If You Need Me: The Uncollected Fiction and Prose* (Harvill, 2000)

was that the writer needs to trust the tale. Lawrence notoriously advised the reader to do so, but the writer has to trust it because it will collaborate in the composition of the work if the work is any good. Carver is impressed by Flannery O'Connor's remark that she started work without knowing where the story was going; when she started 'Good Country People' she didn't 'know there was going to be a Ph.D. with a wooden leg in it'. Carver might have a single phrase in his head as a *donnée*: 'He was running the vacuum cleaner when the telephone rang'. Given time, more sentences attached themselves to this one and finally there is a story called 'Put Yourself in My Shoes', which turns out to be one of the funny ones, though a little sad also.

Here are some of Carver's openings:

I had a job and Patti didn't.
Earl Ober was between jobs as a salesman.
My marriage had just fallen apart. I couldn't find a job. I had another girl. But she wasn't in town.
I was out of work. But any day I expected to hear from up north. I lay on the sofa and listened to the rain.
It was the middle of August and Myers was between lives.

The last of these belongs to a story in the present collection, called 'Kindling'. Myers is a drunk, fresh from twenty-eight days in a drying-out facility, during which time his wife has run away with another drunk. He takes a room he has spotted in a small ad and finds himself shyly sharing a little house with a nervous, civil couple, poor but neither kind nor unkind, neither generous nor mean. Myers keeps himself to himself. When not working, the man of the house watches television, the wife wants to write, and tries to write about Myers. One day a load of wood is delivered. Chopping it up is a big job and the husband has no time to do it. Myers, without payment, without being asked, cuts the wood, though, as requested, he does nothing about the kindling. He finishes the job and writes some words about the experience in his notebook: 'I have sawdust in my shirtsleeves tonight. It's a sweet smell.' Then he ends his stay.

You are entitled to think the woodcutting did him good, even that he was about to start on a new life, but nothing is said directly about the therapeutic effects of hard labour, or of the causes of Myers' spontaneous generosity; these are precisely the sorts of thing Carver by his own hard labour learned not to say. One of his best stories is 'A Small, Good Thing', in the collection *Cathedral*. A woman orders a birthday cake at the local bakery, but her schoolboy son is knocked down by a car on his birthday and dies in hospital. The baker, wanting payment for the uncollected cake, nags her with phone calls. The woman and her husband confront the baker. There are insults, then a humane reconciliation, and they sit and eat some of the baker's richest bread. It would be useless to try in words other than the author's to give an idea of the depth and humanity of this story, a late one, done when Carver was allowing himself to write at greater length, as, in the later years, he decided he ought, citing as a model Chekhov's 'Ward 6'. The title story of the last volume, 'Cathedral', he regarded as a turning point in his career, but the career suddenly came to an end. Perhaps, had he lived, he would have moved on to the novella. One can feel sure that V. S. Pritchett would have admired both these stories, as Carver would have admired Pritchett's favourite among his own, 'When My Girl Comes Home'.

For various reasons the English short story is now a predominantly American form. There aren't many London outlets, while New York still has a few, which sometimes accept British stories, as with Sylvia Townsend Warner and also, of course, Pritchett. There are many annual prizes for stories. Moreover the form fits better than the novel into the pattern of the creative writing courses that are taught all over the country and often by good writers. Carver says it was a struggle to get his first collection, *Will You Please Be Quiet, Please?*, published in 1976. It took thirteen years to write ('the long delay was due in part to a young marriage, the exigencies of child rearing and blue-collar jobs, a little education on the fly') and the publisher took some persuading, but the prospects for American writers were even then better than for their British contemporaries. Later Carver could claim in an optimistic essay that there has never been a better time than the present for his aspiring compatriots and contemporaries; this is not to say it's easy, but it's far less difficult. 'Short stories are flourishing', he says, and the readership is increasing.

Naturally no writer on this side of the ocean sounds very like Carver, deep in what is now a naturalized tradition and in a world of his own. One of his stories reminded me faintly of an excellent one by William Trevor called 'Broken Homes' in which a group of adolescents, from broken homes, sent in as an experiment in 'community relations', cheerfully defile and desecrate the home of an eighty-seven-year-old woman. The story is the more horrible in that the teacher who sent these 'good kids' to the old woman's house is impervious to complaint; the old lady ends by blaming herself for her failure to communicate with the kids, who covered her kitchen and carpets with paint, released her budgerigars, and had sex in her bed. Carver has stories about cruelty and old age, but he is, perhaps curiously, less interested in emphasizing the lurid nastiness of the tormentors. Perhaps a sort of natural piety that shows through in his most serious pieces would have prevented him from imposing such garish humiliations.

Or they may be what his American studies in the craft have taught him to leave out. There seems to be a rule against seeming to be excited by a situation. A good instance is the story 'Vitamins' in *Cathedral*. The narrator has 'a nothing job' and his wife sells vitamins from door to door. He goes on a date with one of his wife's colleagues and takes her to a black bar, where they are menaced by a Vietnam veteran who carries an ear in a cigarette case: 'I took it off one of them gooks. He wouldn't hear nothing with it no more. I wanted me a keepsake.' The vet, drunk but cold, coarse and threatening, propositions the girl. The proprietor arrives to prevent bloodshed and they leave the bar, the little affair already over. The girl says she could have done with the money and resolves to go to Portland; the man goes home and disturbs his sleeping wife, noisily looking for aspirin. There is no actual violence in this desperate tale, though the language of the veteran suggests a whole continent of terror, as the conduct of the narrator and the girl sketches a society in despair.

Indeed there is not much violence in any of the stories, but instead Carver is very good on anomie and also on certain kinds of pain. 'Will You Please Be Quiet, Please?', the story that gave its title to the collection published in 1976, concerns a rather proper young schoolteacher's discovery that years before his wife had had a drunken one-night stand with a friend. This revelation, though the fact was long suspected, caused severe pain, carefully and reticently explored.

Such lesser discomforts as having to be on friendly terms with a wife's ex-lover are equally well managed. Commentators often find themselves talking about Carver's 'clarity' and that is fair enough, but there is always something the reader has to say, and will say confusedly, because of the indefinitely large context it is suggested he or she must supply.

Carver died of lung cancer at fifty. Much that happened in this rather short life was unfavourable to the business of writing. First, he needed to get an education, but making a living in nothing jobs hindered that. Then there were the children: 'They were born before I was twenty, and from beginning to end of our habitation under the same roof – some nineteen years in all – there wasn't any area of my life where their heavy and often baleful influence didn't reach.' In an autobiographical sketch he illustrates this misery by an anecdote. In the mid-1960s he is 'in a laundromat with five or six loads of washing, mostly kids'. He has to wait a long time for a free dryer, is anxious because he is late and has to pick up the kids. His misery is unforgettable; he is almost in tears at being in 'this position of unrelieved responsibility and permanent frustration'. He has a job at a service station, or as a janitor or a delivery man, with the prospect of many more years in this unwriterly posture, so unlike the situation of the well-known writers he admired. And after these destructive years of parenting there was an alcoholic hiatus, ten years of silence, before he joined his present editor, Tess Gallagher, and started writing again.

Carver was sure you could learn to write well, to find out by constant revision what the story you were working on really amounted to, and he more than once records his debts to John Gardner as a teacher, and to Gordon Lish as his editor. Partly by their efforts he became a very famous writer, at any rate in America.

When *Will You Please be Quiet, Please?* appeared in 1976 Gordon Lish sent me six copies, for he was sure I would want to spread the good news. I duly distributed them among my literary colleagues and waited for a response, but there was none. Carver's British reception has taken a little time. The Robert Altman movie *Short Cuts*, of 1993, based on nine stories and a poem of Carver's, helped to get him wider notice. Among the stories incorporated in the film were 'A Small, Good

Thing' – the one about the bereaved couple and the exigent baker – and 'So Much Water So Close to Home', about the girl's body discovered, but not reported, on a fishing trip. These are stories of high quality, as are many of the others. Now one can read almost everything in volumes published by the Harvill Press.

There is quite a lot of verse, most easily found in *Fires* (1984). Americans seem to assume more readily than we do a close affinity between poems and stories. The fact that I am not impressed by the poems may be related to that difference. A collection of prose pieces of varying weight, to be found mostly in *Fires* and in the present volume, are written with the usual care, though not all of them – brief reviews, prefaces to anthologies and the like – seem worth preserving for their own sakes. From this censure the autobiographical material must be exempted. As for the minor pieces, they have been collected as a sort of tribute to the great man, the kind of thing it is seemly to do on the understanding that it is not really these bits and pieces that matter in themselves; what matters is the fact that they were written by the hand that wrote the stories.

21

James Lees-Milne

Of the seven volumes of diaries published over the years by James Lees-Milne two have now been reissued as rather grand paperbacks, along with an eighth, a final hardback selection made by Michael Bloch.* They all have titles like *Ancestral Voices, Caves of Ice, Through Wood and Dale, Midway on the Waves* and *Prophesying Peace,* and it will not escape the notice of the literate public that all these are derived, one with a bit of a spin on it, from 'Kubla Khan'. This sturdy attachment to Coleridge's poem is not easy to explain, as Lees-Milne, for all his curious learning, does not pretend to go in for flashing eyes and floating hair, and the chosen titles seem quite irrelevant to the contents of the books. It is known, for Coleridge mentions it, that Byron admired 'Kubla Khan' and that Lees-Milne admired Byron, for he makes a point of saying so, but the connection still seems tenuous.

Myself a newcomer to the delights of these diaries, which are thought by some to be addictive, I found other obstacles to understanding. The author clearly has many rich and interesting friends, but often makes a point of not being very interesting himself. He is, he says, an opsimath. It takes one to know one, though I suspect he began to acquire his vast knowledge of grand people and grand houses in early youth. He says he is not 'a highbrow with intellectual leanings' but 'a simple, rather stupid man'. This may have been said only to outbid Elspeth Huxley in a modesty contest, but he could sometimes be genuinely over awed by the company. Arriving at a very grand luncheon party,

---

* *Deep Romantic Chasm: Diaries 1979–1981, A Mingled Measure: Diaries 1953–1972, Ancient as the Hills: Diaries 1973–4* (John Murray, 2000)

he saw 'ten sophisticated guests assembled' and would have bolted had his wife not been there to steady him. 'Agoraphobia seizes me on such occasions' (can he have meant quite that?).

A touch of the Prufrocks, perhaps, and a welcome sign of common humanity. Ordinary mortals may suppose that regular frequentation of the multitude of well-born characters mentioned in these books would have eliminated shyness for ever. Many of his women friends are named after counties or important metropolitan districts: Diana Westmoreland, Sally Westminster, Caroline Somerset, Deborah Devonshire. Numerous acquaintances identified in the text by their quite ordinary first names turn out, in the footnotes, to be dukes or earls. Some, by a process of dynastic agglutination, actually have as many as four surnames. One can of course manage with two, but might this not leave one less sure of one's status?

A principal interest, for me, then, was to achieve an understanding of the diarist's social position. A provincial journal (*Gloucester Life*) described him in 1979 as a 'Scholar and Gentleman', but 'these are two attributes I can make no claim to'. He is not an aristocrat ('I have noticed that aristocrats are either like Lord Salisbury, gentle, attentive to their inferiors, courteous, while aware of their superior social status in the world, or provocative and combative and rude like Randolph, Edward Stanley, Nigel Birch and others') and it seems he is unwilling even to be a gentleman. He notes that Somerset Maugham said that Kipling was 'not quite a gent'. When Kipling said of somebody 'He's a white man' Maugham thought, 'How I wish, in order to fulfil my preconceptions of him, he would say he was a pukka sahib. "He's a pukka sahib, all right," continued Kipling.' So that rules him out. But Willie's observations lose authority when one considers that at seventy-nine 'his face is like a nutcracker carelessly wrapped in parchment'. To be a truly admired gent it helps to be young and beautiful, a point made several times in these diaries. There are other ways of qualifying; on the authority of Sir Oswald Mosley Hitler is declared to be 'gentle and gentlemanly. He slipped shyly into a room'.

Still uncertain about rank, one may be helped a little by taking bearings on those who are not gentlemen because far above, or far below that station. Living in a house on the Badminton estate, the diarist could not wholly avoid contact with the Duke of Beaufort, not, of course, a gent but a terrific aristocrat, always known as the Master. When Lees-Milne let his dogs disturb some foxcubs on the Master's land he got a terrible wigging and resolved henceforth to snub the irascible landlord, or anyway to give him no more than a curt greeting, which surely indicates gentlemanliness. When Sally Westminster asked Sir Arnold Weinstock to luncheon to meet the Beauforts, the Master congratulated Sir Arnold on the 'nice coverts' he had in the place he'd just bought, but Sir Arnold said he hated the hunt and wouldn't let it near his land; whereupon the Master went scarlet in the face and said nothing more. This catastrophic exchange had the fortunate effect of expunging the memory of the peccadilloes of the Lees-Milne dogs but showed the Master to be a true aristocrat. Where it left Sir Arnold, socially speaking, one can guess with some certainty. He is described as 'a brash, quick-witted, well-informed, pushing little man, also very ugly' and 'the occasion was like Sir Leicester Deadlock meeting the manufacturer son of his housekeeper ... or the Duke of Omnium keeping his temper in the company of an insolent *arriviste* at Gatherum Castle'.

The Royals, though out of easy social reach, are bumped into from time to time, and are not immune to criticism. With the country suffering from a fuel crisis and endless impudent strikes, Princess Anne's grand wedding went ahead with plebeian approval: 'the public were determined to enjoy the spectacle of this Princess, who is ugly, marrying a handsome boy who is barely a gentleman'. The Queen however, is gracious, and there is always a good seat at Garter ceremonies. Whatever his true rank, the diarist has privileged access almost everywhere, and certainly has more in common with the best people than with the crowd.

From time to time he shows keen interest in people who had no claim whatever to be gentlemen, studying them with an anthropologist's curiosity. The generic description for such people is 'bedint', a term borrowed from Harold Nicolson and Vita Sackville-West; meaning, I suppose, someone who serves, whose manners are appropriate to a subordinate station. They might be 'Liverpool Geordies' (it's hard to tell one bedint from another) or educated at a redbrick university, in which case they affect a 'la-de-dah' accent and are bound to be 'painfully suburban'.

A young man, doctor in history I think from Liverpool University . . . He is writing a book about Princess Winnie [Winaretta de Polignac]. Sensitive, intelligent and earnest. Not handsome, but a fine face, and very long, white, nervous fingers. Pronounces Italian, Itarlian and holds his fork in that ungainly way as though it were a dangerous instrument. Kept saying things like, 'Did the Princess really know Lady Diana Cooper, Lady Cunard, Lady Colefax, Miss Rosamond Lehmann? We almost felt apologetic for knowing them ourselves . . . One wonders how he can and what he will make of such a circle. How can he, born towards the end of the war, and living in a genteel villa in the outskirts of Liverpool, have a clue?

We see this talented young fellow betwixt and between, indulging aspirations that would seem unexceptionable to his teachers, but, under practised scrutiny, quite hopeless. Pardonable, perhaps, and he must have said something to earn the description sensitive and intelligent, though we are not told what it was. Much trouble ensues from the unwillingness of people below the rank of gentleman to stay in their stations. Admittedly they are sometimes very nice, but 'self-motivated'. 'All they want is less work and more money. They have no decent regard for the truth. They are spoilt and rotten. I hope unemployment leaps to astronomical proportions, and that they will be humiliated and come begging cap in hand for work.'

In 1973 the country was clearly in a terrible state, largely because of the unions. Moreover, capital punishment had been unreasonably abolished. Heath was running out of time, the IRA was bombing London, a dangerous oil-crisis loomed. Sacheverell Sitwell passes on the warning of 'influential city friends': ' "we" have only three months to clear out of England.' Another such friend told him to

. . . hoard his cartridges, for there would be shooting within that time . . . Yesterday we lunched with Diana Westmoreland. She was blazing with fury against the Trades Unions and Mr Gormley in particular, for saying over the air that he did not care a damn about the inconvenience he was causing the public, and he was going to have a jolly good Christmas. She wanted to write him a letter. What should she write? I said, ' "The Dowager Countess of Westmoreland presents her compliments to Mr Gormley and begs to inform him that he is a shit".' The Dowager Countess had a better idea. 'No, I will write, "Fuck off to Russia!" '

Meanwhile the wicked Healey was on the air, telling terrible lies about Mr Barber.

What was needed was discipline.

Feebleness has been this country's undoing ... I think it very possible that there may be fighting within four months. If Heath gives way to the Unions this time, the moderates who make up 80% of the population will be in despair. The extremists will press their demands and have to be resisted with force by a super-leader.

Watching the TUC conference on television persuaded him that Communism was unstoppable. Lord Camrose of the *Telegraph* thought the takeover would happen overnight. Years before all this, our diarist had said he would not have dined with the Mosleys had they been Stalinists, 'but I had never felt opposed to Fascists'. His hatred of the Left extends as far as the Communards of 1848 ('loathsome vermin'). By the end of the Seventies 'we' were still around, the pressure to emigrate relieved by Mrs Thatcher. Back on the Badminton estate the Duke's secretary knows which way every single inhabitant of the village voted. 'They subscribe to Tory funds yet vote Labour. Wonderfully cheered by [Thatcher's] victory.' Yet in 1981 he is still fearing a Russian ultimatum 'demanding complete capitulation within a week'. The trouble was 'the people', discontented, greedy and mendacious, one's servants always putting one out so that one can't write.

If the country was still in a fearful mess, the Church was worse. Lees-Milne had been a convert to Rome but now disliked it very much, for it was being propelled down an evil road by 'secret Commies' who perverted the traditional ritual and abolished Latin. The Church of England was only a little better. The diarist's wife was served at Communion with a stale wafer and the clergyman's fingers were none too clean. The Church of England unfortunately offers the sacrament in both kinds; the hour was too early for wine, which in any case was Wincarnis, and the officiating priest wiped the chalice 'in a perfunctory way'. This was perhaps the very priest who detained one in the vestry with horrifying accounts of his bowels. As the populace no longer went to church one's own would doubtless in the near future become a school, and not only a school but a *state* school, its squash court where the diarist now stood. Brave new world, where every comprehensive has its squash court!

It's a national weakness to admire really terrific snobbery, but to me the most pleasing passages in these voluminous diaries were ones that don't seem to be substituting a class identity for a person but instead show a simple interest in the writer's more amiable peculiarities. He chats to himself about his bathroom routines, his marital tiffs, his dreams; or perhaps records a religious or oceanic experience. Reading in bed, he looks up and notices a tapestry on the opposite wall. 'In a flash, so quick that it occupied the fraction of a second, I understood the whole meaning of existence.' When a poet such as Yeats says such things we are disposed to take them more seriously, but although it claims relatively little this passage looks impressive in the context of endless matter-of-fact observations on luncheons and dinners and 'motoring' hither and thither. (Why is the verb 'to motor' upper-class, while the noun 'motor' is plebeian?)

Among these marginal observations there are some that are truly endearing. Driving a small car on the motorway at 70 m.p.h. with another car alongside him, he is impelled to imagine himself in a dodgem, wanting to bounce cheerfully off this other vehicle. He enjoys recording not only his own oddities and gaffes but those of others. A Greek (class not specified) is heard to say to Caroline Somerset, 'I say, your breath smells beastly' when in fact he had merely remarked 'I saw your best friend lately'. There are other bright moments of this kind.

It can't be denied that much of the fun arises from his knowing everybody. There is an excellently observed portrait of Colette, her odd choices of food at luncheon: 'she talked of fish and the superior intelligence of the pike. Her mother, she said, had a tortoise called Charlotte, which slept throughout the winter. There came a day every year when she heard her mother call out: "*Charlotte s'éveille, c'est le printemps*".' Perhaps she was thinking of the tortoise when kissed by Somerset Maugham. This writer is informative on many other subjects; he tells, with apparent authority, the story of how Keats's tomb was broken open and the coffins of Keats and Severn smashed when workmen, told to cut down two nearby pines, tore them out instead. Lees-Milne was a member of the Keats–Shelley committee, but his informant urged him not to tell them about it. The culture of secrecy was no secret to this diarist and his circle.

So one begins to acquire some understanding of him. He was wonderfully learned and terse about furniture, churches, bibelots, houses ('Later eighteenth-century houses must be kept up. They do not decay well'). He liked music (or knew what he liked) and where he was not expert he was still interested. He was fond of beauty in both men and women and sketched them neatly (Graham Sutherland's wife had 'raven black hair as smooth as a gramophone record'). Himself calmly bisexual, he was sympathetic to homosexuals ('buggers are so vulnerable'). His general views on sexual conduct and misconduct are liberal, though no doubt he was making allowances for himself; he valued circumspection more than abstinence. He admired the journalist Patrick O'Donovan, at the time an officer in the Irish Guards, who 'while he took the salute of the King and Queen in the Victory Parade, the upper part of his body out of his tank, his soldier servant was fellating him below'. But he distinguished between lust (unimportant) and love (vital). He imagined that in A. C. Benson's day at Cambridge 'every don was in love with practically every undergraduate'.

The new volume, *Deep Romantic Chasm*, being a work of relatively old age, is in danger, as the author remarks, of turning into an obituary column. Yet he is throughout deep in love with the young man who is now his editor, and enviably active. Here, appended to the normal diary, are accounts of his travels to Normandy, Calabria and Mount Athos, the last pretty arduous. It would be mean to withhold admiration for a man so accustomed to comfort who cheerfully dines on sardines and Kendal mint cake while roughing it in bleak monasteries.

This may cause one to reflect on a certain omission from the diaries: amid all the grand luncheons, the motoring hither and thither, the great houses, the London clubs, the funerals and memorial services, hardly anything is said about the labours of a writer who produced a great many successful books as well as these diaries – a writer who might well have claimed the Renaissance quality of *sprezzatura*, of doing things well yet seeming to do them without pain or care, indeed hardly to be seen doing them at all.

The snobbery can be appalling and comes from deep in the personality (black people have a disagreeable smell). To behave like members of a higher class than one's own is disgusting, but it is easier to tell whether a person has ancestors than to guess his age. And it takes a super snob to write that 'it is astonishing how snobbish the English gentry are. Wherever we go to lunch or dine we are placed at table according to rank' – which presumably means that people intrinsically less interesting or important than oneself are given preference on account of their superior ancestors. So it goes on, volume after volume; all in the dialect of a still powerful tribe. And we pathetic bedints can't help thinking it rather wonderful.

22

Auden on Shakespeare

These lectures* were delivered at the New School for Social Research in Greenwich Village during the academic session 1946–7. Arthur Kirsch has pieced them together from the records of four people who attended them. To have one's lectures assembled from students' notes years after they were given is a rare mark of distinction; offhand I can only think of Saussure and Wittgenstein, though possibly one could add the name of Jesus. Pascal's *Pensées* were put in some kind of order long after his death, but he had written them down, so no allowance needs to be made for mishearing, faults of memory, or the occasional failure of the student to follow the argument. Some disagreement about what was actually said seems inevitable, and it has proved to be so in the case of Saussure. Kirsch, however, has one very dependable witness, Alan Ansen, who was soon to become the poet's secretary. Ansen was an exceptionally alert, well-read note-taker, but he missed a few of the lectures, and for them the editor has to turn to the much less reliable Howard Griffin (who also, in his turn, became Auden's secretary) and to two other volunteers, women who had preserved their notes from the spring term.

The result reads like a remarkably full account of what the poet said about Shakespeare but also about many other matters. At the time of the lectures he was nearing forty and settled in New York. The last few years had been extraordinarily productive even by Auden's standards. *New Year Letter* (or, in the USA, *The Double Man*) appeared in 1941, *For the Time Being* (a volume also containing *The Sea and the Mirror*) in 1944. A 'Collected' came out in 1945 and *The Age of Anxiety*, on

* W. H. Auden, ed. Arthur Kirsch, *Lectures on Shakespeare* (2000)

which he was working at the time of the lectures, was published in 1947. These works, and especially the superb *Tempest* sequel or commentary, *The Sea and the Mirror*, testify to a major poet at the height of his power. A model of professional industry, he was also in these years writing a good deal of prose.

Presumably he agreed to do this heavy lecture course for the same reason he wrote prose, namely because he needed the money, but they show few signs of being put together hastily or impatiently, or treated as a weekly chore. He not only gave the lectures but sacrificed his Saturday afternoons to meet with small groups of students in a situation where they could do some close work and not merely listen to him 'boom away' at them in a large lecture theatre. He must have spent much time on preparatory reading, criticism as well as the actual texts. He didn't write the lectures out but spoke from notes which he later threw away; it does not seem to have occurred to him to use them as the basis of a book. Some of the ideas tried out there do turn up in the group of Shakespearian essays in *The Dyer's Hand*, fifteen years later, but a lot more thinking had been done in the interim. For instance, the well-known piece about *Othello* in *The Dyer's Hand* is remembered for its treatment of Iago as a practical joker, but in the relevant lecture nothing is said about this aspect of Iago's wickedness; instead he is called an 'inverted saint' and credited with an *acte gratuit* of the sort St Augustine committed when he stole some pears he didn't want, and fed them to pigs. Over so long a period alterations of emphasis were only to be expected, and Kirsch has had to be careful about supplementing Ansen's notes from material in the later essays. He does make it clear when and why he occasionally finds it necessary to do so.

Auden was by this time a practised lecturer, and his unprofessorial manner on the platform appealed strongly to his audiences, which were large – as many, it is said, as five hundred. Somebody remarked that the crowd couldn't have been more enthusiastic if Shakespeare had been lecturing on Auden. They might well have been on the look out for the odd joke or teasingly perverse remark, and there are some; but they must also have been willing to listen from time to time to lectures that might quite often have been mistaken for sermons.

Under the influence of Reinhold and Ursula Niebuhr he had been trying to come to terms with Christianity, and from his reading of Pascal (instructive concerning doubt), Augustine (authoritative concerning sin), Buber, Tillich and above all Kierkegaard, he had arrived at a variety of Christian existentialism which is repeatedly expounded in these lectures. He was particularly impressed by Eugen Rosenstock-Huessy's book *Out of Revolution*, which gives a very idiosyncratic account of Christian history, 'tracing patterns unimaginable by others', as Edward Mendelson remarks – a disparaging view the poet himself later accepted. Throughout the time he was working on *The Age of Anxiety* the tone of his thinking was rather bleakly religious. The poem is set on the night of All Souls, a feast of which the establishment in 998 AD seemed to Rosenstock-Huessy, as Mendelson puts it, 'one of the great transforming events of European history'. On the other hand, surrounded by Jewish intellectuals, and now fully conscious of the horror of the Holocaust, another transforming event, he had become very interested in Judaism and even, at one moment, contemplated conversion. At the end of the poem Malin, a Canadian Air Force officer, returns to duty and is 'reclaimed by the actual world where time is real and in which, therefore, poetry can take no interest'. These were some of the preoccupations he brought to his Shakespeare course.

He was almost from the outset offering instruction on the difference between the essential and the existential self. This kind of thing must have been hard going for the audience, which had presumably come to hear about Shakespeare and wasn't expecting Kierkegaard and the like; and it still doesn't always seem very transparent on the page. The excuse for its first appearance is that it leads into a discussion about Richard III's ugliness, which compelled him to make his essential self a not-self and absolutely strong; whereas Don Giovanni, introduced for contrast, has an existential self, and 'the existential drive evolves into an infinite series', hence the list of conquests. There is quite a lot of this kind of thing.

Auden himself had a passion for lists, accompanied by another passion for dividing his topics up into sections, less, one feels, to make the lecture more readily understandable by the audience than to satisfy some personal need. 'We must distinguish the different senses of the term *nature*,' he will begin. 'Two senses are then distinguished, one relating to that which is distinctively human, the other to "the physical frame" in which we have to live. Whereas Classical and Chinese writers use the term in the first sense, the modern West uses it in the second, which can be divided in turn into four subcategories . . .' This by way of introduction to a discussion of *A Midsummer Night's Dream*, where Shakespeare 'mythologically anthropomorphizes nature, making nature like man and reducing the figurants of nature to size in comic situations'. There follows a disquisition on myth, with reference to *Totem and Taboo*, Milton's 'Nativity Ode' and Dante. As to the interference of fairies in human life, we have to accept it as demonstrating the ills, major and minor, that fortune brings on us and which we are obliged to bear. This is a matter of duty: 'our duties are . . . (1) . . . (2) . . . (3) . . .' Along the way he turns aside to explain that nature as manifested in the climate of New York is displeasing to him; Nature, he remarks, never intended anybody to live in such a place, 'only in a little bit of Europe and New Zealand'. A welcome moment of light relief.

In relation to *All's Well*, 'there are two kinds of ego satisfaction . . .' In *Measure for Measure*, there are 'four claims to be made against a law we consider unjust', in *Othello* we can identify 'two types of despair'. To understand *Macbeth* one must recognize 'three classes of crime' and 'three kinds of societies'. The rhetoric of love may also be said to be of three kinds. Less schematic but not a bit less serious are disquisitions on such subjects as the Comic, which includes the observation that masters have essence but servants only existence – it's a pity servants are going out of fashion, they were a useful dramatic resource (see 'Balaam and his Ass' in *The Dyer's Hand*).

These explanations can go on so long that there isn't always time to say much about the plays themselves. Auden's head is full of ideas about Christian ethics and psychology which an encounter with Shakespeare provides an occasion to expound, the more so in that Shakespeare's assumptions concerning these matters are evidently Christian. What is society? How ought I to love my neighbour? How must I love God? 'Beliefs are religious or nothing,' he declared. He thought his own earlier poetry was marred by fake beliefs. Shakespeare's wasn't.

It seemed to follow from these convictions that the aesthetic, art in general and especially his own art of poetry were, when understood in relation to the seriousness of religious belief, pretty unimportant. 'On one side the artist starts with an acute ego problem. Art is completely unnecessary. Like love, it is not a matter of duty.' He accepted Kierkegaard's distinction between the aesthetic and the ethical, which condemns the former as despair. What is important is the ethical-religious awareness of one's relation to God. This view, expressed more directly and forcibly in other writings, affects much that Auden says about Shakespeare, as it was to affect his own poetic practice. Later he tried to write poetry that was as near to prose as possible without sacrificing verse altogether, and here he singles out for admiration a passage from *Cymbeline* v.3.28–51, a speech 'often cut by directors'; it is a 'kind of writing that is not immediately noticeable, but anyone who practises verse writing returns again and again to such passages, more than to spectacular things . . . A writer wanting to learn his trade can find out how to write verse by studying them.'

This is one of Auden's rather rare comments on Shakespeare's language. He might say of a particular passage, like Henry V's soliloquy about the cares of kingship, that it is 'terribly bad poetry', but he doesn't say anything more, except that this 'is just as it should be'. He would read aloud long passages and pass on without recorded comment. The effect is a sort of compliment to the audience; they don't require laborious explanations, for their presence is in itself a claim to be qualified to recognize good writing. His editor says 'he can, of course, respond with perfect pitch to Shakespeare's verse', and this is indeed of course, but he chooses to do so rather rarely. When he does he sometimes depends, wisely, on George Rylands' *Words and Poetry*, a book published in 1928 and, in its kind, never superseded. Auden may very well have said more on the subject of Shakespeare's poetry than has survived; but it is still true that his main interests were elsewhere.

In a sense, he believed that Shakespeare's were, too. 'I find Shakespeare particularly appealing in his attitude towards his work. There's something a little irritating in the determination of the very greatest artists, like Dante, Joyce, Milton, to create masterpieces and to think themselves important. To be able to devote one's life to art without forgetting that art is frivolous is a tremendous achievement of personal character. Shakespeare never takes himself too seriously.'

In the circumstances this is about the biggest compliment he could have offered.

Auden was at this time involved in an anxious love affair, and while he naturally does not refer directly to his own life, he occasionally meditates on love, and, more generally, on the responsibilities of one person to any other person. He quotes Denis de Rougemont (romantic love is a rather absurd illusion), and admires Kierkegaard's lofty view of marriage as the proving ground of a spiritual relationship. Such were his preoccupations; they stem from his own situation in those years, and are of interest to his biographers, though he himself believed that an artist's biography was his work, other talk of his life being objectionable tittle-tattle. Sometimes he does, rather surprisingly, speculate about Shakespeare's life, with the unspoken implication that as a poet he is better equipped to understand it than a non-poet. Artists had to learn and do a job, a job for which they might sometimes, perhaps always, feel some disgust. He is sure Shakespeare did. He identifies a period during which Shakespeare was 'either ill or exhausted' and during which he wrote, or perhaps only partly wrote, *Timon of Athens*, *Cymbeline*, and *Pericles*. And he is fairly sure that Shakespeare would agree with him that art is often 'rather a bore'.

He makes some interesting remarks about the difference between minor and major writers, the latter 'engaged in perpetual endeavours', always trying something new and not caring if it fails, like Shakespeare, Picasso and Wagner, while the minor writer works on one masterpiece with the idea of bringing it to perfection in its kind, like Dante or Proust. The *Sonnets* worry him a little, as does all poetry that concerns itself with what look like private problems such as those caused by sexual desire. 'Why,' he asks, 'should so much poetry be written about sexual love and so little about eating – which is just as pleasurable and never lets you down?' He discusses these matters at some length in his lecture on *Romeo and Juliet*. And although for the most part he proceeds dutifully through the canon he occasionally jibs at plays he despises – *The Taming of the Shrew* is one, *The Merry Wives of Windsor* another. Indeed he declined to discuss *The Merry Wives*, and told the class that they could be grateful it was written because it provided the occasion for 'a very great operatic masterpiece'. He then played a recording of *Falstaff*, a substitution that brought a protest from one of the students in the audience who claimed he was paying to hear Auden talk, not put on records.

Other plays of which he takes an unconventionally disparaging view are *Hamlet*, *Macbeth* and *Coriolanus*. He feels sure Shakespeare was dissatisfied with *Hamlet*, disliking the soliloquies because they are in a way detachable from the play – a fair though contestable point – and, more freakishly, arguing that the whole thing must have been written to spite the actors. Sometimes he may not greatly like a play but still find a lot to say about it, as with *As You Like It*, where he goes conscientiously into ancient primitivism and Empson on pastoral, with quotations from an Old Irish poem, from Goethe, and from *Alice in Wonderland*. Discussing *Love's Labours Lost*, he gives a summary account of Courtly Love based on C. S. Lewis's *The Allegory of Love*, as well as a competent account of Renaissance Neo-Platonism, mostly, and legitimately, cribbed from Erwin Panofsky. He thinks this one of the most perfect of the plays, and says some fine things about its wit.

The chapter on *The Merchant of Venice* is as good as anything I've read on the subject, with a clear view of Shakespeare's idea of Venetian society, an excellent discussion of the usury question, and an account of Shylock that is both plausible and enlightened. But it is on the plays he most admired that he writes best – the *Henry IV* pair, and *Antony & Cleopatra*. The argument of the lecture on the first of these subjects is developed in *The Dyer's Hand*. Auden loathes Prince Henry, the sort of person who becomes a statesman or a college president. (Mendelson describes his reaction to James Bryant Conant, the President of Harvard: 'This is the real enemy.') But he loves Falstaff, not in the old vacant, adoring, incomparable Sir John way, but as a man with a life, and an antitype to the ghastly prince; not a character you would choose to run a country or a university, but a man of style; fat, but compare his way of talking and behaving with Hal's and it is the prince who seems fat. Auden then meditates on the reason why people get fat: they eat humble pie and swallow their pride as drink; and drink destroys the sense of time (time, as he argues, is very important in these plays), and makes one childlike, innocent. He is attached to life through Hal, and when he is rejected he dies. Falstaff would be an artist except that artists need not only the gift of liveliness, language and wit, but also something of Hal's Machiavellianism and prudence.

The Winter's Tale iii.3. is praised as 'the most beautiful scene in Shakespeare – it is the scene on the coast of Bohemia in which Antigonus deposits the baby Perdita and then, as the shepherds discover the child, is eaten by a bear. However, it is the situation, not the language, that Auden admires – he says you could describe it in other words and it would still be beautiful in the way a dream can be. Auden believed in the validity of myths, however they were told; and he distrusted language, which he also worshipped, as only a good poet has a right to do. But the famous speech of the old shepherd in that scene must surely have contributed to his sense of its exceptional beauty.

Otherwise his highest praise is reserved for *Antony & Cleopatra*, of which he speaks with a certain magnificence. He regards with sympathy the love of the principals, so different from that of Romeo and Juliet or Troilus and Cressida; the first pair are just discovering sexual love, the second are coarse and false, but Antony and Cleopatra are having their last affair and its purpose is to enable them to escape the future, old age and death. 'They need the fullest possible publicity and the maximum assistance from good cooking, good clothes, good drink.' The poetry of their love talk is like fine cooking, a technique to maintain excitement even as the senses cool. He makes this point by quoting some 'marvellous' verses, and marvellous they are:

> Lord of lords!
> O infinite virtue, com'st thou smiling from
> The world's great snare uncaught?

and the little scene, certainly a work of genius, in which 'the god Hercules, whom Antony lov'd, / Now leaves him' is called 'beautiful' by a critic who rarely uses such language. This play moved him more than any other, though he also loved some of the late romantic comedies because they represent 'the world as you want it to be, and nothing makes one more inclined to cry'. But he is still more interested in the situation presented in the Roman play – the vast imperial setting, Ventidius doing Antony's fighting for him on the remote eastern frontier, Octavius coldly planning in Rome, the future of the known world in the balance – while this couple, both 'getting on', say wonderful things to one another, and hate as intemperately as they love. 'Tremendous power', says Auden; but there is also a worldliness in which we all share, for 'We all reach a time when the god Hercules leaves us'.

A concluding lecture makes some just remarks about the superiority of Shakespeare to all his competitors in the brief years of flowering enjoyed by the Elizabethan–Jacobean drama. In a few years Shakespeare, serving it, developed his 'middle style', a style 'paced with matter', as Rylands remarked: a style that reaches an extraordinary and difficult maturity in the speeches of Leontes at the beginning of *The Winter's Tale*, which have 'a complete freedom of sentence style'. One wishes there were records of those Saturday afternoon sessions devoted partly to analysis of such passages.

We are left, then, with a Shakespeare who, like his expositor, practised an art without taking it too seriously. 'Increasingly he suggests ... that art is rather a bore.' Yet although this book contains many such remarks, it does take Shakespeare seriously, partly by remaking him in the image of the poet devised by the poet who is discussing him. We may wonder at the intensity of conscience and intellect Auden brought to a task he must sometimes have thought a waste of his time. That it never occurred to him to save the notes and make them into a book strengthens one's respect for the book, now it has appeared. It is the tribute of a mature fellow-craftsman, with as much scholarship as he needed to serve his purpose – certainly nothing like the effort of research that went into John Berryman's book on Shakespeare, but enough to illuminate the subject, and along the way to illuminate the lecturer. It is a remarkable achievement, done, to borrow Milton's phrase, with the left hand.

23

Don DeLillo

The publishers describe this book* as 'lean', which may be taken to refer to its style, though it also serves as a euphemism for 'very short, especially considering the price'. Its immediate predecessor was *Underworld*, at least seven times as long (or as fat). That book, as nearly everybody must know, begins with a chapter about a famous baseball game and a boy who retrieves the ball with which the decisive home run was scored. *The Body Artist* is about as long as the *Underworld* ball game.

DeLillo is a serious and various writer, and we have to take these extremes as deliberately chosen to reflect different aspects of his talent. *Underworld* belongs to the category of the Great American Novel, to which all the really big writers aspire. Structurally it has some resemblance to Pynchon's *Gravity's Rainbow*, and that thought prompts the reflection that Pynchon also wrote an exceptionally fine novella, *The Crying of Lot 49*. If there are two traditions of great American writing it is proper to show up in both of them. One of them may be said to originate with Hawthorne, the other with Melville, one lean and self-absorbed, the other heavy, expansive, determined to contain a world. On the whole the heavyweights have prevailed in recent years; one no longer hears much talk of, say, Glenway Westcott, a lean writer of whom Gertrude Stein remarked that 'he has a certain syrup but it does not pour'. This memory came to me as I read *The Body Artist*. But here the syrup does, slowly, pour.

Underworld aims to put together a complicated image of the desperate condition of the United States in the second half of the twentieth

* Don DeLillo, *The Body Artist* (2001)

century, with some allusion to the rest of the world, since it is still impossible to say everything relevant about life, civilization and the decaying future by talking about America alone. It has a very basic narrative idea; tracing the history of a baseball is a grander version of the exercise one occasionally had to perform at school: the adventures of a sixpence, or the like. However, DeLillo's idea can encompass a vast array of narrative themes and characters, and I have to admit I don't have a firm grasp on every one of them. Garbage is a principal and much reiterated theme. It is taking over the world: 'What we excrete comes back to consume us.'

Baseball has here, as so often, a pastoral simplicity in contrast with pretty well everything else that affects our lives. The seed of the book was probably the fact that the day of the great pennant-deciding ball game was the very day the Soviet Union exploded its first nuclear bomb. What is fallout but more cosmic garbage? It signals the end of any hope that even baseball can remain pure and simple. But in fact the game is already contaminated by the presence of some of the more eminent spectators, such as J. Edgar Hoover and his cronies.

After that critical moment it seems that modern history is all downhill. The Sixties are a decade that has 'paranoid breath'. Evil has formed itself into a system; so thoroughly is the world 'systemed under' that we don't even perceive the connection between orange juice and Agent Orange, which the system 'connects at levels beyond' our comprehension. Even the quite recent pre-system past is food for nostalgia. A tune can take you 'back to your bedside radio and the smells of your kitchen, and the way the linoleum used to ripple near the icebox'. We can even feel nostalgic for the Cold War.

Many things that were anchored to the balance of power and the balance of terror seem to be undone, unstuck. Things have no limits now. Money has no limits. I don't understand money anymore. Money is undone. Violence is undone, violence is easier now, it's uprooted, out of control, it has no measure anymore, it has no level of values.

Underworld is a heroic work, colossal in its assurance, in its temporal and spatial range. Its narrative is propelled by extraordinary imaginative energy, by spectacular feats of dialogue and prose of incessant animation. DeLillo, not for the first time, is writing a great book. Gentler readers may well prefer some of the earlier novels, especially *White Noise*, produced in 1984, back in the good old Cold War epoch; set in a small New England college town, it is dominated by an episode of industrial pollution, a lethal toxic cloud, but it preserves a memory of neighbourly happiness, and is nearly always amusing, sometimes even funny, as well as somehow benign. (In the new book 'somehow' is described as the weakest word in the language, a dishonour Joyce reserved for 'yes'.)

It must have seemed a challenge worthy of a virtuoso to abandon the complex and the extensive, and produce instead an intensive, crystalline novella. The animation of the language, the fervour of the scrutiny applied to a world now grown small, need not be less. All the power of the big book writer must now be applied to a brief scenario and a setting hardly more ambitious than Jane Austen's.

The 'white noise' of the earlier title is death, and DeLillo always has some of the big subjects in mind. In *The Body Artist* they are, as the jacket copy lets us know at once, space, love and death. A man and a woman are in the kitchen of a large rented house in New England, having breakfast on a Sunday morning. He has run out of cigarettes and is looking for his car keys. Instead of coming back with the cigarettes he drives to New York and shoots himself in the apartment of a former wife.

The woman stays in the rented house. A 'body artist', she keeps in trim by day, but at night watches on the internet the videoed traffic on the outskirts of an obscure Finnish town.

Eventually she discovers that the house has a squatter. This strange man speaks a weird dialect of English, having, for instance, no control over tenses, and he is evidently below par in many other ways, but she forms an adhesive relationship with him. He had overheard the husband, a film director, talking into a tape recorder, and discovered that he could mimic the speech of the dead man. The woman accepts the stranger as a member of the household, and tries to capture on the tape recorder her attempts to converse with him. But the conversation fails; it lacks the unspoken contribution of presence, on which personal communication depends. These participants cannot share a sense of inhabiting a particular time between past and future. The man develops a kind of chant in which he seems to identify himself with a moment that is neither the present nor the past nor the future. 'He is another structure, another culture where time is something like itself, sheer and bare, empty of shelter.' Sometimes he repeats sentences spoken by the dead husband, or by the woman herself, either in the past or, less explicably, in the future; for 'this is a man who remembers the future'.

When her guest disappears she mimics his voice on the telephone. She, the Body Artist, gives a performance in Cambridge, Massachusetts, which expresses all that she has discovered about time. As well as miming the interloper she builds into her act many other allusions, and even runs a video of that two-lane highway in Finland. As far as possible her act eliminates the sense of passing time, and a feeling that it may never end causes the more easily bored members of the audience to walk out. Returning to the rented house, she seems to achieve a separation of fact and fantasy, feeling once more 'the flow of time in her body'.

In saying that much about the story I'm not breaking any rules about plot-revelation, for the interest of this book is primarily in its texture. Its repetitive, fragmentary motifs remind one of the old *nouveau roman* – the unavoidable touch of a hand on a newel post, the arm that hits an overhead light when the woman removes her always grubby sweater, the gait of a Japanese neighbour (later incorporated in the Cambridge performance), the behaviour and the noises of birds at garden feeders.

The opening chapter is where you have to learn to read the book. The kitchen detail, how water from the tap looks first clear, then opaque, the toaster where you have to press the lever twice to get the right shade of brown, the cereal box and the handful of blueberries and the soya granules – it's all calculated to make you think the good old days of *choseisme* had come back. The man is trying to remember something he needs to say, remembers it and doesn't say it. The radio plays, he turns it off, turns it on again, remembers he has just turned it off and turns it off again. The husband and wife are in subtle ways separate (had not been long together) though in others they are more at one. She struggles to get rid of a hair in her mouth, he has cut his chin shaving. Although she knows what he was going to tell her, she insists that he do so, but he doesn't. These are seemingly ordinary failures of communication.

When he walked out of the room, she realized there was something she wanted to tell him. Sometimes she doesn't think of what she wants to say to him until he walks out of whatever room they're in. Then she thinks of it. Then she either calls after him or doesn't and he responds or doesn't.

What he had meant to do, though without doing it, was to mention a certain noise in the house, caused, as we are to discover when he has left, by the movements of the intruder upstairs.

And so on. Eventually he asks about his car keys and departs. The interest of this scene lies partly in its skilful use of the old Fifties techniques to establish an aura of hallucinated detail, a brightly lit moment, though we don't of course know that the moment is that of a final parting between the pair. But it also cannily inserts a rather more conventional piece of plotting, the delayed significance of the small noise upstairs.

On a second reading this brief novel strikes one as a demonstration, hardly less impressive than the monstrous *Underworld*, of the writer's virtuosity. All the same I dare say many admirers of *Underworld* will find this new work something of a stumbling block, at least until they see it as what the jacket tells us it is – yet another meditation on time and death, and yet another testimony to the power and scope of this ambitious novelist.

24

Martin Amis

The main title of this collection* may at first seem wantonly non-descriptive, but it turns out to be exact. The first thing to see to if you want to write well is to avoid doing bad writing, used thinking. The more positive requirements can be left till later, if only a little later. Clichés are infallible symptoms of used thinking. Martin Amis has always wanted to be a good writer and he has got what he wanted. He early acquired a habit of vigilance, of stopping clichés at the frontier, and that habit couldn't easily be broken. He is one of the few critics who trouble, even in a shortish newspaper review, to include some consideration of the fabric of a book, the faults of its texture, its clichés.

Over the years Amis has done a lot of virtuous wincing over clichés. John Fowles is a prominent target: 'He managed a wan smile'; 'God, you're so naïve.' No expensive talk about Descartes, Marivaux, Lemprière and Aristophanes, can procure a pardon for that sort of thing. Other reviewers may commend Thomas Harris for committing 'not a single ugly or dead sentence' but Amis finds enough of them to label Harris 'a serial murderer of English sentences' and *Hannibal* 'a necropolis of prose'. He finds the opposite response of other commentators explicable on the assumption that they aren't listening, and, more generally, because their sense of hierarchy has gone. Some writers really are better than others, though these people lack the power to see that it is so; 'there is a levelling impulse at work'. 'Margot laughed in spite of herself' and 'Bob Sneed broke the silence' are not only dead sentences but an unprovoked pain to all good writers. The fact that

* Martin Amis, *The War Against Cliché: Essays and Reviews, 1971–2000* (2001)

Harris, like many others, goes in for the occasional 'fugitive poeticism' only makes things worse. When he says that something is 'truly of the resinous heart' Amis does not know what he means and neither do I, but I catch the poeticism, the theft from Yeats. 'Virtuoso vulgarity', indeed. Amis himself sometimes does a borrowing from high-class literature ('green and pale'; 'promise-crammed'; 'the only end of age') though always when it means something, and where he charitably supposes a decent reader will know not only what it means but where it came from and why it is worth stealing.

And if you quote from memory, get it right. When Andrew Motion, no hero to Amis, says that Larkin's anthology was meant to promote 'the taste by which he wished to be relished' he is adapting a remark of Wordsworth's – 'every author, as far as he is great and at the same time *original*, has had the task of *creating* the taste by which he is to be enjoyed'. But neither Wordsworth nor Amis would have passed 'which . . . wished . . . relished'. These are small matters, perhaps, but not if you think them symptoms of a destructive illness, as Amis does, or even as just bad manners.

For writers are to be polite in every sense, courteous in manner and properly skilled in literature. To 'have to read the sentence twice, even though you didn't want to read it once' is to suffer undeservedly. Worse still is the wince produced by 'genteelisms': 'a forty-minute hike brought the dog and I to the top of the hill'. A belated disciple of Fowler, Amis abhors Elegant Variation: 'If the president seemed to support the Radicals in New York, in Washington he appeared to back the Conservatives'. This is not only Elegant Variation but Pointless Chiasmus, a crime I have only this minute identified.

Bellow and Nabokov apart, nobody can be sure to escape whipping. The severities may seem to be, but aren't, mere pedantries. It might not be worth carrying on a war against the cliché out of nothing more than an usher's blinkered interest in Fowlerian correctness of language. But cliché is a disease that must be stamped out; it infects the mind and even the heart; it makes it impossible to be honest, and that, for Amis is an unquestionable duty of authorship. He says in his introduction that he has tried not to go on as he did in his youth, slashing, burning, jeering; such antics, however pleasing to the author and his readers in their nonage, do not become men of substance in middle life – an attitude more humane than that of Housman, who made up epigrammatic insults and stowed them away for future use. 'Mutton dressed as lamb', says Amis of middle-aged slashing, burning and jeering. This renunciation reflects a firm moral position, but it does not excuse him from duty in the war against cliché and 'scruffy writing'.

Very few are exempt from censure. Angus Wilson, who gets a bit of a drubbing, was capable of writing 'the admirable Admiral Croft' and 'a revolting revolutionary act'. V. S. Pritchett, for whom Amis has a well-considered and affectionate admiration (expressed with less qualification in an earlier essay), doesn't understand the elements of punctuation, his being 'tangled, hectic and Victorian'. Moreover he commits sentences here characterized as 'verbal pile-ups' or 'train-wrecks', over which Amis's pencil, his lifting gear, hovers and is regretfully withdrawn. Iris Murdoch makes a futile attempt to avoid cliché by using inverted commas: 'the wrong end of the stick', 'worth-while activities'. But you can't slip away as easily as that: 'a cliché or an approximation, wedged between inverted commas, is still a cliché or an approximation.' It does not help that Murdoch was also given to 'train-wreck adjectives'.

An especially favoured site of cliché infection is the adverb. When Don DeLillo has a character say something 'quietly' you know he's drawing on a long tradition of 'said quietly' as a conventional announcement that the remark it follows should be taken as particularly impressive. Ordinary reviewers, and even this extraordinary reviewer, cannot manage without the likes of 'genuinely pleased' or 'brilliantly realized', 'brilliantly told'. These are rare instances of Amis himself catching a dose of the disease, and, like much of his rather less brilliant writing, they tend to occur in essays on the authors he most respects, in this case V. S. Naipaul.

Normally he protects his health and virtue by ranging as far as possible from adverbial conventionality. I made a list of recherché adverbs, of which this is a selection: beamingly upbeat, lurchingly written, deeply unshocked, embarrassingly good, tremendously unrelaxed, fruitfully uneasy (Pritchett), pitifully denuded (admittedly apt, for a Leavisian bookshelf), janglingly discursive, remorselessly indulgent, scarily illusionless, hugely charmless, promiscuously absorbed, customarily rotted, chortlingly habituate, finessingly cruel, implacably talented, bicker halitotically.

The great thing about these expressions is that the author can be fairly sure they will never be used again, much less become new enemies of clear thought and virtue. If Amis occasionally allows himself something a bit less 'off the beaten track' (as Miss Murdoch might have said) like 'cruelly burdened' instead of, say, 'crunchingly loaded', or argues that a book has 'aged dramatically' (when he might well judge that adverb, used by another author, to be a vulgarism), or writes that somebody 'espoused . . . free love', he gets off because of the merit acquired by his 'ceaseless labour' of cliché avoidance over such a 'long haul'.

It has not evaded the writer's notice that there are other, equally subtle ways of thwarting clichés, whether of the page, the mind or the heart. He regards Joyce as the great master of the art of 'hoisting' the cliché 'with its own petard'. 'The summer evening had begun to fold the world in its mysterious embrace': so begins the Nausicaa section of *Ulysses*, described here as 'one of the greatest passages in all literature'. Its heroine, Gerty MacDowell, is, as Amis accurately remarks, 'a beautiful slum of clichés'. Observing that 'Joyce never uses a cliché in innocence', he describes the whole novel as being '*about* cliché'. A moderately unhappy consequence of this purgative achievement is that *Ulysses*, being itself, as a whole, a 'structural cliché', can be boring. The scene in the cabman's shelter is a deliberate insult to the very idea of writing: a nightmare of repetitions, tautologies, double negatives, elegant variations, howlers, danglers: 'Mozart's *Twelfth Mass* he simply revelled in, the *Gloria* in that being, to his mind, the acme of first class music as such, literally knocking everything else into a cocked hat'. And after many pages of this sort of thing Amis has had enough: 'This writer has the power to take you anywhere (nothing is beyond him); but he keeps taking you where you don't want to go.' It is relevant that '*Ulysses* takes about a week to read, if you do nothing else'. Amis always feels able to acknowledge greatness without denying that it can be boring and make insolent demands on one's time. This combination of unaffected admiration and critical honesty is very attractive.

He thinks it a pity, but not a pity worth spending much precious time on, that the canon is dead and literary criticism, as he knew it in his youth, a thing of the past. All the same, he has visited the canon and here and there shows a dwindlingly acute interest, not in the great men of the age of literary criticism, like I. A. Richards and F. R. Leavis and Northrop Frye, but in what might be called, rather vaguely, the Hazlitt tradition. Yet he is still mildly bothered by the old Intentional Fallacy, and it causes an occasional disturbance of logic: 'Although writer's lives are no more than optional extras in the consideration of their work, the dull fact of Jane Austen's spinsterhood – her plainness, her childlessness, her virgin death – invests her comedies with disappointment, and with a sense of thwarted homing. It also confirms one's sense of the diminishing physicality of her later heroines . . .' And the virgin Austen is reproved for being cruel to Lydia. 'The reader begins to feel that artists should know better than that; we expect them to know better than that.' For all its 'eternal humour and élan', *Pride and Prejudice* fails the test as art, and the question is, whether we'd have known this if we hadn't also known about the disappointments of the author's plainness and spinsterhood.

That said, or, as Amis allows himself to say, 'simply put', we have here a literary critic of startling power, a post-literary-critical critic who, incorrigibly satirical, goes directly to work on the book. Often being right and being funny are, in this book, aspects of the same sentence. Often, as one reads on, one finds oneself quietly giggling, or gigglingly quiet. The precision of the attack is astounding, and is matched by the bluntness of the condemnation. Alexander Theroux is scolded for 'pseudo-elegant variation' when he switches from 'which' to 'that' in mid-sentence. Worse still, the sentence in question is in any case 'a wreck: ugly, untrue, and illiterate'.

Even greater names are not spared. An essay on *Don Quixote* begins as it means to go on: 'While clearly an impregnable masterpiece, *Don Quixote* suffers from one fairly serious flaw – that of outright unreadability.' Anybody could make bold to say that, but few could justify the remark so lightly and ably as Amis does in this piece. Neat tricks of style cooperate in the business of judgement. Meditating a long-past crisis in the management of the English football team, he decides that 'it is all too easy to blame Ron Greenwood. Yet I think we should blame Ron Greenwood'. Greenwood is then thoroughly blamed, mostly for choosing a goalkeeper who 'came cartwheeling off his line to flail at innocuous crosses; all night he looked capable of being nutmegged by a beachball'. Of course that was twenty years ago, before stern charity and moderation of language became the name of the game.

Amis likes games and seems especially keen on tennis and poker, but he spends more time on chess. He does what might by some be described as a 'splendid job' on Bobby Fischer, and a genial one on George Steiner's book about the great Reykjavik encounter: 'There's not one detailed comparison', he writes admiringly, 'between a middle game and Bach's *Die Kunst der Fuge*. Page after page goes by without any reference to Auschwitz.' All the fine writing (what Amis ungraciously calls 'the old apocalyptic beefcake') is confined to chess itself: 'The dynamic dovetailing of the whole game, the unfolding ramifications of its crystalline armature are implosive in the very first move . . .' The youthful critic, after properly acknowledging the merits of the book, takes the liberty of advising its famous author to cool it, and to discover the difference between brilliance and dazzle.

The kind of writing this writer belongs to is the novelistic kind, so we expect, and get, more detailed comment on novelists, especially twentieth-century novelists, than on poets, playwrights and the like. Here are penetratingly friendly notices of Ballard and Burgess ('the failure is (vexingly, boringly, ineffably) a failure of language'). Michael Crichton has a bad case of cliché rot: 'animals – especially, if not exclusively, velociraptors – are what he is good at. People are what he is bad at. People, and prose'. Crichton has 'herds of clichés, roaming free'. You will listen in 'stunned silence' to an 'unearthly cry' or 'a deafening roar'. Evelyn Waugh 'wrote *Brideshead Revisited* with great speed, unfamiliar excitement, and a deep conviction of its excellence. Lasting schlock, the really good bad book, cannot be written otherwise.' Malcolm Lowry is 'a world-class liar'. The response to John Updike is slightly chilly, but loses its cool when required to be respectful: 'enduringly eloquent . . . in a prose that is always fresh, nubile and unwitherable'. (Yes, it does say 'nubile'.) Philip Roth is admired, though Amis seems uncharacteristically terrorized by *Sabbath's Theater*: 'an amazing tantrum . . . You toil on, looking for the clean bits.' Mailer is 'grandiose and crass'. And so on. It's all deeply interesting and interestingly deep, especially when the subjects are the American masters alongside whom, one can't help feeling, this writer would choose to be assessed. Hence the long eulogies of Nabokov and Bellow: 'the world has never heard this prose before', he writes, all irony discarded, 'prose of such tremulous and crystallized beauty.' Don DeLillo later gets into the side, while Updike still frets on the bench.

There are, however, some good writers on this side of the ocean. The Naipauls and Larkin must be praised. The long central *New Yorker* essay on Larkin is probably the most considered and the most permanently valuable part of the book. It recycles some earlier remarks to great defensive effect. More than any other piece it confirms one's opinion that Amis is the best practitioner-critic of our day – just what Pritchett was in his prime, though without the bad punctuation and the jangling train-wrecks.

25

Ian McEwan

Minor resemblances between this novel by Ian McEwan* and Henry James's *What Maisie Knew* have already been noticed and are of some interest. James left a quite full record of the development of his story, which described modern divorce and adultery from the point of view of a young girl. It had its roots in Solomon's offer to satisfy rival maternal claimants by cutting the disputed child in half, but it grew far more complicated in the years between the first notebook entry on this topic and the completion of the novel about 'the *partagé* child'. First there was a plan for a 10,000 word story, which, in prospect, set delightful technical problems: about 'the question of time' – 'the little secrets in regard to the expression of duration' – and about the need to use the '*scenic method*'. In the Notebooks James prays that he not be tempted to 'slacken my deep observance of this strong and beneficent method – this intensely structural, intensely hinged and jointed preliminary frame'. Only when the frame was built was he ready to start what he called the 'doing'.

Ian McEwan's new novel, which strikes me as easily his finest, has a frame that is properly hinged and jointed and apt for the conduct of the *march of action*, which James described as 'the only thing that really, for *me* at least, will *produire* L'OEUVRE'. Not quite how McEwan would put it, perhaps, but still the substance of his method, especially if one adds to a keen technical interest another Jamesian obsession, the point of view. His central character is a thirteen-year-old girl called Briony, already a maker of stories and plays, and so already a writer of fictions that have only their own kind of truth and are

* Ian McEwan, *Atonement* (2001)

dependent on fantasies readers are invited to share, with whatever measure of scepticism or credulity they can muster.

Briony is the daughter of an important civil servant who has a grand though ugly country house. The year is 1935 and, since a war is threatening, he has exhausting responsibilities in Whitehall. Along with other more genial preoccupations, his London duties keep him off the scene, even on the special occasion during which the story begins. On the hot summer's day of this celebration Briony, in one of those strange moments that chance or fate delivers into the hands of the novelist, or more specifically into Ian McEwan's, happens to see her elder sister Cecilia, just down from Girton, take off her outer clothes and jump into a fountain – this in the presence of Robbie Turner, the son of the family's faithful cleaning lady, who has also been sent, at the expense of the girl's father, to Cambridge. Robbie did well there, but has now decided to start again and qualify as a doctor – one who 'would be alive to the monstrous patterns of fate, and to the vain and comic denial of the inevitable': much as if he had decided to be a novelist. However, the monstrous patterns of fate begin to involve him now, at the fountain, before he can even start a medical career. The episode at the fountain changes his plan, as it changes everything.

McEwan's readers will remember other random and decisive changes of this kind, violent or subtle interruptions of everyday time and behaviour, intrusions of dream-like horror like the snatching of the three-year-old girl in *The Child in Time* or the rogue balloon in *Enduring Love*. The trick works less well, I think, in the more recent *Amsterdam*, with its more slightly ostentatious symmetries, its carefully laid clues concerning euthanasia and crooked Dutch doctors which give the book structure; but the 'doing' is less interesting. The failure of the composer's final symphony, after we have heard so much about the process of composition, might uncharitably be seen as an allegory of the novel it occurs in. There is, however, a finely written scene in which the composer, hiking in the Lakes, declines to help a woman walker when she is violently assaulted; this nasty bit of reality is interfering with the musical thought he had come to work out, and he decides that the music comes first, as his story might to a novelist.

The fountain scene in this new book has as much force, and has also that touch of the grotesque which is one of this author's special talents. Cecilia has been half-playfully disputing with Robbie the right to fill a valuable vase with water from the fountain. He wants to do it for her. Their little struggle proves more serious than it should have been; as they wrestle for the vase two triangular pieces break off its lip and fall into the fountain. (Triangles, by the way, form a minor leitmotif for readers to puzzle over.) Robbie prepares to plunge in and recover the pieces; but Cecilia gets her clothes off and plunges first. The wounded vase will later meet an even worse fate, and this premonitory damage echoes what happens to other fragile objects highly valued but easily ruined, such as Cecilia's virginity, and indeed life itself.

A numerous company is preparing for dinner when Briony, happening to go into the library, finds Robbie and Cecilia violently engaged in the act of sex. Robbie had written Cecilia a harmless letter, but accidentally sent in its place a coarse little meditation on his lust for her, and specifically, the message insists, for her cunt. The letter had been delivered to Cecilia by the hand of Briony, who, being a writer, naturally had a look at it. It was this letter that turned Cecilia on and, when it was circulated, turned everybody else off.

Meanwhile some young cousins, derelict because of a divorce, were staying with the family, and at the awful dinner that evening the unhappy nine-year-old twin boy cousins, one with a triangular piece missing from his ear, ran away. During the search for them their sister Lola, a bit older than Briony, is sexually assaulted, and despite the darkness Briony thinks she is able to identify the assailant as the lustful Robbie. Hence his imprisonment. He is released to the Army, and, in a deeply researched and imagined episode, takes part in the Dunkirk evacuation. A point of interest here is that Robbie and his associates, heading for the coast with a demoralized remnant of the B.E.F., are surprised to see brisk, disciplined Guards regiments going in the opposite direction, presumably to serve as a doomed rearguard. Here as elsewhere we are left to wonder who picked up this point and put it into the story? Did it, in fact, happen? Who will vouch for its truth? Has the author a patriotic weakness for the Guards? It's a small point, but it raises the sort of question that comes up over and over again in this novel. By way of ambiguous answer the narrative, when it ends, is signed 'B.T.', Briony's initials.

Briony's play, *The Trials of Arabella*, written for the house party, but for various reasons not then performed, was the fantasy of a very young writer enchanted by the idea that she could in a few pages create a world complete with terrors amd climaxes, and a necessary sort of knowingness. The entire novel is a grown-up version of this achievement, a conflict or coalescence of truth and fantasy, a novelist's treatment of what is fantasized as fact. Briony is the novelist, living, as her mother is said to have perceived (or the author, or Briony, says she had perceived), in 'an intact inner world of which the writing was no more than the visible surface'. We merely have to trust somebody to be telling something like the truth. In the scene where Robbie and Cecilia make love in a corner of the darkened library (a key scene, terribly difficult for *anybody* to write) Briony, entering, sees her sister's 'terrified eyes' over Robbie's shoulder. Who is saying she is terrified? Who is saying Cecilia 'struggled free' of her heavy partner? Surely she was carried away by lust and henceforth became Robbie's devoted lover? We can only suppose that Briony, writing at the very end of the complex affair, is imagining what she would have made of the scene at thirteen. She must have read the scene wrongly, for we learn that the lovers were actually 'in a state of tranquil joy' as they 'confronted the momentous change they had achieved'. At this moment Cecilia is overwhelmed by the beauty of a face she had taken for granted all her life. Can she also have had terrified eyes? Or could Briony have taken for terror an expression that meant something quite different?

For contrivances such as these the novelist could be forgiven a Jamesian note of self-congratulation and self-encouragement, usually, in the Master's case, expressed in French: *voyons, voyons, mon bon!* Let us see what I, and later what they, can make of this treatment. When Briony comes to the rescue of her cousin Lola the explanation of what happened is not Lola's but Briony's: 'It was her story, the one that was writing itself around her.' Her positive identification of the rapist is not explicitly endorsed by Lola; we are even allowed to suspect that this flirtatious child knew perfectly well the attacker wasn't Robbie, and that it was really a friend of Briony's brother, down there only for a visit but destined to play a heavy part in the sequel. But the less willing Lola was to admit the truth the greater Briony's confidence in her own story, whose impact on reality was so disastrous to Robbie. Her version of the truth was reinforced by that letter and the terrible word it contained. And the girl persisted in it beyond the point where her testimony could be revoked.

To write about the virtuosities of the later pages – what happens to Lola and her assailant, whether Cecilia and Robbie get together, what became of the grand ugly house – would be to deprive readers of satisfactions to which they are entitled; but it leaves the reviewer in a quandary. To discuss the 'doing' properly it would be essential to allude to the whole book. It might reasonably be revealed that both Cecilia and Briony, now totally estranged because of the success of the younger girl's evidence against Robbie, serve in the second war as nurses (again the enviable specificities, the sometimes apparently absurd hospital discipline, the drawing on reserves of endurance, the hideous and hopeless wounds). The title of the book seems to suggest that Briony will do something by way of atonement, but nothing quite fitting that description seems to occur. The problem, we finally learn, and as might have been expected, was this: 'how can a novelist achieve atonement when, with her absolute power of deciding outcomes, she is also God? There is no one, no entity or higher form that she can appeal to, or be reconciled with, or that can forgive her. No atonement for God, or novelists . . .'

These words occur in the Epilogue, as I call it, a final chapter dated 'London, 1999'. Briony now, as again one might have expected, has behind her a successful career as a novelist. At seventy-seven she is suffering from a succession of tiny strokes, and her memory, she is told, is likely to fail progressively. Like Ian McEwan, she has recently been working in the library of the Imperial War Museum. Her book is finished, like Ian McEwan's, and it has apparently exactly the same story. There follow reports of a series of quite implausible encounters. 'If I really cared so much about facts,' she writes, 'I should have written a different kind of book.' And she wishes she could write a happy conclusion, all well and lovers alive and reunited – 'it's not impossible'. In fact she has already written it and we have already read it and probably believed it.

McEwan's skill has here developed to the point where it gives disquiet as well as pleasure. Perhaps to be disquieting has always been his ambition; the first stories were in various ways startling. By now he is such a virtuoso that one is tempted to imagine that the best readers of this book might be Henry James and Ford Madox Ford. It is, in perhaps the only possible way, a philosophical novel, pitting the imagination against what it has to imagine if we are to be given the false assurance that there is a match between our fictions and the specifications of reality. The pleasure it gives depends as much on our suspending belief as on our suspending disbelief.

For example, we are told that Briony, while still a wartime nurse, sent a novella called *Two Figures by a Fountain* to *Horizon*. It was not accepted, but the editor, Cyril Connolly (or anyway someone who signs himself simply as 'C.C.') wrote her a letter running to over a thousand words, with favourable comment on sentences we have already admired. The implication is that the present novel is an expansion of that early work. We can even spot changes from novella to novel (for example, Cecilia goes 'fully dressed' into the fountain) and might attribute the improvements to C.C.'s kindly advice. He wonders if the young author 'doesn't owe a little too much to the techniques of Mrs Woolf'. The novella, he claims, lacks the interest of forward movement, 'an underlying pull of simple narrative'. He thinks the vase should not have been Ming (too expensive to take out of doors; perhaps Sèvres or Nymphenburg?). The Bernini fountain she mentions is not in the Piazza Navona but in the Piazza Barberini (the error is corrected in the novel). He complains that Briony's story ends with the damp patch left by the fountain when Robbie and Cecilia have gone. (It is still there in the longer version but it is there only as a beginning.) Elizabeth Bowen, it seems, read the novella with interest, but thought it cloying, except when it echoed *Dusty Answer*. The author is invited to drop by at the office for a glass of wine whenever she has the time. Had she, by the way, a sister at Girton six or seven years ago? Given her hospital address, is she a doctor or an invalid?

In the first place parody, this brilliant invention does quite a lot of what James called structural work. It is funny because although it sounds rather like him Connolly would never have written such a letter; it lives, like the book as a whole, on that borderline between fantasy and fact that is indeed the territory of fiction. McEwan has examined this territory with intelligent and creative attention, and it could probably be said that no contemporary of his has shown such passionate dedication to the art of the novel.

26

Tom Paulin

This book* is a sequence or collection of poems and other things concerning events in Europe in the period between the Treaty of Versailles and, broadly speaking, the Battle of Britain. Some of the events and personalities, like the Treaties of Versailles and Locarno are considerately annotated, but others, some of them much more obscure than these, are not. Consequently the reader's share, as Henry James called it, is quite half; or, to put it another way, unless you are a polymathic historian with some knowledge of literature you will need to do quite a lot of research to figure out what Paulin is doing.

This is not a complaint; we are dealing with a modern poet and would hardly expect a linked and lacquered historical account of the between-war years, with one thing giving rise inevitably, tragically, to another, although there is some of that in the pages on Versailles, which inescapably had more than economic consequences. Certain aspects have attracted the poet's attention; he confers it, sensing no obligation to say why he wrote about one thing rather than another. There are passages of prose, some by the author, some transcriptions from his sources, some a mixture of both; some in the body of the text and some in the margins. It is sometimes difficult to say who is doing the talking. The reader must decide whether he or she is up to sorting everything out and making some kind of whole of it.

The prevailing or default mode of the book is verse in short rather rackety and sometimes rickety lines. Frequently it is merely chopped prose. In a vignette of Walter Benjamin we find this: 'after he fled Berlin / the Bibliothèque Nationale / was the only place / he allowed

* Tom Paulin, *The Invasion Handbook* (2002)

himself to feel at home in / It couldn't be a sanctuary / for it gave him only / a brief passing illusion / of safety that ended / with the German occupation'. This passage appears as nine lines of verse, divided as above, and without punctuation. I see the point of getting 'safety' and 'ended' into the same short line, but any other advantages over setting it out as prose are hard to descry, except that in general terms it is an advantage to have a routine baseline verse movement to work from. Presumably the line divisions in the following passage have a point, but it escapes me:

> The free world'll punish and blame
> – no, not Trudj–
> – man and the others . . .

As his admirers would expect, Paulin's language within these mostly rough-hewn lines is also, as ever, rough, demotic (Northern Irish slang or dialect) and exotic (lots of German words, passages in French). At a guess, I would say that in developing this style he has been affected by Miroslav Holub, whom he greatly admires, and who can sound like this in English:

> Inside there may be growing
> An abandoned room,
> Bare walls, pale squares where pictures hung,
> a disconnected phone,
> feathers settling on the floor
> the encyclopaedists have moved out and
> Dostoevsky never found the place
> Lost in a landscape
> Where only surgeons
> Write poems –

a passage Paulin has singled out in his praise of Holub, 'the anti-poet' who 'has lived in the truth and spoken it wryly and firmly'. One gets a fair idea of Paulin's method in this book from some of the Holub lines he has quoted:

Pasteur died of ictus,
Ten years later.
The janitor Meister
Fifty-five years later
Committed suicide
When the Germans occupied
His Pasteur Institute
With all those poor dogs –

Paulin has also praised Peter Reading for being 'user-hostile', and for contriving, by avoiding iambs, to demonstrate 'his dissidence from the state'.

The Preface to Paulin's excellent *Faber Book of Vernacular Verse* explains his preference for demotic diction and the natural cadences of Hopkins and Christina Rossetti over upper-class dialects and iambic regularities. Like Donne, he is proud to be harsh. He won't tell the reader what is meant by a 'prittstick' or a 'boortree' or a 'cuas', equally unknown to me and the *O.E.D.* You could probably guess from the context that 'stocious' is Irish for 'drunk' but even an Irishman I consulted could not explain 'pochles', which occurs in the same line. However, 'pobby' means 'swollen' and a 'loy' is an Irish spade. And so on. The 'jeddo' turns out to be the *jet d'eau* in the lake at Geneva. Meanwhile the verses bearing these novelties rattle like unsprung carts over ruts. Wheat dust 'skinks and twindles', sledges 'skitter and slip'. 'There was heard the plockplock of horsehooves / a toltering bustle clipped scatter / like sabots clocking the cobbles.' But they can rise to their occasion, as with this moment in a Czech workers' canteen, come upon in a side street:

. . . oh it was wretched
an unsmiling woman
served us bowls of soup
– dull brown and greasy –
it was intimate and unclean
like eating in a hospital
with a dying man
all we tasted was unhope

So the vernacular style can support such flights. But this vernacular poet is also a very literary poet, and often, when he is at his most elaborate and ambitious, reports can be heard from the not too distant canon. Eliot, whose idea of tradition Paulin particularly reprehends, is contemptuously shown here lunching with Montgomery Belgion, his *Criterion* acolyte, in the Savoy Grill or the Ritz and saying the sort of thing Paulin would expect him to say. But Eliot's verse is another matter, one of the ghosts that haunt the poem. It crops up in the midst of the vernacular, as here, when Clemenceau speaks:

> the Latin orator in the Sheldonian
> made me Christ the tiger
> in the juvescence – wrong springy word –
> of the year . . .

a quotation not less donnish in that while borrowing his words it manages to point out Eliot's mistake. Talk of Hitler brings in the Starnbergersee. A section called 'Chancellor Hitler's Speech' echoes the catalogue of armaments in Eliot's 'Coriolan' and ends with a confession of the theft. (This kind of catalogue, after all an epic convention, recurs in the tallying of the arms abandoned by the British at Dunkirk.) Sometimes the allusion is fugitive: a Dutchman squats on a windowsill, 'above an earth that for some politely / churlish reason / is jampacked with merds not turds'; 'patched and peeled' is borrowed in a passage on the dreadfully burned faces of fighter pilots. Halifax is described as a familiar ghost.

Joyce and his *Ulysses* get a long passage to themselves, along with passing references to agenbite of inwit and commodious recirculation. Hopkins, a favourite because of his liberal views on rhythm, creeps into a meditation of Trotsky's, and is also remembered for celebrating the roll, the rise, the carol of creation. Unsurprisingly, but in the end aptly, there is a fine extended fantasy on the themes of Conrad's *Under Western Eyes*, though neither the title nor the author is mentioned, which is typical of the cloud of reticence that hangs over the whole book. The Auden of *The Orators* has a hand in a surreal catalogue of ailments in the section on 'Weimar', and also in the prose of 'The Invasion Handbook', a document meant to instruct a German invasion force on the geography and social peculiarities of the British (Free-masons mostly); there is a special wanted list consisting of two names, Lascelles Abercrombie and Stefan Zweig. From the list of two thousand people to be eliminated Lloyd George and George Bernard Shaw are expressly exempted. When the invasion has succeeded the Duke of Windsor will resume his throne and Henry Williamson replace the Poet Laureate, John Masefield.

If these instructions and predictions derive from a genuine document, then that document is Audenesque. But Auden's voice can be heard in less fantastic moments: the lights of a car sweeping across a bedroom, as in that fine early poem later named 'The Watershed'; and the 'pluck' of the tide, which remembers 'Look, Stranger!'. Yeats is also a presence, felt in reminiscences of 'Long-Legged Fly' in *Last Poems*. The phrase 'orts, scraps and fragments', which also turns up as '*des bribes et des morceaux*' must come from Virginia Woolf's *Between the Acts*. And I think Pound has made a less obvious contribution; his Cantos may have contributed to the form and structure of these poems.

Milton provides a 'petrific mace' in a context which actually refers, as Milton didn't, to the act of turning things into stone; and he makes a more spectacular appearance in a marginal note which reads thus: 'Du matin jusqu'au midi il roula du midi jusqu'au soir d'un jour d'été et avec le soleil couchant il s'abattit du zénith come une étoile tombante', which is also in the Weimar section. I can't guess why it is in French, or even why it is there at all, but it does sound rather good. Shakespeare is, naturally enough, an important source, providing sometimes a phrase – 'waiting for waftage' from *Troilus and Cressida*, 'millions of strange shadows' from Sonnet 53, bits of *Antony and Cleopatra* and *Hamlet*. Speer at Berchtesgaden remarks that the Germans were already so steeped in blood that they could not go back, and Trotsky also remembers *Macbeth* when he describes his adobe ranch in Mexico as his 'procreant cradle', the expression with which Duncan commends the Macbeth castle on his arrival there; perhaps we are meant to think that the compliment preceded death by dagger or icepick.

The whole book is what Paulin calls a 'loose-leaf epic' and it is easy to see that it is only the first of a series. He has a grand plan and there is no limit to what he can do within it; he need never stop since there are a million incidents, and characters to work on. Among the topics treated are the original Sarajevo assassination (in flashback), the Bauhaus, the Jarrow March, Munich, the German invasions of Poland, Norway, the Low Countries and France, the Battle of Britain, Dunkirk, the Blitz. Among the persons who are spoken for or speak for themselves are Keynes, whose *Economic Consequences of the Peace* has radical impotrance, Austen Chamberlain (upper-class softy, hopelessly outclassed by hard European diplomats), Neville Chamberlain (worse), Lord Halifax, holy fox and privileged schemer, George V, Trotsky, Stresemann, Hitler, Speer, Churchill, Heidegger, Benjamin, Dowding, Richard Hillary, and the Duke of Windsor, who was very thick with Hitler and had an expensive wedding present from him. There are quite a number of others whom I have to admit I know nothing about except what is here more or less obliquely conveyed.

Some of the stories are simple gossip – Richard Hillary and Merle Oberon, for instance, a particularly warm encounter, warmly recorded; but it seems that the blasted and blistered public-school Hillary is not the kind of young man Paulin likes. Yet he is good on heroism and can produce virile narratives of combat, as in 'The Attack in the West', which has strong scenes of action but also the following revealing anecdote: it seems that General Student, against orders, took the most secret invasion plans in a plane. It crashed, and the occupants were prevented from burning the documents, but the wicked Duke of Windsor let the Nazi high command know the Allies had captured them, so this great advantage was lost. And were you aware that Montagu Norman of the Bank of England had 'a secret line to Ribbentrop / who coos to the Queen of England / down cunning corridors', or that Halifax has his own key to the Palace garden?

All this is by the way, and does not prevent Paulin from getting on with the war. The Maginot Line was quite useless, but the inactivity of its defenders allows some nice perceptions:

> we kept still
> and watched their motorcycle patrols
> the flash of field glasses
> like stammering lighthouses

at high noon
as dogs tied to the doors of deserted farms
howled old testament howls
swollenuddered cows bellowed
a French cavalryman
shot a line of horses
one by one
I knew we were finished then

A survivor manages to get to the beach at Dunkirk:

went down like Aeneas
among the living shades
among twentypackets of Players
floating on the tide
the greybrown bloated faces
of drowned soldiers in overcoats . . .

where the demotic arrives just in time to deflate the donnish allusion. Churchill is also credited with thinking of himself as Aeneas glimpsing the Latian shore, but after all he went to Harrow.

The French envy the British their escape, and are permitted to do so in French:

c'est bien beau que les Britanniques
pouvaient ficher le camp
nous n'avons pas le luxe
ils sont retournés chez eux en héros
nous sommes revenus à l'ignominie
à une débacle belle et bien énorme
La France aimerait juste nous oublier
Nous étions comme des mots étrangers . . .

Having got some way, by no means all the way, towards digesting this packed and rather monstrous book, one can certify that it is a work of scope and ambition, with many demonstrations of the poet's power and some irritating features of a kind he can usually be counted on to provide. I daresay many readers would agree that some sort of companion volume, some guide on the lines of all those ancillary efforts devoted to Pound, Eliot and Joyce, would be a help. Paulin often steps out of the mainstream, as in his admiring accounts of Air Marshal Dowding, who, having been more responsible than anybody for our winning the Battle of Britain, was instantly fired and cast into permanent obscurity; Mitchell, designer of the Spitfire; and Churchill, observed at the moment, a most desperate moment, when he and not Halifax got the nod to succeed Neville Chamberlain as Prime Minister. Some of the persons and their adventures are naturally less grandly historical, and it is not always easy to understand what they are doing in the poem. But the poet might well say it's up to us to find out, and it is not improbable that there will be enthusiasts ready to take him at his word. Wanting myself to know more about this extraordinary work, I promise to buy their books.

Notes

1 Poet and Dancer Before Diaghilev

1. *The Art of the Dance in French Literature* (1952).

2. It is quite untrue, by the way, that Fenollosa and Pound 'introduced' the Noh plays; interest in them is at least as old as this century.

3. Mr Ian Fletcher directs my attention to Sabine Baring-Gould's periodical *The Sacristy* (1871–2) where liturgical dancing is discussed with other matters such as liturgical lights and symbolic zoology, and to later ecclesiastical contributions.

4. Still thought of as a female disorder; Freud's Vienna paper on a male hysteric brought him a reproof from a senior who said that if Freud had known any Greek he would have seen that male hysteria is an impossibility. (E. Jones, *Sigmund Freud, Life & Work I* (1953), p. 254)

5. Jones traces the development of Freud's psychoanalysis from this point. By 1892 he knew that 'sexual disturbances constitute the sole indispensable cause of neurasthenia' (I. 282) (he gave up this word later) and by 1895, nine years after his studies with Charcot, the pattern was taking psychoanalytical shape. It was formed by 1897 (I. 294).

6. She was a friend of Marinetti and wrote on the place of women in Futurism. Like Florence Farr, she eventually retreated to the East.

7. This story may not be absolutely true. In the *Magazine of Art* for 1894 there is an article by Percy Anderson, a man so anxious to harry the short skirt from the English stage that he made, for an opera called *The Nautch Girl* (Savoy, 1889) a copy of an 'eastern dancing-dress' in the 'Indian Museum'. 'The great quantity of material used, in order that the dancers might envelop themselves in billowy folds of drapery, seemed to be an obstacle, but the result was curiously graceful. A clever American dancer, who was engaged at the Gaiety Theatre, saw that the idea might be even further developed; so, with the practical instincts of her race, she sped across the ocean and appeared at the New York Casino Theatre in the now famous

"Serpentine" dance which has set the impressionable Parisians frantic with delight ... All this was the result of one dress, which is lying hidden in the security (or obscurity) of the Indian Museum.' This seems a more likely story, though Mr Nicol doesn't accept it, and Fuller was not appearing as a dancer at the Gaiety in 1889. The truth may be that her having such a good idea owed a little more than she admitted to other dancers (like Kate Vaughan) and their dresses. But she made it her own.

8. I ought to say that this passage will make more sense to anybody who has read my *Romantic Image* (1957).

2 Between Time and Eternity

1. See S. H. Butcher, *Aristotle's Theory of Poetry and Fine Art* (1951), p. 331n.
2. See M. P. Tilley, *A Dictionary of the Proverbs in England* (1950).
3. Milton, *Paradise Regained*, i. 269.

3 Solitary Confinement

1. Christopher Burney *Solitary Confinement* (1952) (2nd edn, 1961).
2. Stephen Toulmin and June Goodfield, *The Discovery of Time* (1965).
3. Earl R. Wasserman, *The Subtler Language* (1959).
4. John Denham, 'Cooper's Hill' (1642).
5. Ortega y Gasset, *Meditations on Don Quixote* (1914).
6. J. Hillis Miller, *The Disappearance of God* (1963), pp. 17ff.
7. Kenneth Burke, *The Philosophy of Literary Form* (1941).
8. See Eliot's letters to Sarah Hennell and John Blackwood, quoted in Miriam Allott, *Novelists on the Novel* (1959), p. 250.
9. Joseph Frank, 'Spatial Form in Modern Literature' in *The Widening Gyre* (1963).
10. Arnold Goldman, *The Joyce Paradox* (1966).
11. Philip Larkin, 'Reference Back' in *The Whitsun Weddings* (1964).

4 The English Novel, *Circa* 1907

1. *Letters of Henry James*, ed. Percy Lubbock (1920), ii. 384; quoted by Samuel Hynes, *The Edwardian Turn of Mind* (1969), p. 358. Hynes's book not only characterizes the general mood of the period but provides much helpful detail on the whole 'Condition of England'.

2. Erskine Childers, *The Riddle of the Sands* (1903).

3. H. G. Wells, *The War in the Air* (1908).

4. But one should mention John Fowles, *The French Lieutenant's Woman* (1969), and William Golding, *Rites of Passage* (1980).

5. These quotations are all from Roger Gard, *Henry James: The Critical Heritage* (1968), pp. 149, 269, 347, 382, 349ff.

6. Gard, *Henry James*, pp. 401–7.

7. With the consequence, as Brownell hinted, that the reader gave up James instead: 'I know of nothing that attests so plainly the preponderance of virtuosity in Mr James's art as the indisposition of his readers to re-read his books' (Gard, *Henry James*, p. 404).

8. Quoted in John D. Gordan, *Joseph Conrad: The Making of a Novelist* (1940), pp. 306–8.

9. Paul L. Wiley, *Novelist of Three Worlds: Ford Madox Ford* (1962), p. 40.

10. Alan Friedman, *The Turn of the Novel* (1966), p. 74.

11. See Hynes, *The Edwardian Turn of Mind*, pp. 185ff.

12. Dudley Barker, *The Man of Principle: A Biography of John Galsworthy* (1969), pp. 22–3.

13. Reported in Anonymous [Cecil Chesterton], *G. K. Chesterton: A Criticism* (1909), p. 202.

14. From a late article reprinted in the Penguin edition.

15. Ian Fletcher, 'Bedford Park: Aesthete's Asylum?' in Fletcher, ed., *Romantic Mythologies* (1967).

16. Cecil Chesterton, *G. K. Chesterton*, p. 142.

5 Hawthorne and the Types

1. Quoted by Ursula Brumm, *American Thought and Religious Typology* (1970), p. 106.

2. Brumm, p. 108.

3. It is true that Thomas Maule wrote *The Truth Held Forth and Maintained* in 1695 – a Quaker attack on the Puritan establishment and its witch-hunts that Hawthorne would have known; and that the Revd Thomas Pyncheon elicited from the novelist an apology for the use of his name. This only shows how serviceable were the names Hawthorne invented.

4. It is reproduced in *Proceedings in Commemoration of the One Hundredth Anniversary of the Birth of Nathaniel Hawthorne* (1904), p. 13. Millicent Bell remarks, not unjustly, that the daguerreotype brings out a certain harshness in Hawthorne's face; it lacks the ideality of such portraits as those of Cephas G. Thompson (1850) and George P. A. Healey (1852), also reproduced in the

Proceedings. Hawthorne, who meditated and wrote so much about portraits and their relation to truth, might have endorsed her views (Millicent Bell, *Hawthorne's View of the Artist* (1962), p. 88 and might even have had his own experience in mind when writing about Holgrave's daguerreotype of Jaffrey.

5. *American Notebooks*, edn. of 1911, pp. 372–3.

6. William M. Ivins, Jr, *Prints and Visual Communication* (1953), Chapter III. At the very moment of the advent of the daguerreotype, in 1840, the portrait painter Samuel F. B. Morse hailed it as 'Rembrandt perfected', because no longer dependent on 'the uncertain hand of the artist' (Leo Steinberg, *Other Criteria* (1972), p. 62).

7. The view that there might be 'a gradual evolution of creative power manifested by a gradual ascent towards higher types' was Sedgwick's, though he had been anticipated, in a more mystical way, by Oken and Schelling. See A. E. Lovejoy, 'The Argument for Organic Evolution before *The Origin of the Species, 1830–58*', in Bentley Glass, O. Temkin and W. L. Straus, Jr, *Forerunners of Darwin*, 1745–1859. In Section XXVI of his *Essay on Classification*, ed. E. Lurie (1962), pp. 115–17, Agassiz seems to claim the expression 'prophetic type' as his own invention: 'Prophetic types . . . are those which in their structural complications lean towards other combinations fully realized in a later period.' See, on embryological types, E. Lurie, *Louis Agassiz* (1960). It was the rigour of Cuvier's fixism that eclipsed the earlier *Naturphilosophie* of Oken and Schelling – and also of Goethe, who, it will be remembered, half-thought he might discover the *Urpflanz* on his trip to Sicily.

8. L. Agassiz and A. A. Gould, *Principles of Zoology* (1848), edn of 1851, p. 16.

9. *Principles*, pp. 18–19: 'It is common to speak of the animal which embodies most fully the character of a group, as the type of that group.'

10. *Principles*, p. 182. Assertions of this kind are also frequent in the opening chapter. The Creation was 'the execution of a plan fully matured in the beginning, and undeviatingly pursued, the work of a God infinitely wise, regulating Nature according to immutable laws, which He himself has imposed on her.' (p. 34). A fuller statement occurs in the *Essay on Classification*, which appeared in 1857, on the eve of Darwinism, though of course – like the *Principles* – after Chambers (1844). (See *Essay on Classification*, ed. Edward Lurie (1962), pp. 8–12.) Both works assume that what the biologist studies is something *thought*, which must therefore have a Thinker: 'The character of the connections between organized beings and the physical conditions under which they live is such as to display thought; these connections are therefore to be considered as established, determined and regulated by a thinking being.' They must have been fixed for each species at its beginning . . .' (*Classifications*, p. 16).

Agassiz cleaves to Cuvier's catastrophism (p. 659 ff.) as the only explanation of changes between epochs. *Principles* (p. 26) even uses the analogy of nature as a book in which we study an author. A useful introduction to Agassizz, and selection of his work, is Guy Davenport's *The Intelligence of Louis Agassiz* (1963). Pound's interest is reflected in *Gists from Agassiz* (1953), and the *Rock-Drill* cantos, as well as in the earlier *ABC of Reading* (1934).

11. *Life and Correspondence of Louis Agassiz*, ed. Elizabeth Cary Agassiz (1886), p. 778.

12. The North was nevertheless predisposed to Darwinism by the success of Herbert Spencer and 'the survival of the fittest'; and preachers such as Henry Ward Beecher and Philips Brooks anyway wanted to abandon the fundamentalist position on Genesis. The South, much more preoccupied with fixed types and degeneration, took a more conservative attitude. The judgement at the Scopes trial of 1925 prohibited the teaching of evolution in Tennessee schools, and the ban was lifted only quite recently. On this characteristic repudiation of 'Yankee' thought, hardening as time went by, see W. I. Cash, *The Mind of the South* (1941), Book II, section 12.

13. R. Hofstadter, *Social Darwinism in American Thought, 1860–1915* (1945), pp. 4–6.

14. Lurie, *Louis Agassiz*, p. 307. On the prophetic types, Lurie, p. 162.

15. *Nathaniel Hawthorne, Man and Writer* (1961), p. 27. Wagenknecht, incidentally, is wrong to say that Agassiz is the only modern scientist mentioned by Hawthorne in his writings; see the Conclusion of *The Marble Faun* for a reference to Cuvier.

16. Taylor Stoehr, 'Hawthorne and Mesmerism', *Huntingdon Library Quarterly*, xxxiii (1969), pp. 42–4. Also, for the contemporary interest in mesmerism, spiritualism, and the like, see Howard Kerr, *Mediums and Spirit-Rappers and Roaring Radicals* (1972).

17. Stoehr, p. 54.

18. Marion L. Kesselring, *Hawthorne's Reading* (1949), p. 45. Hawthorne quotes Buffon in a magazine article of May 1836 (*Hawthorne as Editor*, ed. A. Turner (1941), p. 192). Another book he borrowed was Lavater's *Physiognomy*; I do not profess to have mastered the whole vast bibliography of modern Hawthorne scholarship, but I have come across no inquiry into any interest he may have had in Lavater. That it existed seems a highly probable conjecture.

19. Nature allows no 'link in her great work so weak as to be broken'. (*Life and Selected Writings of Thomas Jefferson* (1944), p. 208)

20. Jefferson, p. 205.

21. Jefferson, p. 213.

22. Jefferson, p. 215. For a more extensive account of the controversy, see Daniel J. Boorstin, *The Lost World of Thomas Jefferson* (1948), p. 81 ff.

23. Buffon, *Histoire Naturelle* (15 vols.) (1749–67), iv, p. 209. Agassiz also used the chicken, to illustrate the point that an embryo chicken is nevertheless a chicken and nothing else, 'though if there existed in Nature an adult bird as imperfectly organized as the chicken on the day, or the day before it was hatched, we should assign it to an inferior rank'.

24. In Chapter CIV of *Moby Dick* Melville ventures into palaeontology, citing Cuvier on the 'antichronical' fossil whale which has 'left . . . pre-adamite traces in the stereotype plates of nature'. He implies a certain belief in catastrophism. The following chapter denies the sperm whale has declined in size.

25. It is worth mentioning that in 1850 Hawthorne read Winckelmann, arbiter of the classical epoch and type.

26. Quoted by Wagenknecht, p. 57.

27. *Essay on Classification*, Section xxv.

28. Agassiz mentions ancient Egyptian wheat which, taken from tombs, will sprout and grow (*Principles*, p. 136).

29. See A. O. Lovejoy, 'Buffon and the Problem of Species', in S. Glass, O. Temkin, and W. L. Straus, Jr, *Forerunners of Darwin: 1745–1859*, p. 103.

30. The story called 'The Artist of the Beautiful' is relevant; the artist is a watchmaker, not trusted in his trade, because art – the creation of the beautiful which belongs to the noumenal, not the phenomenal world – has nothing to do with materiality and time.

31. James, p. 156.

32. James, p. 57.

33. James, p. 10.

34. For a more positive statement of the relation between Hester and Anne Hutchinson, see Michael J. Colocurcio, 'Footsteps of Anne Hutchinson: The Context of *The Scarlet Letter*', ELH, xxxix (1972), pp. 459–94.

35. An adaptation of Marvell's conceit at the end of 'The Unfortunate Lover' – 'In a field sable a *lover* gules.'

36. Brumm, p. 147, suggests that Donatello is an emblem of the antique, and Miriam of the Renaissance which, in rediscovering it, corrupted, and also Christianized it.

6 *Wuthering Heights*

1. Leonard B. Meyer, *Music, the Arts and Ideas* (1967), p. 8 (speaking of musical styles).

2. My subsequent reading in *Wuthering Heights* criticism (which has certainly

substantiated my vague sense that there was a lot of it about) has taught me that the carved names, and Lockwood's dreams, have attracted earlier comment. Dorothy Van Ghent's distinguished essay asks why Lockwood, of all people, should experience such a dream as that of the ghost-child, and decides that the nature of the dreamer – 'a man who has shut out the powers of darkness' – is what gives force to our sense of powers 'existing auton-omously' both without and within. (*The English Novel: Form and Function* (1953)). Ronald E. Fine suggests that the dreams are 'spasms of realism' and that Emily Brontë arranged the story to fit them, or as he says, lets the dreams generate the story. He emphasizes their sexual significance, and the structural relations between them, explained by the generative force of a basic dream of two lovers seeking to be reunited ('Lockwood's Dream and the Key to *Wuther-ing Heights*', *Nineteenth Century Fiction*, xxiv (1969–70), pp. 16–30). Ingeborg Nixon suggests that 'the names must have been written by Catherine after her first visit to Thrushcross Grange as a child . . . but they form a silent summary of the whole tragic dilemma'; they indicate three possibilities for Catherine, who of course chooses *Linton*. This is to give the inscriptions the most limited possible 'hermeneutic' sense, reading them back into a possible chronology and ignoring their larger function as literary or defamiliarizing signs ('Note on the Pattern of *Wuthering Heights*', *English Studies*, xlv (1964)). Cecil W. Davies notices that 'Heathcliff' is an Earnshaw name, and argues that this makes him 'in a real, though non-legal sense, a true inheritor of Wuthering Heights' ('Reading of *Wuthering Heights*', *Essays in Criticism*, xix (1969)). Doubtless C. P. Sanger's justly celebrated essay ('The Structure of Wuthering Heights' (1926)) is partly responsible for the general desire to fit everything that can be fitted into legal and chronological schemes; but the effect is often to miss half the point. All these essays are reprinted, in whole or in part, in the Penguin Critical Anthology, *Emily Brontë*, ed. J.-P. Petit (1973). Other collections include one by Miriam Allott in the Macmillan Casebook series (1970), Thomas A. Vogler's *Twentieth-Century Interpretations of 'Wuthering Heights'* (1965), and William A. Sale's Norton edition (1963). Since 1975 there have been innumerable additions to this list.

3. 'Indeterminancy and the Reader's Response', in *Aspects of Narrative*, ed. J. Hillis Miller (1971), p. 42, reprinted in *Prospecting: From Reader Response to Literary Anthropology* (1989).
4. F. R. Leavis and Q. D. Leavis, *Lectures in America* (1969), pp. 83–152.
5. For a different approach to Mrs Leavis's reading see D. Donoghue, 'Emily Brontë: On the Latitude of Interpretation', *Harvard English Studies*, I, ed. M. W. Bloomfield (1970); reprinted in *Emily Brontë*, ed. J.-P. Petit (1973), pp. 296–314, p. 316.

6. E. D. Hirsch, *Validity in Interpretation* (1967), p. 168.

7. F. Jameson, *The Prison-House of Language*, 1972, p. 195, compare the Frege–Carnap distinction between *Sinn* (unchanging formal organization) and *Bedeutung* (the changing significance given to the text by successive generations of readers).

8. Lévi-Strauss, *Structural Anthropology* (1968), p. 198.

9. Jameson (1972), p. 196.

10. '. . . commentaries or interpretations are generated out of an ontological lack in the text itself . . . a text can have no ultimate meaning . . . the process of interpretation . . . is properly an infinite one' (Jameson, p. 176, paraphrasing Jacques Derrida).

11. Picard, p. 135.

12. Barthes, *Critique et Vérité* (1966), pp. 52–3.

13. The 'cultural code' of *S/Z* (1970), serves some of the purposes of Mrs Leavis's archaeological categories, though she is inclined to retain the period elements that he drops.

14. P. L. Berger, 'Secularization and the Problem of Plausibility', extracted from *The Sacred Canopy* (1967), in *Sociological Perspectives*, ed. K. Thompson and J. Tunstall (1971), pp. 446–59; developing the thesis of Berger and T. Luckmann, *The Social Construction of Reality* (1967).

15. William Berg, *The Early Virgil* (1973).

7 The Man in the Macintosh

1. Stuart Gilbert, *James Joyce's Ulysses* (1931), pp. 152f. Gilbert got the idea from Victor Bérard's *Les Phéniciens et l'Odyssée*, in which all the mysterious movements of Theoclymenos are set forth, with the speculation that he may have been a hero in a part of the epic cycle following the *Odyssey* – the *Telegony*.

2. Stanislaus Joyce, *My Brother's Keeper* (1958), p. 165; and articles by John O. Lyons (in *James Joyce Miscellany*, 2nd series (1959), pp. 133f) and by Thomas E. Connolly (in *James Joyce's Dubliners*, ed. Clive Hart (1969), pp. 107f)

3. Robert M. Adams, *Surface and Symbol* (1962), pp. 218, 245–6. Hélène Cixous, *The Exile of James Joyce*, translated by Sally A. J. Purcell (1972), expressly disagrees with Adams, saying that by the time the table emits its loud lone crack Bloom 'knows . . . who M'Intosh was . . . The garment has become transparent to Bloom's "unconscious substance," and he has now to struggle against the truth that is self-imposed' (pp. 712f). How *we* know this is not explained.

4. Note the persistent suppression of Bloom's name in the concluding pages of 'Cyclops'. Indeed, as Gilbert points out, 'the idea of anonymity or misnomer is suggested under many aspects' – perhaps by way of allusion to Odysseus' change of name to No-man in the relevant episode of Homer (*James Joyce's Ulysses*, p. 252).

5. Adams, *Surface and Symbol*, p. 186.

6. *The Pleasure of the Text*, translated by Richard Miller (1975), p. 11.

7. Thomas Kuhn, *The Structure of Scientific Revolutions*, 2nd edn (1970).

8. Taylor, *St Mark*, pp. 561–2.

9. Cranfield, *St Mark*, p. 438.

10. Taylor, *St Mark*, p. 561, Cranfield, *St Mark*, p. 438.

11. Quoted by H. Jonas, *The Gnostic Religion*, 2nd ed. rev. (1963), p. 274. Jonas, describing the Gnostic 'Hymn of the Pearl' or 'Song of the Apostle Judas Thomas', mentions that the symbolism of a garment includes a use of it as the heavenly or ideal double of a person on earth, sometimes the Saviour. That an allegory of Gnostic origin has been intruded at this point in the Passion narrative has not, so far as I know, been proposed by the exegetes, who may well find it wholly counter-intuitive.

12. Morton Smith, *Clement of Alexandria and a Secret Gospel of Mark* (1973); *The Secret Gospel* (1974).

13. Austin Farrer, *A Study in St Mark* (1951); *St Matthew and St Mark* (1954 (2nd edn, 1966)).

14. For the view that Peter's third denial is a formal curse directed against Jesus, see Helmut Merkel, 'Peter's Curse', *The Trial of Jesus*, ed. Ernst Bammel (Studies in Biblical Theology, second series, 13) (1970), pp. 66–71.

15. Schweitzer, *The Quest of the Historical Jesus*, p. 4.

16. For the difficulties that arise when 'history-likeness' is confused with historical reference, see Hans Frei, *The Eclipse of Biblical Narrative* (1974).

17. Richard Ellmann, *James Joyce* (1959), p. 535. He also told Samuel Beckett 'I may have oversystematized *Ulysses*' (Ellmann, p. 715).

18. 'La Construction de la nouvelle et du roman', in T. Todorov ed. *Théorie de la littérature: Textes des Formalistes russes* (1965), pp. 170–96.

19. D. E. Nineham, *Saint Mark* (Pelican Gospel Commentaries) (1963), p. 439.

20. Ellmann, *James Joyce*, p. 536.

21. Ellmann, p. 725. (Translation slightly altered.)

22. J. Jeremias, *The Eucharistic Words of Jesus*, translated by Norman Perrin (1966), p. 132.

23. W. L. Knox, quoted in Taylor, *St Mark*, p. 609.

24. Farrer, *Study*, p. 174.

25. Jonathan Culler, *Structuralist Poetics* (1975), p. 244.

26. Etienne Trocmé, *The Formation of the Gospel According to Mark*, translated by Pamela Gaughan (1975), p. 240.

8 Dwelling Poetically in Connecticut

1. Wallace Stevens, *Opus Posthumous* (1957); hereafter cited as *OP* in the text.
2. *Letters of Wallace Stevens*, ed. Holly Stevens (1966); hereafter cited as *L* in the text.
3. Margaret Peterson, '*Harmonium* and William James', *Southern Review* (Summer 1971), 664ff.
4. Wallace Stevens, *The Necessary Angel* (1951); hereafter cited as *NA* in the text.
5. 'Und keiner Waffen brauchts und keiner / Listen, so lange, bis Gottes Fehl hilft.' Text and translation from Michael Hamburger's complete parallel text, *Friedrich Hölderlin: Poems and Fragments* (1966), pp. 176–7 (translated from *Hölderlin: Sämtliche Werke* [1961]).
6. Friedrich Hölderlin, *Poems and Fragments*, trans. Michael Hamburger (bilingual edition; 1980), p. 250.
7. Ibid., pp. 600–601. The prose poem 'In lieblicher Bläue', from which these lines derive, is not certainly Hölderlin's own, but Heidegger treats it without question as authentic.
8. Thomson, 'The City of Dreadful Night'; Whitman, 'A Clear Midnight'. Both quoted in *NA*, p. 119.
9. Wallace Stevens, *Collected Poems* (1954); hereafter cited as *CP* in the text.
10. Jarrell, *The Third Book of Criticism* (1969), pp. 57–8.
11. Heidegger, *Poetry, Language, Thought*, trans. Albert Hofstadter (1971), p. x.
12. Heidegger, 'The Origin of the Work of Art [Der Ursprung von Kunstwerkes]', in *Poetry, Language, Thought*, pp. 17–81.
13. 'The Thinker as Poet', in *Poetry, Language, Thought*, p. 4.
14. Heidegger, 'Hölderlin and the Essence of Poetry', trans. Douglas Scott, in Heidegger, *Existence and Being*, comp. Werner Brock (1949), p. 310.
15. Commentators on Stevens appear not to have interested themselves much in this affinity, always supposing that it exists. They have not, to my knowledge, spoken of Stevens in relation to late works of Heidegger (that is, from the 1936 Hölderlin essay on). But Richard Macksey freely alludes to *Sein und Zeit* (along with Husserl and Merleau-Ponty) to illuminate late Stevens. He observes, in part, that 'Stevens grounds his poetics and defines his individuality in terms of a death which always *impends* even in 'the genius of summer' (*CP*,

p. 482). See his 'The Climates of Wallace Stevens' in Roy Harvey Pearce and J. Hillis Miller, eds., *The Act of the Mind: Essays on the Poetry of Wallace Stevens* (1965), p. 201. Heidegger argues that *my* death alone achieves and delimits wholeness of Being (cf. 'Every man dies his own death' [*OP*, p. 165]); and the project of the late Stevens recalls Heidegger's *Sein zum Tode* ('when *Dasein* reaches its wholeness in death, it simultaneously loses the Being of its "there"'). Macksey cites as his epigraph Heidegger's favourite Hölderlin quotation ('dichterisch, wohnet der Mensch auf dieser Erde') but does not otherwise refer to the philosopher's later work. An essay by J. Hillis Miller in the same collection sounds as though Miller could have had these later essays in mind, but he does not allude to them explicitly.

16. In *Being and Time*, trans. John Macquarrie and Edward Robinson (1962), p. 80, Heidegger explains (though that is not the right word) that the word *innan (wohnen)* collects the senses of 'to dwell' (*inn*) and 'accustomed', 'familiar with', and 'look after something' *(an)*. But there is no substitute for a reading of that passage and related passages.

17. Quoted by Heidegger in 'Hölderlin and the Essence of Poetry', p. 296.

18. Heidegger, 'Building Dwelling Thinking', in *Poetry, Language, Thought*, pp. 143–62.

19. Heidegger, 'Remembrance of the Poet', trans. Douglas Scott, in *Existence and Being*, p. 281.

20. Heidegger, 'Hölderlin and the Essence of Poetry', pp. 293 ff.

21. Heidegger, 'Remembrance of the Poet', p. 264.

22. Heidegger, 'The Origin of the Work of Art', p. 41.

23. Ibid., p. 47.

24. Heidegger, 'What Are Poets For?' in *Poetry, Language, Thought*, p. 97.

9 Secrets and Narrative Sequence

1. From *Academe* (1979). My thanks to Alexander Baramki, who sent me this book.

2. After this was written, I read Jurij M. Lotman's 'The Origin of Plot in the Light of Typology, *Poetics Today*, 1, nos. 1–2, 1979: pp. 161–84. Lotman speaks of two primeval kinds of plot. The first is 'mythic' and has no 'excesses or anomalies'; it is timeless and motionless. The second is the linear tale about incidents, news, 'excesses'. The two exist in dialectical interaction, and the result is a 'fusion of scandal and miracle'. A secret motivation arising from the 'eschatological' plot intrudes into the linear plot; 'mythologism penetrates into the sphere of excess'. It is from such combinations that we have learnt to interpret reality as we do, plot-wise. Keats's poem foreshadows this theory.

The mythic event is injected into scandal and outrage; beauty subsumes a version of truth which represents it as calamity, decay, and consequence; the assurance that there is a timeless and motionless transcendent world reduces to insignificance the *faits divers* which seem to constitute the narrative of ordinary life.

3. Edward W. Said, *Beginnings* (1975), p. 83.

4. Not forever, I hope; his essay and its 'refined common sense' have powerful implications for a more general narrative theory. [The essay, first presented at the Chicago Symposium on 'Narrative: the Illusion of Sequence', which was also the occasion of the present chapter, is called 'Narration in the Psychoanalytic Dialogue'. It is reprinted in *Narrative*, ed. W. J. T. Mitchell (1981), pp. 25–49. For Hayden White's essay, see *Narrative*, pp. 1–23.]

5. See Chapter 2 of the present volume.

6. Joseph Conrad, *Letters from Joseph Conrad, 1895–1924*, ed. Edward Garnett (1928), p. 234.

7. The trouble is not that there are unreliable narrators but that we have endorsed as reality the fiction of the 'reliable' narrator.

8. Albert J. Guerard, *Conrad the Novelist* (1958); all references to this work will be cited in the text.

9. See Frederick R. Karl, *Joseph Conrad: The Three Lives* (1979), p. 68 n.

10. Conrad, preface to *Chance*, 1920, p. viii.

11. Eloise Knapp Hay, *The Political Novels of Joseph Conrad* (1963); all references to this work will be cited in the text. See also D. C. Yelton's *Mimesis and Metaphor* (1967) which sees a connection between the 'motif of vision' and the phantom but treats it only psychologically.

12. Avrom Fleishman, 'Speech and Writing in *Under Western Eyes*', in *Conrad: A Commemoration*, ed. Norman Sherry (1976), pp. 119–28. After this paper was written, there appeared Jeremy Hawthorn's *Joseph Conrad: Language and Fictional Self-Consciousness* (1979), which contains interesting remarks on Conrad's play with English tenses and argues that when the language teacher tells Miss Haldin that he has understood 'all the words' but without understanding, he is speaking for the reader as Conrad imagined him (see pp. 102–28).

13. See 'The Structures of Fiction,' in *Velocities of Change*, ed. R. Macksey (1974), p. 198.

14. The pun is actually French, since English 'apparition' = 'appearance' is virtually obsolete.

10 Botticelli Recovered

1. Michael Levey, 'Botticelli and Nineteenth-Century England', *Journal of the Warburg & Courtauld Institutes* 23 (1960): pp. 291–306. My opening pages draw freely on this article.

2. Ibid., p. 294. As late as 1887, W. P. Frith, an academician still remembered for the detailed realism of his 'Derby Day', could speak of Botticelli's 'bad drawing and worse painting, and such a revelling in ugliness' (*My Autobiography* [1887], Chapter 2, p. 90 (cited in Levey, p. 305).

3. In 1864 the *Primavera* was moved to the Accademia; it was returned to the Uffizi in 1919.

4. Levey, p. 296.

5. R. N. Wornum, *Epochs of Painting* (1860), p. 160 (cited in Levey, p. 301).

6. Levey, p. 302.

7. Walter Pater, *The Renaissance*, text of 1893, ed. D. L. Hill (1980), p. 39.

8. Ibid., p. 43.

9. Ian Fletcher, 'Herbert Horne: The Earlier Phase', *English Miscellany* (Rome) 21 (1970): pp. 117–57. Professor Fletcher has kindly allowed me to read the not quite complete manuscript of his life of Horne.

10. *Letters of Ernest Dowson*, ed. Desmond Flower and Henry Maas (1967), letter of 4 March 1891 to Arthur Moore; but next day Dowson reported to the same correspondent that the dinner was a success – Horne was 'charming and kind', and afterwards, at 11.30 p.m., they 'strolled Alhambra-wards' but 'were too late for divinities'.

11. *Letters*, 27 January, 1890.

12. On some of the implications of the cult, see Chapter 1.

13. E. H. Gombrich, 'Botticelli's Mythologies', *Symbolic Images* (1972), pp. 31–81. 'Dancing with a slow halting step' is from Apuleius's description of Venus in *The Golden Ass (lente vestigio)*. In Apuleius, also, she is 'slightly inclining her head'.

14. W. B. Yeats, *Autobiography* (1953), p. 191.

15. Fletcher, p. 151.

16. Yeats, p. 182.

17. Herbert P. Horne, *Botticelli, Painter of Florence*. With a new introduction by John Pope-Hennessy (1980), xi. Ronald Lightbrown, *Sandro Botticelli: Life and Works and Complete Catalogue*, 2 vols. (1978) does not dissent from this very usual view, though he notes errors, certain and probable, and also certain disadvantages inherent in Horne's method. For instance, he probably dated the *Primavera* too early: it is a painting for a marriage chamber, made for Lorenzo di Pierfrancesco in 1482–3 (not 1477); it is, therefore,

much closer in time to *The Birth of Venus* (another picture for a marriage chamber) than Horne supposed. The composition of Horne's book began as early as 1903, so he was unable to include information available only after that date; Jacques Mesnil, *Botticelli* (1938), supplements and corrects Horne from his own notes. Finally, Horne's book (of which only 240 copies were printed) is extremely long and has neither chapter divisions nor index, which certainly reduces its utility; but then he liked to think he was writing only for his own amusement.

18. Fritz Saxl, 'Three Florentines', *Lectures* (1957), p. 331 ff.

19. Fletcher, p. 127.

20. Horne, xviii.

21. Horne, xix.

22. Horne, xix.

23. Horne, xviii.

24. Horne, xix.

25. Horne, p. 43.

26. Horne, pp. 59–60.

27. Horne, p. 69.

28. Horne, p. 111.

29. Horne, p. 121.

30. Horne, p. 122.

31. Horne, p. 152.

32. Horne, p. 255.

33. Horne, pp. 333–4.

34. Horne, p. 329.

35. Horne, p. 308.

36. Horne, p. 334.

37. Horne, p. 304.

38. Horne, p. 147.

39. Horne, p. 88.

40. E. H. Gombrich, *Aby Warburg: An Intellectual Biography* (1970), p. 305. I have drawn heavily on this work in my discussion of Warburg.

41. Professor J. B. Trapp reminds me that Warburg dedicated his Botticelli study to Humbert Janitschek and Adolf Michaelis, masters important to him. One should also mention his reverence for Burckhardt.

42. It was Usener who directed Warburg's attention to the work of Tito Vignoli, whose *Mito e scienza* (1879) proved to be of importance to the younger man. Maria Michela Sassi says that Warburg used Vignoli in a very personal way, impressed above all by Vignoli's insistence on fear as the motive behind the tendency to 'animate' the unknown – a tendency that would persist into a scientific age because man 'humanises and personifies images, ideas and

concepts by converting them into living subjects, just as in the beginning he humanised and personified cosmic objects and phenomena'. Maria Michela Sassi, 'Dalla scienza delle religioni di Usener ad Aby Warburg', in *Aspetti di Hermann Usener, filologo della religione. Seminaro della Scuola Normale di Pisa* ... 1982, a cura di G. Arrighetti [etc.], Pisa (1982).

43. 'Sometimes it looks to me as if, in my role as psycho-historian, I had to diagnose the schizophrenia of Western civilisation from its images in an autobiographical reflex', wrote Warburg in relation to the Nympha (Gombrich, p. 303). And it is true that for him the image had a 'manic' quality (he seems, both here and in speaking of his own illness, to have confused the manic-depressive with the schizophrenic). But he was not alone in attaching this sort of significance to the Nympha; Taine had done so, much more palely (see below); and so, a few years later, did Horne, who singles out, in the Sistine fresco of the Temptation, the 'woman with flying draperies, who steps forward, almost in profile, with a bundle of oak faggots on her head. In the blithe, exuberant sense of life which animates this incomparable figure, Botticelli approaches more nearly to the spirit of Greek art than, perhaps, even Donatello himself had done' (Horne, p. 99). Here we may feel a curious affinity between 'Decadent' and 'Greek', which doubtless originates in Pater's essay. Of course it remains true that neither Taine nor Horne was obsessed with the image as Warburg was; we do not sense in what they say anything corresponding to what Gombrich calls 'the subsoil of fear that underlies Warburg's fascination with the Nympha' (Gombrich, p. 305), its association with headhunters, maenads, and ultimately, one supposes, castration fears.

44. M. Podro, *The Critical Historians of Art* (1982), p. 157.

45. The source of this expression, much enquired after, seems now to have been found in Hermann Usener, whose method it was to seek general laws by studying a particular datum (Sassi, p. 86, citing D. Wuttke). Usener has several versions, none completely identical with Warburg's. Sassi shows that Dilthey has the same ideas, differently expressed, and attributes it to Goethe; she is persuaded that Warburg read Dilthey. Here is another indication that Warburg singled out from several diverse threads of the German tradition the theme that had most interest for him as he constructed his own.

46. R. Semon, *Mneme* (trans. 1921).

47. Gombrich, p. 250.

48. Gombrich, pp. 241 ff, 275.

49. E.g. E. Panofsky, *Renaissances and Renascences in Western Art* (1960) (Harper Torchbook, 1969), pp. 191–200; E. Wind, *Pagan Mysteries of the Renaissance* (1958), pp. 100–120; E. H. Gombrich, 'Botticelli's Mythologies' (see n. 13); more recently R. Lightbrown (see n. 17) who finds a simpler message in the 'frank carnality' of the paintings than Neoplatonic or highly ethical programmes account for (Lightbrown, p. 81); and Paul Holberton, 'Botticelli's *"Primavera"*: che volea s'intendesse', *Journal of the Warburg and Courtauld Institutes* 45 (1982), pp. 202–10, argues that Warburg was in general right about sources and themes, though the lady in the central position of the picture is not Venus. Holberton agrees with Gombrich in finding an ethical intention, though for him the subject is not humanitas but the conversion of spring lust into *gentilezza* – love taming savage desire.

50. Gombrich, p. 65.

51. Hippolyte Taine, *Italy: Florence and Venice*, trans. J. Durand (1889), p. 129. Taine speaks also of 'dry outlines, feeble colour, and irregular and ungracious figures' combined with 'deep and fervid sentiment' in the painting of the period. Of the lady and the nymph in the *Nativity of St John*, he adds: 'A fresh smile rests on their lips; underneath their semi-immobility, under these remains of rigidity which imperfect painting still leaves, one can divine the latent passion of an intact spirit and healthy body. The curiosity and refinement of ulterior ages have not reached them. Thought, with them, slumbers; they walk or look straight before them with the coolness and placidity of virginal purity; in vain will education with all its animated elegancies rival the divine uncouthness of their gravity.

'This is why I so highly prize the paintings of this age; none in Florence have I studied more. They are often deficient in skill and are always dull; they lack both action and colour. It is the renaissance in its dawn, a dawn grey and somewhat cool, as in the spring when the rosy hue of the clouds begins to tinge a pale crystal sky, and when, like a flaming dart the first ray of sunshine glides over the crest of the furrows.'

52. Gombrich, pp. 106ff, 169.

53. Sassi, p. 90, records the 'stupefaction' of Ernst Cassirer when he went to the Institute in Hamburg in 1920 and saw that Warburg, then still very little known, had brought together in the library – as if for him personally – all that material, placing books on magic beside those on astrology and folklore, associating art, literature, and philosophy in the manner most suitable for his grasping the relations between the various 'symbolic forms'.

54. Gombrich, pp. 297–302.

55. Gombrich, p. 315.

56. Gombrich, p. 87.

57. Gombrich, p. 238.

58. Gombrich, p. 305.

59. M. Podro, *The Critical Historians of Art* (1982), p. 214.

11 Cornelius and Voltemand

References to *Hamlet* are to the Arden edition, ed. H. Jenkins (1981). For all other works of Shakespeare I refer to The Riverside Shakespeare, ed. G. B. Evans (1974).

1. See Paul S. Conklin, *A History of Hamlet Criticism: 1601–1821* (1957).
2. See L. Jardine, *Still Harping on Daughters* (1983), Chapter 1.
3. It is hard to believe, but I cannot find that anyone has noticed the use here of the *Life of Caligula*.
4. John Carey, *John Donne, His Life and Art* (1981), p. 264 ff.
5. Sir Thopas's reply to Malvolio's complaint that he is being kept in the dark house, 'Why, it hath bay windows transparent as barricadoes, and the clerestories toward the south north are as lustrous as ebony' (iv.2.36 ff), is modelled on the carnival-like inversions of Belsey Bob.
6. L. Sonnino, *A Handbook to Sixteenth-Century Rhetoric* (1968), p. 188 (quoting Richard Sherry).
7. Roman Jakobson, *Selected Writings, III: Poetry of Grammar and Grammar of Poetry* (1981), p. 767.
8. Sonnino, p. 157, quoting J. Hoskins, *Direction for Speech and Style* (c. 1600).
9. Otto Rank, *The Double*, translated by Harry Tucker, Jr (1971; 1979 edn), p. 58.
10. D. Parish, 'Transitional Objects and Phenomena in a Case of Twinship', *Between Fantasy and Reality*, ed. S. A. Goalnick and L. Barkin (1978), pp. 273–87. The case described is of a neurotic younger dizygotic twin who had the tendency 'to view separate people as halves of dyads', especially when he wanted to reject them; however, he mistrusted this feeling. Hamlet certainly tends to think of the dead and living kings as a dyad, and wishes to reject the latter.

12 The Plain Sense of Things

1. See F. O. Matthiessen, *The Achievement of T. S. Eliot*, 3rd edn (1958), p. 90.
2. Northrop Frye, *Anatomy of Criticism: Four Essays* (1957), p. 76.
3. J. Barton, *Reading the Old Testament* (1984), p. 85.
4. *De libero arbitrio*, quoted in *Cambridge History of the Bible*, vol. 3, *The West from the Reformation to the Present Day*, ed. S. C. Greenslade (1969–70), p. 28.
5. John Lyons, *Semantics*, vol. 1 (1977), p. 237.
6. Bruno Bettelheim, *Freud and Man's Soul* (1983).

7. *Cambridge History of the Bible*, vol. 3, p. 11.
8. Gerald Hammond, *The Making of the English Bible* (1982), p. 10.
9. Beryl Smalley, *The Study of the Bible in the Middle Ages*, 2nd edn (1952), p. 15; D. S. Wallace-Hadrill, *Christian Antioch: A Study of Early Christian Thought in the East* (1982), Chapter 2.
10. *City of God*, XVI, 2.
11. *Cambridge History of the Bible*, vol. 2, pp. 252 ff.
12. Smalley, *Bible in the Middle Ages*, Chapter 4.
13. Ibid., p. 151.
14. Ibid., p. 163.
15. Ibid., p. 362.
16. J. S. Preuss, *From Shadow to Promise: Old Testament Interpretation from Augustine to the Young Luther* (1969), p. 53.
17. Ibid., p. 69.
18. Ibid., p. 81.
19. J. T. Burtchaell, *Catholic Theories of Inspiration since 1810* (1969), p. 32.
20. Ibid., pp. 69–70.
21. Ibid., Chapter 5.
22. *Papers of the Institute of Jewish Studies, London*, vol. 1, ed. J. G. Weiss (1964), pp. 141–85.
23. John Searle, 'Literal Meaning', in *Expression and Meaning: Studies in the Theory of Speech Acts* (1979).

13 Mixed Feelings

1. *The English Auden*, ed. E. Mendelson (1977), p. 142.
2. Chorus from 'The Rock', *Complete Poems and Plays, 1909–1950* (1952), p. 103.
3. *Selected Prose*, ed. W. Cookson (1973), p. 249.
4. 'The Desperate System: Poverty, Crime and Emigration', in *Fraser's Magazine* (July 1830), reprinted in G. Levine (ed.), *The Emergence of Victorian Consciousness* (1967), pp. 272–83.
5. See G. Himmelfarb, 'The Culture of Poverty', in H. J. Dyos and Michael Wolff (eds), *The Victorian City* (1973), pp. 707–36.
6. See D. Craig, *The Real Foundations* (1974), pp. 89–90.
7. See S. Marcus, 'Reading the Illegible', in *The Victorian City*, pp. 257–76; and F. Engels, *The Condition of the Working Class in England in 1844*, translated and edited W. O. Henderson and W. H. Challoner (1958).
8. Bagehot is admiring Dicken's talent for dealing with this disconnection. See P. Collins, 'Dickens and London', in *The Victorian City*, p. 34.

9. Louis MacNeice, *The Strings are False* (1965), p. 130.

10. Ibid., p. 135.

11. I take these figures from J. Stevenson, *British Society*, 1914–1945 (1984). In P. Hamilton, *Hangover Square* (1941) – a novel which scrupulously registers the conditions of life immediately before the war – a meal for two at a very expensive London restaurant, together with a great deal to drink, costs £2. 13s. 7d.

12. Cecil Day-Lewis, in *Poetry of the Thirties*, ed. Robin Skelton (1964), p. 69.

13. Ibid., p. 186.

14. *The English Auden*, p. 142.

15. *The Strings are False*, p. 138.

16. K. Allott, *Collected Poems* (1975), p. 17.

17. D. Trotter, *The Making of the Reader* (1984), p. 113.

18. *The English Auden*, pp. 165–6.

19. G. Orwell, *Collected Essays, Journalism and Letters*, ed. S. Orwell and I. Angus (1968), i. p. 230, written in August 1936.

20. *Homage to Catalonia.* (The Penguin edn of 1966, etc. reprints the essay and the poem, pp. 246–7; they originally appeared in *England Your England* in 1953, but are dated 1943 by the author.)

21. S. Spender, *World within World* (1951; 1956 edn), pp. 311–12.

22. W. H. Auden, *New Year Letter* (1941), p. 119.

23. S. Hynes, *The Auden Generation* (1976), p. 317.

24. 'Conversation with Edward Upward', *Review*, pp. 11–12 (1965), pp. 65–7.

25. 'Sketch for a Marxist Interpretation of Literature', in C. Day-Lewis (ed.), *The Mind in Chains* (1937), p. 48.

26. *London Magazine* (July 1985), pp. 3–13.

27. 'Letter to Lord Byron', Part V, in *The English Auden*, p. 198.

28. J. Meyers, *The Enemy: A Biography of Wyndham Lewis* (1980), p. 190.

29. F. Jameson, *Fables of Aggression* (1979), pp. 179 ff.

30. W. Lewis, *The Revenge for Love* (1937; 1962 edn), pp. 201, 206, 225–6.

31. W. Lewis, *The Diabolical Principle* (1931), p. 146.

32. Introduction to *The Revenge for Love* (1962), vii–xvi.

14 Eros, Builder of Cities

1. This is according to MacNeice. Sir Isaiah Berlin told me after the lecture that there was not a word of truth in it.

2. *The Strings are False* (1956), p. 168.

3. G. Rees, *A Chapter of Accidents* (1972), pp. 106, 110.

4. *The English Auden*, ed. E. Mendelson (1977), pp. 208–9.

5. *Autumn Journal* (1939), pp. 16, 17.

6. L. MacNeice, *I Crossed the Minch* (1938), p. 125.

7. See M. Ceadel, 'Popular Fiction and the Next War', in F. Gloversmith (ed.), *Class Culture and Social Change: A New View of the Thirties* (1980), pp. 161–84.

8. Quoted in S. Hynes, *The Auden Generation* (1976), p. 299.

9. S. Spender, *The Thirties and After* (1978), p. 33.

10. *The Strings are False*, p. 169.

11. *The English Auden*, p. 245.

12. G. Orwell, *Selected Essays* (1957), pp. 9–50.

13. B. Everett, *Poets in their Time* (1986), p. 220.

14. *The English Auden*, p. 119.

15. E. Mendelson, *Early Auden* (1982), pp. 246, 142.

16. Reprinted in J. Haffenden (ed.), *W. H. Auden: The Critical Heritage* (1983), p. 231.

17. *The English Auden*, p. 281.

18. *Collected Poems* (1976), p. 546.

19. Ibid., p. 433.

20. *The Thirties and After*, p. 30.

21. *Early Auden*, pp. 200–203.

22. *The Thirties and After*, p. 25.

23. *The English Auden*, p. 155.

24. Ibid., p. 138.

25. Ibid., p. 138.

26. *The English Auden*, p. 212.

27. *Collected Poems*, p. 581.

28. *The Destructive Element* (1935), p. 223.

29. *Forewords and Afterwords*, ed. E. Mendelson (1973).

30. W. H. Auden, review of V. Clifton, *The Book of Talbot*, in *The English Auden*, p. 319.

31. *The English Auden*, p. 156.

15 Memory

1. *Confessions*, X. 8; see Henry Chadwick, *Augustine* (1986), pp. 9–70.

2. Charles Taylor, *Sources of the Self* (1989), pp. 134–6.

3. Taylor, p. 140; Augustine, *Confessions*, I. xiii (21) (Chadwick's translation).

4. Jean Starobinski, *The Living Eye* (1989), p. 177.

5. In a letter to Fliess of 6 December 1896, Freud spoke of 'memory-traces being subjected from time to time to a re-arrangement in accordance with fresh circumstances – to a retranscription.'
6. Starobinski, p. 48, quoting the 'Profession de foi du vicaire Savoyarde'.
7. For an admiring account of Green's theories see E. Nakjavani, 'The Unbinding Process: The Pedagogy of Listening to the Text with the "Third Ear"', *Proceedings of the 9th International Conference on Literature and Psychology*, pp. 25–34.
8. He said this to Maxim Gorky; see J. M. Coetzee, 'Autobiography and Confession', in *Doubling the Point* (1992), p. 264.
9. Vladimir Nabokov, *Speak Memory*, Penguin edn (1969), p. 23.
10. *The Language of Autobiography* (1993), p. 286.
11. Starobinski, p. 232.
12. Sturrock, p. 142.
13. See Jerome Buckley, *The Turning Key* (1984), pp. 87–8.
14. Gibbon, *Autobiography*, ed. Georges A. Bonnard (1966), p. 86.
15. 'Full of Life Now', in James Olney ed., *Autobiography*, pp. 49–72.
16. J. M. Coetzee has some interesting remarks on the problems of ending in confessional writing: there is always, as in Rousseau, the possibility of there being a deeper truth than the confessant allows. And if he allows that, there will be another, each deepened interpretation constituting a Derridean 'supplement' and getting no closer to the inaccessible 'blind spot' or truth ('Confession and Double Thoughts: Tolstoy, Rousseau, Dostoevsky' in *Doubling the Point*, pp. 251–93.
17. From the *Ebauche de Confessions*, Translation from Starobinski, p.64.
18. *William Wordsworth*, ed. Stephen Gill (1984), p. 602.
19. *ibid*, p. 603.

16 Forgetting

1. See 'Botticelli Recovered' above, and E. H. Gombrich, *Aby Warburg: An Intellectual Biography* (1970).
2. Terence Cave, *Recognitions: A Study in Poetics* (1988), p. 212.
3. Peter Brooks, *Reading for the Plot* (1984), pp. 7, 104, 108, 226–7.
4. John Butt and Kathleen Tillotson, *Dickens at Work* (1957), edn of 1968, pp. 21, 30–32, 141–2, 145–6.
5. Patricia McFate and Bruce Goffers list errors in 'The Good Soldier: a tragedy of despair', *Modern Fiction Studies* 9 (1963–4); others are noted by R. A. Cassell, *Ford Madox Ford: A Study of his Novels* (1961), and C. Ohmann, *Ford Madox Ford* (1964). Since this essay was written the matter

has been fruitfully discussed in Martin Stannard's edition of the novel (1995) and in Max Saunders' biography (2 vols, 1996).

6. Paul Ricoeur, *Time and Narrative*, trans. K. Blamey and D. Pellauer, vol. 3 (1988), p. 189.

7. F. C. Bartlett, *Remembering: a Study in Experimental and Social Psychology* (1932).

8. Bartlett, (edn of 1967), Chapters viii, xiv, xv.

9. P. N. Johnson-Laird, *The Computer and the Mind: an Introduction to Cognitive Science* (1988), alludes to Bartlett, and cites a study by Ulric Neisser in which John Dean's memories of pre-Watergate conversations are compared with the record of the tapes. Dean got the gists but lost the non-gist detail. Johnson-Laird remarks that 'the activity of any single unit [in a set of connected inputs] is relatively unimportant. If it malfunctions or is destroyed, the system will not be drastically impaired' (p. 181). This is what happens when novelists are forgetful in what we think of as trivial matters, as in some of the examples above.

10. Rodolphe Gasché, *The Tain of the Mirror: Derrida and the Philosophy of Reflection* (1986), pp. 264–5.

11. Jacques Derrida, *On Grammatology*, trans. G. C. Spivak (1976), p. 18. See the interesting discussion of Derrida's attitude to the Nietzschean concept of forgetfulness ('there could be no present without forgetfulness') in the Preface, pp. xxx–xxxiii.

12. Karlheinz Stierle, 'The Reading of fiction texts', in S. R. Suleiman and Inge Crosman, ed., *The Reader in the Text* (1980), pp. 83–105; Wolfgang Iser, ibid., pp. 106–119; S. Chatman, *Story and Discourse* (1978), pp. 41–2.

13. Percy Lubbock, *The Craft of Fiction* (1965) [1921], pp. 35, 197.

14. S/Z (1971), p. 18. (I have consulted the translation of Richard Miller (1974, p. 10) but have felt it necessary to translate rather more freely.)

15. Annette Lavers, *Roland Barthes* (1982), p. 200.

16. *Le Plaisir du texte* (1973), p. 15. And see Stephen Heath, *Vertige du déplacement* (1974), pp. 155–6.

17. *Of Grammatology*, p. 158; *Positions* (1981), p. 63.

18. R. Scholes, 'Deconstruction and communication', *Critical Inquiry*, 14, Winter 1988, pp. 278–95; John M. Ellis, 'What does deconstruction contribute?' *New Literary History*, 19, Winter 1988, pp. 259–79.

19. *Standard Edition*, vi (1960), pp. 46–7; vii (1953), pp. 174–6.

20. 'Introduction à l'analyse structurale des récits', *Communications* 8 (1966), p. 27.

18 Literary Criticism: Old and New Styles

1. The anecdote is taken from Michael H. Kater, *Composers of the Nazi Era* (2000).
2. See D. J. Gordon's fine essay, 'Name and Fame: Shakespeare's *Coriolanus*', in S. Orgel (ed.), *The Renaissance Imagination: Essays and Lectures by D. J. Gordon* (1975), pp. 203–19.
3. Greenblatt, *Learning to Curse* (1990), pp. 80–88.
4. 'The History of the Anecdote', in H. Aram Veeser (ed.), *The New Historicism* (1989), p. 52.
5. *A Critic's Journey, 1958–1998: Literary Reflections* (1999), p. 227.
6. D. P. Walker, *Spiritual and Demonic Magic, from Ficino to Campanella* (1958), p. 80.
7. *Suffocating Mothers: Fantasies of Maternal Origin in Shakespeare's Plays* (1992), pp. 130–64.

19 Shakespeare and Boito

1. *The Ultimate Art* (1992), p.216. Littlejohn has interesting observations on the pathology of jealous murderers. 'I think much of the potential power of this role is related to the precision with which his behavior conforms not only to actual cases, but to what Freud saw as a near-universal impulse in normal people – in Othello's case, an impulse yielded to so spectacularly that our own healthily repressed instincts may well be touched' (p. 220).
2. I am indebted to Marvin Rosenberg's *The Masks of Othello* (1961).
3. Possibly Trollope was touched in the way Littlejohn says is common. Victoria Glendinning remarks that he repeatedly quotes Brabantio's words about Desdemona forsaking 'the curled darlings of our nation' for Othello's 'sooty bosom' (*Trollope*) (1992), p. 29).
4. Information again from Rosenberg.
5. *Opera as Drama*, edn of 1986, p. 137.
6. 'Affections' in the strong contemporary sense of 'passions'.
7. In A. Groos and R. Parker, *Reading Opera* (1988), pp. 12–59; J. Budden, *The Operas of Verdi*, 3 vols (1981); M. Conati and M. Medici ed., *The Verdi–Boito Correspondence*, trans. and introduced by W. Weaver (1994), p. 89; J. A. Hepokoski, *Giuseppe Verdi: Otello* (1987), p. 25 and *Reading Opera*.
8. E. A. J. Honigmann, (Arden edn, 1997), p. 351.
9. *The Verdi–Boito Correspondence*, p. 63.
10. Ibid., p. 75.

11. Hepokoski, *Otello*, p. 104. Verdi stresses the high importance of clear diction, and says 'in that part it is necessary neither to sing nor to raise one's voice (save for a few exceptions)'.

12. See Gary Schmidgal, *Shakespeare and Opera* (Oxford, 1990), p. 245.

13. Kerman, p. 127.

14. Or, it would be proper to add, cut from the first.

15. E. A. J. Honigmann (Arden edn, 1997), p. 291.

Index

Auerbach, Erich 78
St Augustine 297, 298, 299, 300,
  302, 303, 304, 305, 306
  on choice 35, 36
  Confessions 290–96
  influence/importance 236–7,
    289–90
  his world view 49
Austen, Jane
  Pride and Prejudice 410
Austin, L. J. 27
Avril, Jane 3, 10–12, 29, 187

Backman, Eugene Louis
  Religious Dances 8
Bacon, Francis 33
Bagehot, Walter 249
Barclay, Florence 60
  The Rosary 64–5
Barfield, Owen 7
Barker, George 252–3
Barrès, Maurice 10
Barthes, Roland 114–15, 125, 294,
  309, 319–21
  Le Plaisir du texte 115
  Racine 114
Bartlett, F. C. 315, 316, 329
Barton, John 234
Bastide, R
  'Mémoire collective et sociologie
    du bricolage' 323
Bateson, F. W. 355
  Essays in Criticism 342–5, 355,
    356
  'The Function of Criticism at the
    Present Time' 342
Batteux, Charles 6
Baudelaire, Charles 28
Beardsley, Aubrey 18
Beckett, Samuel 298
Belfort, May 10, 17

Belgion, Montgomery 343, 423
Benjamin, Walter 420–21
Bennett, Arnold 70
  Henry James on 70
  The Old Wives' Tale 60
Benson, R. H
  'On the Dance as a Religious
    Exercise' 8
Bergson, Henri 298
Berlin, Isaiah 268
Bernhardt, Sarah 20
Berryman, John 400
Bettelheim, Bruno 235
Bewley, Marius 339
Blackmur, R. P. 341
Bloch, Mlle ('Gaby') 17
Bloch, Michael
  as editor of James Lees-Milnes's
    diaries 384
Blunt, Anthony 270, 271, 272
Boito, Arrigo
  as librettist of Verdi: *Otello* 357,
    358, 359, 360, 362, 363–73;
    Falstaff 365
Bonniet
  Preface to Mallarmé's *Igitur* 27
Book of Common Prayer 217
Botticelli, Sandro 182–203, 205
  Adoration of the Magi 191
  The Birth of Venus 183, 184
  Herbert P. Horne on 182,
    185–94, 196, 202, 202
  The Madonna of the Magnificat
    184
  Walter Pater on 190–91, 192,
    193, 194
  Primavera 183, 187, 191, 196
  St Augustine 193
Bourguet, M. N. (ed.)
  Between Memory and History
    323